LOGIC
and ONTOLOGY

LOGIC
and ONTOLOGY

Edited by

Milton K. Munitz

New York: NEW YORK UNIVERSITY PRESS
1973

Foreword

The following essays represent the contributions to a seminar on Ontology held under the auspices of the New York University Institute of Philosophy for the year 1970–1971.

The possibility of establishing fruitful links between logic and ontology had already been made evident in earlier work by Frege, Lesniewski, Russell, Quine, and Goodman. More recent investigations have sought to expand and deepen these studies, although by no means always through adhering to paths previously established. Developments in modal logic, model theory, and presupposition-free logics have brought to the fore the need to deal with such central concepts as 'existence,' 'possibility,' 'individuation,' 'identity,' and 'necessity,' among others. The studies here included, by some of the leading investigators in the field, are typical of the most promising and exciting research of recent analytic philosophy. Along with those papers whose orientation to ontology is derived primarily from the preoccupations of logicians, a number of additional studies are included that give testimony to the lively and creative resurgence of interest in ontology in contemporary philosophy.

M.K.M.

Contents

Contents

LOGIC
and ONTOLOGY

On The Theory of the Verb "To Be"

CHARLES H. KAHN

University of Pennsylvania

It seems appropriate to discuss the verb *be* in a seminar on ontology. For of course the very term "ontology" is derived from ὤν/ὄντος, the present participle of the Greek verb *be*. Etymologically speaking, ontology is the theory of being or *what is*. At the same time, it is not entirely clear how far a theory of the verb belongs to linguistics, how far it belongs to philosophy proper. Our topic seems to lie on the border-line between the two disciplines, or in the neutral area where linguistics and philosophy overlap and can scarcely be distinguished from one another. This is generally true for fundamental problems in the study of language. The connection between language and rationality is so close that, if we pursue a linguistic issue deeply enough, we will nearly always come up against its philosophical roots. This is peculiarly true for the theory of *to be*, for in this case the object under discussion, the verb itself, has played a major role in the development of philosophy, not only by providing us with the standard terminology for Being and for Essence (from Latin *esse*), but also by providing us with the linguistic preconditions that make it possible or even natural to form such concepts. Without a verb *to be*, we would be hard put to formulate the concept of Being or the concept of *what there is*. Both historically and linguistically, the philosophical project of ontology seems to depend upon—to have as a necessary condition—the possession of a verb *to be!*

My concern here is neither with the traditional role of *be* in Western metaphysics nor with the general problem of the relation between language and thought. But I shall be at least indirectly concerned with the relation between linguistics and philosophy, since

1

my topic lies somewhere in the no-man's-land between the two. From the linguistic point of view, the theory of the verb which I propose is a novel one, novel in part because the subject has never been studied in a systematic way, and in part because what I have to say differs from the traditional doctrine on *be* in comparative grammar. But the curious fact is that what I might claim as the central novelty in my theory, regarded as a thesis in linguistics, happens to have a close analogue in philosophy which is by no means new and is in fact now generally taken for granted. My linguistic thesis is that the predicative use of *be* as copula is primary and fundamental, whereas the noncopulative uses, including the existential use, are secondary and in a sense parasitic on the predicative use of the verb. (That is, I take the copula *is* as the basic function of *be*, whereas the existential use—as in "I think therefore I am"—is to be regarded as secondary and dependent on the copula verb.) The philosophical analogue which I have in mind is the view prefigured in Kant's claim that existence is not an ordinary predicate and more fully worked out in Frege's doctrine that existence is a second-order concept, a concept of concepts or function of functions, and not a first-order concept which applies directly to individuals. This Fregean view is incorporated into the symbolism of modern logic where existence is normally represented by a quantifier, that is to say, by a kind of sentence-operator, and not by a first-order predicate. An interesting question which I want to raise, but cannot fully discuss, is: What connection is there between this philosophical view of the relation between predication and existence (as embodied in Frege-Russell logic) and the linguistic thesis concerning the predicative and existential roles of *be* which I shall defend? I am sure that there must be some connection, but I would like to make clear from the outset that the connection cannot be a simple or direct one. My theory of the verb *be* was not conceived as a philosophic doctrine concerning the relation between predication and existence. I have worked out my view on the basis of a detailed study of the actual usage of the verb in ancient Greek.[1] I would like to think of this as a theory in empirical linguistics, designed to clarify and interpret the mass of available data concerning a particular verb in the Indo-European family of languages. (However, because of the borderline nature of the subject matter, the linguist may be unwilling to recognize my theory as belonging within this domain. To some linguists I will appear to be discussing philosophical matters, whereas to some philosophers, the issue will seem "merely empirical." See my Afterthought on method at the end of this paper.) Although my detailed work has been

[1] *The Verb "be" in Ancient Greek*, Foundations of Language Supplementary Series, Volume 16 (Dordrecht: Reidel, forthcoming).

on ancient Greek, most of the fundamental features seem to be common to the cognate verbs derived from the root *es of is in other Indo-European languages, particularly in the archaic stage of these languages, but also in their modern form; and I shall, as far as possible, illustrate the different uses by examples from modern English.

By a theory of the verb be I mean a conceptual framework that permits us, first, to describe and distinguish the various uses of be (or is) in Indo-European, and, second, to relate these uses to one another in an intelligible way, so that we can make some sense of the fact that a single linguistic sign has been employed for such a diversity of functions. Thus the theory may be explanatory, but not in any very strict sense of "explanation." The function of the theory is essentially conceptual: to introduce order and clarity into a mass of empirical data. The data include the occurrences of different forms of be (or εἶναι in Greek) in a vast number of sentences. The first conceptual task is to sort these occurrences out into different types or classes, which I call different "uses" of be. For each class I attempt to give a systematic definition in formal or syntactic terms. The next task is to see how these different uses belong together—why does a single verb serve as copula and as expression of existence, for example? Thus the theory I aim at must provide, first, a descriptive analysis and classification of the facts according to the principles of modern syntax, and, second, it should provide some "explanatory" synthesis which makes these facts intelligible by unifying them in some way. My underlying conviction, which I would like to make plausible, is that the diversity of uses for the verb be in Indo-European languages is more than a historical accident, that it represents a cluster of concepts whose interconnections are of permanent importance. In a sense, I would like to defend the verb against some of its critics. But on this occasion I can do little more than sketch the theory, and my defense of the verb will be largely implicit.

We cannot ignore the fact that, after so many centuries of glory, the verb be has recently had a bad press. Philosophers since J. S. Mill have complained that, by combining so many different functions—and above all, by expressing existence and predication with the same word is—the use of this verb in philosophy had led to serious error and systematic confusion. Linguists, on the other hand, have pointed out that the verb be is, after all, a local peculiarity of Indo-European and of no general importance in linguistics. More recently it has been suggested (by Emmon Bach and others) that the verb be is a phenomenon of surface structure only, even in English.[2] It

---

[2] See Emmon Bach, "Have and be in English Syntax," Language, Vol. 43 (1967), pp. 462–85; and John Lyons, Introduction to Theoretical Linguistics (Cambridge: Cambridge University Press, 1968), pp. 322 f., 388.

would seem that philosophical analysis, linguistic relativism, and
depth grammar have formed a kind of conspiracy to undermine the
traditional status of our verb as the expression for fundamental insights into the nature of things. To quote a recent linguist, speaking
of the absence of the copula in Chinese: "There is no concept of
Being which languages are well or ill equipped to present; the functions of 'to be' [as verb of predication in Indo-European] depend
upon a grammatical rule for the formation of the sentence [namely,
that every sentence should have a verb], and it would be merely
a coincidence if one found anything resembling it in a language without
this rule."[3]

My position on these matters is that of a moderate conservative.
We must admit that the logical distinctions between an *is* of existence,
an *is* of predication, and an *is* of identity imply that there can be
no unitary concept of Being in the traditional sense (though the tradition is not as naïve on this point as its critics often suppose). And
we must recognize the fact that the verb *be* (or **es-*) is a peculiarity
of Indo-European. But it does not follow that the traditional doctrines
and concepts built upon this Indo-European verb are a jumble of confusion or a projection onto the world of the surface grammar of Greek
and Latin. Although the diversity of functions serviced by this single
verb may be regarded as a historical accident, I want to suggest that
it was, philosophically speaking, a happy accident and that the proper
subject matter of ontology was in a sense delivered ready-made to
the Greek philosophers in the system of uses of their verb. I want
to claim that an adequate theory of *be* will justify an essential and
not merely etymological connection between the Indo-European verb
and the philosophical project of ontology. But in order to articulate
this claim, we must first have a theory of the verb.

We cannot consider all uses of the verb here. I omit, for example,
the archaic use of *be* to express possession, a use almost extinct in
English but partially preserved in French, where *Ce livre est à moi*
("This book belongs to me") echoes the old Indo-European idiom for
possession. Early Indo-European had no verb *to have*, and the idea of
I have was originally expressed as *est mihi ἔστι μοι* "It is for me." Of
considerable linguistic importance, this possessive use of *be* has exer-
cised no great influence on the philosophical career of the verb. For
entirely different reasons, I shall have nothing to say about the *is* of
identity. This use is of great importance for philosophy but it has no
precise linguistic significance. I mean that neither in Indo-European
nor, as far as I can tell, in any other natural language does the language

---

[3] A. C. Graham, " 'Being' in Classical Chinese," *The Verb 'be' and Its Synonyms,*
Part I (Dordrecht: Reidel, 1967), p. 15.

itself make a formal distinction between a statement of identity and an ordinary predication. From the linguistic point ofi view, an identity statement is a logically (but not linguistically) specal case of predication. We might say that "A is B" is a statement of identity just in case "A is B" and "B is A" are both true. Or, since statements of identity may be false, we may say that "A is B" is an identity sentence when the speaker who asserts "A is B" would also assert "B is A." But this logically special feature is, as a rule, not reflected in the *form* of the sentence. Why natural languages do not regularly mark off predications of identity by a distinct sentence form is itself an interesting question, but not one with which I shall deal. It has more bearing on a theory of the definite article than on a theory of the verb *be*.

Our discussion, then, will be limited to three philosophically central and linguistically distinct uses of *be*: the copula or predicative use, the existential, and what I call the veridical use. I want to suggest that the use of a single verb for these three roles reflects certain deep conceptual connections between the function of predication, the notion of existence, and the notion of truth. But first we must define these three uses of *be*. Now my methodological assumption is that, if we are not going to be satisfied with vague and intuitive notions of "use," to define a distinct use of the verb means to describe a sentence form or syntactic structure in which the verb occurs. But this means that we must have a rather precise syntax at our disposal.

The syntax I make use of is the transformational theory of Zellig Harris, which is closely related to but formally quite different from the generative grammars of Noam Chomsky and his school. In this transformational theory there are no branching tree diagrams and no rewrite rules. The theory consists, on the one hand, of a list of kernel or elementary sentence forms for English and, on the other hand, of a set of transformations defined either as regular relations between sentences forms or as operations (or rules) by which one acceptable sentence form can be derived from another equally acceptable sentence form. We can describe this theory as a kind of axiomatic system designed to derive all English sentences from a small number of elementary forms by means of specified transformations. The elementary sentence forms are the axioms. The transformations are the rules of derivation. Thus the familiar active-passive relation between *John loves Mary* and *Mary is loved by John* is a transformation for Harris as for Chomsky. The passive transformation is the relation between these two, or the rule for forming the second from the first. But Harris also admits a more radical type of transformation where the transform is not a paraphrase of its source. For example, there is a set of transformations which take a sentence as operand and which add an epistemic or intentional concept as operator. The concept of truth like the concept of knowledge is introduced in this way. In Harris' theory, the sentence *It is true that John loves Mary* is a transform of *John loves Mary;* and the sentence *I know that John loves Mary* is a transform of this same kernel sentence, *John loves Mary*. Such transformational operators, which take an embedded sentence or *that* clause as their object or subject, are known as sentence-operators. As we shall see, both the veridical and the most typical existential uses of *be* are of this general form; both are sentence-operators.

We must now define the copula, and the existential and veridical uses.

For a definition of the copula we consider the kernel or elementary sentences of English. (I give Harris' theory in my own, somewhat simplified version.) Elementary sentence forms can be grouped into two classes, symbolized as *NV* Ω and *N is* Φ, where *N* represents an elementary or first-order noun (roughly, a "concrete" noun), *V* represents a standard verb, and Ω represents the (direct or indirect) object of the verb. Ω may be a noun or a phrase, but it may also be empty (where the verb takes no object) or it may be double (where the verb takes two objects). Thus *John sleeps, John loves Mary, John speaks to Mary,* and *John gives Mary a book* represent four subtypes of *NV* Ω which differ only in the form of Ω. Somewhat similarly, the elementary varieties of the copula sentence *N is* Φ differ according to the form of the "predicate," Φ. We can recognize three principal subtypes of the copula, depending upon whether Φ is an adjective, a noun, or a prepositional phrase: *John is tall, John is a man, John is at the office.* We can define the elementary copula as the verb *be* in sentences of this form, *N is* Φ, where Φ ranges over adjectives, nouns, and prepositional phrases. (We could also define second-order and other types of copula by analogy with this form, but for our purposes the elementary copula will suffice.)

Overlooking the distinction between predicate nouns and adjectives, we can focus on the two major subclasses of elementary copula: the nominal copula (where the predicate Φ is a noun or adjective) and the locative or quasi locative copula (where Φ is a prepositional phrase). (By quasi locatives I mean those prepositional phrases where the locative connotation of the preposition is at best metaphorical, as in *John is in a hurry* or *John is at a loss.* Such quasi locative sentences are probably all nonelementary uses of the copula, hence we can omit them here. But, in any case, there is a clear structural analogy between these sentences and properly locative uses of the same prepositions: *John is in a boat; John is at a beach.*)

Thus two basic uses of the copula are (1) to assign a predicate noun or adjective to a concrete subject: *John is a student; John is sad*, and (2) to locate a subject in a given place: *John is at home, John is in Chicago*. In the traditional theory of *be*, the locative copula was strangely ignored. In some recent discussions it has been emphasized, particularly by John Lyons, who has called attention to the systematic connections between expressions for location, possession, and existence in many languages. In English, one obvious connection between locative and existential forms is suggested by the degenerate local adverb *there* which occurs in the existential phrase, *there is*. The locative role of *be* in Indo-European is a topic on which there would be much to say.[4] But we must turn to the two principal non-copulative uses: the existential and veridical. These are both noncopu-lative insofar as they do not conform to the pattern *N is* Φ.

It is difficult to give a formal definition of the existential use, since this is primarily a semantic or lexical notion. In ancient Greek I have found five or six distinct sentence types where *be* would intuitively be said to have existential force. There are parallels to these types in English, but the formal situation is different for us because the existential idea is nearly always expressed in English by the special locution *there is* or by the separate verb *to exist*. In early Indo-European including classic Greek, there was no verb *to exist*, and all existential sentences are formed by the ordinary *is*. In Greek *The gods exist* or *There is no Zeus* is expressed literally as *The gods are* and *Zeus is not:* εἰσὶ θεοί, οὐκ ἔστι Ζεύς. The philosopher may or may not be surprised to learn that such typically existential sentences—what I call here "pure existentials"—which assert or deny the existence of a definite individual or a definite sort of individual, do not occur in the earliest texts. Thus there are no such sentences in Homer. The earliest pure existentials attested in Greece are from the period of the Sophists, and they are nearly always concerned with the existence of the gods. Existential sentences of the form *N is* or *N is not* arise almost as a technical use which seems to be the result of philosophic speculation and theological controversy. In its earliest existential uses, the verb *be* serves not to assert existence in general or absolutely but to provide a subject for further predication, within a definite context.

As a representative of this nontechnical, prephilosophic use of *be* with existential force bound to a specific context of predication, I take

---

[4] In particular, it turns out that the intuitive force of *be* in the existential uses is closely connected with its locative function of locating the subject in a region or group ("in a corner of Argos," among the Trojans"). This locative background of the existential use of *be*, which is reflected in modern idioms like *"there is"* (compare Italian *"ci sono"* French *"il y a"*), is particularly clear in early Greek, where an existential use of ἔστι can often be translated "is present," "is found (there)."

the complex sentence form *There is someone (no one) who* . . . . For example, *There is someone who has betrayed me; There is no one who can fight against the gods.* Notice that in this use the existential verb is almost superfluous; the sentence with *be* is an expressive or emphatic variant on a sentence with indefinite subject and with ordinary verb: *Someone has betrayed me; No one can fight against the gods.* In the existential variant, *there is* serves as a sentence operator which emphatically asserts or denies a subject for the indefinite sentence, transformed as a relative clause: *There is someone who* . . . . I regard this as the typical function of *be* as existential verb: to present or provide (and in the negative form, to deny) a subject for further predication. The resulting sentence form bears an obvious analogy to existential quantification in logic $(\exists x)$ Fx. (I will return to the existential in a moment.)

Finally, we have the veridical use. By this I mean the sentences in which *be* has the value "is true" or "is the case." The most typical ancient specimens are of the form *It is (so)* or *It is as you say.* Familiar English examples are provided by the rather archaic expression *So be it!* and by the not-so-archaic *Tell it like it is.* Notice that in this use the understood or underlying subject, represented in surface structure by *it,* is never a concrete noun or first-order nominal but a sentential subject, that is to say, a syntactical structure equivalent to a *that* clause. For example, "You ask *that your wishes be granted:* so be it!" Or "You claim *that he loves her:* it is as you say." In these examples the *it* refers back to the *that* clause. Here again, then, the verb *be* has the syntactical status of a sentence-operator, since its underlying "subject"—the antecedent of *it*—is sentential in form. The structure of this veridical operator is quite different from the existential type just illustrated (*there is someone who* . . .); but both uses are clearly nonelementary or second order, in terms of transformational syntax. And both the existential and the veridical uses are noncopulative, since neither takes a predicate expression as the copula does in sentences of the form N *is* Φ.

So much by way of a mini-description of the three central uses of *be*: as copula, as existential verb, and as veridical locution. Both in terms of the verb's intuitive "meaning" (or, for the copula, lack of meaning) and in the syntactical form of the sentence, these three uses are quite distinct. We now ask how these uses are related to one another: How is it that these three different functions are performed in Indo-European by a single verb?

The traditional theory of *be* ignores the veridical use (or assimilates it to the existential) and relates the existential and the copula verb as follows. (This is the doctrine of the standard comparative grammars, going back to Brugmann and Meillet.) The verb *be* (or *es-) was originally a verb like other verbs, with concrete meaning. The original meaning was *to exist*, or perhaps something even more concrete like *to be present* or *to be alive*. Predicate nouns and adjectives were originally expressed without any verb, in the so-called "nominal sentence" familiar from Russian and many other languages: *John is wise* was simply *John/wise; John is a man* was *John/(a) man*, and so forth. But in the course of time it became useful to introduce a verb into the nominal sentence, in order to express the tense, person, mood, and other modalities carried by the finite verb in Indo-European. Hence the verb *be* (meaning *exist*) was introduced into the nominal sentence, where it gradually lost its original meaning and degenerated into an "empty" verb or "mere copula," a syntactic device which serves to satisfy the requirement that every sentence must contain a verb.

This historical-sounding theory is enshrined in all the textbooks, but there is precious little evidence in its favor. The notion of an Indo-European language without a copula verb is a pure figment of the imagination. The copula uses of *be* are predominant from the earliest texts: the copula represents something like 80 percent of all uses of *be* in Homer, for example. The notion that the existential uses are somehow more fundamental or more primitive than the copula seems to be a mere prejudice—a prejudice based, perhaps, upon a mistaken philosophical view of existence as an ordinary predicate. Hence I propose a modest Copernican revolution: to reinstate the copula at the center of the system of uses of the verb. Instead of "deriving" the copula construction chronologically from some earlier state of the language without this construction, I propose to take the copula uses as fundamental and primitive for the verb *be* in Indo-European. In some loose sense of the word "derive," I propose that we derive the existential and veridical uses from the copula. This sense of "derive" must be very loose, however, for I do *not* mean that the copula uses are older—for that also there is no evidence. (Nor do I mean that existential and veridical sentences are transformationally or syntactically derived from copula uses of *be*.) I mean simply that if we take the copula use as "original," we can see why the *same* verb should be used to express existence for a subject and also to express truth or being-so for a sentential content or alleged fact.

In order to see these connections we must have a more adequate view of the copula function of *be*. Linguists often speak of the copula as a dummy verb, as a merely formal "bearer" of the verbal marks of tense, person, and the like. There is some truth in this view, but it obscures as much as it reveals. What it reveals is that the copula

be does not function like other verbs which provide specific information content like *runs, eates, loves*. In the copula sentence the informative concept is provided by the predicate word or phrase, not by
the verb. In *John is tall*, the essential information is provided by
tall, whereas *is* might be omitted without loss, as in the nominal
sentence. But as Abelard (who developed the classic doctrine of the
copula) clearly saw, what the copula does is to separate out a function
that is less clearly visible in the case of other verbs just because
it is combined with the expression of a concrete concept or meaning,
like *running, eating, sleeping*.[5] To this extent, the copula is the finite
verb par excellence because it separates out *the function of the finite
verb as such* from the concrete meaning or content which is expressed
by other verbs (and by predicate nouns and adjectives). It is this
idea of copula as verb par excellence which was formulated in the
traditional designation of the copula as a sign of predication. I want
to develop this idea by describing the copula as a sign of predication
at three distinct levels, of increasing generality. The first level is
that of the verb *be* as it is actually used in Indo-European. The
second level is that of the philosophical rewriting of all subject-predicate sentences in the form *S is P,* as in traditional logic. At the
third level the verb *be* is used in complete abstraction from subject-
predicate form, as a general sign for declarative sentencehood or for
the corresponding truth claim or alleged fact, regardless of the form
of the sentence. Let us take these three senses of "sign of predication"
in the order of increasing generality or increasing theoretical
abstraction.

　　1. In its actual use, the copula verb serves not for all subject-
predicate sentences but only for those where the predicate is an adjective, a noun, or a nonverbal phrase. This is the use which I have
defined by contrasting copula sentences of the form *N is* Φ with ordinary verbal sentences of the form *N V* Φ. In the copula sentence
the subject-predicate form is particularly clear, of course. But in this
use the copula also serves two functions which are worthy of note.
The first is peculiar to the Indo-European verb **es-*. The second is
common to all finite verb forms. The special function of **es-* (or
is) is the expression of a static or stative aspect, in contrast to the
kinetic or mutative aspect expressed by *becomes*. The contrast of
is such-and-such to *becomes such-and-such* in nominal predication
is exactly parallel to the contrast of *is somewhere* to *goes somewhere*
or *arrives somewhere* in locative sentences. That is to say, the copula

[5] For Abelard's theory of the copula see his *Logica "Ingredientibus,"* ed. Geyer
(1917–1927), pp. 351 f., 352, 359, 362, and *Dialectica*, ed. De Rijk (1956), pp.
134–38, 161.

is has a static value in nominal predication just as it does in statements of place. This essentially static aspect of *is* deserves a prominent place in any full theory of the verb. But we must pass on here to the more general function of *is*, which it shares with other finite verbs. This is the syntactic mark of sentencehood, and above all of declarative sentencehood, with the corresponding semantic value of a truth claim. To understand the function of the copula as sign of predication, we must consider it both from the syntactic and from the semantic points of view.

I take it for granted that the declarative sentence is the basic form of sentencehood, not only for logical but also for linguistic analysis. The theory of questions, commands, conditions, and other modalities must be built up on the basis of a theory of declarative sentences, as used in statements or assertions. In this sense, the declarative sentence is the primitive sentential form. This means that in Indo-European the indicative is the primitive mood and that the basic use of indicative sentences is for making statements. I shall speak of the declarative sentence form as bearing a truth claim. This locution can be regarded as a short-hand way of saying that the declarative sentence is the form provided by the language as the typical instrument for making statements.

We consider, then, declarative sentences such as *Socrates is wise* or *The cat is on the mat*. The assertion or truth claim is, of course, a function of the whole sentence and not of the verb alone. But there is a clear sense in which the finite verb is the formal mark of sentencehood ("every sentence must have a verb"), and the indicative verb is the mark of declarative sentencehood or truth claim. (Strictly speaking, we would have to mention the declarative intonation here, to rule out questions and unasserted uses of the indicative. But I ignore these complications.) The special declarative role of the verb can be brought out if we emphasize it in pronunciation: "Socrates *is* wise," or "The cat *is* on the mat." Because the copula as a finite verb carries the formal mark of declarative sentencehood, emphasis on the copula expresses a strengthened assertion of the sentence as a whole. For other verbs, similar emphasis requires a periphrase of the verb with *do*: "John *does* love Mary," or "He *did* go, after all." The truth claim of the sentence as a whole is thus associated formally with the finite verb in general, and with the copula in particular.

Underneath the traditional description of the copula as sign of predication, then, lie these two connected functions: the syntactic mark of sentencehood and the semantic mark of truth claim. It is true that one can devise a generative grammar of English in which the copula disappears from deep structure. But then the deep structure must contain other formal indications for declarative sentencehood.

2. The second sense in which *be* serves as a sign of predication is more abstract and philosophical. It is based upon the insight that every finite verb form can be rewritten periphrastically as a combination of *is* and participle: *John runs* as *John is running, John loves Mary* as *John is loving Mary,* and so on. This canonical rewriting is, of course, not always as idiomatic as the original sentence, or it would not normally be used in the same context. But that is not the point. The point is that such rewriting provides a uniform schema for all subject-predicate or noun-phrase-verb-phrase sentences in the language, and that means for nearly all basic or elementary sentences. The philosophical importance of the copula from Aristotle to the *Logic* of Port Royal rests precisely upon this uniform rewriting of sentences in the form *S is P.* And although the copula is no longer so conspicuous in modern logic, essentially the same function is served by the canonical rewriting of sentences in the form *Fa* or *Fx,* to reveal their predicative structure. It is no accident that *Fa* is commonly read as "*a* is *F.*" And if *this* is what we mean by the verb *be* as sign of predication, it should be clear that *be* cannot be eliminated from deep structure so long as deep structure is to retain any analogy with the forms of predicate logic. There must be *something* in the structure of sentences to correspond with the form *Fx,* and hence with *x is F* or *S is P.* In this second sense, then, *be* represents the form of predication in general.

3. Finally, there is a sense in which the verb *be* can serve as sign of predication for any sentence, whether or not it is of subject-predicate (or function-argument) form. Consider the impersonal sentence *It is raining,* which in many languages would be rendered by a finite verb alone, without any dummy-subject *it: pluit* in Latin, *piove* in Italian, for example. Let us assume that these are not subject-predicate sentences. (An indication of this is that it scarcely makes sense to ask "What is raining?") Now if you say "It rained yesterday," I may answer "It is as you say," where "it is" affirms the sentential content which you asserted. In this veridical use of *is* we no longer have the copula, and we have no predication in the ordinary sense. We have only the sign of a sentential form (namely, the form which underlies it as subject of *is*), and the assertion or confirmation of a truth claim. This veridical use of *is,* in *It is so,* or *tell it like it is* is a kind of generalization of its role as mark of declarative sentencehood in copula sentences. Because of this syntactic and semantic continuity with the role of the copula, I would stretch the term "sign of predication" to apply to this generalized

veridical use of *is* to express the content of any sentence whatsoever, including sentences which may not be of subject-predicate form.

We can now see why the verb *be*, whose primary use is that of the copula, is also employed as veridical verb for the assertion of any arbitrary sentence or for its validation in the corresponding fact. In a veridical sentence, for example *Tell it like it is*, the verb *is* serves explicitly to express the fact or real situation. But this is what the copula implicitly claims to do in all declarative sentences. The veridical use of *be* simply makes general and explicit the truth claim which is implicit and particularized in every elementary use of the copula. The veridical use is, of course, second order, since it takes an underlying *that* clause or sentential content as its subject. It thus serves to separate off the truth claim (or the purported positive truth value) as a distinct idea, in order to talk about it, or *thematize* it in Husserl's sense. In the elementary copula use the truth claim is implicit in the declarative form of the sentence but closely associated with the finite verb. In the veridicial use the verb is abstracted from the copula construction and used as a kind of second-order predicate or sentence operator. Since the copula *is*, for various reasons, figures as the finite verb par excellence, the same verb is naturally used for the general form of sentential truth claim, meaning *It is the case that* . . . or *This is how matters stand*. This is the value of the verb *is* in *Tell it like it is*. Thus the veridical use of *be* abstracts out an essential semantic component of declarative sentences in general, and of copula sentences in particular.

We can give a somewhat similar account of the existential use of *be*. Consider a sentence like *John is wise* or *John is at home*. The copula *is*, as finite verb, bears the mark of sentential truth claim for these subject-predicate sentences. Now one of the truth conditions for such a sentence is, of course, the existence of a subject. Regardless whether we consider *John is wise* as false or as nonsensical on the supposition that John does not exist, clearly *John is wise* is true only if John does exist. The existence of the subject is an essential semantic component, a truth condition or presupposition of the simple declarative sentence as a whole. The verb which is uniquely associated with the truth claim of the sentence can thus be used to express the existence of the subject. This is not only conceptually justified in the sense just suggested (namely, because the existence of the subject is a semantic component of the subject-predicate statement). It is also linguistically natural because of various formal connections between the finite verb and its subject. The Indo-European verb agrees with its subject in person and number. Emphasis on the verb can thus serve to focus attention on the subject, to present it in an emphatic way. At least this is true in an ancient language like Greek, where placing the verb in the emphatic initial position makes a copula sentence *look* like an existential: ἔστι Σωκράτης σοφός, with the verb first, could be translated either "Socrates *is* wise" or "There is a wise Socrates." This connection between copula and existential verb is not so obvious in English, where the pre-posed verb must be preceded by the expletive "there."[6] In Greek, but not in English, a so-called existential use often differs from the copula construction only by the emphatic initial position for the verb: ἔστι πόλις Ἐφύρη μύχῳ "Ἄργεος ἱπποβότοιο, which we must render as "*There is a city Ephyre in a corner of Argos.*" Thus the close connection between copula and existential verb is obscured in English by the special "existential" idiom *there is.*

But we can reveal this connection by a little transformational analysis. *There is a man at the door* is related to the copula sentence *A man is at the door* just as *There came a knight ariding* is related to *A knight came ariding.* That is to say, in modern English, where the declarative word order is relatively fixed, we can bring the verb to the head of the sentence only by some special device such as the unstressed adverb *there.* In *There came a knight ariding,* the word *there* serves only to bring the verb before its subject. And in *There is a man at the door, there* serves exactly the same function: to bring the verb to the head of the sentence. Why then, does *there is* seem to us a distinctly existential verb and no longer a mere copula?

The reason lies, I believe, in the typical function of *there is* sentences in ordinary discourse, which is also the typical function of so-called existential uses of ἔστι in nonphilosophical Greek. This is: to introduce a subject for subsequent predication. To show that this is so would require consideration of more examples than we have time for. I can only point out that, in most nontechnical uses of the existential verb, the existential form is strictly superfluous, and we could have the same meaning with an ordinary copula. The copula sentence *Ephyre is a city in Argos,* is a good paraphrase equivalent for our "existential" sentence *There is a city Ephyre in Argos;* and either *Socrates is a wise man* or *A man named Socrates is wise* can serve as paraphrase for *There is a wise man named Socrates.* The peculiar feature of these *there is* sentences in English (and of their Greek originals, where we have an initial ἔστι) is that they introduce a subject—Socrates, the

---

[6] It is worth noting that the use of the unstressed adverb "there" (in our modern idiom "there is") is a relatively late addition to the existential verb, going back to the thirteenth century. In earlier English, as in ancient Greek, this existential use was represented by *be* alone. For the introduction of "there" (as a device for bringing the verb before its subject) see Fernand Mossé, *A Handbook of Middle English,* J. A. Walker (tr.) (Baltimore, 1952), p. 128 (§ 174).

city Ephyre—which will be further described or referred to in what follows. As you know, Plato's sentence actually continues: *There is a certain Socrates, a wise man, a student of things aloft and an enquirer into all things under the earth, who makes the weaker argument the stronger.*[7] We might call this use of ἔστι or *there is* the "existential copula," since the *is* here is transformationally derived from the copula. Realistically described, the function of the "existential" verb in such uses is not to assert the existence of Socrates but to *introduce* Socrates as a subject for predication, as a person about whom more is to be said.

The case is slightly different for what I have taken as the typical existential use, in sentences of the form *There is someone (no one) who.* . . . Here we do have a full-fledged existential use, since the verb does *not* function as copula. (In transformational terms, this use of *there is* can not be derived from the copula.) Here its function is *only* to present (or in the negative, to deny) a subject for the following predication, spelled out in the relative clause. What I suggest is that the verb *be* can *also* function in this way, to present a subject as such, just because it very often functions as existential copula, to introduce the subject of a copula predication.

We may refer to the uses so far described as "bound" existentials, since they are tied to a specific context of predication. The pure or "free" existential, which is so dear to philosophers—as in *There are gods* or *There is no Zeus*—is more difficult to explain in linguistic terms, but I think it can be seen as a natural development from the typical "bound" existential use in *There is someone who.* . . . I believe that here too (in *There are gods*) the verb serves properly to assert or deny a subject for predication—for any and all predication. Hence here too we can see how the predicative verb comes to serve as verb of existence. However, in this use philosophical generality is obtained by the omission of any specific predicates, and as a result the basic predicative connections of the verb are obscured.[8] We seem to have the assertion of a bare subject or the assertion of

---

[7] Plato, *Apology*, 17B6. The other sample is from *Iliad*, VI. 152.

[8] On my view, the pure or "free" existential use (εἰσὶ θεοί "there are gods") arises from (1) the generalization of the bound existential ("there are gods who . . .") by the deletion of every specific predicate, and (2) the reinforcement of the existential value by the influence of the veridical nuance: the negative οὐκ εἰσὶ θεοί "there are no gods" (which is probably more primitive than the corresponding affirmative and thus represents the original form of the "pure" existential) means or suggests: "There is nothing true of the gods, everything said about them is a pack of lies." The basic linguistic function and flavor of the pure existential seems to me expressed by the following equivalences: (1) "x is" $= x$ is something" or, in symbols, $(\exists y)(x$ is $y)$, and (2) "x is not" $=$ "x is nothing" or, in symbols, $\sim(\exists y)(x$ is $y)$.

its mere existence. And hence arises the illusion that *existence* is the predicate! But this purely existential use of *be* is a late development in Greek, and should by no means be considered the original use or basic meaning of the verb. The Greeks, at any rate, seem to have remained sufficiently aware of the basic predicative function of the verb as copula so that they were never seriously tempted to regard existence as itself a predicate. They were protected from this error precisely by their use of the same verb for copula and for existence.

This may serve as my defense of the verb *be* against its critics. What I have tried to show is that there is more to the copula than meets the eye. And I have suggested how, once we have an adequate account of *be* as a sign of predication, a theory of the verb based upon the copula construction can give a reasonable account of the veridical and existential uses as well. Because the copula serves as the typical sign of subject-predicate structure (with sentential truth claim), it can also serve to posit a subject as such, that is, to assert the existence of its subject as a basis for predication. And because the copula verb serves as sign of sentencehood and truth claim, it can also express this claim (or its implied validation in *fact*) for any arbitrary sentence. The permanent fascination of the verb *be* for philosophers derives, on the one hand, from its essential connection with the subject-predicate structure of sentences and, on the other hand, from its more general connection with the semantic function of declarative sentences as saying something (true or false) about something in the world. In the ancient veridical use, which is still alive in our idiom *Tell it like it is*, the verb *is* expresses this fundamental semantic or ontological notion underlying descriptive language as such: the notion of *how things stand* or *what is the case*, which supports the concept of truth and makes the communication of information intelligible, the very same notion which philosophers have called "reality" or "the facts" or "the way the world is."

Perhaps we are better off with a separate verb *to exist*. And of course it is convenient to have a distinct terminology for the veridical concepts: *truth*, *fact*, and *reality*. (However, when we want a veridical *verb*, it is hard to do without "is"!) But as long as ontology is still concerned with the three concepts of predicaton, existence, and truth, it is not in vain that it derives its name from the Indo-European verb *to be*. And the terminology of being (or *what is* or *what there is*) has this advantage over terms like "exists" or "reality": The terminology of being implicitly connects the concept of existence and what is really there in the world with the notion of predication and the concept of truth for sentences. In this sense the verb *be* still properly serves to mark out the central problems of ontology.

* * *

As a conclusion, I might say a word about the problem raised at the beginning of this paper. Let us assume that I am correct in claiming that the predicative use of *be* is primary and that the existential use of the verb is secondary and in a sense parasitic upon this predicative base. How is this new linguistic insight related to the older and now quite standard philosophic view of existence as a second-order concept which presupposes a first-order pattern of predication—the view that existence is parasitic on predication in the sense that $(\exists x)\ Fx$ is parasitic on Fx or on Fa? As I pointed out, my linguistic view was not reached by *applying* the logical analysis of existence to the linguistic data. I began with the traditional assumption that the existential use was primary and only abandoned this view in the face of linguistic evidence —in particular, the evidence that the copula use is overwhelmingly predominant in the oldest texts (and probably in all texts). Still, I am sure that there must be *some* connection between my linguistic "discovery" and the logical account of existence associated with the names of Frege and Russell and embodied in the notation of standard logic. As I see it, there are two ways to explain the connection, both of which have some plausibility. I will call these the Popperian and the Strawsonian account, where it is understood that the proper names are being used metaphorically, to suggest the kind of thing a philosopher like Popper or Strawson *might* say to explain this connection between an older philosophic insight and a new "empirical" thesis in linguistics.

On the Popperian view, the philosophical analysis of existence could stimulate a "conjecture," that is to say, it could suggest an hypothesis to be applied to the empirical data of linguistics and to be tested gainst these data. Only when the factual evidence is seen to corroborate rather than to falsify this thesis is it acceptable as a theory in the empirical study of language. Such a Popperian account is attractive because it does justice to my conviction that it was only the detailed study of the Greek evidence which persuaded me to give up the traditional assumption that the existential use of *be* was primary. I accept the primacy of the copula use only *because* it is factually predominant and *because* in the actual sentences of ancient Greek, (and to some extent in English sentences with *there is*) I can see the existential use emerging from the copula use, but not vice versa. I was no doubt helped to see this, and to articulate it as a theory, by my previous familiarity with the logical notion of existence as a quantifier or operator on predication.

On the other hand, a Strawsonian (or perhaps a super-Strawsonian) account might well hold that, however I may have come to *see* that the existential uses of *be* are linguistically secondary to, and dependent upon, the basic predicative function of the verb, the conceptual relations between existence and predication are such that it *must* be the case that any term which expresses both will first of all and primarily express predication. Now to recast my linguistic "discovery" as the transcendental deduction of an a priori conceptual truth might be going too far, even for a super-Strawsonian. Still, if my thesis is right there is something which makes it right beyond the fact that it introduces order and clarity into the empirical data. As one Hellenist said, in response to my conclusion: "Yes, that is how language is." I for one would be very sceptical of any linguist who claimed to find a natural language with a lexeme whose primitive and basic function was to express the concept of existence. (In this connection, we may note that our own verb *to exist* is derived from a Latin verb meaning *to step out* or *to emerge*.) Although I do not like to talk this way in philosophy, I am inclined to say: It is not really possible to *imagine* a natural language whose basic vocabulary includes a verb which properly and literally means *to exist*. I suspect that it takes philosophy (or philosophically oriented speculation—for example, skeptical doubts about the truth of the traditional accounts of the gods) to discover the need for such a concept. The concept of existence is not only second order; it is philosophically sophisticated. But every language, from the beginning, needs some formal device for predication. Hence when we encounter languages like Indo-European, where a single word serves for predication and existence, we could in a sense know—or reasonably guess—a priori that the predicative use is more basic, that it is not derived from an older existential use. I do not offer this as an *argument* for the truth of my thesis, much less for its a priori truth. I offer it only as a report or perhaps an explanation of my intuitive conviction that this thesis is not just factually correct but that it *must* be right, and that the traditional doctrine that the copula is derived from an existential verb can only be explained by the even more traditional but incoherent view of existence as an ordinary predicate.[9]

I do not apologize for these reflections on the relation between philosophic analysis and empirical linguistics, even though my conclu-

---

[9] I should make clear that my conviction here is based upon the special nature of the concept of existence, as the product of philosophical or quasi philosophical speculation, and not merely upon the fact that it is a concept of the second order. The concept of truth is also nonelementary; its expression is syntactically complex and semantically meta-linguistic. But the notion of truth is indispensable even in the most natural language. And in Indo-European the veridical use of *be*, unlike the pure existential use, is attested in the earliest texts and is demonstrably prehistoric.

sions are obviously very imprecise. We stand, after all, on the border-
line between philosophy and empirical science, where precision may
be particularly difficult to achieve. This does not alter the fact that
it is just in these borderline areas that philosophical reflection may
be most fruitful and most productive.

AFTERTHOUGHT ON METHOD

I have thought of my account of *be* as a theory in empirical
linguistics, whose function is essentially conceptual: to introduce order
and clarity into a mass of empirical data. But a friendly critic, who
is also a very fine linguist, doubts whether my thesis of the primacy
of the copula among the various uses of *be* is clearly enough defined
for a linguist to decide (or even to see how to decide) whether or
not it has been established. My first inclination is to respond by
placing the burden of proof on the opposition: I have given *some*
account of the unity of the system taking the copula as my starting
point. If anyone dissents, it is up to him to show that a *better* account
can be given if we take the existential or some other use as primary.
But this response would be evasive, since what is really in question
is the force of the notion of "primary" here. Can it be given a clear
linguistic sense? In the traditional theory of the verb, although evidence was lacking, the claim was at least clear: The existential use
of the verb was said to be historically older. Since my theory does
not pretend to be diachronic, what is the significance of speaking
of a *primary* use?

I am not sure that I can give an adequate answer to this question.
My notion of the copula as primary rests upon the following three
considerations: (1) in terms of frequency of occurrence, the copula
use is overwhelmingly preponderant from the earliest texts (at least
in Greek); (2) in terms of tranformational syntax, the copula occurs
in elementary sentence forms, the existential and veridical do not;
and (3) it is possible to see (as I tried to show) how a verb whose
typical function is copulative can *also* be used as existential or as
veridical, but not conversely. The third consideration is perhaps the
most decisive for my theory, but it raises similar questions: What
do I mean by "typical function" and what is the status of the claim
that "it is possible to see how"? We are led here into very deep
problems in the theory of linguistic meaning, for which I have no
general solutions. My account of *be* is intended as a small contribution
to the theory of meaning, but it does not constitute such a theory.
Until we have one, it seems we must either abandon the study of
linguistic meaning or make provisional use of such intuitive notions
as primary or typical use and secondary or derivative use, within

a synchronic perspective. Transformational analysis can help to clarify these intuitive notions, but, as far as I can see, it can neither define them adequately nor permit us to dispense with them. Thus we could, for the purpose of my thesis, define a primary use of *be* as one which occurs in elementary sentences. But this definition could not be used to formulate my claim that the existential and veridical uses are *dependent* on the copula, since I do not claim that either of these uses can, in general, be transformationally derived from the copula sentence form. It is true that in some cases the existential and veridical constructions *are* transformationally derivable from the copula. But this is not enough for my purposes. I want to argue more generally for the *unity* of the system of uses for the verb in a sense which I cannot quite make precise. It seems to rely upon a relation of conceptual priority which is roughly of the following sort: the copula use of *be* is conceptually prior to the existential and veridical uses in that it could exist without them but not conversely.

More precision is desirable, and perhaps it can be attained. But the fact that precision is unobtainable (at least for the moment, and for me) does not seem a sufficient reason for abandoning the attempt to see the various uses together, unified by their relation (direct or indirect) to a primary use. If the theory of linguistic meaning is to make progress, we will have to continue to rely upon such *ad hoc* blends of empirical and conceptual considerations, where formal and intuitive principles of description are both employed. If we insist on waiting for an adequate general theory before dealing with particular problems of meaning, we may never get started.

The Content of Existence

JOSEPH OWENS

Pontifical Institute of Medieval Studies

I

The problem of content for existence has a long ancestry. It may be traced back as far as the poem of Parmenides, in which the *estin*—the "exists"—is found to ingest one by one its alleged subjects and its qualitative and quantitative determinations. No room is left for anything whatsoever outside the *estin*. Existence accordingly has a content that is all-embracing. Existence includes in its own intrinsic and undifferentiated unity everything that exists or has existed or will exist or can exist. Outside its own inalienable content there is and can be absolutely nothing.[1]

However, in philosophy, as in ordinary life, an extreme position tends to generate its opposite. The evidence offered by Parmenides could be viewed by other thinkers in a way that reversed the black and white as effectively as a negative print in photography. If all the determinations of things are being and are one, Aristotle noted,[2]

---

[1] Parmenides, *Fr.* 8.1–49 (DK). Interpretations of Parmenides' poem differ radically, but they agree that it presents a view in which human reasoning shows that all things coalesce in being no matter how much they differ in appearance.

[2] *Metaph.* B 3,998b22–28. Cf. "But if there *is* to be a being-itself and a unity-itself, there is much difficulty in seeing how there will be anything besides these,—I mean, how things will be more than one in number. For what is different from being does not exist, so that it necessarily follows, according to the argument of Parmenides, that all things are one and this is being." Ibid. 4,1001a29-bl. Rather, the highest genera are immediately being, without addition of anything else: "But of things which have no matter, either intelligible or perceptible, each is by its nature essentially a kind of unity, as it is essentially a kind of being . . . and so none of these has any reason outside itself for being one, nor for being a kind of being." H 6,1045a36–b5. Explicitly rejected in

21

then being and unity cannot be first principles of things. Obviously, the determinations and the multiplicity of things come first. The fact that each of the things is being and each is one shows rather that neither being nor unity can be a genus that would embrace them all in a single nature. Any notion pertaining to the order of being cannot in consequence have generic content. Subsequent thinkers will show that it cannot have any content at all. The notion of being coincides with that of not being.[3]

Greatly oversimplified, then, the issue would seem to be that all content must be absorbed either by existence or else by its particular determinations. It does not seem that content can be shared by both. If to exist has content of its own, that content, as Parmenides reasoned, will include all determinations and differences, even individual differences. Being contains all its differences. They all exist; they all are being. But if one reverse the perspective, as with Aristotle, the fact that they all are being means that being is nothing but these individuals and determinations. There is no content left over for a generic nature of being.

In a word, the identification of being with its differentiae can be considered in two different ways. If being includes its differentiae, the content of the totality may be ascribed to being and nothing else will be left for the differentiae. If, to the contrary, the content is allowed to remain with the differentiae, being is nothing other than the sum total of these differentiae. It has no content apart from them. It is merely a concept that has to be explained through various references to a single nature or focal point,[4] or in some other way that

the anti-Parmenidean context is the notion of not-being as a nature added for the purpose of distinguishing the various kinds of being: "But it is strange, or rather impossible, that the coming into play of a single thing should bring it about that part of that which is, is a 'this', part a 'such', part a 'so much', part a 'here'." N 2, 1089a12–15. Oxford translations.

[3] For example, Hegel, *Logik*, no. 87; Robin G. Collingwood, *An Essay on Metaphysics* (Oxford: Clarendon Press, 1940), p. 15. Cf.: "If we stop with existence and refuse to go any further, the existent is a perfect and absolute blank, and to say that only this exists is equivalent to saying that nothing exists." J. M. E. McTaggart, *The Nature of Existence* (Cambridge, Cambridge University Press, 1921), Vol. I, p. 60; "The reason that Existence must be empty, diaphanous, blank, neutral, and in sum. *nil* resides in its definitory contrast with Essence. . . . There is no *nature* left for Existence." Donald C. Williams, "Dispensing with Existence," *The Journal of Philosophy*, Vol. LIX (1962), p. 753.

[4] Aristotle's term is "nature" (*physin*), Γ 2,1003a34. In the context, 1003b26–33, substance is shown to be immediately being, that is, without the addition of any further nature. The other categories are being through reference to substance. This has been aptly termed "focal meaning" by G. E. L. Owen, "Logic and Metaphysics in Some Earlier Works of Aristotle," *Aristotle and Plato in the Mid-Fourth Century*, I. Düring and G. E. L. Owen (eds.), (Göteborg: Studia Graeca et Latina Gothoburgensia, 1960), p. 169.

does not require it to function as a generic notion. The alleged identification of being with its differentiae has accordingly appeared on the one hand as eliminating any functional content for the differentiae on the rational level, and on the other hand as eliminating any content for the notion of being as a notion over and above that of the differentiae.

II

Does not this way of approaching the question, though, take for granted that existence and being have exactly the same meaning? Yet was not being in general taken in a quite formal sense by the Greeks? Did not Parmenides view it by comparing it with a well-rounded sphere, with interest in the equal bearing of all its parts upon the common center rather than in the fact whether or not they existed? In explaining Parmenides, could you easily substitute the expressions "the way of existence" and "the way of nonexistence" for the ways of being and of not being? With Plato and with Aristotle "to be" expressly means "to be so-and-so."[5] To say that being is not a genus fits smoothly into Aristotelian language. But is one not hesitant in that context to say "existence is not a genus" or "the existent is not a genus"? Is there not some significant discrepancy between the respective notions in regard to this problem of content?

It is undeniable that in Parmenides the viewpoint in regard to being is quite formal. But it would be difficult to show that the existential facet is ever excluded or that abstraction is ever made from it. The sharp contrast between being and not being that pervades the poem is the contrast between what is there and what is not and cannot be there. True, what is there has to have the formal aspect of being so-and-so. But that in no way eliminates its involvement with existing. The argument against change, moreover, includes the impossibility of springing into being out of not-being.[6] This means clearly enough the coming into existence from non-existence. For Parmenides, being means existence, even though he is centering his attention upon its formal aspects.

Correspondingly, according to Aristotle, even though the form is the cause of being, the form itself is understood to have come into being in matter as a result of motion and efficient causality.[7]

---

[5] Aristotle, Metaph. Γ 4,1006a28–31. Cf. Owen, art. cit., p. 165. With Plato (Tht. 183AB) the emphasis in the distinction between the object of knowledge and that of opinion is that the object of knowledge, in contrast to a flux, is "so or not so."

[6] Parmenides, Fr. 8.6–11. Cf. argument of Gorgias, in MXG 5,979b30–31 (Aristoteles, Prussian Academy edition).

[7] See Metaph. Z 7,1032b9–30; 9,1034b14–19; H 6,1045b21–22.

The form is therefore regarded as existent in matter when it is exercising its causality. The transition from not being to being involves something more than just the presupposed form.[8] This can hardly be anything else than what is regularly called "existence." In fact, the passage in which Aristotle expressly asserts that being adds nothing over and above the notion of thing cannot easily be translated into smooth English except by using the term "existent," as in the Oxford translation "the doubling of the words in 'one man and one *existent* man' does not express anything different (it is clear that the two things are not separated either in coming to be or in ceasing to be)."[9] The Aristotelian tenet that being does not add anything by way of intrinsic content to the natures of things can be phrased just as meaningfully in English by saying that existence does not give any new content to a thing's nature. Being involves for Aristotle the existential as well as the formal function.

The difficulty here is primarily, if not completely, linguistic. In Greek as well as in Latin the one verb covered the senses of the *copula* and the assertion of existence. *Estin* and *est*, used without a further predicate, are normally translated by "exist." But even in English the verb "to be" can be used idiomatically to express this notion of existence, by introducing it with an impersonal "there." "There still are whooping cranes" and "Whooping cranes still exist" assert exactly the same thing.

Whether this modern linguistic distinction between being and existence has any philosophical foundation may for the moment be left open. Certainly the verb "exists" cannot be substituted for the copulative and other uses of "is" that involve a further predicate. Whether this implies a latent philosophical difference that was missed by the Greek and Latin languages and is brought to the fore by modern speech is a new and important enough question. But before the last quarter of the thirteenth century none made such a distinction in philosophical thought. Only during the controversies about the distinction between a thing and its being was the phrase "existential being" (*esse existentiae*) coined and contrasted with "essential being" (*esse essentiae*).[10] "Being" was in this way projected as a wider notion, of which there were two kinds, existential and essential. The

---

[8] For Aristotle the form as well as the matter is presupposed by the exercise of efficient causality. The form has to preexist either in another real individual or in the mind of an artificer. See *Metaph.* Z 7,1032b30–1033a5; 8,1033b5–9; 9,1034b12–19. Only in accidental fashion may the form be said to be produced, Z 8,1033a29–31.

[9] *Metaph.* Γ 2,1003b27–30. Cf. "a man exists" in Apostle tr., *ad loc.*

[10] On the meaning and history of these two expressions, see my article "The Number of Terms in the Suarezian Discussion on Essence and Being," *The Modern Schoolman*, Vol. XXXIV (1957), pp. 150–161.

subsequent controversy centered on the distinction or lack of distinction between these two kinds of being. Against this background being appears as philosophically a wider notion than existence. Everything that is said to be need not be said to exist.[11] But since existence in this perspective is a kind of being, denial of all content to being will thereby entail denial of all content to existence. To say that being is an empty concept would imply that existence, as one of the kinds of being, is likewise void of any distinctive content.

The English translation of the Greek *einai* in terms of being instead of existence, then, need not cut off the present problem of content in regard to existence from Greek sources in Parmenides and Aristotle. In these sources the outlines of a problem emerge quite clearly. Things can be said either to be or not to be. Is anything added to the thing when it comes to be, when it reaches a state in which it can no longer be said not to be? Do Kant's one hundred thalers have any more content when they exist than when they do not exist in reality? The problem seems to be the same no matter which way it is formulated. In ordinary thinking some kind of distinction is made between a thing and its being. Yet on philosophical scrutiny the danger signals begin to appear. If being or existence is allowed any content at all, what limits can be placed to its greed? Does it not engulf everything else as Parmenides would have it? Does it not become a juggernaut that crushes into anonymity all the distinguishing marks of things? How can its tyranny be circumvented except by the uncompromising refusal to allow it any content at all?

Yet throughout the centuries, in spite of fears and protests, the fascination of being and existence has continued unabated. Surely existence must have some content that attracts human intelligence and offers meat for continued digestion. Surely philosophers have not been pursuing a mere phantom all these centuries. At least, the basic problem has been recalled. It is concerned with what we attribute to a thing when we assert that the thing exists, and whether what is asserted can be over and above the thing itself without involving the Parmenidean consequences. It is the problem of "cognitive content" for existence.

[11] For example, *"Being* is that which belongs to every conceivable term, to every possible object of thought. . . . . *Existence,* on the contrary, is the prerogative of some only amongst beings . . . we need the concept of being, as that which belongs even to the non-existent." Bertrand Russell, *The Principles of Mathematics,* 2nd ed. (London, 1937), pp. 449–450. Also in a radically different context: "That kind of Being towards which Dasein can comport itself in one way or another . . . we call *'existence'* (*Existenz*)." Heidegger, *Being and Time,* J. Macquarrie and Robinson (trs.) (London: SCM Press, 1962), p. 32.

III

What, then, is attributed to a thing when the thing is said to exist? Without doubt it is something distinctly meaningful. "The Bronx Third Avenue Elevated Line still exists" has a meaning sharply different from the opposite assertion that it does not exist. Correspondingly "The Manhattan Third Avenue Elevated Line no longer exists" means something definitely other than an assertion than it does exist. What is attributed to the Bronx Elevated Line is something that appears very significant when compared to its absence in regard to the Manhattan Line. Reverse that attribution and the meaningful difference will be only too obvious. The restored existence of the Manhattan Line would stand out like a sore thumb, and the sudden nonexistence of the Bronx Line would cause considerable confusion in the subway station at Grand Concourse and Third. The nonexistence of a golf course and the conditions required for the game on the lunar surface took on a very pictureful meaning in the astronaut's efforts to simulate teeing off. We can easily multiply examples to show the difference that existence makes to the whooping cranes or musk oxen in contrast to its absence for dodos or passenger pigeons, or to New York and Chicago in comparison with cities of the ancient world that have long since ceased to exist.

The meaning of existence is therefore distinctly positive and highly significant. Does it not accordingly exhibit a recognizable content, a content without which everything else in an object would be actually nothing?

Misgivings, however, arise at this further question. The standard example of the one hundred dollars shows that whether the dollars exist in reality or just in imagination they have exactly the same content. In either case the content is one hundred times one hundred cents. The real existence and the imaginary existence respectively add nothing to that content. From the time of Avicenna the tenet that the nature of a thing does not contain either real or cognitional existence has been emphasized[12] No matter how much a thing is conceptualized, it does not in this kind of cognition exhibit any existence. Existence seems to escape conceptualization. It offers no content at all to one's concepts of a thing.

If content were limited to what can be grasped through concepts, it would have to be straightaway denied to existence. But human knowledge is not restricted to what can be attained through conceptualization. There is further knowledge of things, or at least about

---

[12] A discussion of this topic may be found in my article "Common Nature: A Point of Comparison between Thomistic and Scotistic Metaphysics," *Mediaeval Studies,* Vol. XIX (1957), pp. 1–14.

things, that does not consist in the sum of concepts about them. The kind of knowledge expressed mentally in a proposition and verbally in a sentence is radically different from the sum total of the concepts involved. To know that craters exist on the moon is not the same as the adding up of the three concepts of craters, existence, and moon. The three concepts may be had in the notion of "the existence of craters on the moon" and still leave open the question "But do they exist on the moon?" Just in itself the notion "existence" does not indicate whether or not a thing exists.

The knowledge that craters exist on the moon is accordingly something other than what is given through the respective concepts involved. It is knowledge that cannot be obtained merely through conceptualization. Yet would anyone question the claim that it is genuine knowledge? Besides concepts, then, which are expressed by single words, there is another way in which human knowledge is attained. This is the way that is expressed through propositions and sentences. It is only through that type of knowledge that the existence of anything is grasped. No matter how many concepts you form of a thing, none of them just in themselves will ever tell you whether or not the thing exists. After having conceptualized a thing to your satisfaction, you have still to ask the question does it exist.

In sense perception, of course, the two kinds of cognition are not distinguished. Seeing the table in front of you means seeing that it exists. But the intellectual penetration of that datum is more subtle and complicated. What the table is becomes known through concepts, concepts that do not grasp its existence. The existence is grasped simultaneously, but through a judgment and not through a concept. Both a thing and its existence are known intellectually but in different ways.

This means that the complete conceptual knowledge of a thing will not make manifest its existence. It leaves existence outside the thing's content. From the viewpoint of content that can be grasped through conceptualization, existence has none.

But may not the actuality that is grasped through judgment be regarded as content, though of a different kind from that attained through conceptualization? There are difficulties in giving an answer. What we spontaneously represent as content is something that can be conceived as a thing, and that we can spread out, at least figuratively, in a definite measure of perfection. It is taken to be the object of a concept. Restricted in this quite spontaneous way, it does not seem that we can readily apply the notion of content to what is known about a thing through judgment. All the content seems to be concentrated in the thing itself. What is known about the thing, in the fact that it exists, does not appear to be anything that could be brought under the notion of content. The existence may have definite meaning in contrast to nonexistence, but it can hardly be conceived as adding new content. The problem seems to parallel that which arises when Aristotle added form to material parts; that is, the form of a house does not add anything by way of a material part to the building materials.[13]

The notion of content, then, would seem to demand something that can be conceptualized. But may not the actuality originally known through judgment be subsequently conceptualized? Is not this done regularly when existence is thought about, reasoned about, and discussed? We cannot think about anything or predicate anything about it or discuss it without representing it in a concept. The fact that existence is being made the subject of a discussion and that conclusions are being drawn about it is ample evidence that it has been conceptualized. We, accordingly, have a concept of existence.

But how is this concept formed? It is not an immediate grasp of some feature in the thing, in the way the thing's size, color, and shape are grasped through conceptualization. The thing's existence, as has been seen, does not allow itself to be known in this way. Once it has been grasped through judgment, however, it is present before the intellect as a known object and can be represented under the general concept of an object. This concept of an object more naturally applies to things like trees or stones that are known originally through conceptualization, but it allows itself to extend without much difficulty to whatever can be known in any way by the intellect. Similarly the notion of "something," and the notions of "perfection" and of "actuality" can be extended from their original bearing on things to a further bearing upon that which makes the things exist. So existence may be conceived as "the characteristic object of judgment," or as "something that raises a thing from mere nothingness," or as "the perfection of all perfections" or "the actuality of all actualities."[14]

---

[13] ". . . if it is an element the same argument will again apply; for flesh will consist of this and fire and earth and something still further, so that the process will go on to infinity." *Metaph.* Z 17,1041b20–22.

[14] "What is grasped through judgment" would be the spontaneous and affirmative way of conceptualizing existence. The object signified by "what" is the widest generalization of the notion "thing," attained originally through conceptualization but related to cognition as the object of any kind of cognition. Since we are reflexively aware of our judgments, the existence known through them can readily be conceptualized as their object. The conceptualization through contrast with the nothingness that would be the state of the thing without existence, is also quite spontaneous. But it is less satisfactory insofar as it conceives existence through reference merely to the denial of existence. Finally, there is the conception that existence is "the actuality of all acts, and is on that account the perfection of all perfections" (Aquinas, *De Potentia*, VII, 2, ad 9 m). This is positive and exact, but it is the result of involved

In these complex concepts the basic notion has been originally obtained through conceptualization of what is grasped in the natures of things. The basic notion is that of "something," or of "object," or of "actuality." None of these grasp the existence of the thing. None of them can state that the thing exists. Yet they can all be focused on and used to spotlight what is grasped through judgment. Having seen that craters exist on the moon, we can represent this fact conceptually as the existence of these craters.

But this conceptualization of existence is not a victory without casualties. What perishes in the process is that which is most characteristic of existence, the fact that something exists. The concept of brownness represents what is most characteristic of the color brown. But the concept of existence, detached and just in itself, does not give the knowledge that anything exists. In regard to any content that would be characteristic of existence, it is entirely lacking. It is the concept of something else, used to focus upon what is known through judgment. There is no characteristic concept or proper concept of existence. There is merely the use of other concepts to spotlight it and to represent it in this way for purposes of consideration and discussion. But once the notion ceases to spotlight what is known through judgment and accordingly comes to be used as an independent concept, it causes trouble. In the ontological argument for the existence of God, for instance, existence is included as a perfection in the greatest possible object. But does this inclusion of existence allow the inference that the object exists? For one who sees that existence is originally known through judgment and is lost in the detached concept of existence, that conclusion does not follow. Similarly, to say that non-existence exists in one's thought as one reasons about it is not a contradiction. The concept of nonexistence does not, just in itself, entail that non-existence does not exist.

The concept of existence is accordingly not a concept like other concepts, or a predicate like other predicates.[15] It does not have the

---

metaphysical reasoning on the prior and accidential bearing of existence upon essence in finite things.

[15] "The word 'existence' is not a symbol for anything which can be either a constituent or a component of a simple proposition." W. Kneale, "Is Existence a Predicate?" *Proceedings of the Aristotelian Society,* Suppl. XV (1936), p. 164. Aristotle had made a somewhat similar observation in noting that not even the verb taken just by itself tells whether or not what it signifies exists: "When uttered just by itself a verb is a name and signifies something . . . but it does not yet signify whether it is or not. For not even 'to be' or 'not to be' is a sign of the actual thing (nor if you say 'that which is'); for by itself it is nothing, but it additionally signifies some combination, which cannot be thought of without the components." *Int.* 4,16b19–25; tr. J. L. Ackrill. The Oxford translation expresses the notion in terms of judgment: ". . . but they do not, as they stand, express any judgement, either positive or negative." b21–22.

content we would expect in the analogy with other concepts. The
fact that it can be conceptualized does not imply any distinctive
content for it.

IV

But is there no possibility of admitting a content that is not
subject to conceptualization? Is it not possible for us to examine
what is attained through judgment and find in it some genuine content
that entirely eludes grasp by a concept? The existence known through
judgment is certainly meaningful. Should it not therefore consist of
something that offers grist to the intellect, something that may be
rightly described as having a content all its own?

When we undertake this examination, however, existence turns
out to be something despairingly fugitive.[16] It is a temporal continuum,
spread out in parts and consisting of parts. Yet its parts necessarily
have to remain outside itself. Any part of existence in the past no
longer exists, and any part in the future does not yet exist. Only
in the indivisible present is there existence. All else has either ceased
to be existence or is still not existence. Existence would seem to have
as little content as a geometrical point. It appears to elude anything
even remotely resembling the notion of content.

Yet its temporal character requires it to have parts. It is spread
out in parts over the past and the future. But unlike a spatial continuum such as a line or a surface it does not have its parts inside
itself. All its parts are either past or future. They are accordingly
outside itself, for it itself is only in the indivisible present. The past
and future of existence do not exist. If they did, the past and future
parts would be coexistent, and the continuum would no longer be
temporal.

This paradoxical character of existence, when conceived according
to the model of a spatial continuum, has been trenchantly expressed
by Thomas Aquinas: "Now our being has some of itself outside itself;
for there is lacking something of it that has gone by, and that is
to be."[17] At first reading this might seem nothing but the rather trivial
observation that all one's past existence no longer exists and all one's
future existence does not yet exist. For this meaning, however, we
would expect "most of itself" or "nearly all of itself" rather than
just "some of itself." If the whole panorama of one's existence, past,
present, and future, were being viewed, the whole expanse of past

---

[16] On the force of the term "fugitive" in this regard, see A. N. Prior, "Fugitive
Truth," *Analysis,* Vol. XXIX (1968), pp. 5–8.
[17] *"Esse autem nostrum habet aliquid sui extra se: deest enim aliquid quod
jam de ipso praeteriit, et quod futurm est." In I Sent.,* d. 8, q. 1, a. 1,
Solut.; ed. Mandonnet, I, 195.

and future when compared with present existence would appear as much more than *aliquid sui*. Further, this way of speaking can readily be traced back to Aristotle's phraseology when he was considering time, and when philosophical tenets far from trivial were at stake. Finally, Aquinas expressly claims to be drawing his argument in this passage from a statement attributed to St. Jerome that changeable things are, as it were, nonexistent in comparison with what truly can be called existent.[18] The thrust of the argument by Aquinas would accordingly seem to be required to center upon the temporal existence itself, which is had only in the present, and to show that this indivisible needs parts, but parts that are outside itself. In this focus the notion of two parts, one which it terminates, the other which it begins, could quite normally be expressed by the Latin *aliquid sui*.

The Aristotelian background for the phraseology is easily recognizable. In dealing with the nature of time, Aristotle notes that "one part of it has been and is not, while the other is going to be and is not yet."[19] The Greek expresses the contrasted parts merely by the regular *"to men autou"* and *"to de"* without any word for "part." The *"to men autou"* could accordingly appear in medieval Latin as *aliquid sui*. As it is, Aquinas, in explaining the text of the Aristotelian *Physics* at this point, does use *aliquid* with the genitive of the word for time: *"Sed tempus componitur ex his quae non sunt; quia temporis est aliquid praeteritum et iam non est, aliud futurum et nondum est."*[20] The conclusion that time is composed of parts that do not exist can accordingly be transferred to temporal existence. In this way the statement attributed to St. Jerome, that changeable things

---

[18] The notion was expressed by St Jerome: *"Caetera quae creata sunt, etiamsi videntur esse, non sunt; quia aliquando non fuerunt; et potest rursum non esse, quod non fuit." Epist.* XV, 4; *PL,* XXII, 357. The passage attributed to Jerome in Peter Lombard's *Sentences,* upon which Aquinas was commenting, consists of sentences taken from different places in Augustine and Gregory the Great, and found assembled in Isidore, *Etym.,* VII, 1, 10–13; *PL,* LXXXII, 261. It contains Augustine's (*De Civ. Dei,* VIII, 11) statement, made against a strong Platonic background: "... tanquam in ejus comparatione qui vere est quia incommutabilis est, ea quae mutabilia facta sunt quasi non sint." On the Lombard text, see note in the Quaracchi edition, *Libri IV Sententiarum,* I, 57, n. 1.

Another text from Augustine, important for the vocabulary used by Aquinas, is found cited immediately after by Lombard (I,58) as follows: "'Cum ergo nostra locutio per tempora varietur, de eo vere dicuntur verba cuiuslibet temporis, qui nullo tempore defuit vel deest vel deerit." St. Augustine, *In Joann. Ev.,* XCIX, 5; *PL,* XXXV, 1888.

[19] *Ph.* IV 10,217b33–34; Oxford tr. Though the noun "part" is not used expressly in the Greek, it is fully justified by the immediately following context, 218a1–7.

[20] "But time is composed of what does not exist; for one part of time is past and does not now exist the other part is future and does not yet exist." *In IV Phys.,* lect. 15, Angeli-Pirotta no. 1079.

are nonexistent rather than existent, is substantiated by Aquinas. In the pertinent passage of the *Physics*, Aristotle is dealing with the reasons offered for thinking that time "does not exist at all or barely, and in an obscure way" (*Ph.* IV 10,217b32–33; Oxford tr.). The reasons are drawn from the consideration that none of the parts of time can exist: "Further, if a divisible thing is to exist, it is necessary that, when it exists, all or some of its parts must exist. But of time some parts have been, while others have to be, and no part of it *is*, though it is divisble" (218a3–6). Time can exist only in the indivisible "now," yet it cannot be made up of just indivisibles (218a6–30). Aquinas applies these considerations to the temporal character of existence. They show that existence resides in an indivisible actuality that terminates a part already past and initiates a part still in the future. It has to have parts, but its parts have to be outside itself.[21]

If existence, then, has no parts whatsoever within itself, may one correctly ascribe content to it? Can something that has no parts in it at all, like a geometrical point, be accredited with content? Even aside from the conclusion that no characteristic content can be conceptualized for existence, this further scrutiny seems to show that no content can be known in it even though judgment. The parts cannot be grasped in the judgment. Only the existence or the non-existence, sharply differentiated as the principle of contradiction demands, is immediately known. The rest is memory, comparison, and reasoning. Only philosophical reasoning shows that the indivisible existence known through judgment involves parts that are its own

---

[21] "*Unde sicut est idem mobile secundum substantiam in toto motu, variatur tamen secundum esse, sicut dicitur quod Socrates in foro est alter a seipso in domo; ita nunc est etiam idem secundum substantiam in tota successione temporis, variatum tantum secundum esse, scilicet secundum rationem quam accepit prioris et posterioris. Sicut autem motus est actus ipsius mobilis inquantum mobile est; ita esse est actus existentis, inquantum ens est.*" In *I Sent.*, d. 19, q. 2, a. 2, Solut.; ed. Mandonnet, I, 470. The analogy is between movement as the actuality of something mobile and being as the actuality of something existent: "But just as movement is the actuality of the mobile thing insofar as it is mobile, so being is the actuality of the existent thing, insofar as it is a being." Being is accordingly understood in the sense of existence by Aquinas in this text, even though Aristotle, in the example of Socrates in the forum, had meant by "being" one of the accidental categories, that of *where* something is. In a further analogy, the "now" corresponds to the existent thing, changing from the viewpoint of existence while always characterizing the same substance: "Hence just as there is the same mobile thing from the standpoint of its substance in the whole of the movement though it changes from the standpoint of existence, just as it is said that Socrates in the forum is other than himself at home, so the 'now' is also the same from the standpoint of substance in the whole succession of time, changed only from the standpoint of existence, that is, in the aspect it takes on of prior and subsequent."

yet are outside itself. A man, or a tree, or a stone continues to exist in a temporally continuous way, requiring parts for an existence that is never grasped by judgment except in an indivisible "now."[22]

Existence appears accordingly as a surd[23] that can be known, and indicated, and reasoned about in terms of things other than itself. It can be sufficiently controlled for purposes of further philosophical reasoning and demonstration. But, like a surd, it never becomes a closed and definite notion, fully explicable in terms of the natures immediately knowable to human cognition. Like a surd, existence is fuzzy at the edges and tends to keep going on and on. It has to spread outside itself to be itself, yet whatever of itself is outside in this way is not itself. What should appear as its content is not contained by it.

V

These reflections on the data available for an answer to the question about the content of existence do not lead to a simple yes or no. But they do help us to understand the difficulties that have been encountered about existence in the course of Western philosophy. They do show that these difficulties are serious, and are not merely linguistic in nature. The difficulties demand appreciation and careful scrutiny.

If the existence known in observable things is viewed as having a content within itself, it is left open to Parmenides' relentless reasoning. It is almost inevitably regarded as "something." So assessed as a thing or a nature, it refuses to be confined to any particular determination. It leaves no room for anything else when it is considered from the rational viewpoint. There seems no way of avoiding the conclusion, once the starting point is admitted. Where existence is a thing or nature in itself, and not just a nonreified actuality of something else, it will have to include in itself all the perfections of every other thing.[24]

---

[22] Hence the "fugitive" character of truth, supra, n. 16.

[23] George Santayana, *The Realm of Essence* (New York; Scribner's, 1927), pp. 109–110. For Santayana existence may "illustrate" essence but remains irrelevant to it. The metaphor of a "surd," however, may be understood in two senses. There is the mathematical sense, in which a surd is an irrational number, and there is the phonetic sense, in which a surd is a voiceless sound. Applied to existence in the first sense, the metaphor would mean that an endless series is indicated. Yet according to Aquinas, for example, in *De Ente et Essentia*, c. IV (edited by Roland-Gosselin, and reprinted in Paris, 1948), pp. 34.10–35.19, observable existence leads to a first cause that is existence only. Understood in the second sense, the metaphor would imply the possibility of things without existence, just as there can be sonants without consonant sounds.

[24] Aquinas, *De Ente et Essentia*, c. V, p. 38.12–20. For Aquinas this tenet does not entail that no room is left for anything "over against" the one sole

If this conclusion is unacceptable, as it obviously is in the case of observable existence, it would seem to allow this existence no content whatsoever. With Aristotle the existence will not add to the nature of a thing. No generic concept is introduced when things are called beings. With Kant being is not the concept of something that could be added to the concept of a thing. With Hegel and Collingwood it will be the equivalent of nothing, and accordingly a completely empty concept. It may, in fact, be banished from the vocabulary of philosophy.[25]

Both these diametrically opposed conclusions, as I have endeavored to show, follow cogently from the respective ways in which the observable data are read. They are based respectively upon the example of the positive and negative prints of the same photo. But does either tell the whole story?

If added conceptual content is sought, existence presents itself negatively. It does not enter into the positive philosophical consideration. Existence does not show up either as something or as containing its parts within itelf. It gives rise to no concept characteristic just of itself. In these ordinary requirements for the notion of content, it must evoke an empty concept. Yet the existence is highly meaningful, as the contrast of "to be or not to be" makes only too evident. Quite obviously the meaning cannot be located in an emotive reac-

existence. For that objection see Paul Weiss, *Modes of Being* (Carbondale, Ill.: Southern Illinois University Press, 1958), p. 191 (no. 3.08). In subsistent being everything is identical with existence, in things other than subsistent being the perfections are shared in the limiting degree of each essence. On the problem, see G. B. Phelan, "The Being of Creatures," *Proceedings of the American Catholic Philosophical Association*, Vol. XXXI (1957), pp. 118–125.

[25] See note 3. Heidegger, in opposing this tenet describes it as a "dogma" that has been developed from the ancient Greek discussions and which makes being so universal that it becomes most empty: "It is said that 'Being' is the most universal and the emptiest of concepts." *Being and Time*, p. 21. It is of course true that generic concepts decrease in content as they increase in extension. But generic concepts are concepts of a nature confined to some category and accordingly cannot express being: ". . . in every genus some quiddity has to be signified, as has been said, and to its notion being does not belong" (in quolibet genere oportet significare quidditatem aliquam, ut dictum est, de cujus intellectu non est esse). Aquinas, *In I Sent.*, d. 8, q. 4, a. 2, ad 2m; I, 222–223. For Sidney Hook, *The Quest for Being* (New York: St. Martin's Press, 1961), p. 147, truth and falsity suffice for characterizing assertions from this angle, allowing the term "being" to disappear from philosophical vocabulary. Professor Hook's interesting paper finds that being "does not seem to possess an intelligible opposite." This reason does not take account of the contrast of being and thing, a contrast expressed over the last six centuries as the contrast of existence with essence. The opposition here is between what is intelligible through judgment and what is intelligible through conceptualization. Nature or thing, as intelligible through conceptualization, is in this way the intelligible opposite of being.

tion.[26] The meaning is basically cognitive, as the study of judgment has shown. May not this meaning, then, be regarded somehow as genuine cognitive content? It will not come under the ordinary significations of content. It will not be contained within the observable existence itself. But is it not an extension of the notion of content that is required by a philosophy in which observable existence is grasped through judgment without becoming reified in the cognitive process? Does it not indicate supreme content if existence is at all a thing?

The whole story, in consequence, seems to be that existence, as it is immediately known to human cognition, has, in itself, nothing that could ordinarily be described as content, yet that it is rich in cognitive meaning. It is rich in meaning that will allow it the greatest of all content should it be found anywhere as a nature. The tenet that existence is an empty concept accordingly misses the point.[27] Rather, observable existence escapes any conceptualization that would be characteristic of it, and is grasped only in the synthesizing knowledge of judgment. Characteristic content is not to be sought in its conceptualization. But all-embracing content in it is required if what is known of it in a nonconceptual way through judgment be reified anywhere as a subsistent nature.

[26] Cf. approach outlined by Milton K. Munitz, *The Mystery of Existence* (New York: Appleton-Century-Crofts, 1965), pp. 6–7, where the question of "genuine cognitive content" (p. 7) for existence is introduced. The mystery consists "in the mind's inability to find an answer" (p. 32). G. B. Phelan, *art. cit.*, using the terms "the mystery of existence" (p. 119) and "the mystery of the being of creatures" (p. 123), describes the philosophic treatment as "problematizing that mystery in order to increase our insight" (p. 125).

[27] See note 25. Regardless of the difficulties in understanding its meaning, the tendency to question the reasons given for denying existence the status of a predicate has become strong in recent years. See for example, G. Nakhnikian and W. Salmon," 'Exists' as a Predicate," *Philosophical Review*, Vol. LXVI (1957) pp. 535–542; M. Kiteley, "Is Existence a Predicate?" *Mind*, Vol. LXXIII (1964), pp. 364–373; J. Child and F. I. Goldberg, " 'Exists' as a Prediate: A Reconsideration," *Analysis*, Vol. XXXI (1970). pp. 53–57. For a discussion of the two main sources for the contemporary denial that existence is a predicate, see Munitz, pp. 73–90. The classification of a judgment of existence as *analytic a posteriori* (Munitz, p. 77) has its appeal, and against the background developed in the present paper would mean that existence while accidental to thing appears immediately in the analysis of all that is known through the combined intellectual operations of judgment and conceptualization.

Quantifiers, Language-Games, and Transcendental Arguments

JAAKKO HINTIKKA

University of Helsinki

In recent years, we have witnessed something of a revival of interest in Kant's epistemology and metaphysics among analytical philosophers.[1] However, I hope I am not doing an injustice to the philosophers who are responsible for this revival if I say that their efforts have not on the whole been crowned by unqualified success. Perhaps I should say that we have been given interesting general suggestions concerning the interpretation of Kant and concerning his relevance to the contemporary scene rather than sharp, definite results in either direction. If so, there may be a deeper reason for this lack of success (or only partial success). One of the focal points of much of the best philosophy in the Kantian tradition (a German would speak here of *Transzendentalphilosophie*) has been the human activities through which we obtain our knowledge and the contribution of these activities to the total structure of human knowledge. Occasionally, philosophers of this persuasion have even maintained that we can have full-fledged knowledge, such as synthetic knowledge a priori, only of these activities and of what it brought about by ourselves in the course of them.[2] "Reason has insight only into that which

---

[1] Cf. the survey paper, M. J. Scott-Taggart, "Recent Work on the Philosophy of Kant," *Kant Studies To-Day*, L. W. Beck (ed.) (LaSalle, Ill.: Open Court, 1969).

[2] I have tried to survey this tradition briefly in my essay, 'Tieto on valtaa', in Jaakko Hintikka, *Tieto on valtaa ja muita aatehistoriallisia esseitä*, WSOY, Porvoo, 1969, pp. 19–34. Cf. also my paper, "Kant's 'New Method of Thought' and his Theory of Mathematics," *Ajatus*, Vol. 27 (1965), pp. 37–47.

38   *Quantifiers, Language-Games, Transcendental Arguments*

it produces after a plan of its own," Kant writes in his *Critique of Pure Reason* (B xiii).

We do not have to go as far as this, however, in order to find the processes through which we obtain our information about the objects of our knowledge interesting and important. Yet most of the sharp conceptual tools philosophers have recently developed are much better suited for dealing with the structure of the information we have already acquired—the structure of theories, the structure of explanation, and so on—than the activities by means of which it is gathered. The "transcendental" point of view which focuses on the human activities which are basically involved in our obtaining whatever information we have is notoriously absent from recent philosophizing.

This somewhat one-sided epistemological interest is related to, and partly the result of, a parallel neglect manifesting itself in the logical analysis of language. There the study of the relations of our language—or anybody's language, for that matter—to the reality it speaks of has either been left unattended or else has only been discussed in terms of unanalyzed "interpretations," "valuations," "name relations" or comparable static ties between language and the world.[3] Even though it is obvious that these are not natural relations but are only created by and sustained through certain human activities and human institutions, very little systematic work has been done on these vital connecting links between language and reality. In saying this, I am not forgetting the rich Wittgensteinian literature on those "language games" which are supposed to give the expression of our language their meanings. However, I am disregarding these language games because of the unsystematic character of, and lack of specificity in, most of the current discussions about them.

In this paper, I shall try to show that even quite modest systematic efforts in this direction can lead to interesting insights into central Kantian problems. I shall take as my theme one rather small-scale attempt to discuss in precise terms some of those activities that serve to connect, in some idealized but precise sense, certain parts of our language with the world. The expressions I want to find language games for are the usual quantifiers "for at least one" and "for every," in symbols $\lor x$ and $\land x$. I have discussed them in relation to the problems at hand in an earlier paper.[4] The upshot is what I have called "the

---

[3] Cf. the last few pages of my paper, "Logic and Philosophy," *Contemporary Philosophy*, R. Klibansky (ed.) (Florence: La Nuova Italia Editrice, 1968), Vol. 1, pp. 3–30.
[4] "Language-Games for Quantifiers," *American Philosophical Quarterly, Monograph Series, No. 2: Studies in Logical Theory* (Oxford: Basil Blackwell, 1968), pp. 46–72.

game-theoretical interpretation of quantifiers." It turns out that in this case the 'language games' that give our words their basic meanings are not only games in the vague undifferentiated Wittgensteinian sense but also games in the precise sense of the mathematical theory of games. Of course, I am not claiming any radical novelty for this idea. Rather, I want to suggest that this interpretation is merely a clarification and explication of ideas which we all associate with quantifiers, albeit usually tacitly and in a confused fashion. With these—and certain other—qualifications in mind, I have suggested that the primary meanings of quantifiers, and *ipso facto* the content of the ideas of existence and universality they express, is to be sought by examining these games.

Here I cannot motivate or defend my game-theoretical interpretation in any greater detail. Since I want to discuss it, I nevertheless have to explain what it is all about. For this purpose, I associate with each sentence S of an applied first-order (that is, quantificational) language a two-person game. (S may contain, over and above predicates, individual variables and individual constants the two quantifiers Λ and V as well as the connectives $\wedge$, v, and $\sim$.) The players we may call colloquially 'Myself' and 'Nature'. The game is one with perfect information, and it may be considered a zero-sum game.

Since we are dealing with an interpreted language, a domain D of individuals must be given on which all the relations and properties used in S are defined. At each stage of the game, a substitution instance s of a (proper or improper) subformula of S is being considered. The game begins with S, and proceeds by the following rules:

(G · V)   If s is of the form '$Vx\ p$', I choose a member of D, give it a name, say 'n' (if it did not have one before). The game is continued with respect to $p(n/x)$.

Here $p(n/x)$ is of course the result of substituting 'n' for 'x' in 'p'[5].

(G · Λ)   If s is of the form '$\Lambda x\ p$', Nature likewise chooses a member of D.

(G · v)   If s is of the form '$p\ v\ q$', I choose 'p' or 'q', and the game is continued with respect to it.

(G · $\wedge$)   If s is of the form '$p\ \wedge\ q$', Nature likewise chooses 'p' or 'q'.

(G · $\sim$)   If s is of the form '$\sim p$', the game is continued with respect to 'p' with the roles of the two players interchanged.

---

[5] As the reader can see, certain symbols are used in this essay as if they were themselves names or sentences, as the case may be, and not mere placeholders for them.

In a finite number of moves, an expression A of the form '$P(n_1, n_2, \ldots, n_k)$' will be reached, where 'P' is a k-adic predicate defined on D. Since $n_1, \ldots, n_k$ are members of D, A is either true or false. If it is true, I have won and Nature lost; otherwise Nature has won and I have lost.

A few comments may further clarify the nature of these games. Since every sentence of a first-order language can be brought (by means of De Morgan's Laws, the law of double negation, and the interconnection of the two quantifiers) to an equivalent form where negation signs may only occur prefixed to atomic formulas, we may omit $(G \cdot \sim)$ and allow the outcome A to be an atomic sentence or the negation of an atomic sentence. In this way, the exchange of roles could be avoided.

However, $(G \cdot \sim)$ is useful for another elimination. A strange and unrealistic feature of our games may seem to be due to the personification of Nature, who must be thought of as actually choosing individuals if the game is to make sense. Now it is easy to rewrite all universal quantifiers '$\bigwedge x$' as '$\sim \bigvee x \sim$' and all conjunctions '$(p \wedge q)$' as '$\sim(\sim p \vee \sim q)$'. Then rules $(G \cdot \bigwedge)$ and $(G \cdot \wedge)$ become unnecessary, and no personification of Nature is needed. It goes without saying, however, that $(G \cdot \sim)$ is now absolutely vital.

The formulation that will be the most natural will depend on the purpose we hold. In general, it is useful to preserve as much flexibility as possible.

The reason why this game-theoretical interpretation of quantifiers yields a full-fledged semantical theory of first-order logic is that the truth of S in D (with the appropriate predicates defined on D) can be defined in terms of our games. It is easily seen that S is true in the usual sense if and only if I have a winning strategy in the associated game. Hence, in our approach, the truth of S can simply be defined as the existence of such a winning strategy. This definition assumes that truth and falsity have been defined for atomic sentences (plus, possibly, their negations) and serves to extend it for arbitrary truth functions and for quantified sentences.

Since almost everything else can easily be defined as soon as we have the notion of truth at our disposal, the game-theoretical interpretation of quantifiers can serve (in principle) as a foundation of a semantical theory of first-order languages. Here we are more interested in the philosophical perspectives opened by the interpretation, however, than in technicalities. I cannot hope to exhaust even those philosophical applications here, but I can try to convey to you some idea of what is involved.

In the rule $(G \cdot \bigvee)$, we spoke of 'choosing' an individual. It is clear than in an actual play of these games this expression is not very happy. In order for me to win in a game, I usually cannot be content with an arbitrarily chosen member of D. Typically, I have to look around among the members of D for a suitable one. In brief, the step $(G \cdot V)$ involves essentially a *search* for an appropriate individual. Hence, the games we are dealing with are essentially games of seeking and (hopefully) finding various kinds of individuals.

My aim in these games can also be described informally in very simple terms. If we start with the usual definition of truth, instead of defining this notion in game-theoretical terms, we can easily see how I must carry out my moves in order to win. I must choose them so as to make sure that not only the eventual outcome of the game (the sentence A) but also all the sentences which are reached in the course of the game are true (in the usual sense).

What this means is that the game I have described may be thought of as an attempt to *verify* S by searching for and finding suitable individuals in the 'world' D. From this point of view, the function of rule $(G \cdot \Lambda)$ can also be understood. In order to verify a generalization (universal sentence), I must assume the role of a devil's advocate who is trying to find counterexamples to the generalization. If such a devil's advocate can always be defeated, I have won, that is, verified the sentence.

Instead of speaking of verification and falsification, I could have spoken of finding out which sentences of our language are true and which ones are false. Hence the language games governed by the rules (G) can also be looked upon as the activities through which we (in principle) can gather the information about the world which is codifiable in first-order discourse. Here we are perhaps beginning to see the relevance of our games to Kant's transcendental questions. A first-order sentence becomes, as it were, a kind of prediction of what may happen in the game associated with it. This (somewhat imprecise) observation brings out the strong dependence of the meaning of quantified sentences on the language game of seeking and finding.

In general, the informal view suggested by our observations is that the meaning of quantifiers lies in their role in guiding the processes ('games') of verifying (in principle) the sentences of our language. The primary meaning of quantifiers, in brief, is their use in the language games of seeking and finding. A feeling for this may perhaps be engendered by expressing the existential quantifier by the locution 'one can find' and the universal quantifier accordingly by 'one cannot find . . . not . . . '. In some languages this would in fact result in idiomatic native expressions for quantifiers. In such languages, I submit, etymology reproduces ontology more faithfully than in English.

The point may be made especially clear when the interplay of several quantifiers is involved. Consider the sentence 'some Englishman has seen all the countries of the world'. It may be suggested that when this is rewritten as 'one can find an Englishman so that no country can be found he has not seen', it becomes clearer which operations we would have to undertake in order to verify it: We can now see more clearly what kind of entities we will have to look for at the different stages of the verification.

It is obvious that a great deal of idealization is normally involved in speaking of the activities of seeking and finding here. All human limitations have to be abstracted from. The searcher in question will have to be thought of, if not as omnipotent, then at least "omni-nimble," free of all those limitations of access we humans are subject to.

For our present purposes, these scattered hints will have to suffice as an explanation of what the game-theoretical interpretation involves. A couple of matters of principle must nevertheless be dealt with.

W. V. Quine has claimed that my game-theoretical interpretation of first-order sentences confers a kind of substitutional meaning to quantifiers.[6] This is a mistake whose reasons I suspect to be more historical than topical. The demonstrable equivalence of our truth definition with the usual (objectual) one already belies Quine's allegation. Another quick way of seeing the drastic difference between our interpretation and the substitutional one is to observe what assumptions we have to make in order to make sure that our interpretation agrees with the usual "objectual" one, as compared with the assumptions we would have to make in order to force the substitutional interpretation to coincide with the objectual one. In the latter case, we would have to assume that each member of D has a name and that there are no empty names around. In contrast, for the game-theoretical interpretation we do not have to assume anything about there already being names for anything in anyone's language. What we have to assume, say for the purpose of explaining what the truth of a sentence with d layers of quantifiers amounts to, is merely that the speakers of our applied first-order language can give (in the course of a round of our game) names to any d members of D. This assumption is unaffected by the cardinality of D in the way the assumptions that must be resorted to by a defender of the substitution-instance interpretation are not. No fixed totality of names independent of the different strategies the players employ is presupposed here.

---

[6] W. V. Quine, "Replies," *Words and Objections: Essays on the Work of W. V. Quine* Donald Davidson and Jaakko Hintikka (eds.) (Dordrecht: D. Reidel Publishing Company, 1969), especially p. 314.

The whole complex of problems that arise from the different interpretations of quantifiers requires further attention. Here it nevertheless suffices to register the fact that we are on the side of the angels—or at least on the side of Quine and the objectual interpretation.

Another important question here is the following. So far, I have only described to you what the truth (truth *simpliciter*) of an applied first-order sentence means in terms of the game-theoretical interpretation. I have not yet said anything about the role of the actual rules of logic, that is, rules for actually manipulating expressions for the purpose of uncovering *logical* truths, *logical* equivalences, *logical* inconsistencies, and so on—within the game-theoretical interpretation of quantifiers. A special poignancy is lent to this question by the fact that the rules of logic can be put to an extremely interesting general perspective from other points of view. As I have pointed out elsewhere,[7] suitable rules for actually manipulating our formulas for the purpose of proving S may be thought of as governing attempts to describe, step by step, a counterexample to S. And even more: the rules may be thought of as recipes for trying to build, part by part, actual isomorphs ('pictures' in Wittgenstein's sense) to such counterexamples. Thus there obtains an extremely close relationship between the rules of logic and (an extension of) Wittgenstein's picture theory.

A quick comparison between this extension of Wittgenstein's picture theory to quantificational languages and our game-theoretical interpretation of the same languages may also be instructive for purposes other than the problem of understanding the rationale of one's proof techniques in first-order logic. I have shown elsewhere that the kind of extension of Wittgenstein's theory required for the purpose of accounting successfully for quantification theory at the same time destroys the usefulness of the picture theory for other purposes. It destroys all the interest of the picture theory as a realistic model of how first-order languages can actually be used. Two features of the extension cause this failure:

(1) The 'pictures' (model sets) associated with a sentence S are not given by S itself. They are only arrived at by starting from S and constructing 'pictures' (model sets) from it according to certain rules (of model set construction). Sentences, according to this view, are not themselves pictures of states of affairs in which they would be true. They are recipes for constructing a number of alternative pictures.

[7] See, for example, my papers "A Program and a Set of Concepts for Philosophical Logic," *The Monist*, Vol. 51 (1967), pp. 69–92, and "Quantification and the Picture Theory of Language," *The Monist*, Vol. 53 (1969), pp. 204–230.

(2) The 'pictures' (model sets) involved are usually infinite, and an infinite number of them can usually be obtained from a given sentence S.

These facts make it clear that our actual understanding of first-order sentences cannot be based on their 'pictorial' character as Wittgenstein thought. In order to understand S, we just do not construct all the pictures to which S gives rise and compare them with the reality. For this, we typically do not have enough time (or memory-space). Our actual understanding of first-order sentences must accordingly be based on some finite, step-by-step comparisons between the sentence S and the world rather than the (potentially) pictorial nature of S.

What the rules (G) of our games give you is precisely such a method of stepwise confrontation between language and reality. They thus repair the defect which we found in our extension of the picture theory. It nevertheless remains to be seen whether, and, if so, how, our games will suggest an interesting general perspective on the role of logical proofs comparable to the perspective into which the (interpretationally greatly inferior) picture theory puts them.

Such a perspective can easily be obtained. A set of rules for actually manipulating logical formulas may almost be read off from our game rules, which, of course, themselves are of entirely different nature. In the rules (G), we are given a sentence S_0 and a domain D with the predicates of S_0 defined on it, and we are asked whether S_0 is true in D. Now in logic we are typically given S_0 and asked whether there is a D, again with certain appropriate relations and properties defined on it, such that S_0 will be true in D when its predicate symbols are interpreted as expressing these relations and properties.

One natural way of going about answering this question is to ask: If S_0 is to be true in D, that is, if I am to have a winning strategy in the associated game, what other sentences S must there be with the same property in relation to the same D? Assuming for a second that each member of D has a name 'n' $\in N$, it is seen from the rules $(G \cdot V)$, $(G \cdot \bigwedge)$, $(G \cdot v)$ and $(G \cdot \wedge)$ that the totality μ of such sentences must satisfy the following conditions:

$(C \cdot V)_n$ If '$\bigwedge x \, p$' $\in \mu$, then for some 'n' $\in N$, $p(n/x) \in \mu$.
$(C \cdot \bigwedge)_n$ If '$\bigwedge x \, p$' $\in \mu$ and if 'n' $\in N$ occurs in the members of μ, then $p(n/x) \in \mu$.
$(C \cdot v)$ If '$(p \vee q)$' $\in \mu$, then 'p' $\in \mu$ or 'q' $\in \mu$.
$(C \cdot \wedge)$ If '$(p \wedge q)$' $\in \mu$, then 'p' $\in \mu$ and 'q' $\in \mu$.

From our stipulation about how a game ends, we can also see that the following condition has to be satisfied:

(C · ∼)   Not both 'p' $\in \mu$ and '$\sim p$' $\in \mu$ if 'p' is atomic.

For simplicity, we shall here assume that all negation signs in our sentences are pushed inside so they eventually will be prefixed to atomic expressions. Then the conditions (C) given above are precisely the defining conditions of what I have called a model set, provided only that the unnecessary reference to N is dropped from the first two conditions. (The resulting conditions will be called (C · V) and (C · Λ), respectively.)

Since a complete set of Herbrand-type rules for quantification theory may be obtained as (slightly modified) dual inverses of the rules for constructing model sets, we have connected in an extremely simple way our game rules with actual proof and disproof techniques for first-order logic. It is also clear that our rules for model set construction can be interpreted directly as rules for trying to construct an actual D with its relations and properties such that I would have a winning strategy in the game played on D. It may be in order to list the rules here. For the rules, λ is the set of sentences we have reached.

(A · V)   If '$\forall x\, p$' $\in \lambda$ but not $p(n/x) \in \lambda$ for any free singular term (name) 'n', introduce a new name, 'm', and add $p(m/x)$ to λ.

This rule is often known as the rule of existential instantiation.

(A · Λ)   If '$\land x\, p$' $\in \lambda$, if 'n' occurs in the members of λ, and if not $p(n/x) \in \lambda$, add $p(n/x)$ to λ.

(A · v)   If '$(p \lor q)$' $\in \lambda$ but neither 'p' $\in \lambda$ nor 'q' $\in \lambda$, add one of them to λ.

(A · ʌ)   If '$(p \land q)$' $\in \lambda$ but not both 'p' $\in \lambda$ and 'q' $\in \lambda$, add the missing one(s) to λ.

Here (A · v) gives rise to two different lines of construction which have to be examined separately. If all such branches of construction lead to a violation of (C · ∼), S is inconsistent. This result may be said to establish the *soundness* of (A) rules. Conversely, if S is inconsistent, this situation will arise after a finite number of construction steps, by choosing the order of application of the (A) rules in a suitable way. This result may be called the *completeness theorem* for (A) rules. (Neither the soundness nor the completeness of our rules will actually be proved in this paper.)

By inverting the direction of the process and by replacing all expressions by their negations, we obtain a simple proof procedure for first-order logic. This proof procedure is essentially a version of Herbrand-type proof methods.

This serves to connect our game-theoretical rules (G) with the rules of formal logic, for the rules (A) turn out to be nothing but inverses of particularly simple proof rules for first-order logic.

Although the relationship between our game rules (G) and the model set-construction rules (A) might appear almost trivially simple, it nevertheless deserves a few comments. The small differences that there are between the rules (G) and the rules (A) illustrate in fact very nicely certain misunderstandings which easily arise—and have in fact arisen—in the philosophy of logic.

Many such misunderstandings can be traced to a failure to appreciate certain important features of the conceptual situation here.

What we must try to understand is primarily the relationship between two entirely different kinds of activities, namely, those governed by the rules (G) and those defined by the rules (A), respectively. Someone else might call both these activities 'language games'. It is important to realize, however, that they are entirely different sorts of games. The former ones are 'outdoor games'. Each of them is played 'out there in the fields' among the entities (individuals belonging to the domain D) of which our applied first-order language speaks, and it consists of a sequence of searches for suitable entities of this kind.

The latter ones—the games governed by the rules (A) of analysis— are 'indoor games', more specifically board games, played with pen and paper or with a piece of chalk and a blackboard. The objects we are dealing with are not the entities our language speaks of but sequences of symbols, and, instead of searching for and finding suitable ones, we create them with a stroke of the pen. [See, for example, rule $(A \cdot V)$.] Furthermore, the activities governed by the (A) rules are not even real games in the sense that they do not involve any adversary.

The basic philosophical question here arises from the fact that games of the latter kind are obviously not vital to us in the sense the former ones—the actual transactions with the reality we are talking about—can be. Hence what we have to ask here is: How do the (A) games help us in playing the (G) games?

Even though this way of posing the question is natural enough, it is foreign to much of the contemporary philosophy of logic. In it, the language game of proving and disproving formulas is typically dealt with on its own as an independent unit, without any reference to the activities which serve to connect the sentences of an interpreted language with the reality which this language can serve to convey information about. Philosophers habitually ask, for example, what 'intuitions' we have about logical truth and how well an axiomatization of logic serves to do justice to these alleged intuitions. Even some philosophers of logic who have approached logic in a game-theoretical spirit (such as, Lorenzen)[8] have failed to connect their parlour games of 'challenges' and 'responses' with those activities we are engaged in when we are using language to some extra-linguistic purpose. I find this restriction of attention to the one language game of theorem-proving the original sin of much of the recent philosophy of logic, and a source of most of the indecision and confusion which is found in this area.

On the positive side the insight that the language game of formal logic is essentially tied, as far as the logic of existence and universality is concerned, to the language games of searching and finding suggests something about the limits of the applicability of the formal logic of quantification. Just because of this tie, quantificational logic is immediately applicable to a sphere of reality insofar as we can perform the activities of seeking and finding within it. Moreover, it applies directly to a class of objects only insofar as they are potential objects of searching and finding.

However, even when comparisons are made (explicitly or tacitly) between different language games along the lines indicated, it is very easy to get confused and to forget that the comparison must be made between the entire language games and not between their individual moves. This temptation is encouraged by the similarity between the corresponding (G) rules and (A) rules. For instance, it is easy to get perplexed if we start comparing the very similar-looking rules (G · V) and (A · V). The informal meaning of the former is easy to understand. Roughly speaking, it says that in order to verify an existentially quantified sentence we have to find a suitable (that is, a true) substitution-instance of it. (More fully, we have to find an individual whose name yields, when substituted for the bound variable, a true substitution-instance.)

In contrast, in applying (A · V) we do not look for suitable individuals or even suitable substitution-instances at all. Rather, we introduce such a substitution-instance by a *fiat*. A *construction* takes the place of the activities of seeking and finding.

[8] See, for example, P. Lorenzen, *Metamathematik* (Mannheim: Bibliographisches Institut, 1962); P. Lorenzen, "Methodological Thinking," *Ratio*, Vol. 7 (1965), pp. 35–60; P. Lorenzen, "Ein dialogisches Konstruktivitätskriterium," *Infinitistic Methods: Proceedings of the Symposium on Foundations of Mathematics, Warsaw* (London: Pergamon Press, 1961), pp. 193–200; K. Lorenz, *Arithmetik und Logik als Spiele*, Dissertation, Kiel (1961); Wolfgang Stegmüller, "Remarks on the Completeness of Logical Systems Relative to the Validity-Concepts of P. Lorenzen and K. Lorenz," *Notre Dame Journal of Formal Logic*, Vol. 5 (1964), pp. 81–112.

48   *Quantifiers, Language-Games, Transcendental Arguments*

It is not immediately obvious what uses such seemingly arbitrary acts of construction can have in guiding our searches for suitable individuals. Prima facie, they may even seem completely useless for the purpose. They simply do not yield any instructions as to where to find the desired individuals. Moreover, they seem rather strange on their own right. In applying (A · V), we apparently introduce a representative of an individual—that is, a free singular term denoting it—without having found one. We seem to be anticipating a successful outcome of a process of search even when there is no guarantee of an eventual success. As some traditional philosophers might have expressed themselves here: How is it possible to use free singular terms in the absence of any objects they can refer to? What justification can there be for such a procedure? Why is the logical or mathematical knowledge we obtain by means of such anticipatory introductions of new symbols for individuals applicable to anything at all, let alone with a priori certainty, as we usually think of our logical and mathematical truths as being applicable?

Questions arising from this problematic relation of (A · V) to the activities of seeking and finding have also led to more specific puzzles. Among them, there is the problem whether certain rules of logic, especially such rules of existential instruction as (A · V), involve reliance on 'arbitrary' or 'random' individuals, and if so, whether this notion of an 'arbitrary' or 'random' individual is a legitimate one.[9] In an application of (A · V), we often do not—and sometimes cannot—have in mind any particular individual m even when we know that there exist individuals satisfying 'p'. Hence the universal validity of the rule seems to presuppose that m is an 'arbitrary' or 'random' individual satisfying this condition. This pseudo-problem has led to some amount of philosophical controversy.

These recent controversies are closely related to earlier discussions in the philosophy of logic and mathematics concerning the status of the so-called method of exposition or *ecthesis*, which to all practical purposes is just existential instantiation.[10]

[9] A discussion on this subject was carried out in *Analysis* some time ago; see, for example, Nicholas Rescher, "Can There Be Random Individuals?" *Analysis*, Vol. 18 (1957–1958), pp. 114–117; L. Goddar, "Mr. Rescher or Random Individuals," *ibid.*, Vol. 19 (1958–59), pp. 18–20; J. L. Mackie, "The Rules of Natural Deduction," *ibid.*, pp. 27–35.

Although the terminology of "random" or "arbitrarily selected" individuals is not a very apt one, much more is at issue here than "a reification of a notational device."

[10] Cf. E. W. Beth, "Über Lockes 'Allgemeines Dreieck,'" *Kant-Studien*, Vol. 48 (1956–1957), pp. 361–380; E. W. Beth, *La crise de la raison et la logique* (Paris: Gauthier-Villars, 1957); E. W. Beth, "The Problem of Locke-Berkeley," *Aspects of Modern Logic* E. W. Beth (ed.) (Dordrecht: D. Reidel Publishing Company, 1970), pp. 42–62; Jaakko Hintikka, "Kant on the Mathematical

Another (better) way of puzzling ourselves about (A · ∨) is to observe that it, for all practical purposes, has the force of the principle of choice for finite sets of sets. Consequently, many of the general theoretical objections that have been levelled at the other cases of the principle of choice apply against (A · ∨), too.[11] In other words, much of first-order logic ought to be subject to the same doubts as the axiom of choice, if these skeptical objections are to be taken seriously.

The right way out of this kind of problem is to realize, first of all, that we should not be comparing individual applications of (G · ∨) and (A · ∨) but the whole language games governed by the rules (G) and the rules (A), respectively. Moreover, it is important to recall that the language game of formal logic (of quantification) receives its significance from its connection with the activities of seeking and finding and in a sense reflects the structure of these activities. In a sense, then, the truths of logic also reflect only the structure of these human activities—or perhaps rather of the rules that govern them.

Second, a specific connection between the two language games should be noted. In the former, I am trying to win in 'the game of exploring the world'. In the latter, I am asking whether the world could be such that I can win in such a game. A positive answer to the latter question does not tell me much about what will be happening in an actual play of a game of seeking and finding, but a negative answer amounts to a rather severe restriction on what my prospects in a 'game of exploring the world' are. Hence the (A) games of formal logic help me in the (G) games in that they show what my limits of freedom are in these games. Moreover, from a closer examination of the (A) games I can also frequently find out that I can hope to win in a type of (G) game only by playing in certain ways, irrespective of what 'the state of nature' is, as a decision theorist would say.

An example may make this clearer. Consider the following pair of statements

(1)   '∨x ∧y Rxy'

(2)   '∨x ∧y ∼Ryx'

Method," *Kant Studies To-Day* L. W. Beck (ed.) (LaSalle, Ill.: Open Court, 1969), pp. 117–140.
    It seems to me that Beth, too, underestimates the depth of the problems that come up here.
[11] See, for example, the doubts mentioned in R. L. Wilder, *Introduction to the Foundations of Mathematics* (New York: John Wiley, 1952). Some critics of the principle of choice have in fact extended their criticism to the finite case, unaware that they are in effect criticizing first-order logic and not set theory.

In order to verify these two, we would have to find individuals a, b such that the following are true:

(3) '$\bigwedge y\ Ray$'
(4) '$\bigwedge y \sim Ryb$'

In fact, these two expressions are obtained (as members of an approximation λ toward a model set) from (1) and (2), respectively, by $(A \cdot \bigvee)$. Of course, we do not know, sight unseen, whether such individuals can in fact be found. However, the game of formal logic does not pretend to answer this question but rather to see whether statements (1) and (2) can be verified in any case.

If statements (3) and (4) are to be the case, we must also have

(5) 'Rab'
(6) '$\sim Rab$'

These are obtained from (3) and (4) respectively, by $(A \cdot \bigwedge)$. Intuitively, they say that whatever holds for *all* individuals must hold for b and a, respectively.

Of course, (5) and (6) cannot both be true. Hence our little argument shows that even if I should succeed in finding the kinds of individuals I must look for, I cannot win in the game associated with the conjunction of (1) and (2).

This illustrates the way in which the language game of formal logic exposes the limits of what can be accomplished in the language games of exploring the world, although it cannot help to predict in most cases what will actually happen in a game of the latter kind.

By way of a quick popularization of our observations it may be said that the language-games (A) of formal logic deal with the *best possible cases* that can arise in the corresponding 'outdoor' games (G). Just because we are in formal logic asking whether I *can* have—in suitable circumstances—a winning strategy in a certain outdoor game of seeking and finding or whether I am bound to fail 'come what may' against clever enough an opponent, it is pertinent to ask what I can accomplish in the best of circumstances, for nothing can be more suitable than they.

From this point of view the relation of $(G \cdot \bigvee)$ and $(A \cdot \bigvee)$ thus becomes crystal clear. The best situation we can hope to come upon in a game of searching and finding is one in which I always find the individuals I am searching for. What $(A \cdot \bigvee)$ says is, in effect, that this is the situation considered in the language game of formal logic. If I can be defeated even in this optimal case, I am bound to be defeated in *any* circumstances.

From the same point of view, we can also understand the relation of (A · Λ) to (G · Λ). The foremost apparent puzzle here is due to the fact that (A · Λ) seemingly asks me to worry only about those members of our domain of individuals which are chosen earlier by myself in a round of a (G)-game. In other words, in (A · Λ), Nature's moves seem to be restricted in an inexplicable way to the choices I have already anticipated myself. The justification of this restriction may seem problematic until we realize that from the point of view of guarding oneself against counterexamples the optimal case is one in which I only have to worry about the individuals which I have myself come upon in the course of the game. Again, the point of an (A)-game is to set limits on the (G)-games by considering this 'best possible' situation in a (G)-game.

It is interesting to see that puzzles about the interrelation of the two types of language games concern mainly the two quantifier rules (A · V) and (A · Λ). Elsewhere, I have argued that it is the interplay of these two rules, and perhaps especially the use of the former, that makes many quantification-theoretical inferences nontrivial. If we identify this nontriviality with a kind of syntheticity, we may even say that it is the use of existential instantiation that in the first place can make first-order reasoning synthetic in a sense that is related to Kant's.

It still remains to bring our observations to bear on Kantian problems, as I promised in the beginning of this paper. Such an application lies very close at hand, however, for I shall argue that Kant was led to his central doctrines concerning mathematics, space, and time by a line of thought closely related to the problem of justifying the rule of existential instantiation, discussed above. Here problems arising out of our game-theoretical interpretation of the quantifiers actually overlap with questions Kant raises. Moreover, this overlap takes place in an area which is most vital to Kant's own thought. It is here that the role of our games of seeking and finding as especially important activities for acquiring knowledge helps to build a bridge to Kantian doctrines where such activities are consistently emphasized.

This is best seen by considering the way Kant formulates his 'main transcendental question' about the possibility of mathematics in the *Prolegomena*.[12] In spite of the fact that Kant speaks of mathematical knowledge, it is not hard to see that what is at issue in his discussion here (as in so many other passages) is from the modern point of view as much quantificational logic as mathematics. An outline of Kant's argument in the *Prolegomena* can be represented as

[12] Pages 281–284 of the Academy Edition, Vol. 4.

follows: First, he recalls what in his view is the essence of the mathematical method. According to his own explanations, he saw that characteristic feature of the procedure of mathematicians in the use of what he called *constructions*. According to Kant, the 'first and highest' condition of the possibility of mathematical knowledge is that mathematics must be able to 'represent all its concepts *in concreto* and yet a priori, or, as it is called, . . . to *construct* them'.[13] Now for Kant 'to *construct* a concept means to exhibit a priori the intuition which corresponds to the concept'. I have argued elsewhere that by an intuition Kant initially means nothing but a representative of an individual.[14] Hence this definition of a construction means that Kant saw the essence of the mathematical method in the introduction of representatives of individuals which instantiate general concepts. Of such procedures, the rule of existential instantiation offers a paradigmatic case. [Compare step (i) of the outline of the Kantian argument.]

KANT'S ARGUMENT CONCERNING MATHEMATICS:	ANALOGOUS ARGUMENT CONCERNING QUANTIFICATION THEORY:
(i) The essential feature of synthetic reasoning in mathematics is the introduction of new intuitions a priori.	(i)* The essential feature of synthetic reasoning in quantification theory is the use of the rule of existential instantiation.
(ii) In such an operation, we seem to anticipate the existence of an individual with certain properties before experience has provided us with one.	(ii)* In applying it, we seem to anticipate the existence of an individual with certain properties before experience has provided us with one.
(iii) The results of such reasoning are nevertheless applicable to all experience a priori and with absolute necessity.	(iii)* The results of such reasoning are nevertheless applicable to all exerience a priori and with logical necessity.
(iv) This is possible only if the knowledge which we gain by means of these antici-	(iv)* This is possible only if the knowledge which we

[13] *Critique of Pure Reason*, A 713 = B 714.
[14] See "On Kant's Notion of Intuition (*Anschauung*)," in Terence Penelhum and J. J. Mackintosh, eds., *The First Critique: Reflections on Kant's Critique of Pure Reason* (Belmont, Calif.: Wadsworth Publishing Company, 1969), pp. 38–53, "Kant on the Mathematical Method" (note 10 above), and my other papers on Kant.

pations of existence per-
tains to individuals only
insofar as they are objects
of the activities by means
of which we come to know
the existence of individual
objects in general.

(v) The knowledge obtained in
this way will then only
reproduce the structure of
the activities by means of
which we come to know
the existence of individual
objects in general.

(vi) The activity by means of
which we come to know
the existence of individual
objects is *sensation*.

(vii) Hence the knowledge gained
by means of mathematical
reasoning applies to ob-
jects only insofar as they
are objects of sensation
(sensible intuition).

(viii) Furthermore, the interrelations of the individuals
introduced in mathematical
reasoning (and hence also
the interrelations of their
representations or the corresponding intuitions) is
due to the structure (form)
of our sensibility, and reflects it.

gain by means of these
anticipations of existence
pertains to individuals
only insofar as they are
objects of the activities
by means of which we
come to know the exis-
tence of individuals in
general.

(v)* The knowledge obtained
in this way will then only
reproduce the structure of
the activities by means of
which we come to know
the existence of individ-
uals in general.

(vi)* The activities by means
of which we come to
know the existence of in-
dividuals are the activi-
ties of *searching* and
finding.

(vii)* Hence the knowledge we
obtain in quantification
theory applies to individuals only insofar as the
activities of searching
and finding can (in prin-
ciple) be performed among
them.

(viii)* Furthermore, the structure of quantificational
arguments reflects the
structure of the activities
of searching and finding.

Both in the 'constructions' Kant contemplated and in the applications of our rules (A · V) we introduce a representative of an individual
(in Kant's terminology, an intuition, in our terminology, a free singular
term) which does not refer to any known individual. As Kant puts it,

the introduction of an individual takes place a priori. This gives rise to a problem, according to Kant. 'But with this step the difficulty seems rather to grow than to decrease. For now the question runs: *How is it possible to intuit anything a priori?* Intuition is a representation, such as would depend directly on the presence of the object. Hence it seems impossible to intuit anything a priori originally [in German, *ursprünglich*, that is to say, so as to give us the existence of the object in question] because the intuition would then have to take place without any object being present, either previously or now, to which it could refer, and so could not be an intuition . . . '.[15] From this we can see that Kant's problem is to all intents and purposes identical with the problem of the justifiability of the rule (A · V) of existential instantiation which we discussed earlier. In this rule, too, we seem to anticipate the existence of an individual before experience has provided us with one. (Compare the second stage of the appended arguments.)

This creates a problem for Kant because he believed that mathematical knowledge is applicable to all experience a priori and with certainty—quite as much as we believe that our logic is necessarily applicable to all experience. For, we may ask, how can such firm knowledge be obtained by means of an anticipation of the existence of individual objects. (See the third stage of the outline argument.)

Kant's way of trying to solve this problem is closely connected with the basic ideas of his philosophy. His "New Method of Thought" was to assume that "we can know a priori of things only what we ourselves put into them."[16]

This idea has a long and fascinating history which largely remains to be explored.[17] It is one of the tacit presuppositions on which Kant is basing his "transcendental arguments." If these arguments are to have deductive cogency, it must clearly be held that the *only* way in which we can account for our a priori knowledge of certain things is to assume that somehow we have ourselves put the requisite properties and relations into them. [Note the use of the word "only" at stages (iv) and (iv)* of the appended outlines.]

This Kantian assumption is clearly highly interesting, whether it is correct or not. Prima facie, it seems highly dubious. We may try to account for the possibility of our having knowledge of certain objects before having any direct experience of them (and hence for the possibility of having knowledge of them a priori in a sense) in terms of innate ideas or evolutionary adaptation. If this view is

[15] *Prolegomena,* §8.
[16] *Critique of Pure Reason,* B xviii.
[17] Cf. footnote 2 above.

JAAKKO HINTIKKA 55

adopted, arguments based on Kant's assumption have no deductive cogency but at best amount to inferences to the best explanation—a view in effect adopted by some of the foremost Kantian scholars. However, if knowledge a priori is taken to be conceptual knowledge, the situation is different. Then Kant's principle amounts to saying that we can have conceptually guaranteed knowledge of certain things if and only if this knowledge is based on the way in which we come to know them and reflects the structure of this process of coming to know them. Interpreted in this way, the principle is still not obviously correct, but now it is in any case a highly interesting and suggestive idea. I believe it has a great deal of value in conceptual analysis. This point is unfortunately too large to be argued here, however.

Kant's use of his assumption is seen clearly in his theory of space, time, and mathematics. Since mathematical knowledge was assumed by Kant to be a priori, this implies that only such properties and relations of individuals must be anticipated in mathematical constructions as we have ourselves put into objects, and the existence of only such individuals may be anticipated which have been created by ourselves. Now mathematical knowledge is assumed by Kant to apply to all experience (of individuals). But there is, according to Kant's assumptions, only one stage at which we can "put properties and relations into objects" in all the individuals in our experience. This is the process by means of which we become aware of individual objects in general. And this process is according to Kant *sensation*. Kant thought that all "objects are *given* to us by means of sensibility, and it alone yields us *intuitions*," that is, representations of individual objects.[18] Hence the relations and properties with which mathematical reasoning deals and which are anticipated in the a priori intuitions which a mathematician uses must have been created by ourselves in the process of sense perception. Only in this way, Kant thinks, can we explain the possibility of the use of a priori intuitions (introduction of new individuals) in mathematical arguments. If the existence and properties of a triangle had no "relation to you, the subject," then "you could not add anything new (the figure) to your concepts (of three lines) as something which necessarily must be met with in the object, since this object is given antecedently to your knowledge and [on that view] not by means of it." From this Kant concludes that the knowledge we gain through mathematical reasoning applies to objects only insofar as they are possible objects of sensation. He also concludes that the relations with which mathematical reasoning is concerned merely reflect the form (structure) of our sensibility.

[18] *Critique of Pure Reason,* A19 = B31.

This argument is represented in our outline. How is it to be evaluated? We have already seen that no doctrines like Kant's theories of space and time are needed to explain the role of such rules as (A · V). Thus nothing very much seems to remain of Kant's conclusions. However, it is not difficult to recast some of our observations in a form which is in a very deep sense similar to Kant's arguments. These arguments represent a highly interesting line of thought with which we might profitably compare a similar argument which we could try to carry out in terms of quantifiers (second part of the outline). In particular, it seems to me very interesting to try to explain the necessity and strict universality of our logical reasoning in the way Kant strives to explain the necessity and universality of our mathematical knowledge. It seems to me justified to say that, insofar as it is a conceptual certainty that our logic applies to all experience, there must be a conceptual tie between our logical concepts and the ways in which come to have our experience. In the case of the concepts of existence and universality, which constitute the subject matter of quantification theory, the relevant experiences are the ones on which our knowledge of the existence of individuals turns. Quantifiers must, in other words, be essentially connected with the processes by means of which we come to know the existence of individual objects. Now Kant thought that the only process of this kind is sense perception. However, I have already argued that this view is wrong. In an earlier paper[19] I pointed out that it is misleading to say that we come to know the existence of all individual objects by means of sense perception. Saying this overlooks entirely the role which our active attempts to find suitable objects play in the genesis of our knowledge of individual existence. Direct observation may be thought of as a "trivial case" of successful search, but the language games of seeking and finding cannot be reduced to direct observation. Hence we must say that the processes through which we become aware of the existence of individual objects in general are the activities of seeking and finding, not the processes of observation. Hence what Kant ought to have concluded was something rather different from his actual conclusions. He was wrong in concluding that quantificational modes of inference are intimately connected with the mode of operation of our faculty of sense perception. What he ought to have concluded is that quantificational modes of argument are bound up with the structure of our activities of seeking and finding. This bond between them is just what I have tried to spell out in the early part of this paper.

Kant was thus wrong in his attempt to connect all intuitions (in his sense of the word) with sense perception. The connection which he thought there was between sensibility and a posteriori intuitions

---

[19] "Language-Games for Quantifiers" (note 4 above).

does not exist, and, as a consequence, the argument of Kant's (the argument which we have been considering and by means of which he tried to connect the use of a priori intuitions in mathematics with the form of our sensibility) is fallacious.

However, we have seen that this argument (which is essentially the argument which Kant calls "the transcendental exposition of the concepts of space and time") can be recast so as to become a kind of "a transcendental exposition of quantifiers." This strange name is appropriate because Kant explains its meaning by saying that he understands "by a transcendental exposition the explanation of a concept, as a principle from which the possibility of other *a priori* synthetic knowledge can be understood." For what we have obtained is just a modified argument which purports to show that quantificational arguments, including arguments which are synthetic in what I take to be the best modern reconstruction of Kant's notion, apply to all experience. If I do not embrace this argument as wholeheartedly as Kant accepts his, this is merely because I am not fully convinced of the truth of one of its premises. I am not sure whether we should really say that quantificational arguments apply to all experience. But if this assumption is made, I do not see why this "transcendental exposition of quantifiers," or some closely similar argument, should not be fully acceptable. We have already seen that the main conclusions (vii)* and (viii)* of the parallel argument reflect insights into the interrelations of the language games of formal logic and the (G) games of searching and finding.

It would be interesting to see what further changes are necessitated in Kant's philosophy by the switch from his argument concerning mathematics to our argument concerning quantifiers. It seems to me that more light could be thrown on some of Kant's doctrines in this way. It would take us too far, however, to mention more than a single example here. It will be obvious, for instance, that Kant's concept of *Ding an sich* will have to be modified profoundly. Instead of saying, as did Kant, that we can know individual objects only insofar as they are potential objects of sense perception we shall have to say merely that we cannot use quantifiers to describe a class of individual things without considering them as potential objects of searching and finding. In "Language-Games for Quantifiers"[20] I made a number of remarks concerning the conditions in which this is the case. In this way, these earlier remarks can be fitted into a semi-Kantian framework.

There is plenty of room for much further work in this direction, and also on the systematic questions which our observations pose.

---

[20] Cf. footnote 4 above.

On Explicating Existence in Terms of Quantification

ALEX ORENSTEIN

Queens College of the City of New York

This paper is an examination of the most serious account I know of the existential reading of the particular quantifier. W. V. Quine has over a period of years carefully worked out and championed this view. In the first part of this paper I will present his refinement of the thesis that the existential reading is correct, that is, that existence claims are disguised quantifications. In the second part I will present criticisms and try to show that Quine faces difficulties which do not arise for nonexistential readings. Among the nonexistential readings, I will argue for the special importance of the substitutional view.

I

QUINE'S PROGRAM FOR EXISTENCE AND QUANTIFICATION

A. *The Interdependence of the Concepts of Truth and Existence*

The justification for giving a distinctive natural language reading to '∃x' depends upon the semantical truth conditions for sentences containing that sign. Thus the justification for reading '∃x' existentially depends on the fact that the truth of quantified sentences involves the notion of a domain. Here are the conditions usually presented for atomic sentences and those with the particular quantifier.

$$\text{val } (Pt_1, \ldots, t_n) = T \quad \text{iff} \quad \langle \text{val } (t_1), \ldots, \text{val } (t_n) \rangle \in \text{val } (P)$$
$$\text{val } ((\exists x)A) = T \quad \text{iff} \quad (\exists d)(d \in D \ \& \ \text{val } (t/xA) = T)$$
$$\text{where val } (t_1) = d_1, \text{ val } (t_2) = d_2, \ldots, \text{ val } (t_n) = d_n.$$

According to the above an atomic sentence is true when the values assigned to its arguments are members of the values assigned to its predicates. The values assigned to its arguments (the arguments here are singular terms) are the individuals of the domain. The predicates are assigned sets from the domain. An "existential" quantification for an individual variable is true precisely when there is an individual in the domain which would make the appropriate substitution instance, for example, 'Ad' true in the sense just explained for an atomic sentence. Quine himself has not presented truth conditions in exactly this way. I shall nonetheless explain his position in these terms taking care in doing so not to misrepresent it. The values of the variables (in this case individual variables) are the members of the domain. The slogan that to be is to be the value of a variable means that the being or existent is the member of a domain. Quine identifies being and existence and I shall follow him in this practice while explaining his views.

A very important thing to notice about the account given above is that it makes the concepts of truth and existence interdependent. By this I mean that membership in a domain, that is, existence, is the basis for computing the truth of all sentences. Membership in a domain, that is, existence, is the only basis for computing the truth of an atomic sentence, and the truth value of all other sentences are then computed from the atomic ones.

Just as the notion of a domain is central to explaining the existential reading, so is the allied notion of a strong semantical relation. Designation, multiple denotation, and satisfaction are some examples of strong semantical relations, such as designation (an expression designates or names an object), multiple denotation (an expression is true of, applies to, or denotes several objects), and satisfaction (objects satisfy an expression). In each case the relation is between a linguistic entity on the one hand and a member or members of the domain on the other. Throughout the years Quine has used notions such as these to justify his reading of the quantifier. In early papers such as "Designation and Existence" (1939) and "A Logistic Approach to the Ontological Problem" (1939) existential quantification is linked with naming.

Perhaps we can reach no absolute decision as to which words have designata and which have none, but at least we can say whether or not a given pattern of linguistic behavior *construes* a word *W* as having a designatum. This is decided by judging whether existential generalization with respect to *W* is accepted as a valid form of inference. A name—not in the sense of a

mere noun, but in the semantic sense of an expression designating
something—becomes describable as an expression with respect
to which existential generalization is valid. . . . instead of describing names as expressions with respect to which existential
generalization is valid we might equivalently omit express mention of existential generalization and describe names simply as
those constant expressions which replace variables and are replaced by variables according to the usual laws of quantification.[1]

The problem of determining when we can existentially generalize
is linked with that of determining which expressions can be regarded
as nonsyncategorematic, that is, as names.

To ask whether there is such an entity as roundness is thus not
to question the meaningfulness of 'roundness'; it amounts rather
to asking whether the word is a name or a syncategorematic
expression.
    Ontological questions can be transformed, in this superficial
way, into linguistic questions regarding the boundary between
names and syncategorematic expressions.[2]

At this early point in Quine's writings we find a favorite recurrent
theme of his: the explanation of variables in terms of pronouns.

Variables are pronouns, and make sense only in positions which
are available to names.[3]

When Quine later developed the position that individual constants
or names are a derivative type of expression which can be dispensed
with, he ceased to rely on the strong semantical relation of designat-
ing-naming. The thesis of the superfluity of names appeared first
in *Mathematical Logic* (1940) and then in the better known "On
What There Is" (1948). Quine's more recent explanations of the quantifiers now appeal to notions like multiple denotation and satisfaction.
In "Existence and Quantification" (1966) he has said the following:

Another way of saying what objects a theory requires is to say
that they are objects that some of the predicates of the theory

[1] W. V. Quine, "Designation and Existence," *Readings in Philosophical Analysis,*
H. Feigl and W. Sellars (eds.) (New York: Appleton-Century-Crofts, 1949),
pp. 49–50.
[2] W. V. Quine, "A Logistic Approach to the Ontological Problem," *Ways of
Paradox* (New York: Random House, 1966), p. 64. Hereinafter cited as *Ways
of Paradox.*
[3] *Ibid.,* p. 65.

have to be true of, in order for the theory to be true. But this is the same as saying that they are the objects that have to be values of the variables in order for the theory to be true. It is the same, anyway, if the notation of the theory includes for each predicate a complementary predicate, its negation. For then, given any value of a variable, some predicate is true of it; viz., any predicate or its complement. And conversely, of course whatever a predicate is true of is a value of the variables. Predication and quantification, indeed, are intimately linked; for a predicate is simply any expression that yields a sentence, an open sentence, when adjoined to one or more quantifiable variables. When we schematize a sentence in the predicative way "*Fa*," or "*a* is an *F*," our recognition of an "*a*" part and an "*F*" part turns strictly on our use of variables of quantification: the "*a*" represents a part of the sentence that stands where a quantifiable variable could stand, and the "*F*" represents the rest.

Our question was: what objects does a theory require? Our answer is: those objects that have to be values of variables for the theory to be true.[4]

Finally, in his recent *Philosophy of Logic* (1970), Quine has sketched a definition of truth along Tarski's lines relying on the relation of satisfaction.[5] A propositional function is satisfied by objects (or more precisely by sequences) found in the domain. Since Quine now holds that names are not a primitive form of expression, he would not accept the truth conditions presented at the start of this section. For example his semantics would not make use of arguments where *t* is understood as referring to a name. The relations of a predicate being true of and being satisfied rely only on the primitive categories of predicate and propositional function. However, for each of these, as well as for naming, the truth of a sentence depends upon membership in a domain, that is, existence. Put somewhat differently, for Quine truth and existence are interdependent. Let us turn and see how all of this applies to the problem of vacuous singular terms.

B. *The Problem of Empty Individual Constants*

It has become customary in recent years to lay down two requirements for any adequate theory of quantification. The first is that no particular-existential generalization be provable as a theorem. In the paper "Quantification and the Empty Domain" Quine showed how

[4] W. V. Quine, *Ontological Relativity and Other Essays* (New York: Columbia University Press, 1969), pp. 95–96.
[5] W. V. Quine, *Philosophy of Logic* (Englewood Cliffs, N.J.: Prentice Hall, 1970), Chapter 5. Hereinafter cited as *Philosophy of Logic*.

to modify the system presented in his *Mathematical Logic* to attain this end. The second requirement is that there be no restriction on the non-logical constants that fall under the rules of logic. The problem here is that of empty individual constants and rules such as particular-existential generalization. The difficulty is that the presumed-to-be-true 'Pegasus is a flying horse', yields the false, if existentially read '(∃x) (x is a flying horse)'; that is, 'there exists a flying horse'.

Quine has presented two somewhat similar solutions to this problem. The earlier one was stated in *Mathematical Logic*, and the later one in "On What There Is." Common to the two is the basic idea that individual constants are dispensable and not part of our canonical notation. On both of these analyses the troublesome sentence 'Pegasus is a flying horse', turns out to be equivalent to a false sentence, so that the inference to '(∃x)(x is a flying horse)' remains truth-preserving.

The solution offered in *Mathematical Logic* is a variant of Frege's chosen-object theory. Individual constants are defined in terms of definite descriptions. These descriptions are themselves analyzed in terms of class abstraction. Where the name designates a unique object it is ultimately analyzed in terms of a class expression designating a unit class. Where the name or its intermediary description is true either of more than one individual or of none, the class abstract designates the null class. That is to say, the object chosen for improper names and definite descriptions is the null class. 'Pegasus is a flying horse' is presumably false since 'is a flying horse' is a predicate which fails to be true of any individual in the domain (and for that matter of the null class).

There is an odd consequence which follows from the chosen-object theory. Since the null class exists, that is, '(∃x)(x = Λ)' is true, the sentence 'Pegasus exists' turns out to be true. Quine says that when we treat individual constants like 'Europe', 'God', and 'Pegasus' in terms of class abstraction then "There is no question of the existence of these three entities; there is question only as to their nature."[6] I shall comment on this later in the paper.

Quine's more recent and better-known solution is an extension of Russell's theory of descriptions. According to this theory definite descriptions are contextually defined so that they need never be taken as part of our primitive vocabulary. Quine has simply shown that for any individual constant we can construct an equivalent definite description so that the former can be eliminated when we dispense with the latter. For 'Pegasus' we already have the definite description 'the winged horse of Bellerophon'. If we did not have a description, we could easily have constructed one such as 'the unique object which

[6] Quine, *Mathematical Logic*, p. 150.

pegasizes'. The sentence 'Pegasus is a flying horse', becomes in canonical notation

$$(\exists x)(x \text{ pegasizes } \& ((y)(y \text{ pegasizes } \supset y = x) \& x \text{ is a flying horse})$$

Since the "existence" condition is false, that is, the predicate 'is a flying horse' does not apply to anything in our domain, the entire sentence is false. Similarly, the original sentence is false, so that the argument does not constitute a counterexample to particular-existential generalization.

In summary, then, on Quine's later analysis all simple sentences with vacuous singular subjects are treated alike as false.

C. *Quantification for Grammatical Categories Other Than Singular Terms*

The formula that to be is to be the value of a variable as well as the existential reading itself is most plausible where the quantifiers bind individual variables. Here, as we have seen, Quine thinks of variables as linked either to names designating the values of the variables or the values of the variables alone. To say that the paradigm for Quine is quantification of individual variables is as we shall see an understatement. He explains other authors' attempts at quantifications for categories other than singular expressions by construing these in terms of quantification for singular terms. For his own purposes he permits quantification solely for singular terms—individual variables. In this section I will first indicate how Quine understands quantification with respect to propositional positions, such as, 'p', 'q' and for predicate positions, for example, 'F', 'G'. I will then remark on his own method for dealing with expressions in these positions and its bearing on Quine's way of expressing the principles of logic.

Perhaps Quine's first venture into ontology was his 1934 paper "Ontological Remarks on the Propositional Calculus."[7] If we take literally the existential reading and that variables have values and the substituends for these variables name these values, then a problem arises in connection with propositional variables. What sort of object is the value of a propositional variable? If a sentence is the substituend for such a variable, then what sort of object does a sentence designate?

Before proceeding any further we must make some presuppositions explicit. There are at least two different views which we can take about semantical relations and the place of stipulation in semantics. At the one extreme, it is a matter of convention as to which

[7] Quine, *Ways of Paradox.*

categories of expression we consider to be designators—names.[8] According to this view sentences and predicates can be said to designate.
At another extreme is the view which coincides with common usage.
According to this view only names designate. Sentences may be true
or false but they do not designate. Similarly predicates may be true
of or apply to objects but they do not designate. Quine himself accepts
this latter view, as I do also.[9]

It is necessary here to depart somewhat from our attempt merely
to explain Quine's defense of the existential reading, and to voice
a criticism. We cannot consistently maintain that the existential reading is correct for all sorts of variables, that is, to be is to be the
value of a variable for any category of variables, and the view that
only singular terms are designators, that is, individual variables have
values or individual constants that designate those values. The result is
that other forms of quantification than those over singular terms fail
to be explained on the existential reading. Quine himself argues for
restricting quantification to singular terms, and he puts aside the
principle that only singular terms designate when explaining the views
of those who take different styles of quantification seriously.

Returning to propositional variables 'p', 'q', Quine notes the following alternatives. If a principle such as 'p ⊃ (p v q)' is in the object
language, then two different objects can be taken as the values of the
propositional variables. The first is Frege's view that 'p', 'q' have one
of two values; the True or the False. Thus individual sentences, the
substituends for 'p', 'q' designate either the True or the False. The
second choice of values for propositional variables has been propositions.
Propositions here are intensional entities and would be the designata
of the sentences serving as substituends for 'p' or 'q'. Another alternative which Quine mentions but rejects would consist of taking 'p' and
'q' as metalinguistic variables having object language sentences as
their values. But then 'p ⊃ (p v q)' would no longer be an object
language principle.

A similar treatment is accorded quantification of predicates,
such as (∃F)(Fx). The kind of objects that predicate variables have
been said to take as values and predicate constants to designate are
either the extensional entities, classes, or the intensional ones, properties-attributes. Quantification over predicate positions is a part of
higher-order logic. For Quine such quantification—existentially construed—demands values for its variables. Since Quine is an exten-

[8] See Carnap, *Meaning and Necessity* (Chicago: University of Chicago Press, 1956), p. 7.
[9] W. V. Quine, "Logic and the Reification of Universals," *From a Logical Point of View* (New York: Harper Torchbooks, 1961), pp. 112–115. Hereinafter cited as *From a Logical Point of View*.

sionalist the values he opts for are classes. From these two considerations (1) higher-order logic requires values for its variables and (2) extensionalism, it follows that for Quine, to do higher-order logic is to be involved in set theory. In his words, '$(\exists F)(Fx)$' is "set theory in sheep's clothing."[10]

Quine has used these alternative treatments of divergent quantificational contexts to offer what have become influential interpretations of the history of logic in this century. One example, which he has repeated on numerous occasions, is Russell's "no-class theory" of classes.[11] Russell in *Principia* claimed to be contextually eliminating class expressions in favour of quantification over propositional functions. This was analogous to the elimination of definite descriptions in terms of quantification over individual variables. Quine interprets this claim in the following way. If Russell thought that quantification over propositional functions involved only linguistic entities, open sentences, or predicates, then he had confused object and meta-linguistic quantification. A propositional function as an open sentence could be the value of a meta-linguistic variable but never of an object-language one. If, on the other hand, Russell thought quantification over propositional functions involved properties-attributes, then his no-classes theory dispenses with classes in favour of more suspect intensional entities and hence fails to be a significant reduction.

So far we have only shown how Quine interprets different styles of quantification as they were used by authors other than himself. He himself however considers such styles of quantification to be mistaken and restricts quantification to the individual variables of first-order logic. But then how would he permit one to express an ontological commitment to classes or properties given only individual variables and their values? Quine's program for connecting existence and the quantifier must allow people to assert the existence of such entities. His solution is to appeal to the traditional distinction between concrete singular terms and abstract ones.[12] The individual constants which can serve as substituends for the individual variables may be names of concrete individuals, such as 'Bossy', 'Bucephalus' or names of abstract individuals such as classes, for example, 'mankind', 'red', or

---

[10] Quine, *Philosophy of Logic*, pp. 64–65.
[11] See Quine, "Whitehead and the Rise of Modern Logic," *Selected Logical Papers* (New York: Random House, 1966), pp. 21–23; "Russell's Ontological Development," *Journal of Philosophy*, Vol. 63 (November, 1966), pp. 659–661; J. van Heijenoort (ed.), *From Frege to Gödel: A Source Book in Mathematical Logic 1879–1931* (Cambridge: Harvard University Press, 1967), pp. 150–151; Quine, *Set Theory and Its Logic* (Cambridge: Harvard University Press, 1963), pp. 249–254.
[12] Quine, *From a Logical Point of View*, pp. 112–117; also Quine, *Methods of Logic* (New York: Holt, Rinehart and Winston, 1963), pp. 203–204.

properties, for example, 'triangularity', 'redness'. This is one of the most fascinating parts of Quine's program. Whatever exists is an individual member of the domain required for the existential reading of the quantifier. There is only one style of variable—the individual variable—and its values can be concrete individuals, individual classes, individual properties, etc. This is why it is an understatement to say that Quine models quantification on quantification of individual variables. In reality all of his quantification is with respect to individual variables. The slogan 'to be is to be the value of a variable' is similarly misleading. It would be more accurate to say that to be is to be the value of an individual variable.

We have just indicated how Quine can express an existential commitment to different types of entities without quantifying, say, with respect to predicate positions. But there is another difficulty that such positions pose for him. This concerns the ability to express the principles of logic in their full generality. Consider once again the principle of propositional logic 'p ⊃ (p v q)'. Quine, as has been noted above, rejects the view that 'p' has values or that its substituends designate sentences. Moreover it would be distasteful to him to have to expand ontology solely because of propositional logic. Quine's solution to expressing the principles of propositional logic is to regard 'p', 'q', and so on as schematic letters.[13] Schematic letters are described as being dummy expressions or blanks in a sentence diagram. They are not quantifiable, and in this lies their essential difference from variables. The same device of schematic letters enables us to express quantificational principles like '(x)(Fx ⊃ Fx)'. The 'F' and 'G' in quantificational principles are schematic letters and not variables. They are not variables because we do not quantify over them. They are said to be placeholders or unbindable dummy predicates. So 'x + 3 = 7' is an open sentence or propositional function because 'x' is a free but bindable variable. '(x)(Fx ⊃ p)' is not a propositional function but a schema. Neither 'F' nor 'p' are bindable as are variables.

Schematic latters should not be confused with the metalinguistic variables such as, 'φ', 'Ψ' that Quine uses in *Mathematical Logic*.

A schema such as (x)(Fx ⊃ p), ... is not a name of a sentence, not a name of anything; it is *itself* a pseudo-sentence, designed expressly to manifest a form which various sentences manifest. Schemata are to sentences not as names to their objects, but as slugs to nickles. ... The distinction which properly concerns us in the present pages, that between sentence and schema, is not

---

[13] Quine, *From a Logical Point of View*, pp. 107–117; see also Quine, *Methods of Logic*, index entry under "schema."

a distinction between the use and mention of expressions; its significance lies elsewhere altogether. The significance of preserving a schematic status for 'p', 'q', etc. and '*F*', '*G*', etc. rather than treating those letters as bindable variables, is that we are thereby (a) forbidden to subject those letters to quantification, and (b) spared viewing statements and predicates as names of anything.[14]

Though schematic letters are not metalinguistic variables, they are not part of the object language either.

Note carefully the role of the schematic letters 'p' and 'q' in the above explanations. They do not belong to the *object language*— the language that I have been explaining with their help. They serve diagrammatically to mark positions where sentences of the object language are to be imagined. Similarly, the schematic notation '*Fx*' may conveniently be used diagrammatically to mark the position of a sentence when we want to direct attention to the presence therein of the variable '*x*' as a free or unquantified variable. Thus we depict the form of existential quantification schematically as '$(\exists x)Fx$'. The schematic letter '*F*', like 'p' and 'q' is foreign to the object language.[15]

One consequence of this use of schematic letters to express the principles of logic is that none of these principles can be an object-language generalization. This follows from the fact that schema are "foreign to the object language" and that they are not strictly speaking sentences—but only "pseudo-sentences."

D. *Polemical Uses of the Existential Reading*

Let us turn now to review some consequences of adopting the existential reading. The consequences I have in mind amount to a body of criticism directed at higher-order logic, modal logic, doxastic logic, and so on. To begin with, we have seen in the last section how the existential reading can be applied literally to nonindividual variables only if we are prepared to hold that expressions which ordinarily do not designate do designate. The moral or criticism Quine draws from this is that disciplines like higher-order logic or quantified propositional logic should be avoided. A second related criticism is that to indulge in different styles of quantification commits us to

---

[14] Quine, *From a Logical Point of View*, p. 111.
[15] Quine, *Philosophy of Logic*, pp. 24–25.

new sorts of entities. Applying Ockham's razor, that entities should not be multiplied beyond necessity, we find ourselves involved in a program to limit the styles of quantification.

The last criticisms to note, which are associated with the existential reading, occur in connection with quantification into intensional contexts. Later in the paper some of these will be stated and commented upon.

E. *Quine's Metaphilosophy*

In order to evaluate Quine's treatment of quantification in terms of the existential reading a few words must be said about his conception of philosophy. Quine regards his treatment of existence in terms of a special reading of the quantifier as a case of philosophical analysis or explication. To judge whether this explication of existence is or is not successful will depend upon what one's metaphilosophical opinions are about the nature of such analysis.

Let us begin by noting something that philosophical analysis does not do according to Quine. The analysis does not provide us with the meaning of the expression being analyzed. Quine's scepticism about meanings leads him to eschew them in explaining philosophical analysis.

We do not claim synonymy. We do not claim to make clear and explicit what the users of the unclear expression had unconsciously in mind all along. We do not expose hidden meanings, as the words 'analysis' and 'explication' would suggest: we supply lacks. We fix on the particular functions of the unclear expression that make it worth troubling about, and then devise a substitute, clear and couched in terms to our liking, that fills those functions. Beyond those conditions of partial agreement, dictated by our interests and purposes, any traits of the explicans come under the head of "don't cares" (38). Under this head we are free to allow the explicans all manner of novel connotations never associated with the explicandum. This point is strikingly illustrated by Wiener's definition of the ordered pair.[16]

Quine chooses as his paradigm for a philosophical analysis the explication of the notion of an ordered pair. We expect our analysis to provide a substitute for those "particular functions of the troublesome expression that make it worth troubling about." These conditions of partial agreement constitute the material adequacy condition for

[16] W. V. Quine, *Word and Object* (New York: John Wiley and Sons, 1960), pp. 258–259.

the explication. In the case of the ordered pair this condition can be stated succinctly and explicitly as

If $\langle x, y \rangle = \langle z, w \rangle$ then $x = z$ and $y = w$.

Similarly the material adequacy condition for Tarski's explication of truth partially sought to capture certain intuitions about the correspondence theory of truth. This has become known as convention T; for example, 'Snow is white' is true if snow is white is an instance of this convention. In addition to an explication meeting the condition of material adequacy it must also be formally adequate. By this condition Tarski meant that the formal structure of the language used in the definition be specified. This is what Quine has in mind when using the phrase "clear and couched in terms to our liking." The formal semantics provided earlier was formulated to meet this condition. For Quine explication is part of philosophy, and philosophy itself is regarded as being continuous with science. The same kinds of considerations for adopting one theory rather than another are brought to bear on adopting one analysis rather than another, such as explanatory power, relative simplicity, and so on. We must then judge whether Quine's defense of the existential reading of the particular quantifier, that is, that quantification explicates existence, is formally, materially and methodologically adequate.

II

Is the Explication of Existence in Terms of Quantification Adequate?

The evaluation of the adequacy of explicating existence by means of quantification is complicated in at least two ways. In the first place we are not in a position to state a material adequacy condition for 'exists' as exactly as was done in the case of the ordered pair. As Quine himself acknowledges the ordered pair is to this extent not a typical analysandum. Wiener's explication is not a paradigm in the sense of being perfectly typical but rather in the sense of being an ideal. We may wonder, for this reason, whether it is a paradigm at all. It is most typical in philosophy that the material adequacy condition, that is, ". . . how closely we reproduce the presystematically available notion . . . " is itself a bone of contention.[17] The second complication is that adequacy, in the three senses of material, formal, and methodological, applies both to the explicandum 'exists' as well as to facets of the explications, namely, 'some', 'there is', which are equated with 'there exists' and the technical term ' $\exists x$ '.

[17] A. Church, "Ontological Commitment," *Journal of Philosophy,* Vol. 55 (1958), p. 1012.

In what follows three types of criticisms will be offered of this proposed explication. At the same time two nonexistential readings of the quantifier (which are not subject to these criticisms) will be introduced.

F. *The Existential Reading Cannot Provide a Canon of Reasoning*

The upshot of this criticism is that sentences like 'Pegasus is a flying horse' can and should be considered true but that they cannot on the existential reading. Let us begin by indicating why logic should accommodate the truth of such sentences. Most of the people who know what Pegasus is would consider that sentence true, and, to the extent that logic should provide a canon for reasoning, it too should make allowance for this truth. Imagine two students of introductory logic arguing. *A* maintains that Pegasus is a flying horse and *B* that Pegasus is not a flying horse. After consulting a text on mythology they would conclude that *A*'s assertion was true and *B*'s false, and not, as on Russell's theory of descriptions, that both are false. An even more unnatural fate befalls vacuous identity sentences such as "Pegasus is Pegasus'. Even without knowing what Pegasus is most people would consider this sentence true, yet on Russell's and Quine's view it is considered false.

So much for illustration. We can now enunciate another adequacy condition for logic. In Section B we stated two conditions for logic being free of certain assumptions. One of these was that there be no restrictions on the nature of the constants (*salva congruitate*) which the principles should apply to. 'Pegasus' and 'Cerberus' are to be fitting substitution instances. The new, third, requirement is that among the atomic sentences containing vacuous terms some can be true and some false (and following Strawson some neuter, that is, neither true nor false). We want logic to be free of the assumption of the truth of any specific singular sentences.

This view has come to be recognized by many who are concerned with the requirements for a logic being free. Leonard, Shearn, Rescher, van Fraassen, and Thomason are some of the writers who wish to consider 'Pegasus is a flying horse' true.[18] In a different way Strawson

---

[18] H. S. Leonard, "Essences, Attributes and Predicates," Presidential Address for the 62nd annual meeting of the Western division of the American Philosophical Association at Milwaukee, Wisconsin, April-May, 1964, pp. 29–30, 51; M. Shearn, "Russell's Analysis of Existence," *Analysis*, Vol. 11 (1950). p. 127; N. Rescher, *Topics in Philosophical Logic* (New York: Humanities Press, 1968), pp. 152, 159; B. van Fraassen, "Presuppositions, Supervaluations, and Free Logic," and R. Thomason "Modal Logic and Metaphycis," *The Logical Way of Doing Things,* (ed.) K. Lambert (New Haven: Yale University Press. 1969), pp. 89–90, 129.

has argued persuasively that some sentences with vacuous terms, such as 'The present king of France is bald', be considered neither true nor false. Leblanc, Thomason, and van Fraassen have shown that no purely formal considerations about a system of logic prohibit regarding singular sentences as true, false, or neuter.[19]

Thus far the argument has been that some sentences with vacuous terms should be considered true. It remains to be shown that this cannot be accomplished on the existential reading. The essence of the semantics justifying this reading is that being a member of a domain and being an existent are the same. It was for this reason that we said that the concepts of truth and existence are interdependent here. On this view 'Pegasus is a flying horse' must be considered false. Almost all parties agree that Pegasus does not exist. On the existential reading it follows that 'Pegasus is a flying horse' is false since the value of this sentence is computed solely in terms of a domain of existents. For Quine (on one of his approaches) such a sentence would be equivalent to another containing a definite description, that is, 'The one and only object which pegasizes is a flying horse'. The falsity of this would be computed from that same domain of existents. Quite simply, if truth and existence are interdependent, then sentences about non-existents must be false.[20]

A few comments are now in order about Frege's chosen-object theory. According to Quine's version of it in *Mathematical Logic*, improper descriptions always turn out to designate the null class. For Frege only vacuous terms designated the null class. It is a matter of convention which object will serve as the chosen object, the only proviso being that it is included in the domain. Two points must be made about this theory. The first is a criticism. If we take existence seriously, then it simply is false that 'Pegasus exists'. If someone says that on the chosen-object theory, sentences like 'Pegasus is a flying horse' are really about the null class (as is 'Pegasus exists'),

---

[19] See H. Leblanc and R. H. Thomason, "Completeness Theorems for Some Presupposition-free Logics," *Fundamenta Mathematicae*, Vol. 62 (1968), pp. 126–164; also B. van Fraassen, "The Completeness of Free Logic," *Zeitschrift fur Mathematische Logik und Grundlagen der Mathematik*, Vol. 12 (1966), p. 219–239; and B. van Fraassen, "Singular Terms, Truth Value Gaps and Free Logic," *Journal of Philosophy*, Vol. 63 (1966), pp. 481–495.

[20] Another possible way of regarding "Pegasus is a flying horse' is to treat singular sentences as universal conditionals. The sentence above would now be true since the universal conditional 'If anything pegasizes, then it is a flying horse' is on the existential reading vacuously true. Of course this method has the undesirable effect of making 'Pegasus is a flying fish.' and all other vacuous singular sentences true as well. See S. Barker, *The Elements of Logic* (New York: McGraw-Hill, 1965), pp. 75–76; also N. Rescher, *Topics in Philosophical Logic* (New York: Humanities Press, 1968), p. 152.

then we must reply that we are talking about Pegasus and not about the null class, or, in other words, that Pegasus is not identical with the null class. The real trouble with the chosen-object theory is that we turn out to be talking about something other than we thought we were.

A second point about this theory is that it actually reinforces the view that from the standpoint of formal logic it does not matter which singular sentences are true. On Quine's convention 'Pegasus is a class' turns out to be true. If Mount Everest had been our chosen object, then 'Pegasus is the highest mountain' would be a true sentence. Theoretically it would seem possible to choose the objects in just such a way that we could make singular sentences have just the truth values we want them to. In other words, the chosen-object theory furnishes a clue to the fact that a formally correct system of logic need make no commitment as to the truth value of singular sentences.

The moral to be drawn from this discussion is that the truth or falsity of singular sentences, especially those with vacuous subjects, should be regarded as *sui generis* and not computed from considerations about a domain. This is precisely what we can do if we adopt semantical truth conditions appropriate to the substitutional reading of the quantifiers. These conditions justify reading '(x)' as 'always true' and '$(\exists x)$' as 'sometimes true'. An important consequence of this is that questions of quantification can now be separated from questions of existence. One way of stating these conditions is to adopt Carnap's notion of a state description. A state description is a class of all the atomic WFFs belonging to a language or their negations, but not both. There are many state descriptions and Carnap thought of each of them as describing a different Leibnizian possible world. One among these describes the actual world. Carnap supplemented this account of state descriptions with semantical rules which assigned objects from a domain to the predicates and individual constants of the atomic WFFs. Since our interests here center about developing a semantics for the substitutional reading of the quantifiers, we shall forego such talk of worlds-domains and the assignments of objects. This indeed is one way of stating the main difference between a semantics for the existential reading and for the substitutional reading. The former utilizes the notion of a domain, whereas the latter does not. In referential semantics relations such as designation, denotation, or satisfaction are semantical primitives. We adopt a semantical notion which will not involve domains and objects. An obvious choice is to take the predicate 'is true' as the touchstone for our semantics. We can speak either of individual atomic WFFs as true or of classes of them and thus also state descriptions. We use 'S_t' as name for our true state description and proceed then to give the following truth conditions.

$$\text{val } (A) = T \text{ iff } A \in S_t$$

val $((\exists x)A) = T$ iff for some individual constant s of the language V, val $(s/xA) = T$, that is, $(\exists s)(s \in V \ \& \ \text{val } (s/xA) = T)$.

Now with this substitutional semantics an atomic sentence can be true without any reference to whether or not its parts designate a member of a domain. Here the truth of an atomic sentence is entirely divorced from considerations of domains and existence. Truth is broader than existence. If we wish to treat 'Pegasus is a flying horse' as true, we may do so. Furthermore '$(\exists x)(x$ is a flying horse)' is also unproblematically true merely because 'x is a flying horse' has a true substitution instance, namely, 'Pegasus is a flying horse'.

Until now in our discussion of semantics which utilize the notion of a domain we have shown that domains as domains of existents will not allow for the truth of certain sentences. The question must be raised as to why a domain should be limited to existents and not expanded to the broader category of beings. If we wish to consider 'Pegasus is a flying horse' as true, while Pegasus does not exist, then why not consider Pegasus as a non-existent being? Let beings be the objects that make up a domain and not existents. We might take Quine's formula "to be is to be the value of a variable" *au pied de la lettre* and not, as he does, *to exist* is to be the value of a variable. Here too we note that there are no purely formal considerations which mitigate against our following this policy. The truth condition for the existential reading is open equally well to be used in this way.

$$\text{val } ((\exists x)A) = T \text{ iff } (\exists d)(d \in D \ \& \ \text{val } (t/xA) = T)$$

where val $(t_1) = d_1$, val $(t_2) = d_2, \ldots ,$ val $(t_n) = d_n$.

Quine believes that being and existence are not different. To show that this belief is wrong consider the following sentences.

(1) Pegasus is a flying horse.
(2) There *is* a flying horse.
(3) There *exists* a flying horse.

By contrasting sentences (2) and (3), we can indicate that there is a difference. Granted that sentence (1) is true, (2) remains true, whereas sentence (3) is false. Though we wish to distinguish being and existence, we nonetheless find that there is something *ad hoc* about the idea of a domain of beings.

To hold the view that domains are populated by beings as well as existents amounts to abandoning the existential reading for what might be called the neutral 'there is' reading. We however will offer a reason for not adopting this view of domains as populated by beings. As was mentioned above, there appears to be no purely formal reasons against it. There is however a methodological objection which can be raised. The neutral 'there is' reading can be justified by a mixed semantics. In essence this consists of using the substitutional condition to account for truths about non-existent beings, such as the one about Pegasus, and using membership in a domain to account for truths about existent beings.

$$\text{val } (Pt_1, \ldots, t_n) = T \text{ iff}$$
$$\langle \text{val } (t_1), \ldots, \text{val } (t_n) \rangle \in \text{val } (P)$$
$$\text{or } A = Ps_1, \ldots s_n \, \& \, A \in St$$

$$\text{val } ((\exists x)A) = T \text{ iff } (\exists d)(d \in D \, \& \, \text{val } (t/xA) = T)$$
$$\text{where val } (t_1) = d_1, \quad \text{val } (t_2) = d_2, \ldots, \text{val } (t_n) = d_n$$
$$\text{or } (\exists s)(s \in V \, \& \, \text{val } (s/xA) = T)$$

Our objection to positing beings is that this seems to be an *ad hoc* device to account for the truth of Pegasus-type sentences in terms of a domain. If there is no evidence for these beings as members of a domain independent of the truth of certain sentences, then the methodologically correct and simpler procedure would be to treat the truth of such sentences as *sui generis*. This, of course, is what is done in the substitutional reading and in the mixed semantics for the neutral 'there is' reading.

In summary, then, we note that to judge both truth and existence according to membership in a domain precludes the possibility of logic being neutral enough to allow for certain truths about nonexistent objects. By contrast substitutional semantics does not have this shortcoming.

G. *The Existential Reading Cannot Be Used to Express the Kinds of Generality We Expect of the Quantifiers*

The criticisms of this section center about the inability of the existential reading to do justice to quantification for grammatical categories other than that of singular terms. We will show that according to three different intuitions we have about the role of quantification, namely, expansions, pronouns, and formal principles, the notion of quantification, say of a predicate, is as natural as that of a singular term. The difficulty of giving a plausible account of these divergent styles of quantification constitutes a case against referential quantification. At the same time the plausibility of such quantification in the substitutional view is a telling argument as to its being more basic. Some have tried to argue that referential quantification is basic and that substitutional quantification is at best derivative. The force of the present argument is just the reverse. Since substitutional quantification is suited quite naturally to quantification for diverse grammatical categories while the referential variety is natural only for the category of singular terms, the evidence is that the latter view of quantification is a special case of the former.

One of the clearest intuitions as to what we expect of '(x)' and '$(\exists x)$' is that they be analogous to conjunction and alternation. Indeed in the finite case the quantifiers are probably definable in terms of these logical connectives. If it is natural to think of '$(x)Fx$' and '$(\exists x)Fx$' along the lines of

$$\text{'}Fa \mathbin{\&} Fb \mathbin{\&} \text{etc.'} \quad \text{and} \quad \text{'}Fa \lor Fb \lor \text{etc.'}$$

then surely by extension the same applies to thinking of

$$\text{'}(\phi)\phi a\text{'} \quad \text{and} \quad \text{'}(\exists\phi)\phi a\text{'}$$

as

$$\text{'}Fa \mathbin{\&} Ga \mathbin{\&} \text{etc.'} \quad \text{and} \quad \text{'}Fa \lor Ga \lor \text{etc.'}$$

and to

$$\text{'}(p)(p \supset p)\text{'}$$

as

$$\text{'}[\text{John is tall} \supset \text{John is tall}] \mathbin{\&} [\text{Henry is tall} \supset \text{Henry is tall}] \mathbin{\&} \text{etc.'}$$

and to

$$\text{'}(\exists f)(p\!f\!p)\text{'}$$

as

$$\text{'}(p \supset p) \lor (p \mathbin{\&} p) \lor \text{etc.'}$$

A second intuition about quantifiers and variables has been brought to prominence by Quine himself. His intuition is that the role of variables is analogous to that of pronouns in ordinary language. Pronouns are similar to variables in that they are the vehicles of cross-reference in natural languages. Quine has constructed examples showing how the cross-reference achieved in formulas with individual variables can also be achieved (though it is much more cumbersome) with pronouns such as 'it', 'the former', 'the latter', 'the first', and 'the second'.[21] The counterpart of the formula

$$(x)((y)(y < x \lor y > x))$$

assuming that the variables have only numbers as their values, could be expressed in ordinary language using 'the former' and 'the latter' as

> Whatever number you may select, it will turn out, whatever number you may next select, that the latter is less than, equal to, or greater than the former.

If this analogy is helpful and not misleading, then we are very naturally led to the idea of variables for yet other grammatical categories, since pronouns serve equally well as devices of cross-reference to expressions like sentences and predicates.[22] Consider the following examples. 'If the government recalls the ambassador, it means trouble' Here the 'it', in the consequent, cross-refers back to the sentence 'The government recalls the ambassador'. We could thus conclude that there is something such that, if it happens, it means trouble. For predicates consider the following: 'Now while Newton was a bachelor and could concentrate on his work, the former is true of John, while the latter is not'. We might infer from this that something is true of Newton but not of John. That is to say

$$'(\exists\phi)(\phi \text{ Newton } \& - \phi \text{ John})'$$

Our last reason for taking quantification for different types of variables seriously is that principles of logic can be enunciated for them on a par with those applying to quantification and individual variables. Rules of substitution and other quantification principles can be formulated for any grammatical categories. For simplicity's

---

[21] Quine, *Mathematical Logic*, pp. 65–71.
[22] This line of criticism as well as most of the examples is to be found in H. Hiż, "Referentials," *Semiotica*, Vol. 12 (1969), pp. 136–166. Hiż however (pp. 147–148) considers the analogy between variables and pronouns to be somewhat misleading. Here are some of his reasons. (1) The comparison of variables and pronouns does not take into account other referentials such as classifiers like, 'Jean and Peter went to the movies. The man paid for the tickets'. (2) Quine treats the nominal category as the only vehicle of generality and moreover confines himself to pronouns that crossrefer to singular terms. (3) Many referentials are more like constants than variables. For example, in 'John took his book', 'John' is a constant and so is 'his'.

sake consider the following principles for distributing the universal quantifier over a conditional.

$$(x)(Fx \supset Gx) \supset ((x)Fx \supset (x)Gx)$$
$$(p)(p \supset p) \supset ((p)p \supset (p)p)$$

The three kinds of considerations given above provide the following adequacy condition for any account of quantification. Quantification should not be restricted to any one grammatical category. Earlier in Section C we showed how on the existential reading quantification over sentential positions necessitated treating these variables as having values. In other words, it required treating the substituends of the variables, in this case sentences, as designating, that is, naming the objects serving as values. So sentences were said to name either propositions or one of two objects, the True or the False. Further categories such as sentential connectives '$\supset$', '$\&$', 'v', and so on would, because of quantifications like '$(\exists f)(pfp)$', also have to be construed as names. No one has ever commented as to what they would name. It is at the very least unnatural to consider 'John runs', 'runs', and 'and' as names and more likely simply false. Furthermore, there do not appear to be any theoretical advantages that would accrue if we adopted this as a strange but possibly useful convention. Indeed Ockham's razor provides us with an argument for not thinking of logic in terms of domains of such strange objects when we can dispense with them on the substitutional view.

Yet another consideration along these lines is the question of whether we can express certain principles of logic as general truths on the existential reading. Church has given some reasons why we should want to state logical principles in this way.

Against the suggestion which is sometimes made from a nominalistic motivation, to avoid or omit these generalizations, it must be said that to have, e.g., all of the special cases A v − A and yet not allow the general law (p)(p v − p) seems to be contrary to the spirit of generality in mathematics, which I would extend to logic as the most fundamental branch of mathematics. Indeed such a situation would be much as if one had in arithmetic $2 + 3 = 3 + 2$, $4 + 5 = 5 + 4$, and all other particular cases of the commutative law of addition, yet refused to accept or formulate a general law, $(x)(y) \cdot x + y = y + x$.[23]

---

[23] A. Church, "Mathematics and Logic," *Logic, Methodology and Philosophy of Science,* E. Nagel, P. Suppes, and A. Tarski (eds.) (Stanford: Stanford University Press, 1962), pp. 181–182.

As an illustration of a system of logic in which principles are expressed as general truths consider an axiom and a thesis of Lesniewski's prototethic.

Axiom: $(f)(q)[f(p)(p \supset p) \supset (f(p)(p) \supset f(q)]$

This next thesis corresponds to one of the paradoxes of material implication.

$$(p)[(p \supset (p)p) \supset -p]$$

For Quine principles such as $p \supset p$ or $(x)(Fx \supset Fx)$ are not sentences but schemata. 'p' and 'F' are schematic letters. First of all recall that schemata are not part of the object-language. Quine, in a passage quoted earlier, informs us that they are "foreign to the object language." Second, schemata are not strictly speaking sentences, but only "pseudo-sentences." From these considerations it follows that there can be no general object-language truths of logic. Indeed, solely from the fact that schemata are not sentences, it follows that there are no such truths of logic since only sentences are strictly speaking true or false.

A number of other questions can also be raised here. Schematic letters are distinguished from both metalinguistic as well as object-language variables. Furthermore, they are neither names of sentences nor sentences.

A schema such as '$(x)(Fx \supset p)$', . . . is not a name of a sentence, not a name of anything; it is itself a *pseudo-sentence*, ... Schemata are to sentences not as names to their objects, but as slugs to nickels.[24]

Even if a clear semantics for the notion of a schema were provided (Quine does not appear to have done so), would it not be simpler to get on with variables and constants, in the object and metalanguage, rather than introduce a new type of expression? Quine and those who see a genuine reduction in dispensing with individual constants ought to be impressed by a method for dispensing with schemata. A second consideration stems from Quine's own conception of logical truths as continuous with those of science. This continuity thesis clashes with the semantic switch which takes place when we go from the object-language truths of mathematics and physics to the schematic principles (no longer truths) of logic.

[24] Quine, "Logic and the Reification of Universals," *From a Logical Point of View*, p. 111.

Summarizing this section we note that on the existential reading one cannot quantify with respect to different grammatical categories. On the substitutional reading we can. Furthermore on the existential reading there does not appear to be any neutral way in which we can have general truths of logic in the object language.

H. *The Existential Reading Is Not Philosophically Neutral and Creates Special Problems of its Own*

The last criticism concerns the correctness of equating 'some', 'there is', '∃x', and 'there exists'. While no outright contradiction appears if one adopts the existential reading, it is not free of difficulties. There are special problems which attend its acceptance but which do not exist on other readings. These difficulties arise in such problematic areas as modal and doxastic logic, higher-order logic, and set theory, as well as in connection with such unproblematic areas as propositional logic and ordinary categorical sentences.

To begin with consider how Quine employs the existential reading to construct a case against quantified modal logic. He presents the following argument.

(4)　　□9 is greater than 7.
(5)　　9 = the number of the planets.
(6)　　□ The number of the planets is greater than 7. [False]
(7)　　(∃x) □ (x is greater than 7) [from (4) by generalization.]

Quine says

> Now the difficulty [quantification into non-extensional contexts] recurs when we try to apply existential generalization to modal statements. . . . What is this number which according to [6], is necessarily greater than 7? According to [4] from which it was inferred, it was 9, that is, the number of the planets; but to suppose this would conflict with the fact that [6] is false.[25]

The moral he tries to draw from this is that there is something paradoxical about combining quantification and modality. My point is that though the reasoning from statements (4) through (7) is as Quine says it is, nonetheless the moral to be drawn is not the one Quine does. The paradoxical character of modal logic has its locus in line (6). Indeed line (7) is superfluous and merely confuses the issue. To show this, consider that the moral Quine draws depends essentially upon the already problematic line (6), that is, "to suppose

---

[25] W. V. Quine, "Reference and Modality," *From a Logical Point of View,* pp. 143–148.

this would conflict with the fact that (6) is false." The problem here is one of identity and substitutivity in modal contexts and not one of quantification into modal contexts. The former difficulty is primary since it can be stated independently of the latter while the latter supposed difficulty is dependent on the former. We agree that there are problems concerning modal logic, but these have to do with identity and not quantification. On the substitutional reading there is nothing problematic about statement (7) when it is read as 'It is sometimes true of x that x is necessarily greater than 7.' The truth of line (7), so read, is assured, given the truth of (4).

Hintikka, following Quine, asserts that the trouble with the substitutional reading is that it trivializes the problem of quantification in doxastic contexts.[26] Unlike Hintikka we will take the moral of this to be that the problematic character of doxastic logic does not bear on quantification *per se*.

Consider his argument.

(8)   Joe believes that Mary = Mary. [True]
(9)   ($\exists x$)(Joe believes that Mary = x) [(8) Generalization]

When statement (9) is read existentially we have (10).

(10)   There exists an x such that Joe believes Mary = x.

The problem is that statement (10) could be false if, for instance, there were no such person as Mary. But no such problem occurs if we read line (9) substitutionally as in (11).

(11)   For some instance x it is true that Joe believes Mary = x.

Indeed statement (11) is true, if statement (8) is. The moral to be drawn is that the problematic character of doxastic logic is not due to quantification into intensional contexts but rather bears upon identity and substitutivity.

In summary, the existential reading appears to yield problems concerning quantification in modal and doxastic contexts. These problems vanish when we adopt a nonexistential reading. Certainly there are still problems concerning intensional logics, but these appear to center about identity and not quantification.

Next, consider the case of higher-order logic, that is, quantification of predicate positions. On the existential reading, for an exten-

[26] J. Hintikka, "The Semantics of Modal Notions and the Indeterminacy of Ontology," *Synthese*, (1970), p. 414.

sionalist, higher-order logic becomes associated with an ontology of sets or classes. Again we must acknowledge that there are serious problems about higher-order logic, in particular that of a Russell-type paradox for predicates. But this is a logical and not an ontological problem. Similarly for set theory (as distinct from higher-order logic) there are special problems, such as Russell's paradox, but these are not primarily about ontology, that is, the existence of sets as such. In each case an ontological prejudice is created about the problematic area. Even in the otherwise unproblematic case of the propositional calculus, when we follow the existential reading special ontological problems come into being such as an undesirable ontology of either the intensional entities, propositions, or the extensional but mysterious objects, the True and the False.

On the existential reading an ontological stigma becomes attached to these areas of logic. There is a touch in this of the view of metaphysics as the queen of the sciences. By linking the logical with the ontological-metaphysical our metaphysical prejudices provide criteria for making otherwise purely logical decisions. The ontological prejudice against the existence of sets or properties in addition to that of individuals, for example, becomes a reason for avoiding higher-order logic. Certainly the writing of the history of recent philosophy is colored by this approach. Quine and his followers never consider any alternatives to the existential reading. Whenever they encounter quantification they ask what the values of the variables are. Consider what happens in the following three cases: defining identity, Ramsey's treatment of theoretical predicates, and Russell's treatment of classes. No one from this school puts much stock in defining identity in higher-order logic, for example, $x = y = \text{def} \ (\phi) \ (\phi x \equiv \phi y)$ because of the ontic import of the variable 'ϕ'. Similarly Ramsey's suggestion for quantifying over what might be called theoretical predicates poses special ontological problems on the existential reading. This is quite ironic since Ramsey himself appears to have regarded quantification of predicates in a substitutional way.[27]

As a last example, consider Russell's account of class expressions as incomplete symbols which can be defined away contextually. This is Russell's no-classes theory. The contextual definition, however, involves higher-order quantification over propositional functions. Quine, as mentioned earlier in section C, considers that Russell has either made a use-mention error or failed to give a significant reduction because he has merely reduced classes to intensional attributes. Quine does not consider the possibility of construing the higher-order quanti-

[27] F. P. Ramsey, *The Foundations of Mathematics and other Logical Essays* (Paterson: Littlefield Adams and Co., 1960), p. 36.

fication in the no-classes theory substitutionally. While it is true that
Russell frequently made use-mention errors, and that he wished to
accommodate intensional entities, it is nonetheless also true that he
propounded a substitutional view of quantification. Russell never
seemed to notice that he held two different readings of the quantifiers.
We may conclude that on the substitutional reading the no-classes
theory does furnish a significant reduction. Once again it is necessary
to acknowledge that there are difficulties in Russell's philosophy of
mathematics, as in the nonconstructive character of certain axioms,
but these are not ontological in the sense of having to do with the
existence of classes or properties in general.

As a last case in point of the existential reading yielding problems
which do not arise for other readings consider the following sentence
and two renderings of it in colloquial english.

(12) $(\exists x)(x$ is a piece of the puzzle and x does not exist)
(13)   Some pieces of the puzzle do not exist.

It is easy to imagine an occasion for using sentence (13) to make
a true statement. Think of a situation in which someone was un-
wittingly trying to finish a puzzle which lacked a piece. Another person might helpfully offer this information. (One could also show that
sentence (13) is not linguistically deviant by appealing to the intuitions of a native speaker.) Now if we assume that the existential
reading of the quantifier is correct, we must equate 'some' and 'there
exists'. Sentence (12) would be equivalent to sentence (14).

(14)   There exists a piece of the puzzle which does not exist.

In other words, on the existential reading the otherwise contingent
truth (12)-(13) is really a contradiction. To adopt the existential
reading is tantamount to regarding certain hitherto harmless sentences as inconsistent. Some have gone so far as to say that sentence
(13) is meaningless. This point about the existential reading could
equally well have been raised in the prior section: "The existential
reading cannot be used to express the kinds of generality we expect
of the quantifiers." In other words, to adopt the existential reading
is to impair the expressive power of one's language.

CONCLUSION

The negative thrust of this paper has been to undermine the
existential reading of the quantifier by calling attention to some difficulties that result from adopting it. The positive side consisted of

making a case for substitutional quantification. The first two criticisms centered upon the material adequacy of explicating existence in terms of quantification, that is, the success of the explication with regard to our intuitions about the notions involved. The first was that the existential reading could not provide a canon for our reasoning about nonexistent objects. The second criticism concerned the adequacy of the existential reading in accounting for different styles of quantification. While, with the substitutional reading, these presented no special problems, on the existential one, they lead to the false or at least unnatural view of treating ordinarily non-designating expressions as designators. The third criticism attempted to put into perspective the fact that the existential reading is suspect in that it creates special problems which would not exist otherwise. For each of these criticisms we indicated that the problems do not arise for nonexistential readings. Moreover among these nonexistential readings the substititional one takes a position of primacy. The semantics for the substitutional reading seems to be the only one to do justice to the truth values of vacuous singular sentences. Furthermore, quantification of diverse grammatical categories is a natural consequent of the substitutional view. With all these considerations in mind, we might conclude that the time is ripe for more investigation as well as greater employment of the substitutional view. Logic would thus be free of ontology. But what then for ontology? The time is also right for turning to discuss questions of existence in metaphysics proper, so to speak for a metaphysics without logic.

Existence and Presupposition

MILTON K. MUNITZ

New York University

Suppose you and I are sitting at a table and—as I point to a particular bowl on the table—I say: "That bowl is silver-plated." Again, let us suppose that in the course of giving a lecture on ancient philosophy I utter the statement "Socrates often used irony in his remarks." Or, finally, consider the statement we might find in a book on astronomy: "The planet closest to the Sun has an extremely high surface temperature." These would all be examples of singular subject-predicate statements. In each of them the expression serving as the subject refers to some object or person that can be temporally located in the past or present. The expression serving as the subject in the first of the examples above involves the use of a demonstrative pronoun ('that') together with a descriptive expression ('bowl'), the second consists of a proper name ('Socrates'), and the third is a definite description ('the planet closest to the Sun'). They are all examples (though they do not exhaust all the possible types) of referring devices. In normal circumstances the use of one or another of these referring devices accomplishes what we may call, following Strawson, an *identifying reference:* The demonstrative pronoun, proper name, or definite description helps the auditor or reader to pick out a particular object or person.[1] It is this particular object or person about which the predicate of the given statement goes on to say something purportedly informative.

Strawson has argued that in speech-act situations of the kind described, that is, speech acts in which identifying reference is made

[1] Cf. P. F. Strawson, "Identifying Reference and Truth-values," *Logico-Linguistic Papers* (London: Methuen, 1971), p. 75.

by a speaker to an audience by means of a subject term of a subject-predicate statement, there normally would not be an explicit assertion made by the speaker about the existence of the subject being identifyingly referred to. Its existence is presumed to be known or taken for granted, along with other items of knowledge about it in a general background of knowledge. This background of presumed knowledge, for different cases and in different situations, will have varying degrees of richness. Strawson characterizes this presumption of the item of knowledge about the *existence* of the subject a *presupposition.*

A statement *A* is said to *presuppose* another statement *B* if and only if *A* is neither true nor false unless *B* is true (equivalently, the truth of *B* is a necessary condition for the truth or falsity of *A*).[2] Thus the truth of the statement "That bowl exists" (*B*) is a *necessary condition* for the statement "That bowl is silver-plated" (*A*) to be either true or false. The statement "That bowl is silver-plated" *presupposes* the statement "That bowl exists."

The relation of presupposition needs to be distinguished from the relation of entailment. Where *A* entails *B*, the conjunction of *A* and the denial of *B* results in a straightforward contradiction; since the truth of *B* is a necessary condition for the truth of *A*, it would be self-contradictory to affirm *A* and at the same time deny *B*. In contrast, where *A* presupposes *B*, the truth of *B* is a necessary condition for the *truth or falsity* of *A*. Here it would be a "different kind of absurdity," not simply one of contradiction, to conjoin the affirmation of *A* and the denial of *B*.[3]

Despite the above clarification about the basic difference between presupposition and entailment, there are a number of unclarities and ambiguities connected with Strawson's use of the concept of presupposition. Strawson has formulated the presupposition relation in somewhat different ways on several different occasions, and these formulations seem to oscillate between two accounts of what presupposition is.[4] According to the first account "when a meaningful sentence is uttered by a speaker of the language on a certain occasion, then a necessary condition for the statement thus made to have a truth value is that the (main) referring expression in the sentence has,

[2] Cf. P. F. Strawson, *Introduction to Logical Theory,* (London: Methuen, 1952), p. 175; "Reply to Sellars," *Philosophical Review,* Vol. 63 (1954), p. 216.
[3] P. F. Strawson, *Introduction to Logical Theory,* p. 175; cf. Bas C. van Fraassen, "Presupposition, Implication and Self-Reference," *Journal of Philosophy,* Vol. LXV (1968), pp. 136–152.
[4] These have been critically examined in G. Nerlich, "Presupposition and Entailment," *American Philosophical Quarterly,* Vol. 2 (1965), pp. 33–42 and in G. Nerlich, "Presupposition and Classical Logical Relations," *Analysis,* Vol. XXVII (1967), 104–106.

on that occasion, a reference."[5] According to the second account "when a meaningful sentence is uttered by a speaker of the language on a certain occasion, then a necessary condition of the speaker's thereby making a statement is that the (main) referring expression in the sentence has, on that occasion, a reference."[5] Whereas the second account denies that there is any statement at all when there is a reference failure, the first account maintains there is one but only denies that it has a truth value. I shall, however, not stop to explore this ambiguity in Strawson's account, since my concern at the moment is not primarily with the notion of truth-value gaps, but with exploring what we are to make of the status of the presupposed statement having to do with the existence of the referent of the subject term. And here I find that there are other unclarities and ambiguities in Strawson's account to which we must call attention.

For when we examine the various passages in which Strawson appeals to the concept of a presupposition relation, there is a certain ambiguity in the statement of what that relation is. (1) In one sense, the presupposition relation marks, as we have just seen, a logical relation between statements, where the statements so related are fundamentally two, namely, the presupposing statement (A) and the presupposed statement (B). This presupposition relation is to be contrasted with the entailment relation. The difference between presupposition as a logical relation and entailment is one of logical properties: Their tables of truth values (or truth-value gaps) differ. It is thus not a matter principally of what is or is not asserted, for in *both* relations it is necessary to make explicit the respective antecedents and consequents for the respective relations, in order that their corresponding truth values (or truth-value gaps) may be assigned. (2) In another sense, however, Strawson thinks of a presupposed statement in a presupposition relation as one *tacitly accepted as true*, as contrasted with one *explicitly asserted*.[6] Strawson stresses that the presupposition of existence is *not* asserted when he wishes to contrast this sense of presupposition (that is, as something tacitly accepted as true) with what is explicitly asserted. The second of the discriminated senses of presupposition—that which has to do with the matter of *assertion*—comes to the fore when he deals with the

[5] *Loc. cit.*, Nerlich, "Presupposition and Entailment," p. 34.
[6] For example, he writes: "Thus, that there exists a particular item to which the name or description is applicable and which, if not unique in this respect, satisfies some uniqueness-condition known to the hearer (*and* satisfies some uniqueness condition known to the speaker) is no part of what the speaker *asserts* in an utterance in which the name or description is used to perform the function of identifying reference; it is, rather, a *presupposition* of his asserting what he asserts." ("Identifying Reference and Truth Values," *Logico-Linguistic Papers*, p. 80).

use of sentences in speech-act situations, and from the point of view of speech-act analysis. The first sense of presupposition (that which has to do with distinguishing it as a *logical relation* from other types of logical relations) comes to the fore when he wishes to express the distinctive formal logical properties of the presupposition relation.

Thus far I have treated the second meaning of presupposition as having to do basically with a contrast between what is explicitly stated as over against what is not asserted at all, that is, with what is left implicit or tacit. This matter of 'assertion', however, is complicated by a further unclarity or ambiguity in Strawson's account. At one point Strawson remarks (in connection with utterances in which definite identifying reference is made to actual historical individuals): "I shall take it as understood that the existence of the individuals referred to in such utterances is *presupposed rather than implicitly asserted* in the making of such utterances."[7] We must now ask: What does it mean to *contrast* presupposed utterances with those implicitly asserted? Indeed what does the phrase 'implicit assertion' *mean?* According to the way the term is used in this passage, we should need to contrast a presupposed utterance not only with an *explicit assertion*, but with an *implicit assertion* (whatever that means) as well. Are we to say that what is presupposed is always implicit (unexpressed) or is it also capable of being made *explicit?* Obviously it would be necessary for Strawson to allow the latter, since the specification of the logical relation of presupposition, for any given case of statements so related, would require that what is presupposed should be made explicit in order that we would be able to evaluate the truth-values of the presupposing statement, given the truth value of the presupposed statement. But if that which is being presupposed is not even implicitly asserted, what is its logical form when made explicit? Is it a statement? And wouldn't it have to be a statement in order for it to have a truth value so that the presupposing statement can be assigned *its* truth value? One of the preliminary difficulties, then, in Strawson's account of presupposition, as it applies to the matter of existence involved in acts of identifying reference, is that he does not provide any clear way of reconciling the two following apparently conflicting claims: (1) In order for there to be a presupposition relation, there need to be at least *two* statements, each of which can be judged with respect to its truth value. In particular, the presupposed statement '*S* exists' needs to be *true* in order for the presupposing statement to be either true or false. (2) The presupposed 'existence-factor' is not either implicitly or explicitly *asserted*. (But a

---

[7] P. F. Strawson, "Is Existence Never a Predicate?" *Critica*, Vol. 1 (1967), p. 5.

special difficulty of (2) is this: if we could not formulate the existence of the subject to which identifying reference is being made, as a *statement* which *can be* asserted, and its truth value assessed, how can the relation of presupposition hold for A and B?)

The only way I can see of clearing up this unclarity is to say that when Strawson denies that the presupposed statement is an implicit assertion, he is using the term 'assertion' to mean 'making a predication'. We should then need to distinguish two different senses of 'assertion': In one sense of 'assertion' what is asserted, whether explicitly or implicitly, is always an assignment of a predicate to a subject. In another, 'assertion' means whatever is explicitly uttered as a statement. In this sense of assertion, what is presupposed is not asserted because it is not explicit. Let us designate these two different senses of assertion as assertion$_1$ (a statement which qua statement requires a predicate) and assertion$_2$ (an explicit utterance of a statement of any assignable logical form). What Strawson might be taken as saying, here then, is this: Whether a presupposed statement is not asserted$_2$ or is asserted$_2$, in any case it is not asserted$_1$.

If this be accepted, then the question I wish to consider next is this: What can we say about the logical form of the existence-factor statement when it is converted from being a tacit (unasserted$_2$) presupposition to an explicit assertion$_2$? What can we say, in other words, about the logical form of the utterance 'S exists'? How shall this be construed?

Let us begin by recalling the fundamental role which predication plays in the understanding of the logic of statements. Strawson would seem to wish to argue for the logical and philosophical soundness in general of regarding the subject-predicate statement as the basic type of statement, and as adequate to dealing with "most of the propositions we are day by day concerned with."[8] Predication, he tells us, "is the ascribing of something to an individual, or to some, none or all of a class, where the existence of the individual or of the members of the class is presupposed."[9] Accordingly, in a subject-predicate type of statement we can distinguish two main, explicitly present, items: "If we are to be able to say how things are in the world, we must have at our disposal the means of doing two complementary things, of performing two complementary functions: we must be able to specify *general types* of situation, thing, event, etc. and we must be able to attach those general specifications to *particular cases*, to indicate their particular incidence in the world."[10]

[8] P. F. Strawson (ed.), *Philosophical Logic* (London: Oxford University Press, 1967), "Introduction," p. 3.
[9] "Is Existence a Predicate?" *loc. cit.*, p. 12.
[10] "Introduction," *loc. cit.*, p. 3.

Whatever the fundamental role of the subject-predicate statement, it is, at any rate, an open question as to how, for this type of statement, the presupposed existence factor or presupposed existence statement is to be logically classified and its form made clear. That it is not itself an explicit item but only a presupposed item in the initially given subject-predicate statement, attached, as it were, to the referential use of the original subject term, has been brought out. But our question has to do with the logical form of the presupposed sentence '*S* exists' when this is made explicit. What is Strawson's answer to *this* question? Once again, I must report that I do not find a single, clear, positive answer to this question. He has, to be sure, faced this question from time to time, and I shall briefly survey what he has to say by way of giving an answer to this question.

One of the claims Strawson repeatedly makes is that the sentence we are concerned with is *not* to be construed as being of a subject-predicate type, in any other than a purely grammatical sense. He writes: ". . . when an expression which looks as if it might be used to make an identifying reference to a particular (or, for that matter, to a plurality of particulars) is followed in a sentence by the word 'exists' (or 'exist'), we cannot coherently take the first expression as functioning in a particular-referring way, i.e. as making an identifying reference to a particular (or to certain particulars). To attempt to do so would make the sentence unconstruable."[11] The reason why it would be unconstruable as an ordinary subject-predicate statement is that we should be faced with an absurd consequence. We must now stop to explore what this absurd consequence is, according to Strawson, since he does not say what this is, in the passage from which we have quoted. But he does make the point elsewhere. For example, taking as his illustrations the sentences 'The man-in-the-moon does not exist' and 'The man-in-the-moon does exist', he argues that "we cannot coherently construe the substantival expression as a referring expression; for to do so is to construe it as carrying, as a presupposition, precisely that content which the proposition as a whole asserts or denies. We are therefore required, in this case, to find a different way of construing the proposition."[12] In discussing the case of the traditional four basic types of categorical propositions, in his earlier book *An Introduction to Logical Theory*, he points out that "if we tried to assimilate a statement of the pattern '*x*'s exist' to any of the four forms, or to regard it as a subject-predicate statement at all, we should be faced with the absurd result that the question of whether it was true or false could arise only if it were true;

[11] P. F. Strawson, *Individuals* (London: Methuen, 1959), p. 239.
[12] *Ibid.*, p. 227.

or, that, if it were false, the question of whether it was true or false did not arise. This gives a new edge to the familiar philosophical observation that 'exists' is not a predicate. When we declare or deny that 'there are' things of such-and-such a description, or that things of such-and-such a description 'exist', the use of the quoted phrases is not to be assimilated either to the predicative or to the referring use of expressions."[13]

Before going on to consider what positive proposals Strawson makes to deal with this situation, let us stop to examine the argument as he has given it thus far. And let us consider what he has to say in particular with respect to the existential presupposition for a *singular* subject-predicate statement. The presupposed statement for '*S* is *P*' where *P* is some predicate other than 'exists' is '*S* exists.' Now if '*S* exists' were the statement to be analyzed as a putative subject-predicate type statement, then, *on the assumption that every subject-predicate type statement presupposes another statement making an existential claim*, the presupposed statement for the statement '*S* exists' would also be '*S* exists'. And Strawson's argument is that for the *presupposing* original statement '*S* exists' to be true or false, the *presupposed* statement '*S* exists' would need to be true, and this is absurd. Or again, if the *presupposed* statement '*S* exists' is false, the original *presupposing* statement could not be either true or false, since the question would not arise. And this too is absurd. Now, in order for this argument to be valid, we should need, in the first place, to accept the assumption that *every* original subject-predicate statement presupposes another statement expressing the existence claim, and that this would apply to the statement here taken as original, the putative subject-predicate statement '*S* exists'. But why should we make this assumption? What if we were to reformulate the assumption to read that every original subject-predicate statement *except* '*S* exists' presupposes *another* statement expressing the existence claim? This ruling would be tantamount to saying that the presupposition rule (the rule that any ordinary subject-predicate statement presupposes another, an existence statement) does *not* hold for the existence statement itself. Another way of putting this ruling is to say that not every use of a referring expression carries with it a *presupposition* of the existence of the individual referred to by the subject term; specifically, where the referring term occurs in a sentence along with the grammatical predicate 'exists', it does not carry with it any such further presupposition. We should then not be faced with the consequence mentioned. To make this ruling, of course, would require justification, and in particular would involve the decision of how we

[13] *Loc. cit.*, p. 191.

are to treat the term 'exists' in the statement '*S* exists'. Thus we might at least leave the door open to investigate the possibility that this can be done in a plausible or convincing way.

We gain some support in considering this possible emendation by examining another argument for rejecting the classification of the statement '*S* exists' as an ordinary subject-predicate statement. Wherever we have the logical pattern of presupposition, we can always distinguish the original presupposing statement and the presupposed statement since the statements will always be *different:* The presupposing statement will have a *different* (grammatical) predicate from the presupposed statement. And the grammatical predicate of the presupposed statement will always be 'exists'. However, it is by no means clear in what way the application of this pattern to the original statement '*S* exists' as a putative subject-predicate statement, and to its presupposed statement (which is also '*S* exists'), gives us two *distinct* statements. In what way can we *first* evaluate the truth-value of the presupposed statement *before* we evaluate the presupposing statement; or evaluate the presupposed statement as a *condition* for the determination of the truth-value of the original statement? Since there is but *one and the same* statement in both cases which appears both as presupposing and presupposed statements, the operation of *separate* truth-value evaluation breaks down and is inapplicable. This again argues for the possible advantage of not considering the statement '*S* exists' as falling within the *ordinary* pattern of subject-predicate statements.

Rather than explore alternative routes of dealing with '*S* exists' as a subject-predicate statement, though of a *possibly distinctive kind*, Strawson in his *Introduction to Logical Theory* and *Individuals* suggests that we should *abandon* the attempt to treat the use of the sentence '*S* exists' as a subject-predicate type of statement. He proposes instead in *these* writings that we regard the statement as an existential statement, in the sense of modern logic, or rather as part of such an existential statement. "Fortunately," he says, "there are idioms available which allow us to escape from the misleading suggestions of the form described [that '*S* exists' is of the subject-predicate form]; and these are the idioms which are reconstructed in logic by means of the device of existential quantification. The expression which looks as if it might be used in a particular-referring way is replaced by a predicate-expression corresponding to it in sense, and the word 'exists' appears merely as part of the apparatus of quantification. Thus we allow that particulars can be said to exist without committing ourselves to the incoherent attempt to construe existence as a predicate of particulars."[14]

_____
[14] *Individuals*, p. 239f.

I find the foregoing passage quite puzzling. On the one hand, Strawson apparently invites us—by his use of the phrase 'existence-presupposition' earlier in the passage from which the foregoing was taken—to continue to think in terms of his own presupposition theory as the best way, in general, of dealing with subject-predicate statements, in preference to the analysis provided by quantification theory. Yet when he comes to face the question of how to formulate the so-called 'existence-presupposition', he calls upon the resources of the quantification theory, which makes everything explicit and does not appeal to the notion of presupposition at all; *it* treats the existence factor, not as a matter of an existence presupposition, but, as he correctly reports, as conveyed by "a part of the apparatus of quantification." In 'canonical form' the existence condition is explicitly 'asserted', in the sense of being conveyed by the use of the existential operator as applied to a quantified variable. This explicit appearance of the existence factor appears in the standard form of an existential statement of quantificational logic along with two other components in the case of a singular statement, namely, the uniqueness condition and the predicative component. The schema for such a statement reads

$$\text{(1)} \qquad \text{(2)} \qquad \qquad \text{(3)}$$
"[There is] [one and only one x] that [has (or is) P],"

where (1) is the existence factor, (2) the uniqueness factor, and (3) the predicative factor.

Which, then, is Strawson's view of how to treat the existence factor? Can he provide his own analysis of the existence presupposition as a *complete* statement separate from the presupposing statement and as presumably required by his presupposition theory? Or must he call in the apparatus of quantification theory when he has to deal with the existence factor, thereby admitting the weakness and unavailability for this purpose of his own approach? He cannot co herently say that when it comes to stating what the logical form of the existence factor is, we should fall back on the quantificational form, for that is to grant the claim of the logical reconstructionists and is tantamount to abandoning his own point of view. If, in making explicit the existence factor, we need to appeal to the quantificational form, why not do so from the very beginning? And is not this to admit that, whatever be the merits of the presuppositional analysis in pointing out something about the explicit and tacit sayings in a *speech-act* approach, when it comes to giving the explicit *logical form* of what we are committed to in our utterances, the presuppositional analysis fails us, and we need to turn to the logician's reconstruction? I find no clear answer to these questions in Strawson's account.

Strawson himself, I suspect, was aware of this problem, and

undertook to deal with it in a fresh way in his paper entitled "Is Existence Never a Predicate?" [*Critica*, Vol. 1 (1967)]. His answer to the question posed by this title is a qualified *negative*. He there proposes to show how 'exists' *can* be used predicatively, that is as a logical and not simply as a grammatical predicate. In order to do so, Strawson first develops a point originally made by G. E. Moore in the latter's well-known paper "Is Existence a Predicate?" Moore had pointed out in connection with the use of a sentence whose logical subject is 'tame tiger' and whose logical predicate is 'growl' that we can use *any* of the following quantifying adjectives: 'all', 'most', 'many', 'some', 'a few', 'no', 'at least one', to precede the subject term. However, where our subject is 'tame tigers' and the (grammatical) predicate is '*exists*', we can use any of the foregoing quantifying adjectives *except 'all' and 'most'*. Strawson proposes to use this distinction as the basis for determining what are logical subjects and predicates as distinguished from being merely grammatical subjects and predicates. The test is the following: "Given a grammatical subject and predicate, then it is a necessary condition of their counting as a *logical* subject and predicate respectively that if the grammatical subject admits of starting off with *any* of the quantifying adjectives, then it should admit of starting off with them all (with, where necessary, i.e. where 'at least one' is involved, a change from singular to plural or vice versa)."[15]

Strawson now uses this criterion to argue that there are some cases in which 'exists' *can* be used as a logical predicate. He gives the example of a child who is given a classical dictionary to look at, and is told by the person handing him the volume, "A good proportion of the characters listed are mythical, of course; but most of them existed" (or conversely).[16] Since the sentence 'Most of them existed' makes perfectly good sense in this situation, and since, according to the criterion previously stated, wherever a quantifying adjective like '*most*' or *any* of the others can be meaningfully used, we are prepared to say that the subject of a sentence in which this occurs is a logical subject, therefore 'exists', according to the criterion, must be accorded the status of being a logical predicate in this sentence. If so, however, we still have an explanation to seek, for, wherever we have a logical subject used referentially, there is a presupposition of existence connected with the use of that subject. How then, in the present case, are we to satisfy this requirement? What is that whose existence is presupposed in using the subject term, such that we can be said to use the term 'exists' as a logical predicate for

---

[15] "Is Existence Never a Predicate?", *loc. cit.*, p. 12.
[16] *Ibid.*, p. 13.

the subject 'characters in this book'? This is the question to which
Strawson next addresses himself. And in order to answer it he first
introduces the notion of a *presupposed class*. A *presupposed class*
is a class the existence of the members of which is presupposed. According to Strawson, in this situation there is a presupposed class
of characters (those listed in the dictionary). The *existence* of this
class of characters is presupposed since it consists of the class of
characters being *talked about, discussed,* or *described*. However, as
a class it is 'ontologically heterogeneous,' for it includes as *subclasses*
characters which genuinely existed in history, along with those which
are legendary, fictional, and so on. With this approach, therefore,
we can show 'exist' to be used as a logical predicate—that is, where
it makes reference to a certain *subclass of objects or persons talked
about*. In a similar way, Strawson argues, we can show how the term
'exists' can be made to function predicatively relative to subjects
that are conveyed by singular terms. Take the case of the two sentences 'King Alfred did exist', 'King Arthur did not exist'. "We have
only to see the names as serving to identify, within the *heterogeneous*
class of kingly characters we talk about—a class which comprises
both actual and legendary kings—a particular member of that class
in each case; and then see the predicate as serving to assign that
particular member to the appropriate subclass. Thus 'exists' appears
as a predicate, and not as a predicate of a concept; but as a predicate
of some, and not of other members of the heterogeneous class. What,
on this model, we shall have to regard as presupposed by the use
of the name in each case is not the existence in history of an actual
king with certain actual characteristics, or the existence in legend
of a legendary king with certain legendary characteristics, but rather
the existence-in-history-or-legend of an actual-or-legendary king with
certain actual-or-legendary characteristics."[17]

What shall we say of this account? Let us note, to begin with,
that the term 'exists' (or 'existence') is used both in connection with
certain classes and in connection with certain individuals.

1. As for its use in connection with classes, Strawson uses it
in connection both with regard to what he calls a presupposed class
of things talked about as well as in connection with *one* of the subclasses of the presupposed class. The presupposed class is an ontologically heterogeneous class, insofar as its subclasses—those included
among the things talked about—are of diverse ontological types; they
include existence, or the subclass of existing things. This ontologically
heterogeneous class is a presupposed class because its existence is
not explicitly asserted. Yet its existence as the ontologically hetero-

[17] *Ibid.*, pp. 14–15.

geneous class of things talked about is taken for granted in a given context, as in the example given. Now it is worth noting in passing, in connection with this class whose existence is presupposed, that unlike the account which Strawson gives of a subject term that is actually employed in a subject-predicate statement (for example, 'Socrates is wise')—the existence of whose referent is presupposed—the presupposed class in the present use of this term does not function as a *subject term* in a subject-predicate sentence. As a presupposed class its existence is established, not by the use of a term as such, but by the *context of discussion*. Now we might agree that this need not count against the advisability of our thinking of this class as a presupposed class; still we also need to be clear that the notion of presupposition has now been widened to include not only the presupposed existence of an entity being referred to by a term explicitly introduced as a subject term in a statement, but as having to do with a class of matters *not* specifically linked with the use of a subject term in a statement. Allowing for this extension of the notion of presupposed existence, let us now examine somewhat more closely what it means to say *this presupposed class exists* insofar as it is the '*class of things talked about*'. The phrase 'things talked about' is ambiguous. In one sense 'things talked about' is the class of talkings, of things said, of utterances, statements, discussions, and so on. These are all affairs of human beings doing certain things. The episodes and the discussions exist because human beings themselves exist, and their talkings, musings, and interchanges, among others are so many overt or silent *speech acts*. Now if the presupposed class exists in *this sense* (as it undoubtedly does), then are we to say that the subclasses of which it is composed are also so many different species of particular kinds of *speech acts?* Is the subclass of 'existence' or 'fiction' the class of existent things *talked* about, or of fictional things *talked* about? This does not seem likely. We turn then at this point to the other meaning or emphasis to be given to the expression 'things talked about'. For the use of the phrase 'things talked about' can, because of the use of the term 'about', be given another interpretation: It is not the speech acts, the episodes of talking, but rather the referents, the objects or targets of these acts of reference and description to which we should attend.

Of these two meanings of the phrase 'things talked about', I would interpret Strawson to be saying that the presupposed class exists because it is a *class of talkings* and the talkings exist, that is, the *first* of the above discriminated meanings. However, the ontological diversity comes in, not from the fact of talkings, since we could talk history as well as fiction, but in the *different ontological* statuses of what is talked *about*. Accordingly, the subclass of existence, if it is going to be *ontologically* discriminated from the class of fiction, must be a class of *entities* not a class of *talkings*. In this case we should have to say that the sense in which we say 'exists' attaches to the ontologically homogeneous[18] *subclass* of things that exist, does *not* attach to the ontologically homogeneous subclass of fictional entities. And if this is so, it is misleading to speak of the *presupposed class* as *made up* of ontologically heterogeneous subclasses. Indeed, in the sense in which the presupposed class exists, as a class of *talkings*, that class belongs as a subclass to the class of existing things, rather than the other way around. (There are very many other kinds of things that exist and that belong to the class of existing things besides talkings.) Also, if the presupposed class is a class of talkings and the so-called subclasses are classes of entities, then we cannot properly speak of the various *ontological* classes of *entities* as being *subclasses* of the class of *talkings*. However, if Strawson were to say that by the presupposed class he does not mean simply the class of *talkings* but the class composed of the ontologically diverse subclasses of entities of the things talked *about*, then, of course, it makes no sense to say, to begin with, that that class itself *exists*, since at best it only includes as a subclass the things that exist; it includes, however, other types of entities as well, and surely, therefore, the entire class cannot have the same ontological status as belongs only to one of its subclasses. Of course, to put the question this way only reminds us of the greater danger in speaking of the various ontological 'subclasses' as composing or collectively constituting some all-inclusive class, and in assuming, furthermore, that it too can be assigned some ontological status. We might very well be inclined to reject altogether, therefore, at this point any talk of an 'inclusive class' that is allegedly composed of so many 'subclasses'. (To follow through this criticism, which I shall not do at this point, would lead to one possible interpretation of the dictum 'being is not a genus', a dictum I believe to be sound.) Because of the foregoing difficulties and unclarities in Strawson's position, it seems to me he has not fully succeeded in giving an analysis of how 'exists' can be used predicatively in connection with a *plural* subject.

2. Let us now turn to the other prong of Strawson's analysis and see whether he is any more successful in showing how we might use 'exists' predicatively in connection with a *singular* subject. He argues that we can use the term predicatively as in the statement 'King Alfred existed' because we can fall back on a parallel strategy

[18] *Not descriptively* homogeneous.

to that employed in connection with using the term 'exists' in connection with a plural subject (as in 'most of the characters in this book existed'). Once more, to say '*x* exists' (where '*x*' is a singular referring expression) is to use the term 'exists' predicatively, for it takes advantage of a presupposition of *the context of discussion,* rather than of a presupposition in connection with the use of the term '*x*' itself. But what is this presupposition and how does it function to give the desired result? I do not find in the passage quoted earlier, in which Strawson sets out his reply, that he has given us a single reply; indeed I find two. I should like, before moving on to my main critical objection to his approach in general, to stop to briefly call attention to these. The first of these answers appears in the following sentences from the beginning of the passage: "King Alfred did exist, King Arthur did not. We have only to see the names as serving to identify, within the heterogeneous *class* of kingly characters we talk about—a class which comprises both actual and legendary kings—a particular member of that class in each case; and then see the predicate as serving to assign that particular member to the appropriate *subclass.*"[19] Here, as in the case of dealing with predicating 'exist' of a plural subject, the technique is to use this term in the same sense in which it appears as marking off a *subclass* (the class of things that are actual *kings*). (Strictly the subclass 'actual or existent kings' is itself a sub-subclass, since it is included within the wider subclass of *all* things that are actual or exist.) To say 'King Alfred exists' is to take the term 'exists' (or 'is actual') from the sub- (or sub-subclass) 'actual kings'. And this subclass is part of the wider presupposed class of kingly characters talked about, which includes actual as well as legendary kings. The only point I should wish to make in connection with this version of the solution is that it has all of the weaknesses already mentioned when we discussed this type of strategy as used to deal with 'exists' for plural subjects. I shall not repeat these criticisms here.

Let us move on, however, to what seems to be a different answer altogether, one that Strawson offers in the concluding sentence of the passage quoted earlier. He there says: "What, on this model, we shall have to regard as presupposed by the use of the name in each case is not the existence in history of an actual king with certain actual characteristics, or the existence in legend of a legendary king with certain legendary characteristics, but rather the existence-in-history-or-legend of *an* actual-or-legendary king with certain actual-or-legendary characteristics."[20] Now the difference between this version

---

[19] Is Existence Never a Predicate?" *loc. cit.,* p. 14, my italics.
[20] *Ibid.* pp. 14–15, my italics.

of the solution and that quoted earlier is that Strawson here—in appealing to a presupposed background from which to extract the use of the term 'exists'—appeals to a background formulated in *singular* terms. It is no longer, as in the earlier account of presupposition, a matter of representing a *subclass* of actual or legendary kings. He uses the expression '*an* actual-or-legendary king with actual-or-legendary characteristics'. Now this expression, I take it, is intended to identify some special type of *individual* as the presupposed background. I must confess, however, that I find it difficult to understand this. What kind of individual is it that is 'actual-or-legendary' with 'actual-or-legendary characteristics'? Such an 'individual' would seem to be a monstrous ontological hybrid whose only claim to identity as an individual is that which derives in this instance from the spurious use of hyphens. If we were to give the entire passage its most generous interpretation, we should not be obliged to take seriously this (perhaps inadvertent) use of the expression '*an* actual-or-legendary king'; rather we should regard it as simply another way of conveying the basic device mentioned earlier, that, namely, which appeals to the use of *subclasses* as part of a wider presupposed class. If so, our main concern must be with evaluating the soundness or helpfulness of *this* ('subclass') interpretation. And here it seems to me there is an underlying difficulty with this entire strategy, that I have not as yet touched upon, a difficulty, moreover, that is of a far more serious nature than any of the others already mentioned. It is this. Strawson's strategy in attempting to show how 'exists' can be used predicatively in connection with an individual, is to fall back on the use of the term 'exists' as it occurs in marking off a certain *subclass*, the subclass of actual or existent things, which in turn is part of 'the presupposed (ontologically heterogeneous) class'. But have we really helped ourselves very much by falling back on this subclass? Indeed have we not simply postponed and shifted our original question (that is, how to deal with '*x* exists') by saying this is to be done by turning to the *subclass* to which it is related and from which it derives the warrant for the use of the term 'exists'? For how is the subclass itself established or demarcated? If this is to be done extensionally, do we not have to fall back on the *singular statements* out of which the subclass is to be built up—the indeterminately large array of singular statements '*a* exists', '*b* exists', '*c* exists', and so on? And what have we gained thereby? For are we not back with our *original* problem, that is, how we are to understand, for example, '*a* exists'? On the other hand, if we should attempt to avoid this charge of circularity by rejecting the procedure of specifying what the subclass of things actual or existent is in extensional terms, and would wish to say simply that the term 'exists' as it appears in connection with the subclass is to be understood *intensionally*, we then face the question as to what *this* means: Is 'exists' to be thought of as definable, or as a primitive, undefined term? Whichever answer is given, it would seem the *same* answer as is given for the use of the term 'exists' in connection with the *subclass*, can be given for the use of the term 'exists' in connection with an *individual*, as in the statement '*a* exists', and so on. We should not, in other words, have gained any deeper understanding of how 'exists' is to be used predicatively by detouring to the use of this term as applied to an entire *subclass*.

Extension, Intension, and Comprehension[1]

BAS C. VAN FRAASSEN

University of Toronto

The central arguments in this paper concern adverbs. At first sight, adverbs are not a likely subject for philosophical discussion, nor would they seem to be relevant to existence. But these arguments mean to provide the essential tactical support for my overall strategy: My aim is to show that there are distinctions in traditional logical theory to which the orthodoxies in current logical theory do not do justice. These distinctions do concern possible and actual being, but not solely.

This strategy is pursued in sections 1 through 5. Section 6 is a polemic concerning metaphysics and methodology, and the Appendices provide the technical apparatus for a logic of comprehension and adverbial modification.

I

DISTINCTIONS AND THE THEORY THEREOF

In this section, I shall both draw and discuss distinctions. The first distinction is that between *being* and existence. I cannot define

[1] I have benefited much from discussions especially with Professor R. H. Thomason, Yale University; Professor T. Parsons, University of Illinois at Chicago Circle; and Miss Hidé Ishiguro, University College (London). This research was supported first by the Canada Council and then by the John Simon Guggenheim Memorial Foundation.

what existence amounts to, though I can give tautological equivalents: To exist is

to have real being,
to belong to the extension of some predicate,
to be identical with some existent.

Being, however, belongs to any subject of discourse, existent or non-existent, possible or impossible, real or imaginary or unimaginable or inconceivable.

I shall freely say that there are things which do not exist. There are also things that are impossible. I do subscribe to the view that, in moments of high seriousness, a philosopher ought not to use "there is" except when willing to use "there exists." But high seriousness is highly inconvenient in ordinary contexts, and I shall say no more on this methodological point until the final section.

Just as I shall not equate being with existence, I shall not equate being with being possible. But the region of the possibles is as important a subregion of being as the region of existents, for logical theory. Unfortunately, the term "possible" is not univocal. (Perhaps it was to begin in no worse shape than "existent," but we have learned from Quine to insist firmly on the univocity of existence, and I am not inclined to renege on that.) For example, if it is possible that a given thing is possibly a possible entity, does it follow that it is a possible entity? If we say *no*, gradations appear in the region of possible being. But, as is clear from the immediately preceding assertion, we labor under the guidance of a picture in which "possible" has a maximal sense in which it pertains to a region of being including all subregions which qualify as referents of "the region of possible being" in some sense.[2] Hence univocity can be maintained by insisting on that maximal sense.

I turn now to a second set of distinctions, to be drawn between distinctions. Taking the liberty to choose from common but not uniform terminology, I shall describe the medieval distinctions among *distinctions*, extrapolating and reconstructing where I must. Between any two individuals, there is a real distinction; we express this by saying that they are not identical; they could exist separately. In this sense there is no *real* distinction between the evening star and the morning star.

Mobilizing our earlier distinction between being and existence, we might ask whether there is a real distinction between nonexistents.

[2] The grammatical role of *labor* in this sentence is that in "labor under a delusion." Something similar could be said of naïve discourse about sets, though the doubts there would be more acute.

I do not know of any discussion of the matter. Some authors apparently granted only a logical or conceptual status to possibles, and I imagine that there can only be a logical or conceptual distinction between the entities of reason. But the distinction between a real thing and a chimaera is presumably a real distinction.

In any case, distinctions among individuals can be used to distinguish properties in a straightforward way. I shall say that two properties are *existentially* distinct if some existent has the one but not the other, and *conceptually* distinct if some possible has the one but not the other. The question whether the conceptual distinction as well as the existential distinction between properties can be explained in terms of the real distinction is not one that will matter much to us here. What is most interesting is that Medieval philosophers discuss a distinction among properties that is clearly neither of the two above. I refer to the *formal* distinction. Two properties may be formally distinct although they are conceptually identical. Thus Scotus held that the transcendentals are formally distinct.[3] For example, whatever is, is one; whatever is one, is; yet *ens* and *unum* are (formally) distinct properties.

The formal distinction is to be distinguished from a merely verbal distinction. The paradigm of the latter concerns definition: If "human" is completely characterized by saying that it is (introduced as) *short for* "rational animal," then any distinction made between humanity and rational animality must be a purely verbal one (and to think of such a distinction as properly a distinction is to confuse use and mention). There are two defining characteristics of the formal distinction:

(1)   The distinction is objective, founded *a parte rei*.
(2)   If X and Y are formally distinct, not even God's power could separate them.

I take the second characteristic to be very strong: If X and Y are formally distinct properties, the possible instances of X and those of Y must be the same, in the strongest sense of "possible" that we can have.

In a previous paper I argued that the distinction between Being and Non-Being in Plato's *Sophist* is thus.[4] And a platonist today

---

[3] While Scotus did not introduce the formal distinction, he made the most extensive use of it. It should also be noted that he amended the theory of transcendentals; what I refer to above he termed the subclass of *passiones convertibiles,* properties convertible with being.

[4] "Logical Structure in Plato's *Sophist*," *Review of Metaphysics,* Vol. 22 (1969), pp. 482–498.

could easily insist that properties might be distinct, although all their possible instances are the same.[5] But I cannot accept that as an account of the formal distinction; I would require at least non-tautological identity conditions for properties. Distinctions, after all, should not be multiplied beyond necessity. To arrive at an adequate account I shall now detour via some problems concerning adverbs.

II

PREDICATE MODIFIERS AND EXTENSIONALITY

Syntactically there are many kinds of predicate modifiers. He speaks glibly, with a forked tongue, and sometimes tongue in cheek; he is a diplomat, he is a two-faced diplomat, he stoops at nothing, he stoops to conquer, by fair means or foul. The examples I have given show predicates modified by adverbs, adverbial phrases, adjectives, infinitives, and prepositional phrases. In some cases the modified predicate is logically equivalent to a complex of unmodified predicates, but not in all. So, in general syntax, we should recognize a special class of functors, the *predicate modifiers* which turn predicates into predicates. In an extended but practical usage we may call them adverbs.

Superficially, at least, predicate modifiers present a danger to extensionality. Suppose for a moment that those who drive are exactly those who walk; it certainly does not follow that those who drive slowly, walk slowly. Hence it seems that we cannot replace predicates with coextensive predicates within adverbial contexts and hope to preserve truth.

But is this appearance perhaps deceptive, disappearing when we speak perspicuously with the learned? I shall examine now, at some length, an analysis of predicate modification which tends to support the affirmative. I base this analysis on Davidson's analysis of action sentences, but some of its more *outré* moments are due to Gilbert Harman and to my devil's advocacy.[6]

Consider the sentence "John walks slowly." Davidson analyzed this into the counterpart: "There is an event which is a walking, and is of (by) John, and is slow." No wonder then that slow drivers need not be slow walkers even if drivers are walkers, for the events or acts of walking are not those of driving. The analysis seems to have two virtues: It saves extensionality, and is not *ad hoc*, in that there is a definite recipe for going from the vulgar speech to its perspicuous counterpart. I shall in no way criticize Davidson's analy-

---

[5] This was proposed in discussion by Professor F. Fitch, Yale University.
[6] D. Davidson, "The Logical Form of Action Sentences," in N. Rescher (ed.), *The Logic of Decision and Action* (Pittsburgh: University of Pittsburgh Press, 1968), pp. 81–95.

sis of action sentences. But I shall consider the thesis that this analysis leads straightforwardly to an acceptable theory of predicate modifiers in general, and dispute that.

As a first difficulty consider "He drives in imagination." It may be an act, but it is not an act of driving. The answer will have to be that the recipe that transforms English into canonical English is somewhat more complicated for driving in imagination than for driving in sleet or in anger. We must first transform the sentence into "He imagines that he is driving," or perhaps, "He is imagining in a driving way." Then, perhaps, we can apply the old recipe.

As a second difficulty consider "It is brightly colored." This sentence does not describe or ascribe an action. But an analysis similar to Davidson's can be given if we reify a new category of entities, to which colors belong.[7] "It has a color which is bright." Could the reified entity be a set? Well, not the set of colored things, for this set can also be described by some other predicate say, "has a volume" (or "is macroscopic"; by "is colored" I mean "reflects light" to rule out the more traditional parlor tricks with glass and pink ice cubes). In that case the analysans would logically convert with "It has a volume which is bright" or some such attribution that I assume to be nonsensical. Hence the newly reified category must be that of properties (in some sense in which properties are not sets). No one will doubt that extensionality can be saved at the expense of a bloated ontology, but the price is not right.

Returning to acts, consider "Although swimming fast, John crossed slowly." (This kind of example was already discussed by Davidson.) There is here one act, called slow under one description, fast under another. The solution is to argue that "slow" and "fast" are really relational terms. The analysis is, then, "There is an event, which is a swimiming, and which is a crossing, by John, and which is fast among swimmings but slow among crossings."

The crux of the solution to the preceding difficulty is that the two sets of acts are not identical. What if the world contained only mermen who planned mechanized transport but were unable to construct it? They would, in their frustration, declare even their fastest swimmings to be slow crossings, although all their crossings are by swimming. And what if von Braun, with an eye to the future, remarked that all our present spacecraft are relatively slow? If Armageddon occurred tomorrow, they would be the fastest to have existed, but would that mean that his claim was false?

---

[7] This solution was proposed in correspondence from Professor G. Harman, Princeton University. A better example is this: Suppose the red things were exactly the hard ones; then "bright" cannot be construed in "It is bright red" as classifying the set of red things, on pain of the consequence "It is bright hard." The structure of the example is as in the walkers-drivers problem.

In these modifications of the example I am clearly bringing in conceptual elements. For it is by comparison to conceived, as opposed to actualized, possibilities that the terms "slow" and "fast" are now being applied. The answer given by the extensionalist must be that I am not to apply the usual recipes here: Another transformation, into discourse that is perhaps partly metalinguistic, is needed.

I have not tried to argue that the thesis that Davidson's analysis of action sentences has a straightforward extension to a general analysis of adverbial modification is faced with unsolved problems. But I shall now object to it on the basis of a pattern that may be discerned in the solutions to the problems I have displayed. In any explication of a specific area of discourse in natural language there are three factors: the phenomena (actual usage), the canonical language, the formal or symbolic language. The first is given, but imperfectly: We do not have a perfect systematic description of the grammar of actual language in use. The third is described, with both syntax and semantics precisely specified, in (some part of) logical theory proper. The second is circumscribed, in a relatively precise way, as for example by Quine in *Word and Object*. The procedures for transition from the canonical to the symbolic are relatively straightforward, for the canonical language is delimited with an eye to the formal language that is to be used. The procedures for transition from the actual language to the canonical language are relatively imprecise and less straightforward, irremediably so as long as the description of the phenomena is not precise and systematic.

This picture is meant to fit all explications of actual language, those I admire with few qualifications as well as those I cannot accept even with many. Now I can state my objection to the thesis, qualified by a series of problems and solutions given above: Every epicycle occurred not in the formal machinery, which is readily accessible to discursive reflection, but in the paraphrase procedure that leads from ordinary discourse to canonical discourse. Every formal explication incorporates such a paraphrase procedure. But that is the most flexible, most malleable, least tractable, and least disputable part of the explication. Hence in fairness to the opposition, that is where epicycles should *not* be added. And not just in fairness, but in fear: in fear of the flibbertigibbet of glibness that can confound a strong spirit.

III

Semantic Correlates of Predicate Modifiers

We have so far been concerned to explore an approach in which, through appropriate paraphrase, the predicate modifiers disappear in the transition from the linguistic phenomena to be saved to what saves them. I shall now outline the most important alternate to this approach. Language can be syntactically analyzed so that each expression is formed from simpler component expressions in a certain systematic way. This syntactic structure has an exact parallel in the semantics: An interpretation gives each expression a value, which is determined in a systematic way by the values it gives to the component expressions. Now, a predicate modifier turns predicates into predicates; hence it is natural to take the value of a predicate modifier to be an operator that turns values of predicates into values of predicates.[8] Designating the value of expression E as $|E|$, the thesis has a simple formulation:

(1) $|\phi(F)| = |\phi|(|F|)$

for any predicate F and predicate modifier ϕ.

But what values do expressions receive? As a first candidate, let us suppose that $|F|$ is the extension of F. Then equation (1) says that the semantic correlate of ϕ is an operator on sets (subsets of the domain of discourse; for convenience I shall restrict myself to monadic predicates for now). However, that candidate fails, for under this supposition the consequence

(2)   if $|F| = |G|$ then $|\phi(F)| = |\phi(G)|$

has a corollary

(2a) $(x)(Fx \equiv Gx) \supset (x)(\phi(F)x \equiv \phi(G)x)$

which means that the slow drivers are the slow walkers if the drivers are exactly the walkers.

For this reason we naturally turn to a second candidate: intension. If the predicates are assigned intensions as values, the semantic correlates of adverbs are operators on intensions. But what are intensions? Here there are two distinct answers, one simple-minded and one very powerful. I shall give both answers in pictorial, metaphorical language (but postpone to the end my reasons for calling it pictorial). The first answer is that the intension of a predicate is the collection of possibles of which it is true, while its extension is the set of actuals of which it is true. Writing "$(/x)$" for "for all possible entities x," the intensional corollary to equation (2) is

(2b) $(/x)(Fx \equiv Gx) \supset (/x)(\phi(F)x \equiv \phi(G)x)$

[8] Natural bnt not necessary; the general thesis implies only that $|\phi(F)|$ is some function of $|\phi|$ and $|F|$.

And there are possible, nonexistent walkers who do not drive even if all actual walkers do; hence the reasons against equation (2a) do not count against (2b).

The more powerful approach, taken most recently by Parsons and Thomason, interprets the language with reference to a collection of possible worlds, each of which has inhabitants. A predicate F has an extension in each possible world; its intension $|F|$ is the function that maps each world α into the extension of F in α. (I simplify, but not overly for present purposes.) We can now express the identity of intension as necessary coextension; hence equation (2) has the new corollary.

(2c) $\Box(x)(Fx \equiv Gx) \supset \Box(x)(\phi(F)x \equiv \phi(G)x)$

In what follows, nothing hinges on which explication of intension (whether either of the above, or a mixture of the two which replaces the antecedent of equation (2b) by, say, $\Box(/x)(Fx \equiv Gx)$ or $(/x)\ \Box\ (Fx \equiv Gx)$) is used. I have a preference for the first because of its relative simplicity and economy, virtues not to be slighted if other things are equal.

I shall now bring forward two objections to this candidate. If the objections hold, we shall need to look for a candidate for the value of a predicate other than its extension or intension.

The first objection is a problem raised by Thomason.[9] It does not seem that adverbs can always modify negative predicates. "He reluctantly did not go" makes sense, but "He slowly did not go" does not. Thomason concludes that "reluctantly" ought to be construed as modifying the whole sentence ("Reluctantly, he did not go" in analogy with "Possibly, he did not go") and ends his notes with a problem: "there is a certain asymmetry between the syntax and the semantics. Adverbial phrases are not allowed to modify negative predicates, but there is no semantic way to distinguish 'negative' from 'positive' propositional functions."

The second objection is more nearly analogous to the slow-walkers, slow-drivers problem. Its form is simple: identity of intension of F and G is no guarantee of identity of intension of $\phi(F)$ and $\phi(G)$. The following are pairs of cointensive predicates, it seems to me:

(3)   is colored; is extended
       has a mass; has a volume
       thinks; acts
       has a property; is identical with something

[9] R. H. Thomason, "A Semantic Theory of Adverbs," Yale University, May 1970 Xerox.

But consider the following modifications:

(4)   is brightly colored; is brightly extended
      has a mass of 1 kg; has a volume of 1 kg
      thinks before he acts; acts before he acts
      has a property, namely hardness; is identical with some-
      thing, namely hardness

In each case the second member is either nonsensical, or necessarily
false, or false if the first member is true (of whatever subject one
cares to add). I imagine the objection may be attacked by throwing
doubt on the cointensiveness of my pairs of predicates, but I am
prepared to multiply examples (consider having a mother and having
a father, or at any rate a navel, if one more will help).

It may be objected here that I am bending the notion of necessity
to my own ends. Not by pure logical necessity, but by necessity relative to some accepted or background theory, or theory chosen for
the purpose of example, are the predicates coextensive. But in this
I am not diverging from usual practice in philosophical argument
concerning modal logic. (And what is pure logical necessity anyway?
What is tautological in the context of quantification theory is merely
true *ex vi terminorum* in the context of sentential logic.)

Given these problems, it is natural to seek a further semantic
dimension to predicates, and the tradition offers us at least a label:
comprehension. We can look for inspiration to the theories of intension, comprehension, connotation, conventional connotation, multiple
intension, total contingent intension, and so on, by Mill, Bradley,
Keynes, Lewis, Leonard, and so forth. They are not as helpful as
we might wish. Alternatively, we can look to theories of implication
which reject substitution of tautological equivalents, most notably
the relevant logics constructed by Ackermann, Anderson, Belnap, and
their followers. I do not think either coterie of writings is negligible
as a source of inspiration, but there is in fact a fortunate circumstance
to be attended first: Romane Clark's theory of predicate modifiers
is not open at least to our second objection.[10]

For present convenience let me recast Clark's theory in the
present form. Besides an extension and perhaps an intension, each
predicate F has associated with it a mapping $|F|$ of individuals into
sets of facts. This mapping is such that

(5) Fa is true if and only if one of the elements of $|F|$ ($|a|$) is
      the case.

[10] R. Clark, "Concerning the Logic of Predicate Modifiers," *Nous,* Vol. 4 (1970),
pp. 311–335.

If I am allowed to interject my own theory of facts at this point, I can identify the set $|F|(|a|)$ with the set $T^*(Fa)$ defined in an earlier paper.[11] I shall not assume acquaintance with this paper, but offer some intuitive comments that show the main idea. If F is "is colored," then facts to be found in $|F|(|a|)$ are, for example, the fact that a is red, the fact that a is green, and so on (most of which are not the case of course). Supposing ϕ to be "brightly," the corresponding facts to be found in $|\phi(F)|(|a|) = |\phi|(|F|)(|a|)$ are, for example, the fact that a is bright red, the fact that a is bright green, and so on. Note that such facts as that a is brightly six or seven cubic feet do not appear. But they will appear in $|$"is brightly extended"$|$ $(|a|)$, and indeed, I expect that they are all the same, namely the fact that a is a member of the null set.

In other words, the comprehensions of F and G will be distinct if, for some individual a, the fact that a is F is distinct from the fact that a is G. Could this always be taken to be a real individual, and could the facts always be taken to be facts that some real thing belongs to the *extension* of a given predicate? I do not think so if only because the extensions of "is a golden mountain" and "is an existent golden mountain" are the same. But for the pairs of predicates of example (3) it does not seem to matter much whether the facts themselves be construed extensionally or intensionally. For example, if $|$"has a property"$|$ $(|a|)$ is (roughly) the set

$$\{\text{the fact that } |a| \in X : X \text{ a subset of the domain}\}$$

and $|$"is identical with something"$|$ $(|a|)$ is

$$\{\text{the fact that } a \in \{x\} : x \text{ an element of the domain}\}$$

then it is easily seen that the comprehension of "is identical with something" is included in the comprehension of "has a property," and not conversely, which is exactly as it should be.

There is an interesting corollary: If Clark's solution can be construed as I have done, the logic of comprehension is Anderson and Belnap's logic of tautological entailment.[12]

---

[11] "Facts and Tautological Entailments," *Journal of Philosophy*. Vol. 66 (1969), pp. 477–487.

[12] A. R. Anderson and N. D. Belnap Jr., "Tautological Entailments," *Philosophical Studies*, Vol. 13 (1962), pp. 9–24. The technical details supporting this claim are straightforward given the paper cited in footnote 11. For example, to the predicate abstract $[x_1, \ldots, x_n/A]$ give the function which assigns to $\langle \alpha_1, \alpha_2, \ldots \rangle$ the set of facts $T_d^*(A)$ where $d(x_i) = \alpha_i$, $i = 1, 2, \ldots$. Define $F \vee G$ to be $[y/Fy \vee Gy]$ where y is alphabetically the first variable not in F or G; similarly for meet and complement. Define $F \leq G$ to hold exactly if what is given to F is set-theoretically included in what is given to G. This means, for instance, that $[x/Fx] \leq [y/Gy]$ holds in a model exactly if $Fx \; |||{-}\; Gx$ holds for every assignment

IV

Transcendentals and Definitions

In response to logical problems about adverbs, we now have a new semantic analysis of predication, issuing in a logic of comprehension. If you accept the approach of Section III and regard the proffered problems to be genuine, the outcome that predicates have a semantic dimension beyond their (modal) intension is a necessary one. The exact construal of that dimension is not. In this section I shall examine the formal distinction and Thomason's problem of negative predicates from the point of view of comprehension as here construed.

In the history of logical theory, attention has shifted from properties, to concepts, to predicates. What I called the existential, conceptual, and formal distinction among properties I see as exactly parallel to differences of extension, intension, and comprehension among predicates. Scotus saw a formal distinction between such transcendental properties as being, oneness, necessary-or-contingent, infinite-or-finite. Yet no two are conceptually distinct: All possibles have each property. We can show no difference in intension, but can show a difference in comprehension. For instance, the fact that a is a finite being enters the comprehension of "is finite or infinite"; it does not enter the comprehension of "is one thing" or of "is a necessary or a contingent being." (I would pair "has being" with the abstract $[x/(\exists G)Gx]$ and "is one" with $[x/(/\exists y)(y = x)]$, but details of symbolization could be disputed.)

Syntactically distinct predicates may have the same comprehension. While it is not necessary to do so, we would normally give the simplest kind of comprehension to the simplest kind of predicate, a predicate constant.[13] This means that in such cases, identity of intension entails identity of comprehension. But even distinct complex predicates can have the same comprehension; for example $[x/Fx]$ and $[x/Fx \vee Fx]$ do. The paradigm case of sameness of comprehension, however, occurs in the case of explicit definition. Only the Polish logicians have bothered to attempt a thorough logical analysis of this process in theory construction; in current logical practice this process

d of values to the variables. For completeness, consider vacuous abstracts $[x/A]$ with x not occurring in A. (A more straightforward, but less simple, semantic analysis is given in the first Appendix.)

[13] In the simple construal of Section III this is done explicitly (though this could be amended). In the Appendix, properties (candidates for comprehensions of predicates) are constructed without reference to the syntax, so there it is easy to give to a predicate constant or parameter a comprehension of any degree of complexity. This is essential for the discussion of, for example, the relation between "is colored" and "is red."

occurs in the language-in-use but is generally not mirrored in the object language.[14] Think of a language being given piecemeal, a bit at a time, and at a certain point a primitive predicate F is characterized as *short for* a predicate G which has been characterized previously. My analysis of this is: F is assigned the comprehension of G. (In this way a simple predicate can receive a very complex comprehension in a straightforward way.)

The process of explicit definition plays an important role in actual theory construction, and misunderstanding of its nature can produce much confusion. I mention it here because reference is made to the process of definition to explain how formal distinctions are to be distinguished from merely verbal distinctions. Only a full-fledged theory of comprehension can answer every question of the form "Is this a formal or merely verbal distinction?" that is, "Is there a difference in comprehension between these intensionally equivalent predicates or not?" But in the case in which one predicate is introduced by the process of explicit definition, as short for the other, the answer must be the same regardless of the exact construal of comprehensions. Hence the aptness of the reference to explicit definitions.

If the subject of definition is not well understood, it might seem that formal distinctions may be made to disappear at will, to be turned into merely verbal distinctions, by the process of *redefinition*. One predicate is *definable* as another if they have the same intension in the sense of having provably (relative to given theory T) the same extension. So then why not go one step further, and *define* the one as the other? Is this not a common practice in the development of the theoretical sciences, and does it not show that differences in comprehension are there eliminated at will?

If the structure of a theory is so simple that differences of comprehension between intensionally equivalent, syntactically simple predicates cannot be expressed in it, then it should be assumed, it seems to me, that simple predicates (not introduced by definition) have the simplest kind of comprehension. Hence, for them, identity of intension will imply identity of comprehension, and nothing *is* lost if we say (from some point on) that the one is short for the other. But in an extension of the theory in which differences in comprehension can be expressed, this could generally not be done. In that case, eliminating a primitive term (for example by discarding its old comprehension and giving it the comprehension of another term, *or* by removing it from the syntax altogether) might result in an economy because a notion is *discarded* which proved superfluous for some (though not logically for all) purposes.

[14] Cf. E. W. Beth, *Formal Methods* (Dordrecht: Reidel, 1962), Chapter Six.

To illustrate this critique of loose talk about definition is not so easy, since little attention has been paid to differences in comprehension between the fourteenth century and the twentieth. But an example can be taken at a point between, where the smile yet remained if not the cat: a passage by Leibniz which has been discussed at some length by Hidé Ishiguro.[15] Leibniz introduces a notation for the identity of two concepts A and B, and gives as identity criterion mutual substitutivity *salva veritate* everywhere. He adds that certain apparent exceptions to the criterion must be allowed; for example the concept of the trilateral is identical with the concept of the triangular, although we can not say that a trilateral, as opposed to a triangle, contains 180 degrees by its very nature (*quatenus tale*, in so far as it is of such a kind): "*Est in eo aliquid materiale.*"[16]

The point seems to be that triangles contain 180 degrees by definition (the definition of "triangle" being "plane straight-sided figure with three enclosed angles" say), while trilaterals are triangles not by definition although by logical necessity. That is, although nothing about angles appears in the definition of "trilateral," we can infer from its definition that a trilateral has three enclosed angles summing to 180 degrees. Now we could put this as follows: triangularity and trilaterality are distinct features of the figure, although it would not be possible for it to have the one feature and not the other. So the distinction between being a trilateral and having three sides, and so on, is only a verbal distinction, but the distinction between being a trilateral and being a triangle is a formal distinction.

Discussing that passage, Miss Ishiguro points out that Leibniz' closing remark (quoted above) is a reference to the theory of supposition; specifically, to material supposition. Her reconstruction of Leibniz' reaction to such contexts that are opaque to substitutivity of identical concepts is this: Each expression has a meaning which is a function of the meaning of component expressions entering it (or its defining phrase if it is defined). Two expressions may then have distinct meanings, although they stand for identical concepts. It will be clear how I understand that account: I identify what Leibniz-pace-Ishiguro calls meaning with comprehension, concept with intension.

I began by exhibiting the passage as an example of the distinction between what is the case by definition and 'what follows from the definition. Geometry, as it is normally formulated, does not admit

---

[15] H. Ishiguro, "Leibniz and the Ideas of Sensible Qualities," in *Reason and Realtiy, Royal Institute of Philosophy Lectures,* V (London: Macmillan Press, 1972), pp. 49–63.
[16] L. Couturat, *Opuscules et Fragments Inédits de Leibniz,* p. 261.

the expression of this distinction. To add the expression "by definition" (or "by its nature" or *"quatenus tale"*) would be to extend geometry (and not in a way that would serve a geometric purpose. Within geometry proper predicates with the same intension are substitutable everywhere.) But the passage is first and foremost an example of a recognition of distinctions which go beyond the intensional. A similar example, from arithmetic rather than geometry, is furnished by Frege's notion that "2 + 2" and "2²" have the same reference but a different sense.[17] This sense could not be intension, for Frege thinks of numbers as properties of collections, and surely any possible collection having the property 2 + 2 (that is, having 2 + 2 members) has the property 2² and conversely. So the sense of "2 + 2" is not its intension.

V

DETERMINABLES AND NEGATION

In what way are meanings, in the sense of comprehensions, a function of components? I propose that there are two ways; the first is conjunctive and typical of the classical paradigm of definition; the second is disjunctive and typical of the determinable-determinate relationship of modern logic. Let the definition of "human" be "rational animal." Then *humanity* comprehends *rationality* and *animality*. I shall write $\leqq$ for this relationship, and we have no doubt the typical conjunction laws

$$\text{human} \leqq \text{rational}$$
(6) $$\text{human} \leqq \text{animal}$$
$$\text{if A} \leqq \text{rational and A} \leqq \text{animal, then A} \leqq \text{human}$$

But now consider the relation between *being colored* and *being red*. To be red is not to be colored and something else (unless that be red). Yet whatever is red is colored by its very nature. To be colored is to be red, or blue, or . . . To have a finite case, I will introduce an artificial example: Let spin be a quality which has only two varieties, spin +1 and spin −1. Then we have the typical disjunction laws:

$$\text{spin} + 1 \leqq \text{spin}$$
(7) $$\text{spin} - 1 \leqq \text{spin}$$
$$\text{if spin} + 1 \leqq \text{A and spin} - 1 \leqq \text{A, then spin} \leqq \text{A}$$

For color we would of course have an infinite analogue, since there are infinitely many colors. In W. E. Johnson's terminology, color

---

[17] P. Geach and M. Black (eds.), *Translations from the Philosophical Writings of Gottlob Frege* (Oxford: Blackwell, 1966), p. 154.

and spin (and also volume, mass, temperature, and so on) are determinables, and the specific colors and specific spin values are determinates under them.[18]

The tree of Porphyry and Johnson's determinable-determinate hierarchy graphically represent two distinct patterns in conceptual structure. These two patterns must be combined in some integral way if we are to have an adequate representation of how complex meanings are functions of component meanings. For in the building of concepts, one might proceed according to either pattern at any stage. In the logic of comprehension, construed either as in the preceding section or as in the Appendix, these patterns are indeed systematically combined. The way in which they are combined assumes that comprehension is not affected by the standard logical procedure of reducing to 'normal' form. This is a substantial assumption; its justification can consist only in the comparison of Anderson and Belnap's logic of tautological entailment with alternative attempts along similar lines.[19]

In the form adopted, each property (comprehension of a predicate) can be viewed as a determinable, comprising a set of properties (determinates) under it in a disjunctive way. Then each of those properties is this kind of a 'disjunction' only of itself; but it comprises another set of properties in a conjunctive way. Now *these* properties are simplest of all, and comprise only themselves (in either of those ways). These latter are what I called the simplest kind of comprehension a predicate could have: If two predicates have this simplest kind of comprehension, then they have the same comprehension if they have the same intension.

You may wonder what has happened to negation. Well, when a formula is reduced to normal form in ordinary logic, the negations are driven inside, as far as possible. For example, $\sim(p \vee q)$ is reduced to $(\sim p \ \& \sim q)$, by De Morgan's laws. The negation of a disjunction is therefore again a disjunction, which has, however, only one disjunct. In the same way, the very simplest kind of comprehensions have very straightforward complements; complementation of more complex comprehensions is defined in accordance with De Morgan's laws.

Now I can state my solution to Thomason's problem, which I cited in Section III. Most ordinary predicate modifiers (for example, most ordinary adverbs) have an intimate connection with a specific

[18] W. E. Johnson, *Logic,* Part I (Cambridge: Cambridge University Press, 1921), Chapter 11.
[19] This logic is the first-degree fragment of a large family of logics of implication (notably *R-mingle, R,* and *E*), but these do not have to be considered here; we are concerned only with an implication relation among propositions, not with a binary implication operation on propositions.

determinable. They produce nonsense when used to modify something which is strictly outside that determinable. So "is bright not red" ("is brightly uncolored") is nonsense for the same reason that "is brightly extended" is nonsense. And the reason is this: "bright" is intimately connected with the determinable *color*, in this sense, and the comprehensions of "is extended," "is not red," and "is uncolored" are not determinates under this determinable. *Most* adverbs do not sensibly modify negative predicates because complementation *usually* takes one outside the determinable in which the complemented property lay.[20]

Thomason has pointed out that intensions could be grouped in families, and these families called *determinables,* so that exactly this solution to his problem can be had without going beyond intension. This is true; I offer the second Appendix and claim only that the problem has a natural solution in our framework.

VI

METHODOLOGY IN PHILOSOPHICAL LOGIC

Contemporary logical theory often looks like a metaphysician's garden of delights: possibles, properties, facts—is there no end to our weird and wonderful reifications?

Let me say at once that I do not believe a word of it. I can believe in witches and genies; indeed, I can seriously wonder whether I have met those. But I cannot even imagine wondering seriously whether there are sets or properties. Since I talk freely about sets and properties and much other metaphysical flora and fauna, I suppose I have to explain how I feel that I can do this.

My attitude toward mathematical objects such as sets is at least in practice different from my attitudes to the other categories. Specifically, I *use* or *engage in* mathematical discourse to describe other forms of discourse. So I often find myself asserting or assuming that there are sets. Now I do not really believe that there are any. But I do firmly believe that any adequate philosophy of mathematics must show how, nevertheless, we can play the mathematical language game, to the extent that it is needed for all normal scientific and philosophical purposes, in a perfectly sensible way. I grant that neither nominalists nor intuitionists nor constructivists have managed to show this. That means that, in my opinion, there exists today no adequate philosophical account of mathematics. But it would have been foolish not to use normal discourse about motion before Zeno's paradoxes

[20] Similar but more special hypotheses have been offered by Harman and Lakoff.

were adequately handled; it would be equally foolish not to use set theory today.

But, while using mathematical discourse we can, or ought, to provide rational reconstructions of other forms of discourse: modal, epistemic, deontic, discourse about possibles, about implication, about facts, and much more. In the explication of modality, for instance, I distinguish three moments: a language game with modal qualifiers, an account thereof in pictorial language (about possibles or possible worlds), and a formal reconstruction in mathematical language. The pictorial account is a guide to the formal account, but the sole object of semantic analysis is to provide a precise representation of the structure of the language game. (I hold that in addition, a pragmatic analysis is needed for the purposes of philosophical clarification, but our techniques for such analysis have not yet reached maturity.)

The metaphysical language of the second stage I call *pictorial* for a special reason. In any area of discourse, thought and reasoning are guided (and often bewitched) by a picture. The preceding statement is pictorial also. It is an assertion in the kind of language game that I believe to be adequate, on a relatively superficial but not negligible level, to the description of mental activity. That area of discourse is also guided by a picture; a semantic analysis would provide a precise description of the kind of picture that guides it. What it means to call it *adequate*, however, would not be made clear by a semantic analysis; this is a subject in pragmatics.

Given my ontological views, it may be surprising that I do not work within the Quine-Davidson tradition. Superficially, the break is over Tarski's criterion for an adequate theory of truth.

A theory of truth entails, for each sentence s, a statement of the form "s is true if any only if p" where in the simplest case "p" is replaced by s. Since the words "is true if and only if" are invariant, we may interpret them as "means that."[21]

I cannot agree to this. Let some particular fragment of natural language be codified and called Θ. The idea seems now to be that we can frame a metalanguage M, which is part of Responsible Philosophonese, such that (a) M has the structure of the languages studied in ordinary quantificational logic, and (b) M contains an exact copy of Θ. But all sentences of M are bivalent (either true or false, no matter what the facts are like). So how could M contain an exact copy of Θ if Θ is not a bivalent language?

[21] D. Davidson, "Semantics for Natural Languages," *Linguaggi nella societa e nella tecnica* (Milan: Edizioni di Communita, 1970), p. 184.

To this, the following retort is possible: We are not concerned with what language might be like, but only with what it is like—and this language, the language we have, is bivalent. And perhaps the retort could be trivally justified: Is not every language bivalent if by "false" you mean "not true"? But the trivial justification would not be a justification. For the thesis of those who reject bivalence is not that the word "false" has a certain meaning, but that there are important semantic characteristics of and relations among sentences that cannot be explicated in terms of truth (or satisfaction) alone. So the retort, to be effective, must rest on the nontrivial thesis that all important semantic characteristics and relations for natural language are sufficiently like those studied in orthodox formal semantics.

To substantiate this nontrivial thesis, one usually takes recourse to the surface structure/deep structure distinction. It seems fairly certain that Russell held that language has a skeleton, that the philosopher, like Blake's wild beasts, can cleanly separate the flesh from the bones, and that only the skeleton matters. No philosopher today holds this view, I suppose, but the emphasis on deep structure is reminiscent of it. For it is meant, it is not, that there is a hygienic and domesticated fragment of natural language in which all that could be said at all can be said? And that to display the deep structure of a given sentence, one displays its hygienic, domesticated counterpart (or rather, counterparts, to allow for ambiguity)? But the essential philosophical qualification to the earlier view is the present admission of the relative status of deep structure. Davidson (like Harman) proposes that deep structure be identified with logical form, and then adds:

> to give the logical form of a sentence is to give its logical location in the totality of sentences, to describe it in a way that explicitly determines what sentences it entails and what sentences it is entailed by. The location must be given relative to a specific deductive theory; so logical form itself is relative to a theory. The relativity does not stop here, either, since even given a theory of deduction there may be more than one total scheme for interpreting the sentences we are interested in and that preserves the pattern of entailments. The logical form of a particular sentence is, then, relative both to a theory of deduction and to some prior determinations as to how to render sentences in the language of the theory.[22]

[22] D. Davidson, "Action and Reaction," *Inquiry*, Vol. 13 (1970), pp. 140–148.

So the person assigning logical form or deep structure to a given sentence is in the position of a scientist who displays a model of given phenomena: The physical theory he has gives him a certain stock of models for phenomena and rules for selecting the right model. The enterprise falls therefore under the canons of scientific methodology; its hypothetical character is openly granted, as is its nonuniqueness in principle.

From this point of view the difference between the Davidsonian [or (neo?) Quinean or crypto-Russellian] enterprise and our own is that we proceed with reference to a different logical theory. But that is not all: They always seek for logical form in the sense of a model taken from one logic, orthodox quantificational logic, whereas we produce new logical structures to deal with new problems. So this is an inadequate way to characterize the difference. The correct way, in my opinion, is to say that we choose a different *locus for innovation and complication*. The locus they choose is the procedure for fitting the linguistic phenomena (or rather, their surface structure) to the logical theory (what Davidson called in the passage cited above the "total scheme for interpreting the sentences" and "prior determinations as to how to render sentences in the language of the theory"). The locus we choose is the logical theory.

At the end of Section II, I argued against the first (and for the second) choice of locus. Every scientific theory has a precise part and an imprecise part; the procedures for fitting the phenomena to models must belong to the imprecise part if there is no systematic, relatively theory-independent description of those phenomena; complications and innovations ought to occur in the precise part. In our special case, this means that the relation between surface structure and logical form ought to be as close and as direct as feasible. Of course there are also less-official arguments: A stable, well-established, well-understood theory has greater explanatory power, say the others; there is as great a danger of being tyrannized by logic as by society, say we, but a proper understanding sets you free.

To sum up, then, I have offered three theses concerning philosophical logic. The first is that it can be done in such a way as to impute no ontological commitment through any use of language. The second is that orthodox logical theory is inadequate to the analysis of natural language because there are important semantic properties and relations that cannot be characterized in orthodox semantic terms. (As illustrations, but illustrations only, of these two theses I offer my personal rejection of the existence of abstract entities, possibles, and facts, and of the principle of bivalence.) The third is that, in the special situation of philosophical logic, correct methodology requires innovations and complications to occur on the side of the formal apparatus.

Appendix I

THE LOGIC OF COMPREHENSION[23]

In Section III I defined the comprehension of a predicate by combining Clark's theory of predicate modifiers with my representation of facts. The fact *that Fa*, for example, is represented as the unit set $\{<[F],|a|>\}$ where $[F]$ is the intension of F (or its extension, depending on how deep our analysis needs to go) and $|a|$ is the referent of a. Clearly the facts that make a sentence true are determined then by the intensions (or extensions) of the predicates involved, and by the referents of the singular terms involved. Put it this way, it would seem that the comprehensions of predicates could perhaps be constructed directly from intensions, bypassing the individuals and the facts. This more direct approach I shall pursue in these two appendices.

In this first appendix I shall give a representation of *properties*. Each property Z will have a corresponding *attribute* $[Z]$ and in each possible world α, Z will determine a set of existents $[Z,\alpha]$. When a language is interpreted, the value assigned to a predicate is such a property. If $|F| = Z$, then we also say that Z is the comprehension of F, $[Z]$ the intension of F, and $[Z,\alpha]$ the extension of F in possible world α. A more-complicated scheme, in which intensions may also differ from world to world, presents only routine difficulties. The value of a predicate modifier will be an operation on the set of properties. While I shall consider only monadic adverbs, which are not themselves given as functions of anything else, the extension to more complex cases again presents only routine difficulties, I think (although it might suggest interesting new logical problems). So, for example, "continually," as in "He continually jumped and ran about," is perhaps best seen as polyadic, since running and jumping cannot be done simultaneously. On the other hand, in "He ran to Bath and to Bournemouth," we should perhaps regard the value of "to" as mapping places into operators on properties.

I shall construe properties in such a way that the values of relational and complex predicates can be properties. The maneuver is simple: as extension of "——$_1$ is father of ——$_2$" I take the set of

---

[23] An earlier draft of these Appendices was presented in my "Adverbs: Some Logical Problems," University of Toronto, August, 1970. Mimeographed.

all infinite sequences of objects such that the first is father of the second. So extensions are sets of infinite sequences, the members of which tend to become irrelevant after some initial segment. The same holds for intensions: the elements of the sequence are then possible individuals. If, in the language, complex predicates are made up by abstraction or definition, the syntactic operators ought to be regarded as corresponding to operations on properties; for example

$$||[x/Fx \ \& \ Gx]|| \ = \ |F| \wedge |G|$$

whatever we eventually mean by the meet of two properties. Similarly universal quantification will correspond to infinite meet, the indexing being through the possible individuals.

From here on I shall disregard existence, which is a predicate without intension or comprehension, and the sole use of which is to determine extensions. (This limitation does not appear if we regard an intension as a function assigning extensions to possible worlds, but I do not think that we need go to that length to encounter any of the problems *peculiar* to the logic of adverbs.) We assume given a set H (the set of possible individuals, the logical space). H^ω is the set of all denumerable sequences of elements of H. I define

(1) (a)   a *point* is an element of H^ω.
     (b)   an *attribute* is a subset of H^ω, that is, a set of points.
     (c)   a *molecule* is a nonempty set of attributes.
     (d)   a *property* is a nonempty set of molecules.

The molecules play a purely expository role. We shall use variables

x over the points
X over the attributes
Y over the molecules
Z over the properties

in each case with or without sub- or superscripts. We say that

(2) (a) x has X iff $x \in X$.
    (b) x has Y iff x has each element of Y.
    (c) x has Z iff x has some element of Z.

Clearly if $Z = \{Y\}$, then x has Y if and only if x has Z; for that reason the molecules are really inessential.

Each property determines an attribute as follows

(D3) $[Z] = \{x : x \text{ has } Z\}$

Using the convenient molecules, it is easy to see how this can be defined set-theoretically

(4)(Da) $[Y] = \cap \{X : X \in Y\}$
   (b) $[Z] = \cup \{[Y] : Y \in Z\}$

That is, equations (3) and (4a) imply (4b); (4a) and (4b) imply (3). As the capital letter "D" indicates, I regard (3) rather than (4b) as the correct definition.

The properties are ordered, and this ordering carries over to the corresponding attributes. We read $\le$ as "coerces."

(D5)(a) $X \not\le X'$ iff $X \subseteq X'$
   (b) $Y \not\le Y'$ iff every X' in Y' is coerced by some X in Y
   (c) $Z \not\le Z'$ iff every Y in Z coerces some Y' in Z'

(6)(a)   If $Z \not\le Z'$, then $[Z] \subseteq [Z']$
   (b) $Z \not\le Z$; and, if $Z \not\le Z'$ and $Z' \not\le Z''$, then $Z \not\le Z''$

We shall now show that we can with much convenience and no loss of generality restrict our attention to a certain kind of properties, *closed properties*.

(D7)(a) $Z^* = \{Y : Y \not\le Y' \text{ for some } Y' \text{ in } Z\}$
   (b) Z is *closed* iff $Z = Z^*$

(8) $Z \not\le Z^*$ and $Z^* \not\le Z$

To prove equation (8), note first that $Z \subseteq Z^*$. Hence each molecule in Z is identical with, and hence coerces, some molecule in Z^*. Therefore $Z \not\le Z^*$. But conversely, every Y in Z^* coerces some Y' in Z by definition. Therefore $Z^* \not\le Z$. Thus Z and Z^* are indistinguishable by our ordering, and there is no difference between calling Z the comprehension of a predicate F, or Z^*. Henceforth the variable

P ranges over closed properties

used with or without sub- or superscripts.

(9) $P \not\le P'$ iff $P \subseteq P'$

(If $P \subseteq P'$, then $P \not\leq P'$, as for any pair of properties. Suppose therefore that $P \not\leq P'$. Then each Y in P coerces some Y' in P'. But then each Y in P belongs to P'^* by the definition of closure. Since P' is already closed, $P \subseteq P'$.)

The closed properties form a set-theoretic lattice. That is, intersections and unions of closed properties are closed again. Let Y be in $P \cap P'$ and let Y' coerce Y. Then Y is in P and also in P'. Hence Y' is in P and also in P' (they are closed), and therefore Y' is in $P \cap P'$. On the other hand let Y be in $P \cup P'$, and $Y' \leq Y$. Then Y is either in P or in P', and Y' is in the same part. None of this reasoning depends on the finitude of the case, hence we conclude

(10)   The closed properties form a complete set-theoretic lattice.

We may note that the null element of this lattice is $\{\{\Lambda\}\}$, which is also the null element among all properties. This gives us automatically the interpretation in comprehension of conjunction, disjunction, and quantification, provided the comprehensions we assign are closed. And there could be no advantage in doing otherwise, as equation (8) shows.

However, for the purely expository purpose of facilitating the discussions of complementation and completeness to come, I shall now give meets and joins for properties in general.

(D11)(a) $X \wedge X' = X \cap X'$; $X \vee X' = X \cup X'$
    (b) $Y \wedge Y' = Y \cup Y'$; $Y \vee Y' = \{Y, Y'\}$
    (c) $Z \wedge Z' = \{Y \cup Y' : Y \in Z \& Y' \in Z'\}$
        $Z \vee Z' = Z \cup Z'$

(12) $[Z \wedge Z'] = [Z] \cap [Z']$; $[Z \vee Z'] = [Z] \cup [Z']$

Infinite analogues are obvious. For example, if $Z_i = \{Y_{ij}\}$, $j \in J$ for each $i \in I$, and we denote the set of maps from I into J as J^I. Then

$$\bigwedge_{i \in I} Z_i = \bigwedge_{i \in I} \{Y_{ij}\}, \quad j \in J$$
$$= \{\bigcup_{i \in I} Y_{if(i)} : f \in J^I\}$$

It can easily be checked that the lattice laws hold among the properties. In addition, $P \wedge P' = P \cap P'$. (That $P \wedge P' \subseteq P \cap P'$ follows from the definition of coercion and the fact that $P \cap P'$ is closed. On the other hand if Y is in both P and P', then $Y \cup Y = Y$ is in $P \wedge P'$.)

How shall we define complementation? There is a natural complement on attributes, and this we can extend to molecules and properties with the De Morgan relations in mind.

$$(D13)\ (a)\quad \bar{X} = H^\omega - X$$
$$(b)\quad \bar{Y} = \vee\{\bar{X} : X \in Y\} = \{\{\bar{X}\} : X \in Y\}$$
$$(c)\quad \bar{Z} = \wedge\{\bar{Y} : Y \in Z\}$$

$$(14)\quad [\bar{Z}] = H^\omega - [Z]$$

I have left the consequences for corresponding attributes mostly unproved so far, but equation (14) is less simple than the others. We have to use the law of *complete distributivity* for sets:

$$(15)\quad \bigcup_{i \in I}\left(\bigcap_{j \in J} X_{ij}\right) = \bigcap_{f \in S}\left(\bigcup_{i \in I} X_{if(i)}\right)$$

where $S = J^I$, the set of all mappings of I into J.

First, let us write henceforth

$$Z = \{Y_i : i \in I\} = \{\{X_{ij} : j \in J\} : i \in I\} = \{\{X_{ij}\}, j \in J\}$$

$i \in I$, and let $S = J^I$. Then we can express the complement by

$$(16)\quad \bar{Z} = \bigwedge_{i \in I} \bar{Y}_i = \bigwedge_{i \in I} \{\{\bar{X}_{ij}\} : j \in J\}\}$$
$$= \{\bigcup_{i \in I} \{\bar{X}_{if(i)}\} : f \in S\}$$
$$= \{\{\bar{X}_{if(i)} : i \in I\} : f \in S\}.$$

by equations (13) and (15). (In applying equation (15), let $Z_i = \bar{Y}_i = \{Y_{ij}\}, j \in J$ where $Y_{ij} = \{\bar{X}_{ij}\}$; remember that $\bar{Y}_i$, unlike Y_i, is a property. In the same symbolism,

$$(17)\quad [Z] = \bigcup_{i \in I} [Y_i] = \bigcup_{i \in I}\left(\bigcap_{j \in J} X_{ij}\right)$$
$$= \bigcap_{f \in S}\left(\bigcup_{i \in I} X_{if(i)}\right)$$

So by De Morgan's laws,

$$(18)\quad H^\omega - [Z] = \bigcup_{f \in S}\left(\bigcap_{i \in I} \bar{X}_{if(i)}\right)$$

But, from equation (16), we can derive

$$(19) \quad [\bar{Z}] = \bigcup_{f \in S} [\{\bar{X}_{if(i)} : i \in I\}]$$
$$= \bigcup_{f \in S} (\bigcap_{i \in I} \bar{X}_{if(i)})$$

which agrees exactly with equation (18), thus proving consequence (14). And consequence (14) is, in my opinion, a prime criterion for the correct definition of complement in this context.

Turning now to the formal principles obeyed by complementation, we find

$$(20) \quad \bar{\bar{Z}} = Z$$

To prove equation (20), and writing the bar to the left instead of above when convenient, and "$\bar{X}_{f,i}$" for "$\bar{X}_{if(i)}$," we find

$$(21) \quad \bar{\bar{Z}} = -\{\{\bar{X}_{if(i)} : i \in I\} : f \in S\}$$
$$= -\{\{\bar{X}_{f,i} : i \in I\} : f \in S\}$$
$$= \{\{\bar{\bar{X}}_{f,g(f)} : f \in S\} : g \in I^S\}$$

by applying equation (16) *mutatis mutandis* to the case $Z' = \{\{X_{f',i}\} \ i \in I\}, f \in S$.

Of course $\bar{\bar{X}} = X$. Hence we see that each molecule $\{\bar{\bar{X}}_{f,g(f)} : f \in S\}$ in $\bar{\bar{Z}}$ is a subset of molecule $Y_{g(f)}$ in Z. To see the converse, let $g(f) = i$, and let X_{ij} be in Y_i. There is certainly an f in S, such that $f(i) = j$. Hence $X_{ij} = X_{if(i)} = X_{f,i} = X_{f,g(f)}$ for some f in S. Therefore the two molecules are identical. But this mapping of Z into z is really *onto* Z, since, for each i in I and f in S, there is a mapping of g such that $g(f) = i$.

This is not enough to qualify the operation formally as a complement; we need also at least

$$(21) \quad \text{If } Z_1 \angle Z_2, \text{ then } \bar{Z}_2 \angle \bar{Z}_1.$$

Let $Z_1 = \{Y_i\}, i \in I = \{\{X_{ij}\}, j \in J\], i \in I$, as above, and let $Z_2 = \{Y_k\}, k \in K = \{\{X_{km}\}, m \in M\}, k \in K$, and let there be a mapping $g : I \to K$ such that Y_i coerces $Y_{g(i)}$. Then there is, in addition, a mapping $h : K \times M$ into J such that $X_{g(i)m}$ is coerced by $X_{ih(g(i)m)}$. That is, the latter is a subset of the former.

Now let us consider an arbitrary member $Y_f = \{\bar{X}_{kf(k)} : k \in K\}$, where f is in M^K, of $\bar{Z}_2$. We must show that, for some g in S, Y_f forces $Y_g = \{\bar{X}_{ig(i)} : i \in I\}$. Hence we must show that for that function g,

$\bar{X}_{ig(i)}$ has a subset $\bar{X}_{kf(k)}$ for an appropriate choice of k. So, for a given i, and $f(k) = m$, we must choose g and k such that $X_{ig(i)} \subseteq X_{km}$. Well, let k be $g(i)$. So we must have $X_{ig(i)} \subseteq X_{g(i)m}$. To have that, let $g(i) = h(g(i), m)$, for we do indeed have $X_{ih(g(i),m)} \subseteq X_{g(i)m}$.

We turn back now to closed properties; clearly our complementation does not preserve closure. However, if $Z_1 \not\leq Z_2$, and conversely, then $\bar{Z}_1 \not\leq \bar{Z}_2$, and conversely, and for each Z there is a unique closed property that coerces and is coerced by Z, namely Z^*. Hence we can define

(D22) $\tilde{Z} = \bar{Z}^*$

and prove that this yields a complement of the same kind on the closed properties. First, $\tilde{\tilde{P}} = \bar{\tilde{P}}^* \lessgtr \tilde{P} \lessgtr \bar{P}^* \lessgtr \bar{P}$ (because, as we said, if $Z_1 \lessgtr Z_2$, then $\bar{Z}_1 \lessgtr \bar{Z}_2$, by equation 21, and, of course, $\bar{P}^* \lessgtr \bar{P}$). Second, if $P_1 \subseteq P_2$, then $\tilde{P}_2 = \bar{P}_2{}^* \lessgtr \bar{P}_2 \not\leq \bar{P}_1 \lessgtr \bar{P}_1{}^* = \tilde{P}_1$. Therefore the analogues of equations (20) and (21) hold, and

(23)   The closed properties form a De Morgan lattice of sets.

This means that the logic of tautological entailment is a sound logic of comprehension (by standard results of the former subject) and we wish now to show that it is also complete.

As appropriate syntax, take the variables x_1, x_2, . . . , to be nouns, and if A_1, A_2 are nouns, so are $\bar{A}_1$, $A_1 \wedge A_2$, $A_1 \vee A_2$. Call a noun *atomic* if it has either the form x_i or the form $\bar{x}_j$. If A_1, A_2 are nouns, $A_1 \leq A_2$ is a statement. A statement is *valid* if it is true under the interpretation of the signs, $\wedge$, $\vee$, $-$, $\leq$, regardless of what properties are assigned to the variables and regardless of the choice of set H.

(24)   If A_1, . . . , A_m, B_1, . . . , B_n are atomic nouns, then $A_1 \wedge \cdots \wedge A_m \leq B_1 \vee \cdots \vee B_n$ is valid (if and) only if A_i is the same noun as B_j for some i and j.

This follows because we can clearly choose subsets X_1, . . . , X_{m+n} of H^ω such that $X_i \not\subseteq X_j$ and $X_i \not\subseteq H^\omega - X_j$ for all $i, j \leq m + n$. In that case, we note

$$\bigwedge_{i=1}^{m} X_i{}^1 \not\leq \bigvee_{j=m+1}^{n} X_j{}^1$$

that is,

$$\{\{X_1{}^1, \ldots, X_m{}^1\}\} \not\leq \{\{X_{m+1}{}^1\}, \ldots, \{X_n{}^1\}\}$$

where $X_i{}^1$ is either X_i or $H^\omega - X_i$, for $i = 1, \ldots, m + n$.

Call A a *primitive* conjunction (disjunction) if it has the form $A_1 \wedge \cdots \wedge A_m (A_1 \vee \cdots \vee A_m)$ where $A_1, \ldots, A_m$ are atomic.

(25) If $A_1, \ldots, A_m$ are primitive conjunctions and $B_1, \ldots, B_n$ are primitive disjunctions, then $A_1 \vee \cdots \vee A_m \leq B_1 \wedge \cdots \wedge B_n$ is valid (if and) only if $A_i \leq B_j$ for each i and j.

Let $|A_i| = \{\{X_1{}^i, \ldots, X_{m_i}{}^i\}\}$ and $|B_j| = \{\{V_1{}^j\}, \ldots, \{V_{m_j}{}^j\}\}$, where $|A|$ is the value of noun A. For

$$\bigvee_{i=1}^{m} |A_i|$$

to coerce

$$\bigwedge_{j=1}^{n} |B_j|$$

each $|A_i|$ must do so. But then $|A_i|$ must coerce $\{\{V_{f(1)}{}^1, \ldots, V_{f(n)}{}^n\}\}$ for a certain mapping f such that $f(j)$ is in $\{1, \ldots, m_j\}$. So each $V_{f(j)}{}^j$ must have a subset $X_{g(f(j))}{}^i$ for a certain mapping g such that $g(f(j)) \in \{1, \ldots, m_i\}$. In that case, however $\{\{X_1{}^i, \ldots, X_{m_i}{}^i\}\}$ coerces $\{\{V_{f(j)}{}^j\}\}$, and hence $|B_j|$.

Because of the normal form theorems for tautological entailment, these two results imply the completeness of this logic as a calculus of comprehension.

Appendix II

THE CLASS OF ASPECT MODIFIERS

The usual pattern of predicate modification at the center of the discussions by Reichenbach, Davidson, and Thomason, is this: A subject is qualified by a number of expressions, each of which qualifies this predicate in some particular respect. These qualifiers answer such questions as:

Where?
How?
With what?
When?
To whom?
While what else happened?
How much?

I shall call this *aspect modification*. As an example, we have, say,

He buttered the toast *at midnight*$_1$ *in the shower*$_2$
with a knife$_3$.

If this is done perspicuously, the aspect in question can be determined
by looking at the modifier. The modifiers do not interfere (hence
their order is, at most, of stylistic importance), and all the modifiers
clearly pertain to the original predicate. The following three principles
hold:

I. $\qquad \phi(F)x \vdash Fx$
II. $\qquad \phi\phi'(F)x \vdash \phi'\phi(F)x$
III. $\quad \phi(F)x \,\&\, \phi'(F)x \vdash \phi\phi'(F)x$

where ϕ, ϕ' range over aspect modifiers.

I maintain that the aspect modifiers constitute the paradigm and
most pervasive class of predicate modifiers in our language. Of course,
no theory holding only for them is an adequate theory of predicate
modification, but any adequate theory must give a special account
of them. Now I shall offer as theses some further principles beyond
the three above and a construction that is in accordance with them;
I hope that this will qualify as an acceptable rational reconstruction
of this class of modifiers, and will serve as a guide to the reconstruction of other wider such classes.

IV. $\qquad \phi\phi = \phi$
V. $\quad \phi(Z \lor Z') = \phi(Z) \lor \phi(Z')$
VI. $\quad \phi(Z \land Z') = \phi(Z) \land \phi(Z')$

I realize that, in offering theses **IV** through **VI**, I run the danger
of seriously limiting the class to a subclass of that discussed by
Reichenbach and Davidson.[24] For example, with respect to thesis **VI**,
does Davidson recognize the existence of acts described by conjunctions which cannot be analyzed into sets of acts done conjointly?
I don't know.

In addition to the six theses I have listed, I offer the informal
thesis that each aspect modifier is intimately connected with a certain
determinable, in the sense that it makes nonsense of what does not fall
under that determinable. For example, "bright(ly)" in "brightly
colored" or "bright red" is an aspect modifier (indicating, roughly, the

[24] Cf. Lakoff, "Is There a Distinction between Adverbs and Modal Operators?"
University of Michigan, August 1970, pp. 5–7. Mimeographed.

degree of a certain aspect of the property). It belongs intimately, in this sense, to the determinable *color*. (Of course, words in natural language tend to play many roles; we also speak of bright minds. But this complication I shall ignore here.) Suppose that the intension of "is red" is X and its comprehension is of the simplest kind, namely $\{\{X\}\}$. Then the intension of "is bright red" is, say X_1, a proper subclass of X, and its comprehension should be $\{\{X_1\}\}$. Similarly, if the comprehension of "is hard" is $\{\{X_2\}\}$, then the comprehension of "is bright hard" should be $\{\{\Lambda\}\}$. In this sense "bright(ly)" makes nonsense of "is hard." Note that the comprehension of this *nonsensical* predicate is very different from that of the *self-contradictory* predicate "is hard and is not hard," which is $\{\{X_2, H^\omega - X_2\}\}$.

What exactly is the effect of "bright(ly)" on "is red"? The example above is not accurate because we let the comprehension be a property that is not closed. *Really* we should say that

$$\text{"is red"} = \{\{X\}\}^*$$

and this has as members $\{X_1\}$ as well as $\{X'\}$ for every other subset X' of X. So the effect of the modifier is to reduce $\{\{X\}\}^*$ to its proper subclass $\{\{X_1\}\}^*$. We can do this by saying that ϕ, the corresponding operator, acts as follows (for a certain family $\mathbf{F}$):

(a) $\quad \phi(X') = \begin{cases} X' & \text{if } X' \subseteq X_1 \in \mathbf{F} \\ \Lambda & \text{otherwise} \end{cases}$

(b) $\quad \phi(Y) = \{\phi(X) : X \in Y\}$

(c) $\quad \phi(Z) = \{\phi(Y) : Y \in Z\}$

When ϕ fulfills equations (a) through (c) for some family $\mathbf{F}$ of subsets of H^ω I shall call ϕ a *projection*. Now I offer as a basic thesis, from which equations I through VI follow:

VII.   An aspect modifier is an operator ϕ^* defined by

$$\phi^*(Z) = \phi(Z)^*$$

for some projection, ϕ, on all (closed) properties Z

The need to use ϕ^* instead of ϕ is clear if we wish to deal with the family of closed properties alone; it must be remembered however that this is mainly a matter of mathematical regimentation.

I shall briefly analyze two examples. Consider the sentence

It is bright (red and hard).

Perhaps no one would say that; perhaps there are no nonartificial examples of this sort. Let us assume that "is red" and "is hard" both have simple comprehensions, $\{\{X\}\}^*$ and $\{\{X'\}\}^*$. Then "is red and hard" has $\{\{X, X'\}\}^*$. Now this is exactly $Z = \{Y : Y$ contains some subset of X and some subset of $X'\}$. The operator ϕ corresponding to "bright(ly)" takes subsets of X_1 into themselves and subsets of X' into Λ; where $X_1 \subseteq X$. Hence

$$\phi(Z) = \{Y : Y \text{ contains } \Lambda \text{ and some subset of } X_1\}^*$$
$$= \{\{X_1, \Lambda\}\}^*$$

So the above sample sentence amounts exactly to

> It is bright red and bright hard.

This is not pure nonsense, it is mixed sense and nonsense; and cannot be true, because the mixture is conjunctive.

As second example, consider then

> It is bright (red or hard).

with the same assumptions about "is red" and so on. Then

$$\text{"is red or hard"} = \{\{X\}, \{X'\}\}^*$$

which is

$$Z' = \{\{X\}\}^* \cup \{\{X'\}\}^*$$
$$= \{Y : Y = \{X_2\} \text{ for some subset } X_2 \text{ of } X \text{ or of } X'\}$$

Hence $\phi(Z') = \{Y : Y = \{\Lambda\} \text{ or } Y = \{X_2\} \text{ for some } X_2 \subseteq X_1\}^*$ but since $\Lambda \subseteq X_1$ also, that means

$$\phi(Z') = \{\{X_2\} : X_2 \subseteq X_1\}^* = \{\{X_1\}\}^*$$

So the sentence amounts to exactly

> It is bright red.

which is the same as

> It is bright red or it is bright hard.

just because we have construed pure nonsense to imply everything (as contradictions would in the modal approach).

This last consequence is probably less welcome than the others; the way to eliminate it is to leave the values of some predicates [for example, $\phi(Z)$ for some Z] undefined. The technical details could be adopted from Thomason's handling of similar problems within an intensional (modal) context.[25] I am prepared to be faced with counterexamples and undesirable consequences; but I hope I have given evidence of the possibility of systematic reconstruction of classes of predicate modifiers in the present framework.

[25] R. H. Thomason, "A Semantic Theory of Sortal Incorrectness," *Journal of Philosophical Logic* 1(1972), pp. 209–258.

Whither Russell's Paradox of Predication?*

NINO B. COCCHIARELLA

Indiana University

Russell's paradox has two forms or versions, one in regard to the class of all classes that are not members of themselves, the other in regard to "the predicate: to be a predicate that cannot be predicated of itself."[1] The first version is formulable in the ideography of Frege's *Grundgesetze der Arithmetik* and shows this system to be inconsistent. The second version, however, is not formulable in this ideography, as Frege himself pointed out in his reply to Russell.[2] Nevertheless, it is essentially the second version of his paradox that leads Russell to avoid it (and others of its ilk) through his theory of types.

The first version is of course the relevant version with respect to any formulation of the theory of types in which membership in a class is the fundamental notion, that is, a formulation utilizing 'ϵ' as a primitive binary predicate constant.[3] However, Russell's theory of types (even ignoring its ramification) is essentially concerned with the notion of predication, and only indirectly through the (philosophically questionable) interpretation of predication as the membership relation is the first version of his paradox relevant to this formulation.

* The Author was partially supported in the research for this paper by NSF grant GS-28605.
[1] "Letter to Frege," reprinted in [10], p. 125.
[2] "Letter to Russell," *ibid.*, p. 128.
[3] Cf. [5], p. 140 for a specific formulation of this kind of type theory.

Apparently, Russell saw his paradox as generating an aporetic situation in regard to two fundamental "notions," namely, the notion of membership (in a class) and the notion of predication (of an attribute).[4] In regard to the notion of membership, the application of Russell's paradox is not here brought into question. However, in regard to the notion of predication, the applicability of the reasoning grounding Russell's paradox will here be very much brought into question. Indeed, I shall claim that in this case the paradox fails.[5]

Paradoxical reasoning, of course, is inapplicable within any "reasonable" system, since an inconsistent system is *eo ipso* "unreasonable." That is not the point. Rather, it is that the original context of the reasoning grounding Russell's paradox of membership involved deep metaphysical assumptions, some logical, such as the principle of excluded middle, and some ontological, namely the comprehension principle for sets, which really are collectively inconsistent. The joint inconsistency of these assumptions does indeed constitute appropriate motivation for philosophical perplexity (*aporia*) regarding the notion of membership in that original context. On the other hand, the metaphysical assumptions (especially in regard to the "nexus" of copulation) of the original context supposedly grounding Russell's paradox of predication are not, I shall want to argue, after all inconsistent; for once we rigorously specify the essential features of the original context within which the reasoning is supposedly codified, we shall see that the reasoning involves a trivial violation of the restrictions imposed for the *proper substitution* of a formula for a predicate variable in the specification law for predicate variables. These restrictions, I shall argue, are essential not because they preserve consistency—which would be an *ad hoc* justification, a charge, I believe, that it is appropriate to make against the theory of types with its restrictions on grammatical well-formedness—but rather because they are the intuitively natural and appropriate restrictions to make when we are dealing with the notion of predication as opposed to that of membership. (It is assumed throughout that these two "notions" are not the same.) The "loosening" of these restrictions required to "validate"

---

[4] Gödel (cf. [6], p. 131f.) distinguishes these two forms of Russell's paradox by referring to them as the "extensional" and the "intensional" forms, respectively. For the purposes of the present paper, this distinction is preferable to Ramsey's different but better known distinction between "logical" and "semantical" paradoxes.

[5] With this failure of course goes a primary if not sole motivation for the simple theory of ontological types of third and higher order. The ontological scheme of second-order logic remains unaffected, having as it does a natural motivation of its own. Ramification also has *its* own motivation, and it may be appended to second-order logic (cf. [2], §58.) even though historically it was first appended to the simple theory of types.

the paradox of predication does not, I believe, result in a collection of philosophical assumptions that constitute appropriate motivation for philosophical perplexity.[6]

I

THE LOGICAL CONTEXT OF RUSSELL'S PARADOX
OF PREDICATION

Russell's formulation of the set-theoretical version of his paradox is applicable to a certain type of logical context, one formulation of which is Frege's *Grundgesetze*.[7] The central notion of such a context is the membership relation.[8] What, on the other hand, is the type of logical context to which supposedly the paradox of predication is applicable? Obviously, one central notion of this type of context is predication *cum* quantifiable predicate variables, and therefore the context involves at least second-order logic. Equally obvious, the context is not that of (simple or ramified) type theory, for the latter is Russell's proposed replacement for that context, since supposedly by his paradox it was shown to be inconsistent. Accordingly, the syntactical representative of the type of logical context in question is somehow an extension of second-order logic but not an extension in the manner of type theory.[9] We are concerned of course with syntax

---

[6] This is not to say, however, that the context of Russell's paradox of predication (formalized below as T* and shown to be consistent) is philosophically unobjectionable—at least certainly not simply because it is consistent after all. Since there is no paradox, such philosophical objections cannot, of course, be construed as "lessons" of the paradox. Rather, they will arise at a conceptionally prior stage, as, for example, the nominalistic objection against allowing quantifiable predicate variables, and will, of course, beg the metaphysical issue in question by presupposing their own ontological paradigm. For myself, I have deep misgivings about allowing attributes a "double existence," one expressed through quantifiable predicate variables (but only in the predicate position—a mode of attribute existence which I do accept), the other expressed through additionally allowing predicate variables to occupy subject or nominal positions, thus construing attributes as a special (though perhaps secondary) breed of individual, the two breeds constituting a "two worlds" ontology.

[7] An alternative but more compact formulation is The Ideal Calculus, K, described in [5], Chapter III, Section 1.

[8] By a "logical context" I mean more than an uninterpreted calculus. The context is syntactically represented when formalized by the construction of a calculus. But the calculus alone is not an adequate representative of this context. What remains is the semantical or ontological background motivating the construction of that calculus.

[9] F. P. Ramsey (cf. [9], pp. 118–120) and R. Grossman (cf. [7]) might object here to standard second-order logic since the comprehension principle for complex attributes is here a theorem, whereas both Ramsey and Grossmann deny that there are complex attributes. However, a primary, if not sole, motive for the denial of complex attributes is to avoid Russell's paradox of predication, and in this regard any formulation of predication *cum* quantifiable predicate variables proposed by such a view is, vis-à-vis the paradox of predication,

(though not with syntactical considerations alone) since it is within a syntactical formulation of the logical context that the paradox is to be derived.

Now, although second-order logic is essentially incomplete, there exist formulations which are at least complete in a secondary sense and within the relevant extension of which Russell's paradox should be derivable if it is derivable at all within the intended logical context. Consider, for example, Church's formulation of the pure functional calculus of second order.[10] For convenience I shall refer to this calculus as the system T. Our question now is: How is T to be extended to a system T* which can be construed as an adequate syntactical representative of the type of logical context in which Russell's paradox of predication is formulable?

Obviously, a minimum requirement for the relevant extension of T is that we extend the notion of (well-formed) formula to allow predicate variables to occupy subject (or nominal) positions as well as predicate positions—for how otherwise could we represent "the predicate: to be a predicate that cannot be predicated of itself"?

Our grammar is specified as follows. We shall assume that there are enumerably infinite and pairwise disjoint sets of variables: individual variables and, for each natural number n, n-place predicate variables. (Propositional variables are 0-place predicate variables.) We shall use 'α', 'β', 'γ' to refer to individual variables, also called *subject terms*, and 'π', 'ρ', 'σ', 'τ' to refer to predicate variables (of arbitrary many places), also called *predicate terms*. We understand a *term* to be either an individual variable (subject term) or a predicate variable (predicate term). We shall use 'μ', 'ν' to refer to terms. As logical particles we shall use $\sim$, the negation sign, $\rightarrow$, the conditional sign, and $\wedge$, the universal quantifier. Other logical particles, such as $\leftrightarrow$, the biconditional sign, and $\vee$, the existential quantifier, are assumed to be defined (as syntactical abbreviations in the metalanguage) in the usual manner. An *atomic formula* is, for some natural number, n, the result of applying an n-place predicate variable π to n terms $\mu_0, \ldots,$ $\mu_{n-1} : \pi(\mu_0, \ldots, \mu_{n-1})$. If $n = 0$, this result is understood to be π itself. (Observe that though a predicate term is not a subject term, a predicate term may occupy a subject position in an atomic formula.

on a par with Russell's proposal of type theory. (And so too is my own preferred view disallowing predicate variables in subject or nominal positions!) That is, such a proposal amounts to a replacement of the original type of logical context to which the paradox of predication supposedly is applicable. Our present concern is not the evaluation of alternatives to this type of context but rather a clarification of its characterization and a reassessment of the reasoning supposedly grounding the paradox of predication within it.

[10] [2], Chapter V. In what is to follow, we shall use a notational style variant to Church's.

A subject term, on the other hand, is not allowed to occupy a predicate position.) A *formula* is any member of the intersection of those sets K containing the atomic formulas and such that $\sim\varphi$, $(\varphi \to \psi)$, $\bigwedge\mu\varphi$ are in K whenever φ, ψ are in K and μ is an individual or predicate variable. We shall use 'φ', 'ψ', 'χ' to refer to formulas. Bondage and freedom of (occurrences of) variables is understood in the usual manner.

We now have the grammatical context for Russell's paradox of predication. Before specifying the transformational context, T*, let us review the informal reasoning grounding the paradox. We quote Russell:

> Let w be the predicate: to be a predicate that cannot be predicated of itself. Can w be predicated of itself? From each answer its opposite follows. Therefore we must conclude that w is not a predicate.[11]

We paraphrase Russell in preferring 'property' to 'predicate'. The statements that there exists and that there does not exist such a property as described by Russell are formulated within the present grammar by

(A) $\bigvee\tau\bigwedge\pi[\tau(\pi) \leftrightarrow \sim\pi(\pi)]$
(B) $\sim\bigvee\tau\bigwedge\pi[\tau(\pi) \leftrightarrow \sim\pi(\pi)]$

respectively, where τ, π are distinct 1-place predicate variables. The presumed argument for expression (B) with respect to the yet-to-be specified transformational system T* seems to be the following:[12]

(1) $\vdash_{T^*}\bigwedge\pi[\tau(\pi) \leftrightarrow \sim\pi(\pi)] \to [\tau(\tau) \leftrightarrow \sim\tau(\tau)]$

by special specification law for predicate variables;

(2) $\vdash_{T^*} \sim [\tau(\tau) \leftrightarrow \sim\tau(\tau)]$

by sentential logic;

(3) $\vdash_{T^*} \sim \bigwedge\pi[\tau(\pi) \leftrightarrow \sim\pi(\pi)]$

by (1), (2) and sentential logic;

(4) $\vdash_{T^*} \bigwedge\tau \sim \bigwedge\pi[\tau(\pi) \leftrightarrow \sim\pi(\pi)]$

[11] *Op. cit.*
[12] We indicate that φ is a theorem of T* by writing '$\vdash_{T^*} \varphi$'. By a theorem of T* we understand any formula terminating a finite sequence of formulas, where each constituent of the sequence is either an axiom of T* or is obtained from preceeding constituents by one of the inference rules of T*.

by (3) and (universal) generalization;

(5) $\vdash_{T^*} \sim \sim \bigwedge \tau \sim \bigwedge \pi [\tau(\pi) \leftrightarrow \sim \pi(\pi)]$

that is,

$\vdash_{T^*} \sim \bigvee \tau \bigwedge \pi [\tau(\pi) \leftrightarrow \sim \pi(\pi)]$

by (4) and sentential logic.

A minimum basis for T* which recognizes the above reasoning can now be described. As inference rules we retain, without regard for redundancy (in T*), the inference rules of T by understanding the latter now to apply to all formulas (as defined by our present grammar) as well as to those that are wffs of T. These are (1) the rule of *modus ponens*, (2) the rule of generalization (applied to predicate and individual variables), (3) the rule of alphabetic change of bound individual variables, and (4) the rule of substitution for individual variables.

We provide a complete basis for the tautologous formulas by stipulating the following to be axiom schemata of T* (thereby extending the sentential axioms of T to all the formulas):

(A1) $\varphi \rightarrow (\psi \rightarrow \varphi)$
(A2) $(\varphi \rightarrow [\psi \rightarrow \chi]) \rightarrow ([\varphi \rightarrow \psi] \rightarrow [\varphi \rightarrow \chi])$
(A3) $(\sim\varphi \rightarrow \sim\psi) \rightarrow (\psi \rightarrow \varphi)$

The confinement laws for the universal quantifier (when applied to both individual and predicate variables) are collapsed into one axiom schema:

(A4) $\bigwedge \mu(\varphi \rightarrow \psi) \rightarrow (\varphi \rightarrow \bigwedge \mu\psi)$

where μ is a predicate or individual variable which does not occur free in φ.

What remains to codify the above argument for (B), the sentence of T* denying the existence of "the Russell property," is a special specification law for predicate variables corresponding to the specification axiom +509 (of T) for individual variables.[13] We shall state this law so as to encompass +509 as well. For its formulation, we understand two variables to be of *the same type* if either both are individual variables or, for some natural number n, both are n-place

---

[13] *Op. cit.*, p. 297.

predicate variables. Where μ, ν are variables, whether of the same type or not, we take

$$\varphi \begin{bmatrix} \mu \\ \nu \end{bmatrix}$$

to be the result of replacing each free occurrence of μ in φ by a free occurence of ν, if such a formula exists; otherwise

$$\varphi \begin{bmatrix} \mu \\ \nu \end{bmatrix}$$

is understood to be φ itself. The special specification axiom replacing +509 of T is now formulated as:

$$(A5) \quad \bigwedge\mu\varphi \to \varphi \begin{bmatrix} \mu \\ \nu \end{bmatrix}$$

where μ, ν are variables of the same type.

By the reasoning in (1) through (5) above, we conclude that so far as T* is concerned, "the Russell property" does not exist:

$$\vdash_{\mathrm{T^*}} \sim \bigvee\tau\bigwedge\pi[\tau(\pi) \leftrightarrow \sim\pi(\pi)]$$

II

The Nondefinability of "The Russell Property"

Let us now consider (A), the sentence of T* affirming the existence of "the Russell property." We note first that the truth of (A) is affirmed by Russell through a simple specification of "the predicate: to be a predicate that cannot be predicated of itself."[14] Most writers on the paradox construe such a specification to be a definition in the object language of a (1-place) predicate constant t, read 'is impredicable'[15]:

$$(C) \quad t(\pi) \leftrightarrow \sim\pi(\pi)$$

Since definitions when construed other than as syntactical abbreviations in the metalanguage amount to additional axioms, expression (C) as an axiom added to T* yields:

$$(D) \quad \bigwedge\pi[t(\pi) \leftrightarrow \sim\pi(\pi)]$$

[14] Throughout we ignore Russell's use of the modal 'cannot (be)' and read 'is not' in its place. Even were the modal to be distinguished through extending T* to include modality, the same issue of trivial violation of proper substitution remains.

[15] Cf. Carnap [1], p. 83 and Hilbert and Ackermann [8], p. 145.

from which (A) follows by existential generalization. Existential generalization here amounts to extending the special specification axiom (A5) to a form (A5') which allows specification to constants of the same type as the generalized predicate variable. It would seem then that the reasoning supposedly grounding expression (A) is to be viewed as being codified within that portion of T* described so far in Section 1 [with the replacement of (A5) by (A5')], which we shall call T_0*, plus the so-called "definitional" axiom (C):

(a) $\vdash_{\overline{T_0*+(C)}} \Lambda\tau \sim \Lambda\pi[\tau(\pi) \leftrightarrow \sim\pi(\pi)] \rightarrow \sim\Lambda\pi[t(\pi) \leftrightarrow \sim\pi(\pi)]$

by special specification axiom (A5');

(b) $\vdash_{\overline{T_0*+(C)}} \Lambda\pi[t(\pi) \leftrightarrow \sim\pi(\pi)]$

by "definition" (C) and generalization; and therefore

(c) $\vdash_{\overline{T_0*+(C)}} \sim\Lambda\tau \sim \Lambda\pi[\tau(\pi) \leftrightarrow \sim\pi(\pi)]$

that is,

$\vdash_{\overline{T_0*+(C)}} V\tau\Lambda\pi[\tau(\pi) \leftrightarrow \sim\pi(\pi)]$

by (a), (b) and sentential logic.

But is (C) a legitimate definition; that is, is T_0* + (C) really a definitional extension of T_0*? One necessary condition for a definition is that it be *noncreative,* and in the present case this means that for any formula φ in which the defined predicate constant t does not occur, if

$\vdash_{\overline{T*+(C)}} \varphi$

then

$\vdash_{\overline{T_0*}} \varphi$

Accordingly, if T_0* + (C) really is a definitional extension of T_0*, then expression (A), as well as (B), is already provable in T_0*, that is, T_0* is inconsistent. The following argument, however, shows to the contrary that T_0* is consistent. Moreover, its consistency can be proved by the same "very elementary syntactical argument"[16] which proves the consistency of T, our present version of standard second-order logic.

In the proof of consistency, we shall associate with each formula φ (of our present grammar) a wff $f(\varphi)$ of the extended propositional

[16] [2], p. 306.

calculus, that is, a wff of T in which occur no variables other than propositional (0-place predicate) variables. We observe that the extended propositional calculus is not only consistent but provides an effective test for validity.[17]

We first characterize the following function g defined recursively on the set of formulas:

(i) $g(\pi(\mu_0, \ldots, \mu_{n-1})) = \pi$

where $\pi(\mu_0, \ldots, \mu_{n-1})$ is an atomic formula

(ii) $g(\sim\varphi) = \sim g(\varphi)$
(iii) $g(\varphi \to \psi) = [g(\varphi) \to g(\psi)]$
(iv) $g(\bigwedge \alpha \varphi) = g(\varphi)$

where α is an individual variable

(v) $g(\bigwedge \pi \varphi) = \bigwedge \pi g(\varphi)$

where π is a predicate variable

Observe that g assigns to each formula an expression which consists only of logical particles and predicate variables. Now since the set of predicate variables is equinumerous with its proper subset of propositional variables (both being of cardinality $\aleph_0$), we have a one-to-one function * correlating different propositional variables with different predicate variables. We define recursively the function h, the domain of which is the range of g:

(i) $h(\pi) = \pi^*$

where π is a predicate variable

(ii) $h(\sim\xi) = \sim h(\xi)$
(iii) $h(\xi \to \theta) = [h(\xi) \to h(\theta)]$
(iv) $h(\bigwedge \pi \xi) = \bigwedge \pi^* h(\xi)$

We now take f to be the relative product g/h, that is, $f(\varphi) = h[g(\varphi)]$, for each formula φ. Quite obviously, if φ is an axiom of T_0^*, then $f(\varphi)$ is a valid formula of the extended propositional calculus. Moreover, each inference rule of T_0^* is easily seen to preserve validity under the transformation f. Accordingly, if

$\vdash_{T_0^*} \varphi$

[17] *Ibid.*

then $f(\varphi)$ is a valid wff of the extended propositional calculus. Therefore, if T_0^* were inconsistent, then the extended propositional calculus would also be inconsistent, which it is not. Accordingly, T_0^* is consistent after all. We conclude then that $T_0^* +$ (C) is not a definitional extension of T_0^*, that is, expression (C) cannot be construed as an innocuous definition.

III

THE NONCOMPREHENSIBILITY OF "THE RUSSELL PROPERTY"

Why should it ever have been thought that expression (C), or its closure (D), was a legitimate definitional form? More specifically, at least relative to our present context, where t is a (1-place) predicate constant and φ is a formula in which t does not occur and whose only free variable is μ, what are the exact conditions under which the formula

(E) $t(\mu) \leftrightarrow \varphi$

(or its closure) can be legitimately construed as a definition (relative to T*), that is, under what necessary and sufficient conditions can T* $+$ (E) be construed as a definitional extension of T*? Obviously, T* $+$ (E) is a definitional extension of T* when and only when

$$\vert_{\overline{T^*}} \; \bigvee\tau\bigwedge\mu[\tau(\mu) \leftrightarrow \varphi]$$

where τ is a 1-place predicate variable distinct from μ and not occurring free in φ. Accordingly, it is not the so-called "definition" (C) of "the Russell property" which shows (A) to be provable in T*. Rather conversely, it is the provability of (A) in T* which would show that (C) can reasonably be construed within the type of logical context in question as a definition of a property, specifically "the Russell property."

Of course, if T*, our representative of the type of logical context in question, were inconsistent, then (A) would be provable in it and therefore (C), relative to T*, would be an "acceptable" definition. Moreover, since T_0^* is a fragment[18] of T*, (B) is provable in T*; and, accordingly, were we to assume (A) as an axiom of T*, we would immediately have its inconsistency. But there is simply no

---

[18] According to the observations made in Section 1, T* is to be an extension of T. But T contains as theorems instances of the comprehension principle for complex properties and these are not provable in T_0^*. Their provability in T requires the general specification laws *509$_0$ and *509$_n$ (*op. cit.*, p. 297), and for these laws some account has yet to be given.

point in assuming the context to be inconsistent only to show that a paradox is provable within it. The logical context of the reasoning supposedly grounding Russell's paradox of predication cannot be based simply on the assumption of (A) as an axiom—not at least without surrendering its philosophical significance—unless that assumption is a consequence of a more general principle comprehending the conditions under which a formula is understood to "determine" or "represent" a property. Clearly, the correct characterization of such a principle is the central difficulty in the specification of the system T*.

We note that in regard to the system T, standard second-order logic, such a principle has already been appropriately characterized. Specifically, it is the principle which concerns the conditions under which a formula may be construed as a substituend of a generalized predicate variable. For, as, and only as, such a substituend does it "represent" a value of that predicate variable. Accordingly, it is the general specification law for predicate variables which comprehends the conditions under which a formula is understood to "determine" or "represent" a property. For the wffs of T, the law is schematized as:

$$\bigwedge \pi \psi \rightarrow \check{S}^{\pi(\alpha_0 \dots, \alpha_{n-1})}_{\varphi} \psi|$$

where π is an n-place predicate variable and $\alpha_0, \dots, \alpha_{n-1}$ are distinct individual variables.[19] Note that from this axiom schema we are able to derive the comprehension principle for properties. For since

$$\check{S}^{\pi(\alpha)}_{\varphi} \sim \bigwedge \alpha[\pi(\alpha) \leftrightarrow \varphi]| = \sim\bigwedge\alpha[\varphi \leftrightarrow \varphi]$$

where π is not free in φ, then

$$|_{\overline{T}} \bigwedge \pi \sim\bigwedge\alpha[\pi(\alpha) \leftrightarrow \phi] \rightarrow \sim\bigwedge\alpha[\phi \leftrightarrow \phi]$$

by the general specification axiom for predicate variables, and therefore:

$$|_{\overline{T}} \bigvee\pi\bigwedge\alpha[\pi(\alpha) \leftrightarrow \varphi]$$

The question now is: How are we to extend in an intuitive and natural way the notion of the proper substitution of a formula for a predicate variable so that we can apply the notion to all formulas as well as the wffs of T? Needless to say, the extension of this notion is not to violate the distinguishing feature of predication as reflected

[19] Cf. [2], p. 297.

by our grammar, namely, the distinction between subject positions on the one hand and predicate positions on the other. To nullify this distinction by construing predicate positions as "argument" positions on a par with subject positions is to depart from predication as our central concept and to turn rather to membership or a membership type of *relation*.[20]

Because of notational differences, we paraphrase rather than directly quote Church's definition of substitution for T.[21] In doing so, however, we shall understand

$$\varphi \begin{bmatrix} \mu_0 & \cdots & \mu_{n-1} \\ \nu_0 & \cdots & \nu_{n-1} \end{bmatrix}$$

to be the result of *simultaneously* replacing all the free occurrences of $\mu_0, \ldots, \mu_{n-1}$ in φ by free occurrences of $\nu_0, \ldots, \nu_{n-1}$, respectively, if such a formula exists; otherwise it is φ itself.

If π is an n-place predicate variable and $\alpha_0, \ldots, \alpha_{n-1}$ are distinct individual variables, then

$$\check{S}^{\pi(\alpha_0, \ldots, \alpha_{n-1})}_{\varphi} \psi|$$

shall be ψ unless the following conditions are satisfied: (1) no free occurrence of π (in predicate position) in ψ occurs within a subformula of ψ of the form $\bigwedge \mu \chi$, where μ is a predicate or individual variable distinct from $\alpha_0, \ldots, \alpha_{n-1}$ and occurring free in φ; and (2) for all individual variables $\beta_0, \ldots, \beta_{n-1}$, if $\pi(\beta_0, \ldots, \beta_{n-1})$ occurs in ψ in such a way that the occurrence of π is a free occurrence, then for each $i < n$, there is no subformula of φ of the form $\bigwedge \beta_i \chi$ in which α_i has a free occurrence. If these two conditions are satisfied, then

$$\check{S}^{\pi(\alpha_0, \ldots, \alpha_{n-1})}_{\varphi} \psi|$$

is the result of replacing, for arbitrary individual variables $\beta_0, \ldots, \beta_{n-1}$, each occurrence of $\pi(\beta_0, \ldots, \beta_{n-1})$ in ψ at which π is free by an occurrence of

$$\varphi \begin{bmatrix} \alpha_0, & \ldots, & \alpha_{n-1} \\ \beta_0, & \ldots, & \beta_{n-1} \end{bmatrix}.$$

If we extend this notion of substitution so that it applies to our broader notion of what a formula is, we observe that clause (1)

---

[20] What Grossmann (*op. cit*) calls "exemplification" is an example of such a membership type of relation.
[21] *Op. cit.*, p. 192 f.

remains quite appropriate as it is and requires no addition. Clause (2), to the contrary, does. We replace clause (2) by:

(2′)   for all *terms* (predicate or individual variables) μ_0, . . . , μ_{n-1}, if $\pi(\mu_0, \ldots, \mu_{n-1})$ occurs in ψ in such a way that the occurrence of π is a free occurrence, then for each $i < n$, there is no subformula of φ of the form $\bigwedge \mu_i \chi$ in which α_i has a free occurrence.

When conditions (1) and (2′) are satisfied, we take the substitution to be the result of replacing, for arbitrary *terms* (predicate or individual variables) μ_0, . . . , μ_{n-1}, each occurrence of $\pi(\mu_0, \ldots, \mu_{n-1})$ in ψ at which π is free by an occurrence of

$$\varphi \begin{bmatrix} \alpha_0, & \ldots, & \alpha_{n-1} \\ \mu_0, & \ldots, & \mu_{n-1} \end{bmatrix}.$$

We observe that the restrictions regarding proper substitution, that is, the two restrictions, (1) and (2′), are required in order to avoid a "clash" of bound and free variables. The first restriction makes the reasonable demand that other than the indicated *subject terms* α_0, . . . , α_{n-1}, no variable free in φ, the substituend, is to become bound upon the substitution of φ (relative to the subject terms α_0, . . . , α_{n-1}) for π in ψ. This restriction is already essential even for standard second-order logic. The second restriction, however, requires that no subject or predicate term occupying, say, the kth subject position of a free occurrence of π in ψ becomes bound when that term replaces a free occurrence in φ of its associated subject term α_k. That this restriction should apply to predicate as well as subject terms occupying subject or "argument" positions of a free occurrence of π is a natural requirement, once we allow predicate terms to occupy subject positions. The restrictions then are quite in order.

Accordingly, we replace axioms *509$_0$ and *509$_n$ of T by a single axiom schema:

(A6) $\bigwedge \pi \psi \rightarrow \overset{\vee}{S}{}^{\pi(\alpha_0, \ldots, \alpha_{n-1})}_{\varphi} \psi \mid$

where π is a n-place predicate variable and α_0, . . . , α_{n-1} are distinct individual variables

We have now accounted for and replaced every axiom (and inference rule) of T by an analogue appropriate to all the formulas and not just the wffs of T. The system resulting from T by this replacement is $T_0^* + (A6)$. The question now is: Is $T_0^* + (A6)$ an *adequate* syntactical representative of the logical context within which the reasoning supposedly grounding Russell's paradox of predication is to be represented? That is, is $T^* = T_0^* + (A6)$?

In evaluating this question, let us note that the notation:

$$\breve{S}^{\pi(\alpha_0, \ldots, \alpha_{n-1})}_{\varphi} \psi \mid$$

is not defined when $\alpha_0, \ldots, \alpha_{n-1}$ are not all of them (distinct) *free subject terms* (individual variables) of φ.[22] In other words, predicate terms are not allowed to indicate the "argument" positions of our formula substituends.

In order to see why this should be so within the context in question consider the attempt to prove (A), the formula of T^* affirming the existence of "the Russell property," in a manner analogous to our proof above of the comprehension principle in T for properties. If we were to grant the initial step of this proof, namely,

$$\bigwedge \tau \sim \bigwedge \pi[\tau(\pi) \leftrightarrow \sim\pi(\pi)] \to \sim\bigwedge\pi[\sim\pi(\pi) \leftrightarrow \sim\pi(\pi)]$$

then expression (A) would follow as a trivial consequence. It is quite obvious, of course, that this initial step cannot be justified by (A5) since the substitution of $\sim\pi$ for τ in $\sim\bigwedge\pi[\tau(\pi) \leftrightarrow \sim\pi(\pi)]$ results in replacing a free occurrence of τ by a bound occurrence of π. In addition, of course, (A5) applies only to terms and $\sim\pi$ is not a term. The relevant law here, if any, is not (A5) but (A6), where supposedly we are to substitute $\sim\pi(\alpha)$ for τ. But

$$\breve{S}^{\tau(\alpha)}_{\sim\pi(\alpha)} \sim \bigwedge\pi[\tau(\pi) \leftrightarrow \sim\pi(\pi)] \mid$$

---

[22] This is not entirely correct in that $\alpha_0, \ldots, \alpha_{n-1}$, on the definition given, are not required to even occur no less occur free in φ. This, however, is merely a matter of logical economy. For in place of φ we can always put $(\varphi \wedge \alpha_0 = \alpha_0 \wedge \ldots \wedge \alpha_{n-1} = \alpha_{n-1})$ and then interchange (as based on provable equivalence) in the substitution result all occurrences of

$$(\wedge \alpha_0 = \alpha_0 \wedge \ldots \wedge \alpha_{n-1} = \alpha_{n-1}) \begin{bmatrix} \alpha_0 \cdots \alpha_{n-1} \\ \mu_0 \cdots \mu_{n-1} \end{bmatrix}$$

that replaced an occurrence of $\pi(\mu_0, \ldots, \mu_{n-1})$ in ψ by

$$\varphi \begin{bmatrix} \alpha_0 \cdots \alpha_{n-1} \\ \mu_0 \cdots \mu_{n-1} \end{bmatrix}$$

Identity is understood to be defined as follows:

$$\mu = \nu = df \wedge \sigma[\sigma(\mu) \leftrightarrow \sigma(\nu)]$$

where σ is the first 1-place predicate variable distinct from μ and ν.

is not identical with $\sim\bigwedge\pi[\sim\pi(\pi) \leftrightarrow \sim\pi(\pi)]$, for π occurs free in $\sim\pi(\alpha)$ but becomes bound in the replacement of $\tau(\pi)$ by

$$\sim\pi(\alpha) \begin{bmatrix} \alpha \\ \pi \end{bmatrix}$$

in the formula $\sim\bigwedge\pi[\tau(\pi) \leftrightarrow \sim\pi(\pi)]$. In this case we have a violation of our first restriction, namely, clause (1), which was designed to prevent just such a "clash" of variables. However, because π is not a *subject term* (individual variable), even though in $\sim\pi(\pi)$ it occupies a subject position, we cannot construe the substitution to be:

$$\overset{\vee}{S}{}^{\tau(\pi)}_{\sim\pi(\pi)} \sim \bigwedge\pi[\tau(\pi) \leftrightarrow \sim\pi(\pi)] \mid$$

since substitution in this case is not defined. Note, however, that if it were defined, in this case we would have a conflict between the occurrence of π in the subject position and the occurrence of π in the predicate position in $\sim\pi(\pi)$. For, intuitively the occurrence of π in the subject position would be allowed to become bound upon substitution,[23] whereas the occurrence of π in the predicate position would not. The reason for this last claim is that the replacement of $\tau(\pi)$ by $\sim\pi(\pi)$ by "substituting" $\sim\pi(\pi)$ for τ in $\sim\bigwedge\pi[\tau(\pi) \leftrightarrow \sim\pi(\pi)]$ would be the same replacement of $\tau(\pi)$ by $\sim\pi(\pi)$ except by *improperly* substituting $\sim\pi(\alpha)$ for τ in the same formula. The two substitutions do exactly the same job except that there is readily recognized to be a "clash" of variables in the one, and therefore this substitution is improper, but supposedly (?) there is no "clash" of variables in the other, and therefore this substitution would be said to be proper. Indeed, this is essentially the point of our not defining substitution where the "argument" positions of the substituend are allowed to be occupied by predicate variables. Every substitution effected by allowing predicate terms to indicate the subject positions, construed as the "argument" positions of the substituend, can also be effected by allowing only subject terms to indicate these same "argument" positions. The real difference between the two is that, where some substitutions of the latter kind indicate a clear "clash" of variables and therefore are *improper*, their corresponding substitutions of the former kind fail to indicate the "clash" of variables involved and therefore would be unreasonably recognized as proper. The two substitutions do the same job, except that the one shows itself to be improper, whereas the other fails to do so. Our procedure has been to discriminate in favor of those

---

[23] Note that in the definition of substitution the variables indicating the "argument" positions in the substituend are allowed to be bound in the formula resulting by proper substitution of that substituend.

that indicate "clashes" of variables that intuitively are really there in the logical context in question.

Now I do not believe that our discrimination here is adventitious. There is, I should like to argue, an ontological basis for it. Furthermore, this basis is to be found in the ontological background implicit in the logical context in question.

IV

THE ONTOLOGICAL BACKGROUND OF RUSSELL'S PARADOX OF PREDICATION

In discussing the ontological background of T* let us note that within it there is an explicit ontological distinction being made analogous to that of Aristotle's between primary and secondary being (*ousia*). Retaining this terminology somewhat, we shall call *primary* those "individuals" of the background ontology which can be a value of an individual variable but which cannot be a value of a predicate variable. The remaining "individuals" of the ontology we shall call *secondary individuals*.

Now it may seem dubious to refer to the nonprimary individuals as "individuals" even if they are secondary. Propositions, properties, and attributes, in general, are not normally thought of as "individuals." Propositions are the kind of entity that is asserted, denied, believed, known, conjectured (whether), and so on, in short the kind of entity that is represented only by a complete sentence or formula. Similarly, properties and attributes are the kind of entity that is predicated, ascribed, attributed, that is, the kind of entity that is represented only by predicate expressions (complex or otherwise). All this may be so, and the background ontology of T* agrees up to a point. What this ontology explicitly denies, however, is that propositions, properties, and attributes can be represented only by sentence and predicate forms, respectively. Propositional (0-place predicate) variables are allowed to occur not only in propositional contexts as whole formulas but also in subject or argument positions of predicate variables. Similarly, property (1-place predicate) variables and attribute (*n*-place predicate) variables, in general, are allowed to occur not only in predicate positions but also in subject positions of themselves as well as of other predicates. Accordingly, predicate variables are being construed as substituends of individual variables, and the values of predicate variables are therefore also values of the individual variables. It is in this fact of the grammar we have constructed as a syntactical representative of this background ontology that we are confronted with an extension of the usual view of the nature of propositions, properties, and attributes. Actually, however, it is more an extension of the notion of *individuality:* the characteristic of being that type of entity for which it is ontologically significant that *it* be a subject of predication, that is, that type of entity which can be *referred to* through the subject expressions of the sentences and formulas of the ontological language in question.

Now it is a noteworthy fact of the constructed grammar that a proposition is entified *qua* proposition and that in general an *n*-ary attribute is entified *qua* being an *n*-ary attribute only through quantification binding distinct types of predicate variable, specifically 0-place predicate variables for propositions and *n*-place predicate variables for *n*-ary attributes. Consequently, implicit in the background ontology of T* is the assumption that what we have called the secondary individuals do not form a unified ontological category *qua* secondary individuals. Otherwise, the grammar should include a generic type of predicate variable or some such logical element designating or having as its values all and only the secondary individuals. Though less obvious, a similar observation applies to the primary individuals.[24]

However, what is also implicit in the background ontology is that the "individuals," the primary and secondary individuals together, do form just such a unified ontological category. This ontological category is represented in our grammar by allowing any term to occupy any subject position of any predicate variable. The category of being of the values of terms that occupy subject positions is comprehended through quantification binding variables whose essential feature is to represent and to represent no more than the being of a "subject," an individual. What we have called individual variables are exactly such variables as described. No external meaning—especially from the point of view of an ontology construed as an alternative to that grounding T*, for example, the point of view of the theory of types, which, at least for Russell, replaced the point of view of the ontology of T*—should be given to our use of 'individual' here.

If this assessment of T*'s ontological background is correct, then the conditions under which a formula "determines" or "represents" an attribute, that is, the conditions under which the formula might be said to "define" an attribute, must be conditions comprehending

---

[24] Accordingly, the ontological content of our generic phrase 'secondary individual', as well as that of 'primary individual', is not expressible in T*. Our present perspective, however, is that of general metaphysics and we shall allow ourselves phraseology not permitted in the logistic system T* whose purpose is to be an adequate syntactical representative of the logical context to which supposedly Russell's paradox of predication is applicable.

all the individuals, both primary and secondary. Each attribute must result in a proposition when "applied" or attributed to *any* individual (or n-tuple of individuals if the attribute is n-ary). The resulting proposition will either be or not be the case, though it may be either on ontological grounds.[25] In effect, the relevant "argument" positions of open formulas defining attributes must be occupied only by subject terms (individual variables). Thus "the Russell property," not being "determined" or "represented" by a definiens, which can be significantly predicated in T* of either primary individuals or secondary individuals other than properties, fails to exist as a property in the ontology of T*.

Let us note that every proposition, property, or attribute which can be "determined" or "represented" by a formula of T* is so determined by the comprehension principle for attributes. This principle is already provable in T_0* + (A6) in exactly the same manner described earlier for T; where φ is a formula and $\alpha_0, \ldots, \alpha_{n-1}$ are all (or even, only some of) the distinct *individual* variables (*subject terms*) occurring free in φ (regardless of the order of their occurrence in φ), then

(CP) $\big|_{\overline{T_0^* + (A6)}} \; \bigvee \pi \bigwedge \alpha_0 \ldots \bigwedge \alpha_{n-1}[\pi(\alpha_0, \ldots, \alpha_{n-1}) \leftrightarrow \varphi]$

where π is an n-place predicate variable which does not occur free in φ.

Observe that no instance of this comprehension principle can be construed as affirming the existence of "the Russell property." For, although an individual variable has all the properties among its values, the variable itself still cannot occupy a predicate position; that is, $\bigvee \pi \bigwedge \alpha[\pi(\alpha) \leftrightarrow \sim \alpha(\alpha)]$ is not a formula according to the grammar of the logical context in question. And the reason for this is precisely our respect for the distinction between predication and membership or any membership type of relation. Indeed, predication is not to be construed as a *relation* at all, and the singular way our present grammar has of expressing ("showing forth") this "ontological fact" is through distinguishing *subject terms* (individual variables) from *predicate terms* (predicate variables) and by refusing to allow subject terms to occupy predicate positions. Were prediction to be misconstrued as being a relation, there would be no ontological point to the grammatical

---

[25] For example, consider the property of being an n-nary attribute:

$$\Pi_n(\alpha) \; = \; df \; \bigvee \pi \bigwedge \sigma[\sigma(\alpha) \leftrightarrow \sigma(\pi)]$$

where π is an n-place predicate variable and σ is the first 1-place predicate variable distinct from π (in case $n = 1$). This property on ontological grounds will be only falsely attributable to primary individuals or secondary individuals other than n-ary attributes.

distinctions we have made, and Russell's paradox of predication would be but a "funny" way of expressing his paradox of membership.[26]

Finally, we may return to our original inquiry regarding whether $T_0^* + (A6)$ is an adequate syntactical representative of the logical context within which the reasoning supposedly grounding Russell's paradox of predication is to be represented, that is, our inquiry whether $T^* = T_0^* + (A6)$.

Now, in so far as $T_0^* + (A6)$ fails to fully express the ontological fact of T^* that every proposition, property, and attribute in general is an *individual* of the background ontology, that is, that it is a value of a bindable individual variable, our response here must be in the negative. One way of supplementing $T_0^* + (A6)$ with this additional ontological content is by stipulating that whatever is true of every individual is therefore true of every secondary individual of any specifiable type as a value of a predicate variable of that type:

$$(A7) \quad \bigwedge \alpha \phi \to \bigwedge \pi \phi \begin{bmatrix} \alpha \\ \pi \end{bmatrix}$$

where α is an individual variable and π is any predicate variable which does not occur in ϕ. With the desired additional content expressed in this manner, we may finally identify T^* as the system $T_0^* + (A6) + (A7)$. Russell's paradox of predication, of course, is no longer derivable in its original form since that form involves, as we have seen, a violation of the restrictions imposed for the proper substitution of a formula for a predicate variable in the specification law (A6). Nevertheless, these restrictions, I have argued, are intuitively natural and appropriate from the perspective of the ontology of the type of logical context in question.

Incidentally, it is noteworthy to point out here that relative to the fragment $T_0^* + (A7)$, the comprehension principle (CP) and the

---

[26] Predication as an ontological category amounts to what I have called the category of *modes of copulation* [3]. In the present grammar only two unary modes, misconstrued nominally as "truth" and "falsity," are represented, the latter by $\sim$, and the former by an implicit interpretation of the concatenation factor between a predicate and its argument expressions. (The addition of a "modal" operator corresponding to the English 'It is true that' would be redundant here. Notice how this redundancy (and the redundancy of any finite iteration of such an operator) along with the view that predication is not a relation answers Bradley's infinite regress argument for predication!) Extensionalists, of course, deny that there are any unary modes of copulation other than truth and falsity and that all n-ary modes, for $n > 1$, are truth-functional (a thesis not being challenged in the present paper). Needless to say, truth and falsity so construed are not to be confused with *semantic* truth and falsity, the latter being *properties of sentences* (and dependent in their analysis on the former).

specification law (A6) for predicate variables determine the same logical conditions; that is, the systems $T_0^* + (A6) + (A7)$ and $T_0^* + (A7) + (CP)$ are equivalent. This shows that the relationship between the comprehension principle (CP) and the specification law (A6) is really about as intimate as I have indicated.[27]

V

THE CONSISTENCY OF T*

It may be thought that all of our formal reconstruction comes to naught, for do we not now have a variant of Russell's argument in which rather than "the predicate: to be a predicate that cannot be predicated of itself" we consider that property: *to be an individual which is identical* (in the sense of having all properties in common) *with a property which that individual does not have?*[28] The existence of such a property is guaranteed in the ontology of T* by the comprehension principle (CP):

$$\vdash_{\overline{T^*}} \bigvee\tau\bigwedge\alpha[\tau(\alpha) \leftrightarrow \bigvee\pi(\alpha = \pi \wedge \sim\pi(\alpha))]$$

where identity is understood to be as it is defined in footnote 22.

[27] The equivalence can be shown in the manner indicated in [4] where it is proved that (CP) and (A6) as formulated for T, standard second-order logic, determine the same logical conditions relative to the remaining axioms of T. Moreover, by utilizing essentially the same arguments of [4] we can prove T* to be equivalent to a substitution free axiomatization the only inference rule of which is *modus ponens*. The axioms of this substitution free axiom set are all (universal) generalizations of all instances of (A1) through (A3), (CP), and formulas of the following forms (where identity is understood as defined in footnote 22):

$$\bigwedge\mu(\phi \to \psi) \ \to \ (\bigwedge\mu\phi \to \bigwedge\mu\psi)$$
$$\phi \to \bigwedge\mu\phi$$

where μ is a predicate or individual variable which does not occur (free) in ϕ,

$$\bigvee\alpha\mu = \alpha$$

where μ is a predicate or individual variable distinct from α,

$$\bigvee\pi\sigma = \pi$$

where π, σ are distinct n-place predicate variables,

$$\mu = \nu \to (\phi \to \psi)$$

where ϕ, ψ are atomic formulas and ψ is obtained from ϕ by replacing an occurrence of ν in *subject position* by an occurrence of μ.

[28] This version of Russell's argument was first suggested to me by Professor Max Zorn.

We note that by (A7), that is, the thesis that every property is an individual,

$$\vdash_{T^*} \Lambda\alpha[\tau(\alpha) \leftrightarrow \bigvee\pi(\alpha = \pi \wedge \sim\pi(\alpha))] \to [\tau(\tau) \leftrightarrow \bigvee\pi(\tau = \pi \wedge \sim\pi(\tau))]$$

and therefore by generalization and distribution over a conditional of a universal into an existential quantifier:

$$\vdash_{T^*} \bigvee\tau\Lambda\alpha[\tau(\alpha) \leftrightarrow \bigvee\pi(\alpha = \pi \wedge \sim\pi(\alpha))] \to \bigvee\tau[\tau(\tau) \leftrightarrow \bigvee\pi(\tau = \pi \wedge \sim\pi(\tau))]$$

That is, within the ontology of T* there is a property which has itself if and only if it is identical with a property which it does not have:

$$\vdash_{T^*} \bigvee\tau[\tau(\tau) \leftrightarrow \bigvee\pi(\tau = \pi \wedge \sim\pi(\tau))]$$

The claim that such a result is counterintuitive presupposes the principle that identical properties are co-extensive:

$$(Id^*) \quad \Lambda\pi\Lambda\tau(\pi = \tau \to \Lambda\alpha[\pi(\alpha) \leftrightarrow \tau(\alpha)])$$

For, by (Id*), any property identical with a property which it does not have *eo ipso* does not have itself. That is, since

$$\vdash_{T^*+(Id^*)} \tau = \pi \to [\tau(\tau) \leftrightarrow \pi(\tau)]$$

by (Id*), (A5), and (A7), then

$$\vdash_{T^*+(Id^*)} \bigvee\pi(\tau = \pi \wedge \sim\pi(\tau)) \to \sim\tau(\tau)$$

by generalization, (A4) and sentential logic.
But within T*, by law (A5), any property which possesses every property with which it is identical therefore possesses itself:

$$\vdash_{T^*} \Lambda\pi(\tau = \pi \to \pi(\tau)) \to \tau(\tau)$$

and therefore by contraposition

$$\vdash_{T^*} \sim\tau(\tau) \to \bigvee\pi(\tau = \pi \wedge \sim\pi(\tau)) \quad \text{[29]}$$

---

[29] We might note as an incidental consequence of this last theorem that the property of being an individual identical with a property which that individual does not have is a property which possesses itself; and therefore since, by (CP), this property exists in T*, we have $\bigvee\tau\tau(\tau)$ as a theorem of T*.

Accordingly, given (Id*), a property is identical with a property which it does not have if and only if that property does not have itself:

$$\Big|_{\overline{T^*+(Id^*)}} \sim\tau(\tau) \leftrightarrow \mathsf{V}\pi(\tau = \pi \wedge \sim\pi(\tau))$$

And therefore, by sentential logic, generalization, and quantifier negation, within T* + (Id*) there is no property which has itself if and only if it is identical with a property which it does not have:

$$\Big|_{\overline{T^*+(Id^*)}} \sim\mathsf{V}\tau[\tau(\tau) \leftrightarrow \mathsf{V}\pi(\tau = \pi \wedge \sim\pi(\tau))]$$

But, as I have shown above, there is such a property within T* and therefore also within T* + (Id*). Consequently, T* + (Id*) is inconsistent. Or, equivalently, ($\sim$Id*) is a theorem of T*.[30]

Although such a result is contradictory within the ontological framework of type theory, it really is very much in accordance with the ontological framework of T*, at least in regard to some of its consequences. For according to the ontological background of T*, *predication is not a relation*, and within T* this significant ontological fact is actually implied by ($\sim$Id*). The proof is as follows, where $\sim\mathsf{V}\rho\wedge\pi\wedge\alpha[\rho(\pi, \alpha) \leftrightarrow \pi(\alpha)]$, since it denies the existence of any relation which is coextensive with predication, is understood to express in T* the ontological fact that predication is not a relation. We have first by (A6):

$$\Big|_{\overline{T^*}} \wedge\sigma[\sigma(\pi) \leftrightarrow \sigma(\tau)] \rightarrow \mathsf{S}^{\sigma(\beta)}_{\rho(\beta,\alpha)}[\sigma(\pi) \leftrightarrow \sigma(\tau)] \Big|$$

that is,

$$\Big|_{\overline{T^*}} \pi = \tau \rightarrow [\rho(\pi, \alpha) \leftrightarrow \rho(\tau, \alpha)]$$

and therefore

$$\Big|_{\overline{T^*}} \pi = \tau \rightarrow \wedge\alpha[\rho(\pi, \alpha) \leftrightarrow \rho(\tau, \alpha)]$$

by generalization, (A4), and sentential logic; but then

$$\Big|_{\overline{T^*}} \wedge\pi\wedge\alpha[\rho(\pi, \alpha) \leftrightarrow \pi(\alpha)] \rightarrow (\pi = \tau \rightarrow \wedge\alpha[\pi(\alpha) \leftrightarrow \tau(\alpha)])$$

---

[30] A similar argument applies to relations of arbitrary many places. For example, in the case of a binary relation (CP) guarantees

$$\Big|_{\overline{T^*}} \mathsf{V}\rho\wedge\alpha\wedge\beta[\rho(\alpha, \beta) \leftrightarrow \mathsf{V}\sigma(\alpha = \sigma \wedge \sim\sigma(\alpha, \beta))]$$

But with Id* extended to apply to binary relations as well—call it Id₂*—we can show that no such relation exists in T* + (Id₂*) and, accordingly, that ($\sim$Id₂*) is a theorem of T*.

It is noteworthy, however, that apparently Idₙ*, for each natural number *n,* is disprovable in T* only for (*n*-ary) attributes of a rather peculiarly "self-reflexive" and impredicative kind.

by (A5) and elementary quantificational logic, and therefore

$$\vdash_{\overline{T*}} \wedge\rho\wedge\pi\wedge\alpha[\rho(\pi,\ \alpha) \leftrightarrow \pi(\alpha)] \rightarrow (\text{Id}^*)$$

by generalization, distribution over a conditional of a universal into an existential quantifier, and deletion of a vacuous quantifier. But since $(\sim\text{Id}^*)$ is a theorem of T*, it follows that

$$\vdash_{\overline{T*}} \sim\vee\rho\wedge\pi\wedge\alpha[\rho(\pi,\ \alpha) \leftrightarrow \pi(\alpha)] \quad {}^{31}$$

Aside from yielding such desirable consequences as the above and thereby being of positive significance to T*, the claim that $(\sim\text{Id}^*)$ cannot consistently be a theorem of T* is simply false. For the consistency of T* is easily shown by the same "very elementary syntactical argument" which proves the consistency of T and which earlier we utilized to prove the consistency of T_0^*. And this is the case because, by definition of the transformation of any formula of T* into a formula of the extended propositional calculus, the transform of any instance of (A7), being a conditional whose consequent is a vacuous quantification of its antecedent, clearly results in a valid formula. Similarly, the transform of any instance of the comprehension principle for T* results in an instance of the comprehension principle for the extended propositional calculus; and therefore $T_0^* + (A7) + (CP)$ is consistent. But, because this system is equivalent to T*, it follows that T* is consistent.[32]

In addition, we might note that the following version of the axiom of choice is formulable in T*:

$$(\text{AC}^*) \quad \wedge\alpha\vee\pi\phi \rightarrow \vee\rho\wedge\alpha\check{S}^{\pi(\beta_0,\ ...,\ \beta_{n-1})}_{\rho(\alpha,\beta_0,\ ...,\ \beta_{n-1})}\phi \;\vert$$

[31] A similar argument utilizing (Id_n^*) shows that $\sim\vee\rho\wedge\pi\wedge\alpha_0 \ldots \wedge\alpha_{n-1}$ $[\rho(\pi, \alpha_0, \ldots, \alpha_{n-1}) \leftrightarrow \pi(\alpha_0, \ldots, \alpha_{n-1})]$ is a theorem of T*.
[32] Without going through the consistency of the equivalent system $T_0^* + (A7) + (CP)$, a more direct proof of T*'s consistency utilizes the lemma that if

$$\check{S}^{\pi(\alpha_0,\ ...,\ \alpha_{n-1})}_{\phi}\psi \;\vert\; \neq \psi$$

then

$$f(\check{S}^{\pi(\alpha_0,\ ...,\ \alpha_{n-1})}_{\phi}\psi \;\vert) = \check{S}^{\pi^*}_{f(\phi)}f(\psi) \;\vert$$

This lemma is proved by a simple inductive argument on the structure of ϕ. From this lemma it follows that the transform of any instance of (A6) is an instance of the general specification law of the extended propositional calculus.

where α, β_0, . . . , β_{n-1} are distinct individual variables, π is an n-place predicate variable, ρ is an $(n + 1)$-place predicate variable, and ϕ contains no bound occurrences of either ρ or α.[33]

Furthermore, since the transformation into the extended propositional calculus of the antecedent of any instance of (AC*) differs from the transformation of its consequent by an alphabetic change of a bound propositional variable, it follows that the transform of such an instance is valid ; and therefore T* + (AC*) is consistent, but again proved to be so within a decidable fragment of elementary syntax.

In regard, however, to the addition to T* (or T* + (AC*)) of an axiom of infinity, such as

$$\text{(inf)} \quad \bigvee\pi(\bigwedge\alpha\bigvee\beta\pi(\alpha, \beta) \wedge \bigwedge\alpha \sim \pi(\alpha, \alpha) \wedge \bigwedge\alpha\bigwedge\beta\bigwedge\gamma[\pi(\alpha, \beta) \wedge \pi(\beta, \gamma) \rightarrow \pi(\alpha, \gamma)])$$

the situation is somewhat different. For the negation of the transform of (inf) is valid in the extended propositional calculus. Therefore, T* + ($\sim$inf), with or without (AC*), is consistent; that is, (inf) is not provable in T*, with or without (AC*). Consequently, establishing the consistency of T* + (inf) requires a different type of proof.

VI

T* IS A CONSERVATIVE EXTENSION OF T

One significant syntactical difference between (inf) and (AC*) is that the former but not all instances of the latter is a wff of T, and T + (inf), as is well-known, is consistent. Accordingly, to show that T* + (inf) is consistent it more than suffices to show that T* is a conservative extension of T, that is, that any theorem of T* which is a wff of T is already a theorem of T. For in that case, if T* + (inf) were inconsistent, then ($\sim$inf) would be a theorem of T* and therefore a theorem of T, which, by the existence of finite models of T, we know it not to be. Such an argument shows, of course, the much stronger result that any wff of T which is consistent in T is therefore a formula which is consistent in T*.[34]

We note first that the cardinality of the set of terms of T*, that is, of the set of all predicate and individual variables together, is $\aleph_0\aleph_0$,

---

[33] Cf. [2], p. 131.
[34] The argument that T* is a conservative extension of T was communicated to me by my colleagues Robert Meyer and Max Zorn independent of each other.

which by infinite cardinal arithmetic is $\aleph_0$, and, accordingly, there exists a one-to-one correspondence between all the terms and the individual variables. For convenience, let $\bar{\mu}$, where μ is a predicate or individual variable, be the individual variable associated with μ under such a one-to-one correspondence. We define recursively the function s whose domain is the set of formulas of T* and whose value for any such formula is a wff of T:

(i) $s(\pi(\mu_0, \ldots, \mu_{n-1})) = \pi(\bar{\mu}_0, \ldots, \bar{\mu}_{n-1})$

(ii) $s(\sim\phi) = \sim s(\phi)$

(iii) $s(\phi \to \psi) = (s(\phi) \to s(\psi))$

(iv) $s(\bigwedge\alpha\phi) = \bigwedge\bar{\alpha}s(\phi)$

(v) $s(\bigwedge\pi\phi) = \bigwedge\bar{\pi}\bigwedge\pi s(\phi)$

The claim now is that for any formula ϕ, if $\vdash_{\mathrm{T}^*} \phi$, then $\vdash_{\mathrm{T}} s(\phi)$. Obviously, if ϕ is an axiom of T* by (A1) though (A4), then $s(\phi)$ is an axiom of T for the same reason. In regard to (A5), we note that

$$s\left(\bigwedge\alpha\phi \to \phi\left[\begin{array}{c}\alpha\\\beta\end{array}\right]\right) = \left(\bigwedge\bar{\alpha}s(\phi) \to s(\phi)\left[\begin{array}{c}\bar{\alpha}\\\bar{\beta}\end{array}\right]\right)$$

$$s\left(\bigwedge\pi\phi \to \phi\left[\begin{array}{c}\pi\\\sigma\end{array}\right]\right) = \left(\bigwedge\bar{\pi}\bigwedge\pi s(\phi) \to s(\phi)\left[\begin{array}{c}\pi\\\sigma\end{array}\right]\left[\begin{array}{c}\bar{\pi}\\\bar{\sigma}\end{array}\right]\right)$$

and therefore the s transform of any instance of (A5) is clearly a theorem of T by the specification laws of T. In regard to (A7), observe that

$$s\left(\bigwedge\alpha\phi \to \bigwedge\pi\phi\left[\begin{array}{c}\alpha\\\pi\end{array}\right]\right) = \left(\bigwedge\bar{\alpha}s(\phi) \to \bigwedge\bar{\pi}\bigwedge\pi s(\phi)\left[\begin{array}{c}\bar{\alpha}\\\bar{\pi}\end{array}\right]\right)$$

and therefore the s transform of any instance of (A7) is a theorem of T by the rule of alphabetic change of bound individual variables and the insertion of a vacuous quantifier phrase. Finally, since

$$s(\bigvee\pi\bigwedge\alpha_0 \ldots \bigwedge\alpha_{n-1}[\pi(\alpha_0, \ldots, \alpha_{n-1}) \leftrightarrow \phi])$$
$$= \bigvee\bar{\pi}\bigvee\pi\bigwedge\bar{\alpha}_0 \ldots \bigwedge\bar{\alpha}_{n-1}$$
$$[\pi(\bar{\alpha}_0, \ldots, \bar{\alpha}_{n-1}) \leftrightarrow s(\phi)]$$

then the s transform of any instance of (CP) is an instance of the comprehension principle of T prefixed by a vacuous quantifier on an individual variable (since π does not occur free in ϕ); and therefore the s transform of any instance of (CP) is a theorem of T. But because s clearly preserves theoremhood in T under the inference rules of T*, and because T* is equivalent to T* + (A7) + (CP), then it follows that for every formula ϕ of T*, if $|_{\overline{T^*}}\,\phi$, then $|_{\overline{T}}\,s(\phi)$.[35]

Finally, observe that if ϕ is a wff of T, then $s(\phi)$ is an alphabetic variant of ϕ with possibly the insertion of some vacuous quantifiers of the form $\bigwedge\bar{\pi}$ or $\bigvee\bar{\pi}$; and, accordingly, $|_{\overline{T}}\,s(\phi)$ if and only if $|_{\overline{T}}\,\phi$. We conclude then that if ϕ is a wff of T and a theorem of T*, then ϕ is already a theorem of T. Consequently, T* + (inf) is consistent.[36]

Bibliography

[1] Carnap, R., *Introduction to Symbolic Logic and Its Applications*. New York: Dover, 1958.

[2] Church, A., *Introduction to Mathematical Logic*. Princeton, N.J.: Princeton University Press, 1956.

[3] Cocchiarella, N., "Existence Entailing Attributes, Modes of Copulation and Modes of Being in Second Order Logic," *Nous*, Vol. III, No. 1 (1969), pp. 33–48.

[4] Cocchiarella, N., "A Substitution Free Axiom Set for Second Order Logic," *Notre Dame Journal of Formal Logic*, Vol. X, No. 1 (1969), pp. 18–30.

[5] Fraenkel, A., and Y. Bar-Hillel, *Foundations of Set Theory*. Amsterdam: North-Holland Publishing Company, 1958.

[6] Gödel, K., "Russell's Mathematical Logic," *The Philosophy of Bertrand Russell*. P. A. Schilpp (ed.). Chicago: Northwestern University Press, 1944.

[7] Grossmann, R., "The Lessons of Paradox," unpublished paper read to Indiana University Philosophy Department Colloquim, December, 1969.

[8] Hilbert, D., and W. Ackermann, *Principles of Mathematical Logic*. New York: Chelsea Publishing Company, 1950.

[9] Ramsey, F. P., *The Foundations of Mathematics*. Patterson, N.J.: Littlefield, Adams and Company, 1960.

[10] Van Heijenoort, J., *From Frege to Gödel*, Cambridge: Harvard University Press, 1967.

[35] Retaining (A6) in place of (CP) we note that

$$s(\bigwedge\pi\psi \to \breve{S}^{\pi(\alpha_0,\ldots,\alpha_{n-1})}_{\phi}\psi\;|) = (\bigwedge\bar{\pi}\bigwedge\pi s(\psi) \to \breve{S}^{\pi(\bar{\alpha}_0,\ldots,\bar{\alpha}_{n-1})}_{s(\phi)}s(\psi)\;|)$$

and therefore the s transform of any instance of (A6) is a theorem of T by the specification laws of T.

[36] We perhaps should point out that although T* + (AC*) and T* + (inf) have both been shown to be consistent, the two proofs we have given cannot be joined to show that T* + (AC*) + (inf) is consistent. For as I pointed out above, (AC*) has instances that are not wffs of T, and unless we can show that such instances yield no more consequences in T* than do those that are wffs of T, the above proof does not suffice to establish the consistency of T* + (AC*) + (inf) relative to the consistency of T + (AC) + (inf).

Existence and Predication

FRED SOMMERS

Brandeis University

I

1. To contemporary philosophers the question whether 'exists' is a predicate is a syntactical question. Using an older terminology, it is the question whether 'exists' is an autocategorematic or a syncategorematic expression. In more recent parlance it is the question whether 'exists' belongs among the formative-logical signs or among the descriptive-extralogical signs of a logically adequate language.

Those who give canonical status to the idioms of quantification theory have a ready answer to this question. In the syntax of modern logic 'exists' is a syncategorematic expression. In canonical translations 'exists' is never a predicate. To accept this popular view is to assume that the formative expressions enumerated in the formation rules for predicate logic constitute a definitive list. But this overlooks the fact that the line distinguishing certain signs as formative, logical, or syncategorematic from other signs that are descriptive, extralogical, or autocategorematic has been arbitrarily drawn. How, indeed, do we decide whether a sign is syncategorematic or autocategorematic?

There is, of course, the indirect appeal to the power of a logic with this or that list of formatives. For example, if identity is added to the list of logical signs of the lower functional calculus, there is a significant increase in inference power. This, however, is an argument for adding identity to a system whose logical syntax has already been determined by an arbitrarily enumerated list of formatives. It can, for example, be shown that identity is not needed in a logical

159

language whose syntax differs radically from that of the standard first-order functional calculus.[1] The point is that the question whether a certain sign is formative or descriptive cannot be fruitfully answered by considering how an already-constituted logical language will fare with this sign or without it. This retail approach begs the more fundamental question raised by the distinction between logical and extralogical signs: What principle governs the distinction; what distinguishes the logical signs from the extralogical signs?

2. The problem in this general form has been raised by Tarski and since discussed by many other writers, most notably by Pap, Popper and Quine. However, the state of the problem has not been significantly advanced beyond the conclusion tentatively offered by Tarski:

> Perhaps it will be possible to find important objective arguments which enable us to justify the traditional boundary between logical and extralogical expressions. But I also consider it quite possible that investigation will bring no positive results in this direction so that we shall be compelled to regard such concepts as 'logical consequence', 'analytic statement' and 'tautology' as relative concepts which must, on each occasion be related to a definite, although in greater or less degree, arbitrary division of terms into logical and extra-logical.[2]

In this larger perspective the syntactic status of existence can only be determined within some general theory of logical syntax that "justifies" and sharpens the boundary between logical and extralogical signs. As Tarski noted, such a theory will have important bearing on such fundamental notions of logical theory as tautology and validity. But it should also, and, as it were, incidentally, answer our own question, namely, whether 'exists' is a syncategorematic or autocategorematic expression.

3. We shall, in consequence, devote a good deal of space to presenting, in outline, a general theory of logical signs.[3] We shall see that certain signs possess a common feature that defines them as logical or syncategorematic. Signs like 'not', 'every', and 'if . . . then' all possess the feature I have in mind. But 'exists' does not. Thus, according to the theory of logical syntax that we shall present, 'exists'

---

[1] See my paper "Do We Need Identity?" *The Journal of Philosophy* (August 7, 1969).

[2] Alfred Tarski, *Logic, Semantics, Metamathematics*, (Oxford, 1956), p. 420.

[3] Some of the results given here are published elsewhere in a more technical paper on a calculus for a logic of terms. See "The Calculus of Terms," *Mind* (January 1970). But the syntactic questions were there unexplored.

is not a syncategorematic sign. Syntactically, anyway, existence is a predicate. The question whether existence is a predicate thus reverts to an older semantic issue. For we can still ask whether the predicate 'exists' satisfies certain semantic conditions that most other predicates satisfy. For example, since 'fails-to-exist' is not true of anything, 'exists' differs from most predicates in not having an applicable contrary. This has led Kant and others to say that 'exists' is not a *real* predicate. The traditional question whether 'existence'—syntactically in predicate position—is a "real" predicate does not occur at all to anyone who maintains that in a logically adequate language 'exists' does not appear in predicate position. I shall be content to have shown this popular view to be mistaken. For the rest, the question whether 'exists' is a real predicate appears to me to invite a not very interesting dispute over the question whether an autocategorematic expression whose contrary is inapplicable should be considered a "real" predicate.

II

4. A presystematic partial list of formative or syncategorematic signs could include the following words, expressions, and particles:

is, isn't, not, no, un-, -less, non-, every, some, and, if . . . then, or

If we examine this list, we note that 'is' and 'isn't' are *opposed* as positive and negative signs, and that 'not', 'no', 'un-', '-less', and 'non-' are negative particles. Some signs, then, are "plus," others are "minus." Of the rest, only the word 'and' has a "plus" or "minus" signification; 'and' is, in fact, used as a synonym for "plus" in the sense of addition. We represent these findings in the following table:

$$
\left.\begin{array}{l}\text{is}\\\text{and}\end{array}\right\} + \qquad \left.\begin{array}{l}\text{isn't}\\\text{not}\\\text{un-}\\\text{no}\end{array}\right\} - \qquad \left.\begin{array}{l}\text{every}\\\text{some}\\\text{if . . . then}\\\text{or}\end{array}\right\} \ ?
$$

Looking over these correlations we note the preponderance of negative elements that have no explicit positive elements opposed to them. In natural languages the opposition between contrary words like 'wise' and 'un-wise' is signified by the presence or absence of a single negative sign. The *absence* of 'un-' in 'wise' is tantamount to the presence of a positive sign. If we represented 'unwise' by '—W' we could represent 'wise' by '+W'. In natural languages the implicit "plus sign" for positive terms is never made explicit. This corresponds to arithmetical practice. A negative number is represented by '—X' while the corresponding positive number is represented by 'X'—and only rarely by '+X'. The difference between arithmetic and linguistic notation is that natural language altogether lacks an explicit positive sign for positive terms.

What holds for the opposition between positive and negative terms holds also for the opposition between positive and negative modes of predicating. The following pair of contradictory sentences illustrates this:

(1)   Scientists were attentive.
(2)   No scientists were attentive.

In (2) the word 'no' signifies that the predicate 'were attentive' is *denied* of the subject 'scientists'. A corresponding sign for predicative *affirmation* is missing in sentence (1). If we represent the positive copula 'were' by a plus sign then sentences (1) and (2) would be written as follows:

(1) $S + A$
(2) $-(S + A)$

We could make all positive signs explicit. Formulas (1) and (2) would then look like this:

(1) $+((+S) + (+A))$
(2) $-((+S) + (+A))$

The signs immediately preceding the letters are positive signs indicating that the terms are positive. The initial sign in formula (1) is a sign that the predicate '$+ (+A)$' is affirmed of the subject '$(+S)$'.

5. We have so far found that a number of formatives are "oppositional" in nature. Consider now the following schedule of four propositions:

Schedule I	(1)	$S + A$	Scientists were attentive.
	(2)	$-(S + A)$	No scientists were attentive.
	(3)	$S + (-A)$	Scientists were inattentive.
	(4)	$-(S + (-A))$	No scientists were inattentive.

In propositions (1) and (2), the positive predicate 'were attentive' is, respectively, affirmed and denied. Similarly in propositions (3) and (4), the negative predicate 'were inattentive' is positively and negatively predicated. The affirmative propositions (1) and (3) are weakly interpreted to claim that scientists—some anyway—were (in-)attentive. So interpreted, propositions (1) and (3) respectively contradict (2) and (4).

At the price of arbitrarily representing the formative sign 'some' by a plus sign we can get a schedule of four propositions arithmetically and logically equivalent to those of Schedule I.

Schedule II	(1*)	+S + A	Some scientists were attentive
	(2*)	−(+S + A)	NOT (Some scientists were attentive)
	(3*)	+S + (−A)	Some scientists were inattentive
	(4*)	−(+S + (−A))	NOT (Some scientists were inattentive)

Schedules I and II do not contain the word 'every'; neither schedule uses the *difference* between 'every' and 'some' in a logically discriminating way. In both schedules the operative differences are oppositional: *a positive or negative predicate is affirmed or denied.*

Schedules I and II are called primary schedules. In a primary schedule only oppositions of "quality" differentiates one proposition from another. The difference of "quantity" is inoperative. It will be convenient to distinguish between the two qualitative oppositions of the primary schedule. The opposition of *contrariety* between positive and negative terms or predicates will be referred to as "C opposition." The opposition of *contradiction* between positive and negative predication will be referred to as "P opposition." A primary schedule will be called a PC Schedule. The logical form of the propositions in a primary schedule is fully specified by signs of P- and C-opposition.

There are cases when both negative propositions in a primary schedule are true. In the schedule presented above the second and fourth propositions may both be considered true if there were no scientists at all. Similarly since prime numbers are not the kind of thing that eat or fail to eat, it is as true to say that no prime number is unfed as it is true to say that none is fed. When the contrary denials of a PC Schedule are both true, we cannot legitimately infer 'every X is Y' from 'no X is un-Y' or 'every X is un-Y' from 'no X is Y'. For example, since prime numbers are neither fed nor un-fed, we cannot infer 'every prime number is fed' from 'no prime number is un-fed'. The move from the negative proposition 'no X is Y' to affirmative proposition 'every X is un-Y' is known as obversion. When both contrary denials are true, obversion is not a valid inference. Valid obversion presupposes non-vacuous contraries.

6. When the semantic condition for valid obversion obtains, we may use the primary schedule to derive a new and equivalent schedule all of whose propositions are affirmative.

Primary Schedule (A)	Derived Schedule (B)
1. Some X is Y	Some X is Y
2. No X is Y	Every X is un-Y
3. Some X is un-Y	Some X is un-Y
4. No X is un-Y	Every X is Y

Represented arithmetically the relations between the primary and derived schedule form four equations:

$$
\begin{array}{ccc}
 & A & B \\
1. & +X + Y & = +X + Y \\
2. & -(+X + Y) & = -X + (-Y) \\
3. & +X + (-Y) & = +X + (-Y) \\
4. & -(+X + (-Y)) & = -X + Y
\end{array}
$$

The propositions of the derived B schedule make use of a new opposition defined by distributing the sign for negative predication in equations (2A) and (4A) into the expression in parentheses. The initial minus sign in equations (2B) and (4B) is then interpreted as 'every', and the logical difference between 'some' and 'every' stands revealed as an "oppositional," plus-minus, difference.

The new opposition between the signs of quantity 'some' and 'every' will be referred to as Q-opposition. It must again be stressed that Q-opposition is a defined logical relation derived from the more-primitive qualitative oppositions of contrariety and contradiction. More particularly, Q-opposition is only defined for the range of obversible inferences. When propositions of form (1A) and (3A) in the primary schedule are both false an opposition between 'every' and 'some' is logically *meaningless*. We shall have occasion to return to this point (see Section 15).

7. We have so far given plus-minus assignments to the following signs: is (+), isn't (−), un- (−), no (−), not (−), some (+), every (−), and (+).

With the exception of 'some' and 'every', these assignments are intuitively acceptable. Even so they could well be logically arbitrary, providing no more than a stenographic way of representing categorical propositions. That they are not arbitrary is conclusively proved by the fact that, so represented, the propositions can be reckoned with arithmetically in a manner that preserves logical validity. In other words, the oppositional way of representing logical signs gives us an arithmetic calculus. The arithmetic is logically efficient; this must mean that the oppositional representation of the syncategorematic signs reveals logical form.

To show this we shall consider some simple inference types. We begin with "immediate" inferences from a single premise.

When the premise and conclusion of an immediate inference are both universal or both particular, the inference will be called regular; otherwise, it will be called irregular. Only regular inferences are valid. The full condition for validity is this: An immediate inference 'P, hence C' is valid if and only if

(1)   it is a regular inference
(2) $P = C$

When we represent 'P, hence C' as the equation '$P = C$', we read the sign of equality as 'hence' or 'therefore'.

Applying the above principle to the following inferences we find the first two valid, the last two invalid.

(1)   Every A is B $\therefore$ Every un-B is un-A $-A + B = -(-B)$
$+ (-A)$
(2)   Some A is B $\therefore$ Some A isn't un-B $+A + B = +A - (-B)$
(3)   Some A isn't B $\therefore$ Some B isn't A $+A - B = +B - A$
(4)   Every A is B $\therefore$ Some B isn't A $-A + B = +B - A$

Inference (3) is invalid because $P \neq C$. Inference (4) is irregular.

8. Syllogisms and sorites are inferences with n premises and $n + 1$ terms. A syllogistic inference is regular if (1) its conclusion and all of its premises are universal, or (2) its conclusion and exactly one premise are particular. Arithmetically a syllogism has the form: $P_1 + P_2 + \cdots + P_n = C$. Only regular syllogisms are valid but regularity is not sufficient for validity.

A syllogism or sorites is valid if and only if

(1)   it is regular.
(2) $P_1 + \cdots + P_n = C$

The following three forms illustrate this:

(1)   Every M is P and every S is M ∴ Every S is P.

This syllogism is regular and its equation is true: $(-M + P) + (-S + M) = -S + P$. Note the use of '+' for 'and'.

(2)   Every M is P and no S is M ∴ No S is P.

$$(-M + P) + (-(S + M)) = -(S + P)$$

This equation is false and the syllogism is invalid.

(3)   Some M is P and some S isn't M ∴ Some S isn't P.

$$+M - P + S - M = +S - P$$

Though the equation is true, the inference is irregular.

The requirement of regularity for immediate and syllogistic inference rules out "weakened" forms like 'All X is Y, hence some X is Y'. It is, however, easy to reinstate inferences of this kind if we consider them as enthymemes with a tacit premise of form 'Some X is X'. The inference then turns out to be a valid syllogism. For example, we have $-X + Y + X + X = +X + Y$. It is not necessary to interpret '$+ X + X$' as asserting the existence of things that are X. In any case tacit premises of form '$+X + X$' are not analytically true. On the other hand the form '$-X + X$' representing 'every X is X' *is* analytic.

9. Propositions with *relations* are easily represented in the logico-arithmetic notation. Furthermore, we can continue to reckon them arithmetically. Consider the following statement:

No sailor buys a trinket in every port.

This is represented as

$$-(S + b + T - P)$$

which is arithmetically and logically equivalent to

$$-S - (b + T - P)$$

That is, every sailor fails to buy a trinket in every port. Or to

$$-S + (-b) - T + P$$

every sailor fails-to-buy ("passes up") every trinket in some port. Adding 'Some trinkets are metal' to the last formulation we get

$$(-S + (-b) - T + P) + (+T + M) = -S + (-b) + M + P$$

that is, every sailor fails-to-buy some metal thing in some port.

Other relational inferences preserve arithmetical form. For example, the formula

$$-C + F = -(d + C) + (d + F)$$

is a true equality and it represents the valid inference: Every circle is a figure, hence everyone who draws a circle draws a figure.[4]

10. Singular propositions are treated as indifferently universal or particular.[5] Thus, 'Socrates is wise' is treated as either 'Some Socrates is wise' or 'Every Socrates is wise', and, generally, when 'S_i' is a singular term, a proposition of form 'S_i is P' is represented as $\pm S_i + P$. Because singular statements have "wild" quantity we are able to handle inferences like

Socrates is wise

Socrates is a good man

∴ Some good man is wise

The corresponding equation is:

$$(+S_i + W) + (-S_i + G) = +G + W$$

In this syllogism, the first premise is particular, the second is universal.

11. Identity statements can also be represented and reckoned with arithmetically. An identity statement is a singular proposition with singular terms in both subject and predicate positions. The expression 'is identical with' is represented by a plus-sign. Thus, both 'Tully is Cicero' and 'Tully is identical with Cicero' are represented by '$T_i + C_i$'. An inference like

Tully is identical with Cicero

Tully is not identical with Plutarch

∴ Cicero is not identical with Plutarch

---

[4] For a more complete account of the logical arithmetic see my article "The Calculus of Terms," *Mind* (January 1970).

[5] See my paper "Do We Need Identity?" *Journal of Philosophy*, Vol. LXVI, No. 15 (August 1969). See also, Leibniz, *Logical Papers*, G. H. R. Parkinson (ed.) (Oxford, Clarendon Press, 1966), p. 115.

would be shown valid by the syllogistic equation

$$(+T_i + C_i) + (-T_i - P_i) = +C_i - P_i$$

We have been arguing (1) that syncategorematic signs are signs of opposition and, conversely, (2) that any sign whose oppositional representation is logically efficient is a syncategorematic sign. If we are right, identity is syncategorematic, a fact that cannot occasion much surprise.

12. If all signs are made explicit, the general form of the proposition is

$$\pm(\pm(\pm X) \pm (\pm Y))$$

where X and Y are autocategorematic expressions (terms) and the signs of opposition are the "syncategorematic," "logical," or "formative" elements.

The signs furthest to the left are signs indicating whether the predicate '$\pm(\pm Y)$' is affirmed or denied of the subject '$\pm(\pm X)$'. The next signs signify *some* ($+$) or *every* ($-$). The signs immediately preceding 'X' and 'Y' are signs of term quality, *plus* for positive terms, *minus* for negative terms. The middle signs are for the positive and negative copula. X and Y may be relational expressions, that is, expressions of form '$R \pm A \pm \cdots \pm K$', where R is a relative expression and A, . . . , K are objects of the relation R. Also X and Y may be singular terms. In the next section we shall show that X and Y may also represent propositions and that the general categorical form is also the general form of a truth-function.

13. Our theory of the syncategorematic signs has been described and been partly justified. It is the theory that all such signs are "oppositional" and that logical form is arithmetical. According to the theory, every logical sign can be efficiently represented in a plus-minus way. We now turn to some signs that appear to resist this thesis. What possible "oppositional" way is there of saying 'or' or 'if . . . then'?

To get at the oppositional nature of 'if . . . then' [or 'or'] we use a method similar to the one used for getting a "minus" assignment for 'every'. We take a formula that is logically equivalent to a conditional proposition and give *that* formula an arithmetic representation. We then equate the conditional to its logical equivalent.

We know that 'if P then Q' is logically equivalent to 'not (P and not Q)'. Now the signs of this latter formula are fully oppositional: $-(P + (-Q))$. Now

$$-(P + (-Q)) = -P + Q$$

If this true arithmetic equation is to represent the logical equivalence of 'not (P and (not Q))' and 'if P then Q', we must read the ordered pair of signs '— . . . + . . . ' as 'if . . . then'. Note that '—P + Q' has the form of a universal categorical proposition: Every (state of affairs in which) P is (a state of affairs in which) Q. By a similar technique we can define 'or' and all other logical connectives. A more extended account of propositional logic in arithmetic form is found in my paper "The Calculus of Terms" (*Mind*, January 1970). The "logical arithmetic" of truth-functions does not completely coincide with ordinary arithmetic. It is, however, close enough to support the oppositional account of formative signs. The general form of molecular propositions is isomorphic to the form of categorical propositions:

$$\pm(\pm(\pm P) \pm (\pm Q))$$

where 'P' and 'Q' may themselves be molecular. For example, the fully explicit way of representing $-((N \cdot S) \supset Q)$ would be

$$-(-(+(+N) + (+S)) + (+Q))$$

Notational economies would reduce this to

$$-(-(N + S) + Q).$$

That the general forms of molecular and categorical propositions coincide means that the oppositional theory gives a unified account of all syncategorematic signs, including propositional connectives along with 'every', 'is', and so forth. This account is in the spirit of Leibniz's program for an arithmetical "Characteristic."[6]

14. We have indicated how the quasi-arithmetical notation may felicitously be used for logical reckoning. What are the implications of this fact? No more than a brief discussion is possible here.

The Implication for Logic

Modern logic is relatively complex and its syntax is foreign to the syntax of natural language: It is complex in several ways:

(1)   Two calculi are used—the predicate calculus and the calculus of propositions. The foundation rules for predicate logic are syntactically innovative. In contrast to this, a term logic is syntactically

---

[6] "If, as I hope, I can conceive all propositions as terms, and hypotheticals as categoricals . . . this promises a wonderful ease in my symbolism and analysis of concepts and will be a discovery of the greatest importance." Leibniz, *op. cit.*, p. 66, G. H. R. Parkinson (ed.) (Oxford, 1966), p. 66.

uniform for propositional compounds and categorical propositions. (2) The syntax of modern logic is complex, consisting of "connectives," individual symbols, predicates, and quantifier operators. In contrast to this the syntactical elements of the arithmetic term calculus are basically of two kinds, *terms* and *signs of opposition*. Various kinds of brackets may be used to indicate whether a term is ordinary, propositional, composite, or relational.

(3) The syntax of modern logic is unrelated to that of natural language and the logical translations are quite strange to the uninitiated student. Moreover, these translations are ptolemaically complex in comparison to the direct transcription of the arithmetized logic of terms. For example, the translation of 'Every censor withholds some book from every minor' is

$$(x)(Cx \supset (\exists yBy \cdot (z)(Mz \supset Wxyz)))$$

For every X, if X is C, then there is a Y such that Y is a book and for every Z if Z is a minor then X withholds Y from Z.

In contrast to this, the logic of terms represents this sentence as:

$$-C + (w + B - M)$$

The standard symbolic translation is used today because it is believed that with a "mere" logic of terms we cannot achieve adequate inference power. Perhaps enough has been shown to cast serious doubts on this universally accepted belief.

Grammatical Implications

As a science linguistics does not yet exist and even a brief remark about the relations of grammar to logic must be highly speculative. Part of the trouble lies with linguists themselves. Even those who know logic hardly bother to mention it. A recent major work by Chomsky[7] argues for a universal grammar common to all natural languages on the ground that linguistic competence is hardly plausible without it. Amazingly, even with this thesis as its burden, Chomsky does not mention logic and so does not discuss how such a universal grammar could be related to the logical constraints that are surely a necessary (universal) condition of linguistic competence. There is little point in investigating the possibility of a universal grammar until the relation of such a grammar to logic itself is clarified. This is not to say that the relation must be fully specified in advance.

[7] Chomsky, *Aspects of the Theory of Syntax*.

But even at the outset, the investigation into this possibility must be undertaken with some idea of the difference between logic and grammatical structures. However, the foregoing account of the way declarative sentences may be transcribed into logical arithmetic form suggests the possibility that Russell and other logicians are basically right in their belief that linguists have all along been hampered by an outmoded informal constituent analysis which obscures the "logical form" of the sentence. It suggests that a truly formal syntax, closely correspondent to surface structure, but considerably abstracting from certain details, may be a universal element in all grammars. A syntactic analysis which—as it were incidentally—exposes the inference capacity of declarative, information-bearing, sentences of natural language is truly and literally a logical syntax. That logical syntax is a universal condition of linguistic competence is not a novel thesis. What is perhaps surprising is the close correspondence of simple arithmetic to the logical structure implicit in natural syntax. Leibniz believed that such a correspondence existed. And Aristotle himself did not distinguish between natural syntax and logical form. The idea that a universal grammar is logical syntax is thus very old. And the idea that logical signs are arithmetical signs is not so very young. In ending my account of the oppositional theory I cannot do better than to quote Leibniz himself:

Thomas Hobbes, everywhere a profound examiner of logical principles rightly stated that everything done by the mind is a *computation*, by which is meant either the addition of a sum or the subtraction of a difference (*De Corpore* I.i.2). So, just as there are two primary signs of algebra and analytics, + and —, in the same way there are, as it were, two copulas 'is' and 'isn't'.[8]

III

15. What, finally, of existence? The answer given by the theory of opposition is clear. In representing a statement like 'unicorns exist' we do *not* give 'exist' an oppositional representation. Thus 'exist' is no more syncategorematic than 'runs'. The logical form of 'unicorns exist' and 'unicorns run' is the same:

$$U + E \qquad \text{unicorns are existent}$$
$$U + R \qquad \text{unicorns are running}$$

'Exists', then, may appear in predicate position. There is, however, an important logical difference between statements predicating 'exists'

[8] Leibniz, *op. cit.*, p. 3.

and other statements. The difference I have in mind is observed by Moore when he points out that we never say 'some unicorns do not exist' or 'every tiger exists'. The reason for this is that the Q-opposition between 'every' and 'some' is *not defined* for statements predicating existence. To see this we first form a primary schedule:

Schedule III (1) Some unicorns exist $+U + E$
              (2) Some unicorns are inexistent $+U + (-E)$
              (3) No unicorns exist $-(U + E)$
              (4) No unicorns are inexistent $-(U + (-E))$

(1) is factually false. (2) is false since 'is inexistent' is never true of a thing. Both (3) and (4) are true and so neither is obversible. This being so, we can neither infer 'every unicorn is inexistent' from (3) nor 'every unicorn exists' from (4). And this means that the "Q-opposition" between 'every' and 'some' is not defined for statements with 'exists' in predicate position. Since obversion fails, a schedule with existence in predicate position is *essentially* "primary."[9] Moreover, since the contrary of 'exists' is *never* applicable, C-opposition is also irrelevant. The primary schedule given above is reduced to a two-entry P schedule: 'unicorns exist', 'no unicorns exist'.

The sum of our discussion of existence so far is this: 'Exists' is not a syncategorematic sign. However, existence statements are logically primitive and essentially confined to P-opposition.

16. A logical syntax in which 'exists' is not syncategorematic has certain advantages. I shall briefly touch on several.

In standard logics we use special rules enabling us to get from 'Adam is created' to 'Something is created' and from 'Everything is created' to 'Adam is created.' In a logical system that treats 'exists' as a predicate, these rules are not needed. For we can form a sentence like 'Adam exists' or 'Adam is an existent' and use it as a premise in a syllogism. The inference 'Adam is created, therefore Something is created' is a valid enthymeme whose tacit minor premise is 'Adam exists':

(Every) Adam is created
(Some) Adam is existent
∴ Some existent is created

The syllogism is valid since the two singular premises may be assigned opposing quantities (see Section 10 above). And the syllogism is sound since the minor premise is (assumed) true. And, generally, the move from 'α is P' to 'Something is P' is syllogistic; we do not need a

[9] See Section 6 above.

special principle of existential generalization. The principle of universal instantiation is similarly unnecessary. Syllogistic reasoning is wholly adequate if 'exists' is in predicate position:

> Every existent is created
> Adam is an existent
> ∴ Adam is created

Since we do not make use of special principles we do not have the problem of making exceptions to them. The move from the true proposition 'Pegasus is a flying horse' to the false conclusion 'A flying horse exists' is blocked on syllogistic grounds since we cannot truly assert the missing minor premise 'Pegasus exists'.

If existence is an implicit syncategorematic element of a proposition of form 'Some A is B', the truth conditions are ontologically strong. In the case where no A exists the proposition must be counted false. This seems too strong for certain propositions that are considered true despite the obvious vacuity of their subjects. A proposition like 'Some ideal gases are colorless' or 'Some frictionless motion is constant' does not have truth conditions which include the existence of an ideal gas or a case of frictionless motion. The standard overtly existential interpretation of particular propositions is known to give trouble in another quarter. The usual translation of 'John saw a cat' is: 'There exists a thing such that it is a cat and John saw it'. A similar translation fails for 'I want a cat". The existential interpretation proces too strong for such contexts. If 'exists' is a predicate we have room to distinguish between the existentially overt and false proposition 'A colorless ideal gas exists' from the merely particular proposition 'Some ideal gases are colorless'. Nor do we need to assume that 'I saw a knife' differs from 'I want a knife' in entailing 'A knife exists'.

If existence is syncategorematic then all general propositions—and perhaps singular propositions as well—are interpreted as affirming or denying existence claims. On this view modern predicate logic amounts to a system of formal ontology. The idea is attractive because truth conditions for overtly existential propositions are clear and well-understood. It must be confessed that a logic that relegates 'exists' to predicate position has no adequate semantics for propositions that are not overtly existential. But it is not clear that quantificational logic possesses a permanent truth advantage. So the semantic inadequacy of the older term logic may be temporary.

On the other side it is apparent that the traditional treatment of 'exists' as a predicate is simple and natural. And more generally, as I have tried to show, a logical syntax along traditional lines that excludes 'exists' from the canonical list of logical elements can give a coherent representation to all of its logical signs. This kind of syntactic unity is altogether lacking in the artificial syntaxes for standard systems of modern logic.

17. I have been arguing against the popular view that existence is syncategorematic. The average reader may find that my negative conclusion goes too far. He is, I think, prepared to acknowledge that predicate logic is not the only possible adequate logic and that other logics differing in syntax from modern standard logics are possible. He would not be surprised that in these variant logical systems, 'exists' is treated as autocategorematic and not as syncategorematic. But even the sympathetic reader may balk at the position I have taken. I say: 'exists' is not syncategorematic; it is autocategorematic. Shouldn't I say instead that, in certain systems, adequate for certain logical purposes, existence is autocategorematic and not syncategorematic?

Our "average reader" is here pleading for the wrong kind of logical tolerance. The choice between the syntax of modern predicate logic and the syntax of an oppositional logic is the choice between a logical language without a unified conception of its formative elements and a logical language in which all formative elements are uniformly characterized and uniformly represented. The reason for saying that existence is not syncategorematic comes to this: The question whether a given sign is syncategorematic or auocategorematic can only be answered by a theory that does not arbitrarily enumerate the syncategorematic expressions of a logically adequate language. We have shown that a unified theory of logical syntax that illuminates the idea of "syncategorematic sign" can be developed. According to the theory all syncategorematic elements are represented as signs of opposition, and no element that is incapable of such representation is syncategorematic. We saw, for example, that the expression 'is identical with' can be represented as a plus sign for purposes of logical reckoning. But 'exists' is not an expression of this kind.

On Assertions of Existence

H. HIŻ

University of Pennsylvania

The problem to which I am addressing myself may be illustrated by a painting by Jean Dubuffet entitled 'Ampliation du robinet' ('Amplification of the Tap'). We may think that the subject matter of that painting is awkward and ill-chosen, that amplifications, and, in particular, amplifications of taps, do not exist. For it is not a tap itself which has been painted here, but rather an amplification of a tap, and we do not see such in actuality. We have here only a mental deformation of a tap. If we think the painting to be about an odd and unreal thing, we take a concretistic attitude. Concretism is deeply rooted in our tradition, the tradition of believing in the existence of a particular tap in Monsieur Dubuffet's bathroom, or other such fixtures, and of disbelieving the existence of abstractions, of properties, abilities, relations, functions, or distortions. In opposition to concretism, I will claim that it is hard to assert the existence of such things as a particular tap, but more reasonable to claim the existence of such things as amplifications of taps. It seems to me that the concept of an individual thing, such as this or that tap, is a degenerate relic of the naïve religious belief in the soul. The soul was supposed to be unique, indecomposable, and fundamental, existing independently of other things. Just as souls were supposed to think and imagine, although they were not thoughts and imaginations, so individual things are supposed to be green and cold and moving, but are not greenness, coldness, or motion. Individual things are supposed to be related to other things, but are not supposed to be relations themselves, just as a man is supposed to perceive,

175

but is not to be identified with perception. The belief in *res cogitans* was extended to *res extensa*. *Res extensa* assumed similar characteristics to that attributed to the soul. It was to be a *substantia prima*, a substance which was not to be predicated of anything, but of which predication can be made. This anthropomorphism treated material things as fundamental components of the world, themselves not composed of other entities in the sense in which, say, a binary relation is composed of pairs of objects between which it holds. A thing like a tap is supposed to persist, to be the same tap no matter what happened to it in time, just as a man remains the same throughout his life.

We may have the impression that in science individual things are sometimes assumed to exist. But this is an illusion. A mathematical logician speaks about a model of a theory. For a model he often takes a structure, that is, a set U together with operations on the members of U with values in U (each operation forms an element of U out of a number of elements of U) and along with relations among members of U. We may also include in a model higher-order operations and relations among lower-order operations and relations. The entire model is anchored on the elements of U which is sometimes called 'a universe of discourse'. It may appear that the world view expressed in such a model is essentially the same as that of Aristotle, with his first substances as the universe of discourse and various derived *substantiae secundae*.[1]

But a modern theoretician of models notices that his structure is not the only model; there are other models of the theory. For instance, as the universe of discourse we may take a suitable subset of the relations among the elements of the original set U. Instead of individuals we may start with some relations and treat them in the same way as individuals were treated before. It is rare that a theory accepts only models which are isomorphic, that is, that do not differ in any respect studied by that theory. Such theories are called 'categorical.'[2] Most of the usual scientific theories are not categorical. If a theory is categorical, its different models are indistinguishable by formal means alone. The models may be seen as different when they are studied by means beyond the reach of the science to which these models apply. Thus, to take a trivial example, the

---

[1] The modernity of considering operations as well as relations is absent in Aristotle.

[2] The concept of categoricity of a theory was introduced by O. Veblen in "A System of Axioms of Geometry," *Transactions of the American Mathematical Society*, Vol. 5 (1904). A very clear presentation of the concept and its methodological importance is given by Andrzej Grzegorczyk in "On the Concept of Categoricity," *Studia Logica*, Vol. 13 (1961).

arithmetic modulo 5 has as a model the fingers on my left hand (with addition being a passage from a finger to another finger) and as another model the fingers on my right hand, or any other ordered set of five elements. The models are arithmetically indistinguishable. Yet the fingers on my left hand are physically different objects from the fingers on my right hand.

Today set theory comes close to Aristotle's writings about substance in general and about other categories as related to substances. It may be again viewed as a general theory of being. There is no definite formulation of set theory. Some systems of set theory accept individuals; other systems do not. Anyway, it is possible to base modern science on a theory which does not accept anything which is not a class, a property (in the broadest sense).[3] We do not have in science a fixed, unique universe of discourse from which we develop the construction of the scientific world. Science never asserts that there are some things, if by this phrase we mean the existence of something as a fundamental entity about which the science is supposed to speak. Therefore, science does not assert the existence of taps themselves.

With amplifications the job is easier. The amplifications do not remain the same when their properties change, as it was mysteriously assumed for individual men and individual things. Still it is the same amplification which applies to a variety of things. Amplification is an operation, a function, and it is not proper to ask, 'Where is amplification?' Amplification of the tap is not in the artist's bathroom; it is nowhere. Though, to be sure, once the painting was called 'Amplification of the Tap,' 'Amplification of the Tap' became the name of that painting, and, in this meta-graphic sense, *Amplification of the Tap* hangs in a museum.

First, notice a minor ambiguity: amplification of a tap may be either the function of amplifying or else the result, the value of that function. This kind of ambiguity is met often; for instance, when we speak about the summation of two numbers, we may wish to speak either about the operation or about the result of the operation. This can easily be clarified. It is more difficult to determine whether the operation is really performed, or only performable, or even perhaps cannot be performed. If the phrase 'amplification of the tap' is understood as referring to the function itself and not to the value of the function, then we are talking not about performed, realized amplifications, but simply about amplification. We are talking about the "concept" of amplification, whether applied to something or not, whether

[3] See, for example, Paul Bernays, *Axiomatic Set Theory* (Amsterdam, 1958), and comments on that topic in Patrick Suppes, *Axiomatic Set Theory* (Princeton, 1960).

actually applicable, as in the case of a concert, or not at all, as in the case of a tap. Taps are not easily, if at all, amplifiable. But amplification of the tap is something worth considering even if there will never be such things as amplified taps. What I am asking, therefore, is: Does amplification exist? What is its domain? What is its counter-domain? The conclusion of my comments will be that, in a specific sense, amplification does exist, but a tap does not.

Abstracting from the defense of amplification, we may ask what does it mean to say that something exists. There are many different senses of the phrase 'exists', 'existence', and all other derivatives. English exhibits an impressive variety of meanings of these words. Here are a few representative sentences containing the phrase 'exist':

Does life exist on Mars?
Do you believe in the existence of ghosts?
When did this world come into existence?
The roots of this polynominal do not exist in real numbers.
There is no law in existence which regulates advertising.
She exists on very little.
What a miserable existence!
Let's co-exist.

It would be futile to try to find a common meaning for all the uses of 'exist' in fluent English. Moreover, philosophers often equate the meaning of 'exist' with the meaning of 'there is', 'there are', and by so doing, depart somehow from fluent English. We can compile a list of meanings in which the phrase 'exist' is used by various English speakers. Philosophers should be included among English speakers, and their use of 'exists' as equal in meaning to 'there is', should be in that list.

Now the tap in the bathroom of Monsieur Dubuffet, the tap which served him as his model in 1965 and which serves us here as an example, twinkles with ontological ambiguity. On the one hand, if someone should consider the tap to be a particular piece of metal, then he would suppose it to be the carrier of the tap's properties though itself not a property. As Aristotle would put it, it can neither be predicated of anything nor is it in anything. Or, to state the matter linguistically, the phrase 'the tap which served as a model for Monsieur Dubuffet' is a proper name. On the other hand, that tap can be taken as a predicate, as a property. We may ask about something: Is that the tap which served as a model for Monsieur Dubuffet? And this question may be understood as inquiring whether that something has the property of having served as a model for Monsieur

Dubuffet. In that sentence the grammatical category of the string 'the tap which served as a model for Monsieur Dubuffet' is a functor, a verb phrase and not a proper name, as before. If to different grammatical categories different ontological categories correspond, then to a proper name there corresponds an individual, a thing, whereas a functor represents an attribute. This, rightly or wrongly, is the usual way philosophers link phrases with entities, and grammatical categories with ontological categories. That philosophical tradition, in a variety of formulations, dates at least from Frege; names stand for individuals, predicates for attributes, transitive verbs for binary relations, and so on. When, instead of speaking about the tap that served Monsieur Dubuffet as a model, we speak about being the tap that served Monsieur Dubuffet as a model, then we change the ontological category of the tap from a thing to an attribute. They differ in kind.

There are reasons for recognizing the tap in its attributive rather than in its substantive guise. In the first place, whatever factual information we can convey by using the proper name of the tap, we can convey it as well without using that proper name. We can rephrase the entire statement, except for the indication of the ontological status of the tap. But the ontological status of the tap, just as the ontological status of anything, is unclear anyway. All taps leak ontologically.

Instead of saying

(1)   The tap that was a model for M. Dubuffet was made of iron.

we may equally well say

(2)   The tap that was a model for M. Dubuffet $\{x\}$ and was made of iron $\{x\}$, for some x.[4]

If this sounds strange, we can paraphrase it:

(3)   Something is the tap that was a model for M. Dubuffet and it was made of iron.

or in some other more fluent way. We can profit from the schematic formulation (2) because of its widespread applicability even though its "surface" rendering may vary considerably from case to case. Generally, instead of any sentence

(4) $S\alpha$

---

[4] We use here a notation similar to that used in arithmetic where instead of '2 is even' we write 'even $\{2\}$', and generally instead of 'α has property ϕ' we write '$\phi\{\alpha\}$'. Below we use some standard logical notations: '$\bigwedge$' = 'for all'; '$\bigvee$' = 'for some', '$\wedge$' is a sign for conjunction, and so on.

containing α which is taken here to be a proper name, we can use

(5) $\bigvee x[\alpha\{x\} \wedge S\{x\}]$

where α is used as a functor. The problem of the ontological status of the tap is partly the choice between formulas (4) and (5). The sentence

(6) Here is the tap which was the model.

may be analyzed grammatically in two different ways, each with different ontological significance. We may divide sentence (6) into three main parts: *here, is,* which serves as the verb, and *the tap which was the model,* which is a noun phrase and a description.[5] This grammatical analysis seemingly induces an ontology which takes the tap to be a thing. However sentence (6) can be analyzed into only two main parts: *here* and *is the tap which was the model.* The second analysis does not induce an ontology of things. Rather, it calls for an ontology of the attribute of being the tap which was the model.

In favor of formula (5) we can cite the fact that formula (5) is much more general than formula (4). If we want to speak about the boredom of fairytales, the cruelty of justice, the relative primeness of 21 and 22, we do not want to make fairytales, justice, and numbers into things. In order to have a broad, uniform way of speaking, we can either choose to reify relations, attributes, events, ways of behaving, or else we can choose to treat the individual things as attributes. The first approach is taken by many philosophers, by reists, by Descartes and Leibniz, by Brentano, by the so-called American nominalists, and, more or less explicitly, by all those who think that homogeneous systems of logic are philosophically more acceptable than systems in which not every two variables have necessarily the same range.

Those philosophers try to reduce all cases to an exceptional case because individual substances behave very differently from the rest of entities. The opposite, namely the elimination of the exceptional

---

[5] It was Bertrand Russell who stressed that descriptions, that is, phrases of the form *the β such that γ, the β which δ,* function like proper names in that they call for a single entity to be their denotation. Here γ is a sentential function, a phrase like a sentence except that it contains, instead of a phrase, a free variable β, or in a natural language a referential to β. Referentials and their similarities to variables are spoken of in my paper "Referentials" in *Semiotica,* Vol. 2 (1969). δ above is a phrase with a zero referential. The Russellian views on descriptions are questionable. See Beverly Robbins, *The definite article in English transformations* (The Hague: Mouton, 1968). Here we will not need to go into the grammatical or ontological nature of descriptions.

case, is much easier however, and is therefore preferable, if it does not prevent us from stating the facts in one way or another. As each case of formula (5) is a paraphrase of the corresponding case of formula (4) and as sentence (6) asserts the same in either of the two analyses, the last condition is satisfied by the policy of eliminating *substantiae primae* from our topics.

We may recall a similar argument which Berkeley used effectively. He insisted that by rejecting independently existing entities we do not have to exclude anything from our knowledge. The philosophy of Berkeley has, of course, little to do with the point of view I am presenting. Neither his subjectivistic idealism nor his antimaterialism are in any way relevant here. What is relevant is his argument that without speaking about substantial individuals we can still say all we know. If we abandon individual names, if we do not use proper names as denoting individuals, we may still say whatever we would have said about amplification of the tap, but we now do not have to take the tap as a nonproperty.

The next and perhaps crucial argument against taking proper nouns in our language as denoting things, or in favor of looking at the alleged proper nouns as predicate phrases, as functors, is that we cannot define in the object language the concept of being in the lowest grammatical category.

There is no way of saying in the object language that there is no lower grammatical category than that of a particular phrase. This is so not merely because we cannot speak about grammatical categories in the object language at all, but also because when this phrase occurs in a grammatical category which is not the lowest grammatical category, then the string in which it occurs is not a well-formed string. We would have to exhibit an ill-formed string and say that it is not well-formed. The ontological counterpart of this grammatical consideration is even more striking. We cannot say in the object language that a given entity cannot be a property of another, for this would involve saying that it is not a property; that is, that for no entity is it its property. To say that x is an individual would mean that there is no y such that $x\{y\}$.

(7) $\bigwedge x$ [individual $\{x\} \equiv \sim(\bigvee y \, [x\{y\}])$]

However, (7), if true, if it conveys what it was intended to convey, is not well-formed. It is not well-formed because in the right-hand side of the equivalence 'x' occurs not in the same grammatical category as the occurrence of 'x' on the lefthand side. 'y' should be in a lower grammatical category than 'x' in front of it. But then the grammatical category of '*x*' in that definiens is not the lowest. The definiens, as it stands, rather asserts that *x* is an empty property, an attribute of nothing at all and not an individual. Either, therefore, (7) is to be a definition of the empty class, which is not an individual, or it is not well-formed. In the first case it should, perhaps, make clear that '*x*' is not in the same category as '*y*':

$$(7') \quad \Lambda x \,[\text{empty } \{x\} \equiv \sim(\vee y\, [x \{y\}])]$$

where the difference in the shape of parentheses indicates the difference of the grammatical categories. To say that something is a *substantia prima*, that is, an individual thing, is nonsense in the object language. One perhaps can, meta-systemically, conclude that something is treated as a prime substance by observing that it was never said of anything. But this conclusion has a very weak basis. It is, at best, a conclusion from somebody's speech, from a finite part of what he might have said. We conclude only that his speech is in accordance with the rule of treating an entity as an Aristotelian prime substance, as a thing, as *res;* we cannot conclude that he really takes it to be so. The rule of treating something as a prime substance—or better, an individual substance—is only a meta-systemic rule, which does not go into the description of the world itself, but rather into the description of our description of the world. Moreover, this is not a productive rule as are rules of inference; it is rather a prohibitive rule, so that we never observe an instance of its usage.

Therefore, one would like to give a paradoxical answer to the question of what there is. The answer would be: Everything, except the things. But even this cannot be said.

In the systems of logic which accept individuals it is a striking feature that none of the individuals is definable in the system. Such is the case in the *Principia Mathmetica* of Whitehead and Russell and such is the case in Quine's *Mathematical Logic.*[6] Quine considers an individual to be a class which is its own sole member, but individuals do not play any role in his system. (See *Mathematical Logic*. p. 135). In Zermelo's set theory the axiom of regularity (*Axiom der Fundierung*) asserts that there is no infinite descending chain of membership—but one does not deal there with any particular individual which is not a set.[7] It is the same in Aristotle, who in *Categories* and in *Metaphysics* accepted prime substances, but in the systematic work of *First Analytics* excluded them from the range of his variables.

---

[6] W. V. Quine, *Mathematical Logic*, revised edition (New York: Holt, Rinehart & Winston, 1951).

[7] See W. V. Quine, *Set Theory and its Logic* (Cambridge: Harvard University Press, 1963), p. 285.

Finally, I come to considerations about assertions of existence. These considerations also favor not speaking about individuals. The main claim will be that in logic (and therefore in any systematic knowledge) there are at least two senses of existence and that each is applicable in exactly the same manner to all properties, relations, properties of properties, and so on, and therefore that there is no need, nor even any possibility, of distinguishing any individuals which exist not as properties. The two senses of 'exists' I will call '*quantificational*' and '*predicative*'. There are also in logic some variants of the two concepts, but we will not go into these details. The two concepts are linked in an important way. [See (a) through (e) below.] I will not say which concept is better, which refers to "truer" existence. I will not ask which of the two concepts is closer to English and which (perhaps a different one) is closer to Czech.

Many logicians, particularly Quine, attribute existential import to the quantifier. There is no doubt that a quantified sentence says, in a sense, that something exists, that there is something satisfying a condition recited under the quantifier. Quine's doctrine in this matter is well-known and does not require repeating here. But several comments, mostly sceptical, are in order. When a phrase β is used in a true sentence α, then you can conclude as true that for some x, ϕx, where 'ϕx' is a sentential function obtained from the sentence α by replacing with 'x' one or more occurrences of β in α. Thus if Peter drives fast, then also for some x, x drives fast. But also it is quite convincing that if Peter drives fast, then for some x, Peter x fast; and also that for some x, Peter drives x (or x-ly). Quine limits the reasoning by "existential generalization," as he calls it, to noun phrases. This limitation is dictated by some of his philosophical opinions, as well as by ways in which he insists in rendering his philosophical opinions in the language of logic. But neither a practicing mathematician nor an English speaker would hesitate to draw conclusions by "existential generalizations" without Quinian restrictions. From '$5 < 7$' we conclude that for some r, 5 r 7, or, in other words, that there is a way in which 5 and 7 are related, or differently yet and perhaps better, '5 and 7 are related in a way' (or 'by a relation'). Similarly from 'Peter drives fast' English allows us to conclude 'Peter does something fast' and 'Peter drives with a velocity'.

The restrictions on this kind of reasoning should be of a very general nature only, say, that a phrase which is replaced by a variable be of a grammatical category. Somebody would violate this restriction should he try to conclude from '$2 \cdot (3 + 7) = y$' '$\bigvee f\,[2f3 + 7) = y]$'. The string composed of the multiplication symbol followed by the left-hand parenthesis is not a phrase of any grammatical category. The proposed conclusion is not well-formed. Similarly in English, if somebody concludes from 'Peter has not eaten any apple' that 'Peter has done something to apple', his supposed conclusion is not a grammatical sentence. The reason clearly is in the fact that the "existentially generalized" phrase *not eaten any* is not of a grammatical category. There are also cases when the requirement of the phrases thus generalized is violated, in which the alleged conclusion is a well-formed grammatical sentence, though the argument is not valid. For instance, if somebody concludes from 'Peter ate almost all the apples' that 'Peter has done something to all the apples', his reasoning is not sound. Here again *ate almost* is not a phrase of any grammatical category whatsoever, though it is a contiguous string. Incidentally, both in mathematical and natural languages, there are phrases which are of a grammatical category which are not contiguous. The well-known examples are 'either . . . or', 'both . . . and', 'is . . . ing' (like in 'is driving'). There are techniques to apply the "existential generalization" rule to discontiguous phrases, but we will not go into that technicality here.

We may phrase our conclusion not solely by means of an explicit existence assertion. We may say not only 'There exists a relation which 5 bears to 7' but also, as we have just done, '5 and 7 are related in a way'; not only 'There is a velocity with which Peter drives', but also 'Peter drives with a velocity' or 'Peter drives somehow'; and not only 'There exists somebody who drives', but also simply 'Somebody drives'.

In a natural language we use indefinite pronouns in these cases, or some other indefinite classifiers like 'a speed'. It is perhaps more prudent to name the rule involved *'the rule of indefinite pronominalization'*, or—more generally—*'the rule of indefinite replacement'*. The existential import of the use of the rule is much diminished by a less existential phrasing of the indefinite promorphemes.

Let me add that the very term 'existential quantifier' seems misleading. Indeed, in the Warsaw school it was not used; instead the term 'particular quantifier' was employed. This had a double advantage. First, it avoided the suggestion that this quantifier must be interpreted as carrying existential claims. Second, and quite properly, it linked the sentences with the two quantifiers of modern logic—the universal and the particular—to the terminology of traditional logic, where universal sentences were contrasted with particular sentences. In traditional logic, the contrast was just the same as the contrast made nowadays between the two quantifiers, though the applicability of the current quantifiers is much greater.

The use of the particular, or—if you insist—existential, quantifier is a source of some perplexities. To start with, its use is not necessary.

It is not necessary in two ways. First, every use of it is equivalently replaceable by a phrase which utilizes the universal quantifier. This is a well-known procedure. The customary statement of that procedure is to replace '$\bigvee x\,[f(x)]$' with '$\sim(\bigwedge x\,[\sim(f(x))])$'. The second way in which the use of the particular quantifier is not necessary arises from the fact that no special rule of inference refers to it. The universal quantifier is referred to by the rule of substitution and by the rules of distributing the quantifier, for instance by the rule of distributing the quantifier over implication. These rules, to a large extent, determine the sense of the universal quantification. But no primitive rule of inference refers to the particular quantifier except through the direct translation of the substitution and the distribution rules.

The very statement of the procedure to rewrite any phrase containing the particular quantifier by a phrase without it, is puzzling, in that it is not a definition in a usual sense.

(8) $\bigwedge f\,[\bigvee x\,[f(x)] \equiv \sim(\bigwedge x[\sim(f(x))])]$[8]

Formula (8) does not satisfy the usual requirements of a definition. The proposed *definiendum* is not what it should be; it should be a constant functor followed by a number of variables which occur free in the *definiendum*. On th econtrary, the 'x' on the left-hand side of the equivalence is bound in the would-be *definiendum*. And so formula (8) cannot be accepted on the basis of the usual rule of definition. It requires a special *ad hoc* rule. Formula (8) would be the only case of its use in standard logic. We could think of introducing a lot of other different quantifiers, such as 'for infinitely many', 'for at most one', 'for exactly three', 'for any finite number', 'for non-denumerably many', among others, but this is not done in logic yet.[9]

At present, if we have a rule that allows us to accept formula (8), then it would be the only formula so accepted. That means that it is an axiom. It is hard to see what this axiom is going to accomplish in the system; it is not going to change anything semantically for the system. Whatever was a model of the system without axiom (8) remains a model of the system augmented by (8) and *vice versa*. If somebody attributes to sentence (8) some semantical importance, it is perhaps because he has preassigned a meaning to the phrase

---

[8] The underlined parentheses in formula (8) indicate that (8) holds for any shape of parentheses whatsoever. The underlined parentheses are used similarly in other formulas.

[9] Instead of (8) logicians often accept a meta-systemic rule that allows us to write $\bigvee \alpha\,[\phi(\alpha)]$ in place of $\sim(\bigwedge \alpha\,[\sim(\phi(\alpha))])$. The problem remains under what conditions such a definitional rule can be accepted for the system.

'for some'. The existential meaning and the concept of existence is limited for him by his personal persuasions on what there is. These persuasions are not stated in the system of logic, but only in his personal constraints on the kind of models he will use. It would be better to state explicitly one's ontological opinions rather than to pretend that they are somehow included in the meaning of a quantifier, which they are not.

The use of variables and quantifiers binding them often has the effect of changing the domain of our discourse. The equating of the sentence

(9)   There is an oak in front of my window.

with

(10) $\bigvee x$ [x is an oak in front of my window],

or more exactly, from the point of view that rejects (8),

(11) $\sim(\bigwedge x$ [x is not an oak in front of my window])

is questionable because in the first sentence I am speaking about an object, the oak in front of my window. I do not really know, or need to know, on what level of ontological abstractness this object is here being considered. It may be just a property. For we speak about properties, often without the slightest indication of what entities these are properties. We speak about transitivity of relations, without entering into the problem of what sort of beings are related by these relations.

The second concept of existence, the predicative concept, was originated by Leśniewski's theory in which

(12) $\bigvee x$ [ex $\{x\}$ $\equiv$ $\bigvee y$ [$x\{y\}$]].

For example, exist {dog} because $\bigvee y$ [dog $\{y\}$].
Similarly, ex {transitivity of relations} because $\bigvee y$ [y is a transitive relation], or $\bigvee y$ [trans $\{y\}$]. For functors of more than one argument we need also

(13) $\bigwedge x$ [ex $\{x\}$] $\equiv$ $\bigvee y$ $\bigvee z$ [$x\{yz\}$]]
(14) $\bigwedge x$ [ex $\{x\}$ $\equiv$ $\bigvee y$ $\bigvee z$ $\bigvee w$ [$x\{yzw\}$]][10]

This concept of existence is closest to English 'there is' or 'there are'. Existence, so defined, is a predicate, a property. To say that

_____

[10] The parentheses are not necessarily fixed; this means that grammatical categories are not fixed. But the shapes of parentheses here indicate schematically the mutual dependence of the grammatical categories involved.

existence is a property is an ontological statement. To this ontological statement corresponds a linguistic formulation: the phrase 'exists' is a functor which forms a sentence with an appropriate argument, an argument of a suitable grammatical category. If the variable 'x' is of the grammatical category a, then 'exists' is of the grammatical category of a functor that forms a sentence when combined with a phrase of the category a.

The predicative concept of existence, as I here defined it, applies well to all the grammatical categories, except the lowest one, if there were such. Equivalently the concept of existence may be defined by the Leśniewski kind of ϵ but not of the lowest type.

(15) $\bigwedge x \, [\text{ex} \, \{x\} \equiv \bigvee y \, [\epsilon\{yx\}]]$

To say that there are x's is to say that for some y, y is an x. Thus, to say that there are relations is to say that there is something which is a relation. More exactly, $\bigvee y \, [\epsilon\{yx\}]$ means that

(16) $\bigvee a \, \bigvee b \, [y\{ab\}] \wedge \bigwedge a \, \bigwedge b \, [y\{ab\} \supset x\{ab\}] \wedge$
$\bigwedge a \, \bigwedge b \, \bigwedge c \, \bigwedge d \, [(y\{ab\} \wedge y\{cd\}) \supset (a = c \wedge$
$b = d)]$

The connection between the two concepts of existence, the predicative and the quantificational, can be seen by the following example.

From '5 < 7' we conclude, as we have seen,

(a') $\bigvee x \, [x\{5, 7\}]$

Now we adopt a definition

(b') $\bigwedge y \, \bigwedge z \, \bigwedge x \, [\text{rel} \, \langle yz \rangle \{x\} \equiv x\{yz\}]$

The number 5 bears to 7 many relations: smaller than, is different from, is the relative prime of, is the prime next smaller than the prime, when doubled is more than, and infinitely many others. With definition (b') we define the general concept of a relation which y bears to z. This concept is predicated of a relation x any time x holds between y and z. Substituting in definition (b'), '5' for 'y' and '7' for 'z',

(c') $\bigwedge x \, [\text{rel} \, \langle 5, 7 \rangle \{x\} \equiv x\{5, 7\}]$

Because of (a') from (c')

(d') $\bigvee x \, [\text{rel} \, \langle 5, 7 \rangle \{x\}]$

Using now the definition of predicative existence

(e′)   ex {rel ⟨5, 7⟩}

In our conclusion (e′) 'rel ⟨5, 7⟩' is of the grammatical category of a functor which forms a sentence with one argument which, in turn, is of the same grammatical category as 'is smaller than'. In statement (e′) we assert the existence of a property of relations. In statement (a′) the existence of a relation is asserted. From sentence (e′) we can also derive sentence (a′). Thus they are inferentially equivalent.

More generally, suppose that

(a) $\bigvee x \,[\phi(abx)]$

where '$\phi(abx)$' is a sentential function in which 'x' occurs as the only free variable and 'a' and 'b' occur as constants. We accept a definition

(b) $\bigwedge y \,\bigwedge z \,\bigwedge x \,[\alpha\langle y, z\rangle\{x\} \equiv \phi(yzx)]$

where '$\phi(yzx)$' differs from '$\phi(abx)$' only by replacing some occurrences of 'a' and 'b' by occurrences of 'y' and 'z' respectively. By substituting in definition (b) 'a' for 'y' and 'b' for 'z', we obtain

(c) $\bigwedge x \,[\alpha\langle ab\rangle\{x\} \equiv \phi(abx)]$

combining sentences (a) and (c),

(d) $\bigvee x \,[\alpha\langle ab\rangle\{x\}]$

Using the definition of 'ex',

(e)   ex {α⟨ab⟩}

Similarly, if we suppose sentence (e), we obtain sentence (a). Thus they are inferentially equivalent.

It is necessary to shift the category of existence here. There are quantificationally existing attributes which do not exist predicatively. We may have

(17) $\sim(\bigvee x \,[f\{x\}])$

and therefore,

(18) $\sim(\text{ex } \{f\})$

But we can at the same time conclude from (18) itself that

(19) $\bigvee x\, [\sim(\text{ex } \{x\})]$

and therefore,

(20)   ex {non-ex}

where non-ex is defined as

(21) $\bigwedge y\, [\text{non-ex } \{y\} \equiv \sim(\text{ex } \{y\})]$

Or we may say according to assertion (20) that *nonexistence exists.*

So far we were dealing with many concepts of existence; for each grammatical category we formed a separate concept. We schematize it by underlining the parentheses in 'ex $(\underline{x})$', but, of course, if the grammatical category of 'x' is α, then the grammatical category of 'ex' is $(s;\, \alpha)$. If the grammatical category of 'x' is $(s;\, \alpha)$, then the grammatical category of 'ex' is $(s;\, (s;\, \alpha))$, and so on. The question arises whether we can generalize the concept of existence. To this the answer is partly positive. In order to arrive at such a generalization we must form abstract sets, which are abstracted from the level of less abstract sets. We may, for instance, accept as a rule: If a concept is defined in the system of type theory, then we can also accept a set which is its abstraction, namely a set which has as its members all and only particular sets defined in the type theory, provided that their definientia differ only by the types of some of their phrases.

Thus we have several empty sets, for each grammatical category separately:

(22) $\bigwedge x\, [\Phi\{x\} \equiv \sim(\bigvee y\, [x\{\{y\}\}])]$

also

(23) $\bigwedge x\, [\Phi\{x\} \equiv \sim(\bigvee y\, [x\{y\}])]$

and so on. Therefore, generalizing definitions (22), (23), and infinitely many similar cases,

(24) $\bigwedge x\, [\Phi_a[x] \equiv \sim(\bigvee y\, [x[y]])]$
              $a\ a$ $a\ a$

The subscript 'a' indicates in definition (24) and in subsequent formulae that we do not consider 'x' or 'y' or 'Φ' as phrases of any particular grammatical category; rather we generalize over all empty sets and form an abstract empty set. For variables, we can substitute constants marked by subscript 'a', so we may ask, for instance, whether or not $\Phi_a[\Phi_a]$. The answer is in the negative; the concept of an empty set is not empty; that is, there are empty sets.

$$(25) \quad \Phi_a[\Phi_a] \equiv \bigwedge y \, [\sim(\Phi_a[y])]$$

But the right-hand side of sentence (25) implies, by substitution of an abstract for a variable inside parentheses marked with 'a', that $\sim(\Phi_a[\Phi_a])$. Therefore,

$$(26) \quad \sim(\Phi_a[\Phi_a])$$

If we abandon the theory of types and reach for a greater generalization, as we have just done, we may substitute any phrase marked by subscript 'a' in place of any variable which occurs as an argument inside parentheses marked by subscript 'a'. We may also speak about properties of abstract sets. However, not all properties of abstract sets are themselves abstract sets. Only those properties are abstract sets which are indeed abstractions of the theory of types. Thus, we can define a Russellian set

$$(27) \quad \bigwedge x \, [R[x] \equiv \sim(x[x])]$$

For instance, the abstract empty set is Russellian; that is $R[\Phi_a]$. But we cannot put the subscript 'a' under 'R'; R is not an abstract set, though it is a property of abstract sets. This precludes substituting 'R' for 'x' and obtaining an antimony.

After these preliminary comments we may ask again whether the concept of existence can be generalized. It is obvious that it can, as it was introduced for any particular case in accordance with the type theory. Therefore,

$$(28) \quad \bigwedge x \, [\mathrm{ex}_a[x] \equiv \bigvee y \, [x[y]]]$$

The definiens in definition (28) is just a negation of the definiens in definition (24), which defined the abstract empty set. We can now substitute 'ex' for 'x' in definition (28) and obtain

$$(29) \quad \mathrm{ex}_a \, [\mathrm{ex}_a] \equiv \bigvee y \, [\mathrm{ex}_a \, [y]]$$

Applying definition (28) to theorem (29),

(30) $\text{ex}_a \; [\text{ex}_a] \equiv \bigvee y \; \bigvee x \; [y[x_a]]$
        $\quad a \quad a \qquad\qquad\quad a \quad a$

which says that the existence class exists, if and only if something can be predicated of something else.

There are cases when we say that there are some entities but we are not able to show them. When we say

there are x, such that $f \, [x]$
            $\qquad\qquad\qquad a \quad a$

someone may meaningfully ask for an example of such an x. The concept of existence needed for modern science is broad enough not to be able to provide an answer. And in some cases the very question itself is not sound.

First, recall the many nonconstructive theorems of mathematics. The famous mean-value theorem states that for any function f differentiable between a and b, there is a number for which the derivative of the function is equal to the slope between $f(a)$ and $f(b)$. But, usually we are not able to compute that number. Moreover, in physics we say

A body has lost 150 calories.

To this the question 'which ones?' is silly. Still, calories exist, and their existence is confirmed strongly by physical theories. I am inclined to think that most fundamental scientific entities are like calories rather than like individual taps.

Transworld Identity or Worldbound Individuals?

ALVIN PLANTINGA

Calvin College

The idea of *possible worlds* has seemed to promise understanding and insight into several venerable problems of modality—those of essence and accident, for example, necessary and contingent truth, modality *de dicto* and *de re*, and the nature of subjunctive conditionals. But just what is a possible world? Suppose we take it that a possible world is a *state of affairs* of some kind—one which either obtains, is real, is actual, or else *could have* obtained. But then how shall we understand "could have" here? Obviously no *definition* will be of much use: Here we must give examples, lay out the connections between the concept in question and other concepts, reply to objections, and hope for the best. Although I cannot do this in detail here,[1] I do wish to point out that the sense of possibility in question is wider than that of *causal* or *natural* possibility—so that *Agnew's swimming the Atlantic Ocean*, while it is perhaps causally or naturally impossible, is not impossible in the sense under discussion. On the other hand, this sense is narrower than that captured in first-order logic, so that many states of affairs are necessary, in the sense in question, although their corresponding propositions are not provable in first-order logic. Examples of such states of affairs would include those corresponding to truths of arithmetic and mathematics generally,

---

[1] See my "De Re et De Dicto," *Nous* (September 1969) and "World and Essence," *Philosophical Review* (October, 1970).

as well as many more homely items such as *Nobody's being taller than himself, red's being a color,* (as well as *a thing's being colored if red*), *Agnew's not being a composite number,* and the like. Other and less homely candidates include *every person's being conscious at some time or other, every human person's having a body at some time during his career,* and *the existence of a being than which it's not possible that there be a greater.*

In the sense of necessity and possibility in question, furthermore, a pair of states of affairs S and S' may be so related that it is not possible that both obtain, in which case S *precludes* S'; and if it is impossible that S obtain and S' *not* obtain, then S *includes* S'. So, for example, *Agnew's having swum the Atlantic* includes *Agnew's having swum something or other* and precludes *Agnew's not being able to swim.* Still further, a state of affairs S may be such that for any state of affairs S', S either includes or precludes S', in which case S is *maximal.* Now we may say that a possible world is just a maximal possible state of affairs. Corresponding to each possible world W, furthermore, there is a unique class of propositions, C, of which a proposition P is a member just in case it is impossible that W be actual and P be false. Call this class *the book on W.* Like possible worlds, books too have a maximality property: each book contains, for any proposition P, either P or the negation of P. And the book on the actual world, obviously, is the set of true propositions.

Now it is plausible and natural to suppose that the same individual exists in various different states of affairs. There is, for example, the state of affairs consisting in *Paul R. Zwier's being a good tennis player;* this state of affairs is possible but does not in fact obtain. It is natural to suppose, however, that if it *had* obtained, Zwier would have existed and would have been a good tennis player. That is, it is natural to suppose that Zwier *exists in* this state of affairs. But, of course, if he exists in this state of affairs, then he exists in every possible world including it; that is, every possible world including *Zwier's being a good tennis player* is such that, had it been actual, Zwier would have existed. So Zwier exists in many possible worlds. I say it is natural to make this supposition; but many philosophers otherwise kindly disposed towards possible worlds are inclined towards it denial. Among them, there is, for example, Leibniz, whose credentials on this subject are certainly impeccable; Leibniz apparently held that each object exists in just one world.[2] The idealists, furthermore, in arguing for their doctrine of internal

[2] As has been argued by Benson Mates. "Leibniz on Possible Worlds," *Logic, Methodology, and Philosophy of Science* 3rd, ed. Amsterdam: Van Rootselaar and Staal, 1968).

relations, were arguing in essence that an object exists in exactly one possible world—indeed, some of them may have thought that there is only one such world. More recently, the view that individuals are thus confined to one world—let's call it The Theory of Worldbound Individuals—has been at least entertained with considerable hospitality by David Kaplan.[3] Roderick Chisholm, furthermore, finds difficulty and perplexity in the claim that the same object exists in more than one possible world.[4] Still further, The Theory of Worldbound Individuals is an explicit postulate of David Lewis' Counterpart Theory.[5] In what follows I shall explore this issue. Now perhaps the most important and widely heralded argument for the Theory of Worldbound Individuals (hereafter 'TWI') is the celebrated *Problem of Transworld Identification*, said to arise on the supposition that the same object exists in more than one world. Accordingly I will concentrate on these two topics: TWI and the problem of Transworld Identity.

Why, then, should we suppose that an individual is confined to just one world—that you and I, for example, exist in this world and this world only? According to G. E. Moore, the idealists, in arguing for their view that all relations are internal, were really arguing that all relational properties are essential to the things that have them. The argument they gave, however, if it is sound, establishes that *all* properties—not just relational properties—are thus essential to their owners. If this is correct, however, then for no object x is there a possible state of affairs in which x lacks a property that in fact it has; so x exists only in the actual world, the world that does in fact obtain.

Now an argument for a conclusion as sweeping as this must pack quite a punch. What did the idealists come up with? A confusion, says Moore. What the idealists asserted is

(1)   If P be a relational property and A a term to which it does in fact belong, then, no matter what P and A may be, it may always be truly asserted of them, that any term which had *not* possessed P would necessarily have been other than numerically different from A. . . . [6]

[3] "Transworld Identification," read at an APA Symposium, Chicago, 1967.
[4] "Identity through Possible Worlds: Some Questions," *Nous*, Vol. I, No. 1 (1967), p. 1.
[5] "Counterpart Theory and Quantified Modal Logic," *Journal of Philosophy*, Vol. LXV, No. 5 (March 1968), p. 113.
[6] "External and Internal Relations," *Philosophical Studies* (London: Routledge and Kegan Paul Ltd, 1922), p. 287.

Perhaps we may put this more perspicuously as

(1′)   If x has P, then for any object y, if there is a world in which y lacks P, then y is distinct from x

which clearly entails the desired conclusion. What they suggested as a reason for accepting (1), however is

(2)   If A has P and x does not, it *does* follow that x is other than A.[7]

If we restate (2) as the claim that

(2′)   For any object x and y, if x has P and y does not, then x is distinct from y

holds in every world, we see that (2) is just the thesis that the Indiscernibility of Identicals is necessarily true. This thesis seems accurate enough, but no reason at all for (1) or (1′). As Moore, says, (1) and (2) are easily conflated, particularly when they are put in the idealists typically opaque and turgid prose; and the idealists seized the opportunity to conflate them.

Initially, then, this argument is unpromising. It has a near relative, however, that we may conceivably find in Leibniz and that often surfaces in contemporary discussion. Leibniz writes Arnauld as follows:

> Besides, if, in the life of any person and even in the whole universe anything went differently from what it has, nothing could prevent us from saying that it was another person or another possible universe which God had chosen. It would then be indeed another individual.[8]

This is on its face a dark saying. What Leibniz says here and elsewhere, however, may suggest the following. Suppose Socrates exists in some world W distinct from the actual world (which for purposes of easy reference I shall name "Charley"). Taking the term 'property' in a broad sense, we shall be obliged to concede that there must

[7] *Ibid.*, p. 289.
[8] Letter from Leibniz to Arnauld, July 14, 1686. Leibniz makes very nearly the same statement in a letter to Count von Hessen-Rheinfels, May 1686 (p. 111), *Discourse on Metaphysics* (La Salle, Ill.: Open Court, 1962), p. 127–128. published in the *Discourse* as well.

be some property that Socrates has in Charley but lacks in W. (At the very least, if we let 'π' name the book on Charley, then one property Socrates has in Charley but lacks in W is that of being such that every member of π is true.) So let us suppose that there is some property—snubnosedness, let us say—that Socrates has in Charley but lacks in W. That is, the Socrates of Charley, Socrates-in-Charley, has snubnosedness, while the Socrates of W does not. But surely this is inconsistent with the Indiscernibility of Identicals, a principle than which none sounder can be conceived. For according to this principle, if Socrates-in-Charley has snubnosedness but Socrates-in-W does not, then Socrates-in-Charley is distinct from Socrates-in-W. We must conclude, therefore, that Socrates does not exist both in Charley and in W. There may be some person in W that much resembles our Socrates, Socrates-in-Charley; that person is nonetheless distinct from him. And of course this argument can be generalized to show that nothing exists in more than one world.

Such an argument, however, is less than impeccable. We are asked to infer

(3)   Socrates-in-Charley is snubnosed and Socrates-in-W is not

from

(4)   Socrates is snubnosed in Charley but not in W

We need not quarrel with this request; but the Indiscernibility of Identicals in no way licenses the inference that Socrates-in-Charley and Socrates-in-W are distinct. For, contrary, perhaps, to appearances, there is no property that (3) predicates of Socrates-in-Charley and withholds from Socrates-in-W. According to (3) [so taken that it follows from (4)], Socrates-in-Charley (that is, Socrates) has the property of being snubnosed, all right, but *in Charley*. Socrates-in-W, however, lacks that property *in W*. But this latter, of course, means only that Socrates-in-W has the property of being such that, if W had obtained, he would not have been snubnosed. And, of course, this property—the property an object x has iff x would not have been snubnosed, had W obtained—is not the complement of snubnosedness. Indeed, this property is not even incompatible with snubnosedness; Socrates himself is snubnosed, but would not have been had W been actual. So the Indiscernibility of Identicals does not apply here; there is no property P which (3) asserts that Socrates-in-Charley has but Socrates-in-W lacks. To suppose that Socrates has

P in the actual world but lacks it in *W* is to suppose only that Socrates does in fact have *P* but would not have had it, had *W* been actual. The Indiscernibility of Identicals casts not even a hint of suspicion upon this supposition. This objection, therefore, is a snare and a delusion.

A more popular and more promising argument for TWI is the dreaded *Problem of Transworld Identity* said to confront anyone who rashly supposes the same object to exist in more than one world. Here the claim is that there are deep conceptual difficulties in *identifying* the same object from world to world—difficulties that threaten the very idea of Transworld Identity with incoherence. These difficulties, furthermore, presumably do not arise on TWI.[9]

But what, exactly, *is* the problem of Transworld Identity? What difficulties does it present for the notion that the same object exists in various possible worlds? Just how does this problem go? Although published statements of it are scarce,[10] the problem may perhaps be put as follows. Let us suppose again that Socrates exists in some world *W* distinct from this one—a world in which let us say, he did not fight in the battle of Marathon. In *W*, of course, he may also lack other properties he has in this world—perhaps in *W* he eschewed philosophy, corrupted no youth, and thus escaped the wrath of the Athenians. Perhaps in *W* he lived in Corinth, was six feet tall, and remained a bachelor all his life. But then we must ask ourselves how we could possibly *identify* Socrates in that world. How could we *pick him out?* How could we *locate* him there? How could we possibly tell which of the many things contained in *W* is *Socrates?* If we try to employ the properties we use to identify him in *this* world, our efforts may well end in dismal failure—perhaps in that world it is Xenophon or maybe even Thrasymachus that is Plato's mentor and exhibits the splendidly single-minded passion for truth and justice that characterizes Socrates in this. But if we cannot identify him in *W*, so the argument continues, then we really do not understand the assertion that he exists there. If we cannot even identify him, we would not know whom we were talking about, in saying that Socrates exists in that world or has this or that property therein. In order to make sense of such talk, we must have a *criterion* or *principle* that enables us to identify Socrates from world to world. This criterion must include some property that Socrates has in each

[9] So David Lewis: "P_2 [the postulate according to which nothing exists in more than one world] serves only to rule out avoidable problems of individuation" (op. cit.)

[10] But see R. Chisholm, "Identity through Possible Worlds: Some Questions," *Nous* Vol. I, No. 1, pp. 1–8.

world in which he exists—and if it is sufficient to enable us to *pick him out* in a given world, distinguish him from other things, it must be a property he alone has in these worlds. Further, if the property (or properties) in question is to enable us to pick him out, it must in some broad sense be "empirically manifest"—it must resemble such properties as having such-and-such a name, address, Social Security number, height, weight, and general appearance in that we can tell by broadly empirical means whether a given object has or lacks it. How, otherwise, could we use it to *pick out* or *identify* him? So, if it is intelligible to suppose that Socrates exists in more than one world, there must be some empirically manifest property that he and he alone has in each of the worlds in which he exists. Now obviously we do not know of any such property, or even that there is such a property. Indeed, it is hard to see how there *could* be such a property. But then the very idea of Transworld Identity is not really intelligible—in which case we must suppose that no object exists in more than one world.

The first thing to note about the objection outlined above is that it seems to arise out of a certain *picture* or *image*. We imagine ourselves somehow peering into another world; we ask ourselves whether Socrates exists in it. We observe the behavior and characteristics of its denizens and then wonder wonder which of these, if any, is Socrates. Of course, we realize that he might look quite different in W, if he exists there at all. He might also live at a different place, have different friends and different fingerprints, if, indeed, he has fingers. But how then can we tell which one he *is?* And does it so much as make sense to say that he exists in that world, if there is no way in principle of identifying him, of telling which thing there *is* Socrates?

Now perhaps this picture is useful in certain respects; in the present context, however, it breeds nothing but confusion. For it is this picture that slyly insinuates that the proposition *Socrates exists in other possible worlds* is intelligible to us only if we know of some empirically manifest property that he and he alone has in each world in which he exists. But suppose we consider an analogous temporal situation. In Herbert Spiegelberg's book *The Phenomenological Movement* there are pictures of Franz Brentano at ages 20 and 70 respectively. The youthful Brentano looks much like Apollo; the elderly Brentano resembles nothing so much as Jerome Hines in his portrayal of the dying Czar in Boris Godounov. Most of us will concede that the same object exists at several different times; but do we know of some empirically manifest property P such that a thing is Brentano at a given time t if and only if it has P? Surely not; and this casts no shadow whatever on the intelligibility of the claim that Brentano existed at many different times.

Still, isn't the argument made above available here? No doubt there was a time, some fifty years ago, when Spiro Agnew was a precocious baby. But if I understand that assertion, must I not be able to *pick him out, locate* him, at that time? If I cannot identify him, if I cannot tell which of the things that existed at that time was Agnew, than (so goes the argument) I cannot make sense of the claim that he existed at that time. And I could identify him, at *t*, only if I know of some empirically manifest property that he and he alone has at *t*.

But here the argument is manifestly confused. To suppose that Agnew was a precocious baby at *t* it is not necessary that I be able to pick his picture out of a gallery of babies at *t*. Of course I must know *who he is* to understand this assertion; and perhaps to know that I must know of some property that he and he alone has. Indeed, we might go so far as to concede that this property must be 'empirically manifest' in some sense. But surely it is asking too much to require that I know of such a property that he and he only has *at every time at which he exists*. Of course I must be able to answer the question "Which of the things existing at *t* is Agnew?" But the answer is trivial; it's that man sitting right over there—the Vice President of the United States.

If this is correct, however, why suppose otherwise in the Transworld case? I understand the proposition that there is a possible world in which Socrates did not teach Plato. Now let *W* be any such world. Why suppose that a condition of my understanding this is my knowing something about what he would have looked like or where he would have lived, had *W* been actual? To understand this proposition I must know who Socrates is. Perhaps this involves my knowing of some property that is empirically manifest (whatever exactly that comes to) and unique to Socrates. But what earthly (or otherwise) reason is there for supposing that I must know of some empirically manifest property he has *in that world W?* The picture suggests that I must be able to look into *W* and sift through its inhabitants until I run across one I recognize as Socrates—otherwise I cannot identify him, and hence I do not know whom I am talking about. But here the picture is not doing right by us. For, taken literally, of course, this notion makes no sense. All I know about this world *W* is that Socrates would not have taught Plato had *W* obtained. I do not know anything about which other persons would have existed, or—except for his essential properties—which other properties Socrates has in that world. How could I know more, since all I have been told about

W is that it is one of the many worlds in which Socrates exists but does not teach Plato?

Accordingly, the claim that I must be able somehow to identify Socrates in W—pick him out—is either trivial or based on a confusion. Of course, I must know which of the persons existing in W—the persons who would have existed, had W been actual—I am talking about. But the answer, obviously, and trivially, is Socrates. To be able thus to answer, however, I need know nothing further about what Socrates would have been like had W been actual.

But let us imagine the objector regrouping. "If Socrates exists in several worlds," he says, "then even if there need be no *empirically manifest* property he and he alone has in each of them, there must at any rate be some property or other that he and only he has in each world in which he exists. Let us say that such a property is an essence of Socrates. Such as essence meets two conditions: (1) Socrates has it in every world he graces, and (2) nothing distinct from him has it in any world. (By contrast, a property need meet only the first condition to be *essential* to Socrates.) Now a property P entails a property Q if there is no world in which there exists an object that has P but lacks Q. So any essence of Socrates entails each of his essential properties—each property that Socrates has in every world in which he exists. Furthermore, if E is an essence of Socrates, then the class C of his essential properties—the properties he has in each world in which he exists—will obviously entail E in the sense that there is no world in which something exemplifies all of these properties but does not exemplify E. (What makes this particularly obvious is that any essence of Socrates is essential to him and hence is a member of C.) An essence of Socrates, therefore, is, in this sense, equivalent to the class of his essential properties; and Socrates exists in more than one possible world only if he has at least one essence in the explained sense. But at best it is far from clear which (if any) of Socrates' properties are essential to him and even less clear that he has an essence. Nor does there seem to be any way of determining whether he has such a property or, if he does, which properties are entailed by it. So is not the suggestion that he has an essence both gratuitous and problematic? We can and should avoid this whole problem by accepting TWI." Thus far the objector.

What can be said by way of reply? First, that if we follow this counsel, we gain all the advantages of theft over honest toil, as Russell says in another connection. The question is whether Socrates has an essence and whether objects do or do not exist in more than one world—not whether we would be saved some work or perplexity if we said they did not. But more fundamentally, TWI does not avoid the question which of Socrates' properties are essential to him. Obviously it gives an answer to that question, and an unsatisfactory one at that; for it says that *all* of his properties are essential to him and that any property he alone has—that of being married to Xantippe, for example—is one of his essences.

These caveats entered, however (and I shall return below to the second), let us consider the objector's main complaint. Is it really so difficult, on The Theory of Transworld Identity, to determine whether Socrates has an essence? In fact, in the actual world, Socrates has the property of being snubnosed. But now consider a world W in which he is not snubnosed. Had W obtained, Socrates would not have been snubnosed; we may say, therefore, that Socrates is non-snubnosed-in-W. In general, where P is a property and W a world, to say that x has P-in-W is simply to say that x would have had P if W had been actual. So Socrates has the property of *being non-snubnosed-in-W;* that is, he has this property in Charley, the actual world. In W, on the other hand, Socrates has the property of *being-snubnosed-in-Charley.* Indeed, in *any* world in which Socrates exists, he has the property of being snubnosed-in-Charley.[11] This property, therefore, is essential to him. And of course we can generalize the claim: Where P is any property Socrates has, the property of having-P-in-Charley is essential to him. But now consider some property P that Socrates has in fact and that he alone has—*being married to Xantippe*, perhaps, or *being born at such and such a place and time*, or *being A. E. Taylor's favorite philosopher.* The property *having-P-in-Charley* will, of course, be essential to Socrates. Furthermore, each thing distinct from Socrates has its complement essentially, for everything distinct from Socrates has the complement $\bar{P}$ of P; hence each such thing has $\bar{P}$-in-Charley, and has it essentially, that is, in every world in which it exists. But then everything distinct from Socrates has the complement of *having-P-in-Charley* and has that property essentially. So there is no possible world in which some object distinct from Socrates has the property of having P-in-Charley. Not only, then, is this property essential to him; it is also one of his essences. And obviously we can find as many essences of Socrates as you like. Take any property P and world W such that Socrates alone has P in W; the property of having P in W is an essence of Socrates.[12]

---

[11] If, as I do, we make the S_5-like opposition that if a given state of affairs (or proposition) S is possible, then S is possible in every world. See "World and Essence," p. 475.

[12] For more discussion of his essences (and for discussion of more of his essences) see "World and Essence," pp. 487 ff.

Now you may think the very idea of a property like *being snub-nosed in Charley* is muddled, perverse, ungainly, or in some other way deserving of abuse and contempt. But where, exactly (or even approximately), is the muddle? We must not let this terminology mislead us into thinking that if there is such a property, then Charley must be a geographical unit or place—like Wyoming, for example—so that this property would be like *being mugged in New Jersey*. Socrates elected to remain in Athens and drink the hemlock, instead of fleeing to Thebes. He had the opportunity to take the latter course, however, and it was certainly possible that he do so. So there are possible worlds in which Socrates flees to Thebes and does not drink the hemlock. Now let *W* be any such world. Certainly it is true of Socrates that if *W* had been actual, he would have fled to Thebes; but that is all that is meant by saying that Socrates has the property of fleeing-to-Thebes-in-*W*. It is certainly not easy to see that this property is mysterious, underhanded, inelegant, or that it merits much by way of scorn and obloquy.

The objector, therefore, is right in claiming that if Socrates exists in several worlds, he must have an essence. His objection to the latter idea, however, is not impressive. Is there really something problematic or untoward in the idea of Transworld Identity? Is there really a problem of Transworld Identification? If there is, I am at a loss to see what it might be.

Of course there are legitimate problems in the neighborhood—problems that often are exposed when the subject ostensibly under dicussion is Transworld Identity. For we might ask such questions as these: Is there a world *W* and an object *x* existing in *W* such that *x* is identical with Socrates, and *x*, let us say, was born in 1500 BC or was an eighteenth-century Irish washerwoman? These questions advertise themselves as questions about Transworld Identity; in fact they are questions concerning which of Socrates' properties are essential to him. Could he have had the property of being disembodied-at-some-time-or-other? Or the property of having-an-alligator-body-at-some-time-or-other? These are legitimate questions to which there are no easy answers. (Socrates himself suggests that everyone actually has the former property, while some of his more snappish acquaintances may have the latter.) These are real questions; but they need not shake our confidence that some of Socrates' properties are ones he could have lacked, so that Charley is not the only possible world in which he exists. The fact that we are not confident about their answers means only that Socrates has *some* properties such that we cannot easily tell whether or not they are essential to him; it does not so much as suggest that *all* his properties are thus inscrutable. And further, of course, the Theory of Worldbound Individuals, as so far explained, does not avoid these questions; it simply answers them by fiat in insisting that each of Socrates' properties is essential to him.

II

The arguments for the Theory of Worldbound Individuals, then, are based upon error and confusion. But are there positive reasons for rejecting it? I think there are. The basic thrust of the theory is the contention that no object exists in more than one possible world; this implies the outrageous view that—taking property in the broadest possible sense—no object could have lacked any property that in fact it has. Had the world been different in even the tiniest, most Socrates-irrelevant fashion, Socrates would not have existed. Suppose God created n electrons. The theory in question entails the absolute impossibility of His having created both Socrates and $n + 1$ electrons. It thereby fails to distinguish the relation in which he stands to inconsistent attributes—being both married and unmarried, for example—from his relation to such attributes as *fleeing to Thebes*. It is as impossible, according to this theory, that Socrates should have had the latter as the former. Consider furthermore, a proposition like

(5)   Socrates is foolish

a proposition which predicates of Socrates some property he lacks. Now presumably (5) is true, in a given possible world, only if Socrates exists in that world and has the property of being foolish therein. But on TWI, there is no such world, and (5) accordingly, is necessarily false, as will be any proposition predicating of Socrates a property he does not in fact have. In the same vein, consider any proposition P that is false but contingent. Since *Socrates exists* is true only in Charley, where P is false, there is no world in which P and *Socrates exists* are both true. The latter, therefore, entails the denial of the former. Accordingly, *Socrates exists* entails every true proposition. And all of this is entirely too extravagant to be believed. If we know anything at all about modality, we know that some of Socrates' properties are accidental, that *Socrates is foolish* is not necessarily false, and that *Socrates exists* does not entail every true proposition.

But here we must consider an exciting new wrinkle to this old theory. Embracing the Theory of Worldbound Individuals, David Lewis adds to it the suggestion that a world-bound individual typically has *counterparts* in other possible worlds:

The counterpart relation is our substitute for identity between things in different worlds. Where some would say that you are in several worlds, in which you have somewhat different properties and somewhat different things happen to you, I prefer to say that you are in the actual world and no other, but you have counterparts in several other worlds. Your counterparts resemble you closely in content and context in important respects. They resemble you more closely than do the other things in their worlds. But they are not really you. For each of them is in his own world, and only you are here in the actual world. Indeed we might say, speaking casually, that your counterparts are you in other worlds, that they and you are the same; but this sameness is no more a literal identity than the sameness between you today and you tomorrow. It would be better to say that your counterparts are men you *would have been*, had the world been otherwise.[13]

Fortified with Counterpart Theory, TWI is no longer obliged to hold that each of Socrates' properties is essential to him; instead, a property is essential to him if and only if each of his counterparts (among whom is Socrates himself) has it. Accordingly, while indeed there is no world in which Socrates, *our* Socrates—the object that in our world is Socrates—lacks the property of being snubnosed, there are no doubt worlds containing *counterparts* of Socrates—counterparts which are not snubnosed. So the property of being snubnosed is not essential to him.

And let us now return to

(5) Socrates is foolish.

TWI seems to imply, paradoxically enough, that this statement is necessarily false. Can Counterpart Theory be of help here? Indeed it can, for, no doubt, Socrates has foolish counterparts in other worlds; and this is sufficient, according to TWI fortified with Counterpart

[13] "Counterpart Theory and Quantified Modal Logic," *Journal of Philosophy*, Vol. LXV, No. 5 (1968), p. 114–115. I said David Lewis embraces TWI; but this is not entirely accurate. Speaking of the Counterpart Relation, he says, "Yet with this substitute in use, it would not matter if some things *were* identical with some of their counterparts after all! P₂ [the postulate according to which objects are worldbound] serves only to rule out avoidable problems of individuation." One may offer and study means of formalizing modal discourse for a variety or reasons, and TWI is not really essential to Lewis' program. What I shall be quarrelling with in ensuing pages is not that program, but the view which takes TWI as the sober, metaphysical truth of the matter.

Theory, for the contingency of (5). This proposition is contingently false if there is another world in which it is true; but its truth in a given world does not require the existence, in that world, of what is denoted by 'Socrates' in this. Like 'the first man to climb Mt. Rainier', 'Socrates', according to the present view, denotes different persons in different worlds. Or, as we may also put it, in different worlds different things have the property of being Socrates—just as, in different worlds, different things have the property of being the first man to climb Rainier.

Socrateity, then, or the property of being Socrates, is not the property of being identical with the person who in Charley, the actual world, is Socrates; it is not the property of being that person. It is, instead, a property that could have been had by someone else; roughly, it is the property that is unique to Socrates and his counterparts. You may think it difficult to see just what property that is; and indeed that *is* difficult. In the present context, however, what is important to see is that Socrateity is had by different objects in different worlds. Indeed, on counterpart Theory an object may have more than one property in a given world; so no doubt there are worlds in which several distinct things exemplify Socrateity. And the point is that (5) is true, in a world W, just in case W contains an object that is both Socratic and foolish—that is, just in case Socrates has foolish counterpart and Socrateity a foolish instance in W. So what (5) says is or is equivalent to

(6)   Something exemplifies both Socrateity and foolishness.

And, of course, this proposition will be true in some but not all worlds. But what about

(7)   Socrates exists?

If nothing exists in more than one world, then presumably Socrates does not, in which case on TWI, (fortified with Counterpart Theory though it be), (7) still seems to be true in just one world and still seems paradoxically to entail every true proposition. But here perhaps appearances are deceiving. Counterpart Theory affords the means of denying that (7) is true in only one world. For this proposition, we may say, is true in any world where Socrateity has an instance; since there are many such, there are many worlds in which it is true; hence there are many worlds in which both (7) and some false propositions are true. So the former does not entail every true proposition. But if (7) is true in many worlds, how does the central claim of

TWI—that nothing exists in more than one—fit in? If Socrates, along
with everything else) exists in only one world, that is, if

(8)   Socrates exists in more than one world

is false, how can (7) be true in more than one world?

But perhaps the partisan of TWI can go so far as to deny that
his theory commits him to the falsity of (8). Perhaps he can construe
it as the entirely accurate claim that *Socrates exists* is true in more
than one world. But how, then, does (8) comport with the central
claim of TWI? According to the latter, nothing has the property
of existing in more than one world. How, then, can TWI sensibly
hold that (8) is true? As follows, perhaps. Suppose the predicate
"exists in more than one world" expresses a property that, according
to TWI, no object has. Then (8), if true, must not, of course, be
seen as predicating that property of Socrates—if it did, it would
be false. Perhaps it *looks* as if it predicates that property of Socrates;
in fact, however, it does not. What it does instead is to predicate
truth in more than one world of *Socrates exists*. There is an instructive
parallel between (8) so construed and

(9)   The number of planets is possibly greater than nine.

Read *de dicto*, (9) quite properly predicates possibility of

(10)   The number of planets is greater than nine.

It is plausible to add, furthermore, that the words "is possibly greater
than nine" express a property—the property a thing has just in case
it is possibly greater than nine. Every number greater than nine enjoys
this property; that is to say, each number greater than nine is *possibly*
greater than nine. The number of planets, however, being nine, does
not have the property in question. (9), therefore, can be read as
a true *de dicto* assertion; but, thus read, it does not predicate of
the object named by "the number of planets" the property expressed
by "is possibly greater than seven."

Similarly, then, for (8); the words "exists in more than one
world" express a property that (if TWI is true) nothing has; the
proposition in question, however, does not predicate that property
of anything and hence need not (at any rate on that account) be
false. Furthermore the argument from

(11)   Nothing exists in more than one world

to the falsehood of (8) is to be rejected. We may compare this argument with another:

(12)   Every number greater than seven is necessarily greater than seven

(13)   The number of planets is greater than seven.

Hence

(14)   The number of planets is necessarily greater than seven.

If we construe (14) as the *de dicto* claim that

(15)   The number of planets is greater than seven

is necessarily true, then it obviously fails to follow from (12) and (13). (12) says that every number meeting a certain condition has a certain property—that of being necessarily greater than seven. According to (13), the number of planets meets that condition. (14), however, is not the consequent *de re* assertion that the number of planets has that property; it is instead the false (and inconsequent) *de dicto* assertion that (15) is necessarily true. But now the same can be said for (8). This is not the *de re* assertion that some specific object has the property that (11) says nothing has. *That* assertion, indeed, is precluded by (11) and thus is false on TWI. Instead, we must look upon (8) as the *de dicto* allegation that *Socrates exists* is true in more than one world—an allegation quite consistent with (11). What we have here, then, as in the inference of (14) from (12) and (13), is another *de re-de dicto* ambiguity.

So the partisan of TWI need not hold that Socrates has all his properties essentially, or that *Socrates exists* entails every true proposition. Indeed, he can go so far as to join the upholder of Transworld Identity in affirming the truth of sentence (8). You may think this course on his part less ingenuous than ingenious; and so, perhaps it is. Indeed, as we shall see, a certain disingenuousness is perhaps a salient feature of TWI. But so far the addition of Counterpart Theory seems to provide TWI with a solution for difficulties it could not otherwise cope with.

Despite its fortification with Counterpart Theory, however, the Theory of Worldbound Individuals is open to a pair of decisive objections. Perhaps we can approach the first of these as follows. Consider the following eccentric proposition:

(16)   Everyone is at least as tall as he is.

It is plausible to consider that this proposition predicates a certain property of each person—a property that is universally shared. It predicates of Lou Alcindor, for example, the property of being at least as tall as he himself is, a property that in no way distinguishes him from anyone else. But the proposition also predicates of each person a property he need not share with others. For what it also says of Lou Alcindor is that he has the property of being at least as tall as Lou Alcindor—a property he shares with nearly no one. The same things hold for

(17)   Everything is identical with itself.

This proposition predicates of each object the property of being self-identical—a property it shares with everything else. But it also says of any given object x that it has the property of being identical with x—a property unique to x. Socrates, for example, has the property of being essentially identical with Socrates, as well as that of being essentially self-identical. It is natural to say that these two properties *coincide* on Socrates in the sense that it is impossible that he have one but not the other.

But in TWI (henceforth understood to include Counterpart Theory) these two properties come apart. For while Socrates, of course, has no counterparts that lack self-identity, he does have counterparts that lack identity-with-Socrates. He alone of all of his counterparts, in fact, has the property of being identical with Socrates—the property, that is, of being identical with the object that in fact instantiates Socrateity. It is true, no doubt, that each of Socrates' counterparts has Socrateity, so that a counterpart (Socrates$_w$, say) of Socrates in a world W has the property of being identical with the thing that *in W* is Socrates or has Socrateity. But, of course, Socrates$_w$ is *distinct from* Socrates—the person who *in fact* is Socrates. Accordingly, some of Socrates' counterparts have the property of being distinct from Socrates. This means that (according to Counterpart Theory) the two properties predicated of Socrates by (17) do not coincide on Socrates. Indeed he has the property of being essentially self-identical, but he does not have the property of being essentially identical with Socrates. And this is the first of the two objections I promised. According to Counterpart Theory, the property of being identical with myself, unlike the property of self identity, is not essential to me. Hence I could have been someone else. And this, I take it, is genuinely paradoxical. I could have been different in many ways, no doubt; but it makes no sense to suppose that I could have been someone else—someone, who, had he existed, would have been distinct from me. And yet Counterpart Theory, thus explained, implies not merely that I *could* have been distinct from myself, but that I *would* have been distinct from myself had things gone differently in even the most miniscule detail.

We can approach the same matter a bit differently. According to Counterpart Theory,

(18)   I could have been taller than I am

is no doubt true. For what (18) requires is that there be a world in which I have a counterpart whose height exceeds the height I actually enjoy. But then similarly

(19)   I could have been a different person from the one I am

will be true just in case there is a world in which I have a counterpart who is a different person from the one I actually am. And of course the Counterpart Theorist will hold that I do have such counterparts; so he must hold that (19) is true. Indeed, he must put up with something even worse; Counterpart Theory implies, not merely that I *could* have been a different person from the one I am, but that I *would* have been a different person, had things gone differently in even the most miniscule detail. More exactly, what Counterpart Theory implies is the truth of

(20)   If *S*, then either I would not have existed or I would have been a different person from the one I am

where '*S*' is replaced by any false sentence. For such an instance of (20) will be true if every world in which *S* holds is one in which I lack a counterpart or have one that is a different person from the one I am. And, of course, if *S* is false, then every world in which it holds *is* one in which I either lack a counterpart or have one who is a different person from the one I am. If a leaf deep in the mountain fastness of the North Cascades had fallen in October 31, 1876, the day before it actually fell, then (according to Counterpart Theory) I should have been either nonexistent or else a different person from the one I am. And surely this is false.

According to TWI-Counterpart Theory, therefore, I have self-identity essentially but identity with myself accidentally. Although I could not have had self-diversity, I could have been diverse from myself, I could have been someone else. But there is a related and perhaps more important objection. The characteristic feature of TWI is that each of us (and everything else) would not so much as have existed had things been different in even the most insignificant fashion. This is itself not at all easy to believe. Asked to think of possible but non-actual states of affairs, we come up with such items as *Paul's being a good tennis player;* we suppose that there is a possible state of affairs such that, had it obtained, Paul himself—the very person we know and love so well—would have existed and had some property that, lamentably enough, he lacks. Perhaps this point becomes even more poignant if we take it personally. According to TWI, I would not have existed had things been in even the slightest way different. Had I had an extra cornflake for breakfast, I should not now exist. A narrow escape if there ever was one! The very idea fills one with existential Angst; the merest misstep has dramatic consequences indeed.

But of course the Angst is misplaced. For, according to TWI, there is no world in which I have that extra cornflake; it is not logically or metaphysically possible that I should have done so. And this holds whether or not TWI is fortified with Counterpart Theory; the latter's promise to relieve the former of this embarrassing consequence is not fulfilled. I am now confronted with what seems to me to be a choice; I can load my pipe with Dunhill's Standard Mixture or with Balkan Sobranie, both being available and congenial. I believe that it is possible for me to do either of these things and that which I do is up to me. According to TWI, however, one of these events will take place and the other has not so much as a ghost of a chance. For one of these takes place in the actual world and the other occurs in no possible world whatever. If I shall, in fact, smoke Sobranie, then smoking Dunhill is as far out of the question as smoking the number 7. No doubt the partisan of TWI will protest that it is possible for me to take an action A if there is a world—in which I have a counterpart who takes that action. But is not this just to redefine, change, the meaning of the locution 'it is possible for me'? Of what relevance to my being able to take an action A is the fact, if it is a fact, that there is a possible state of affairs such that, had it obtained, someone very like but distinct from me would have taken A? Surely this gives me no reason at all for supposing it possible that I take this action. Of course we can give a new sense to the terms involved; but to do so is just to change the subject.

The difficulty with TWI in its original Leibnizian forms, I said, was that it implied that each object has each of its properties essentially; and the original attractiveness of Counterpart Theory was its promise to overcome that difficulty. This promise, I think, is illusory. Of course we can define the locution 'has P essentially' in the way suggested by Counterpart Theory; and then we will be in verbal agreement with the truth that objects have some of their properties accidentally. But the agreement, I suggest, is *only* verbal. For according to TWI, if in fact I have a property P, then there is no possible world in which I lack it. It is not possible that I should have lacked it. Of course there may be a state of affairs S such that had it obtained, there would have existed someone similar to me that would have lacked P; but how is this even relevant to the question where I could have lacked P—whether it is possible that I should not have had P? This seems no more to the point than the possibility that there be someone with my *name* who lacks P. And hence I do not think Counterpart Theory succeeds in overcoming the main objection to TWI; that difficulty remains.

By way of summary and conclusion, then: our initial insight into these matters is that objects have only some of their properties essentially; and an object x has a property P contingently only if there is a possible state of affairs S such that x would not have had P had S obtained. This joint affirmation obviously implies that the same object exists in more than one possible world—an idea that some find difficult or incoherent. The objections to this idea, however, do not withstand careful scrutiny. To reject it, furthermore, is to hold that an object exists in exactly one possible world, and this alternative entails—with or without the fortification of Counterpart Theory—that each object has each of its properties essentially.

The Ontology of the Possible

NICHOLAS RESCHER

University of Pittsburgh

I

PRELIMINARIES

The sphere of the possible covers a wide range. There are as-yet unrealized possibilities that await us in the future. And there are the possible albeit unrealized doings of actual things such as my possible attendance at the film I failed to see last night. There are those things which are "possible for all I know," many of which will be as real as anything can be. But some states of affairs and some things are *merely* possible. They are not going to come to be realized in the future. Further inquiry is not going to have them turn out to be real. They are not simply alternative permutations of the actual. They are wholly unreal—*merely* possible in the most strictly hypothetical sense. These possible things and states of affairs—we may call them *hard-core possibilities*—are paradigmatic of what I have in mind here in speaking of "the possible." These hard-core, totally unactualized possibilities will be central to the ensuing discussion.

The conception of "nonentities," or "unactualized possibles," or "negative things," or "unreal particulars," or "nonexistent individuals" is among the most ancient and persistent notions in the history of philosophy. In surveying this area of conceptual historiography it is my aim to show the idea of nonexistent individuals to be historically respectable in its antecedents, as well as to have substantial philosophical interest.

The fountainhead of subsequent discussions of nonexistent individuals is to be found in the dialogues of Plato. In the *Sophist*[1] Plato espoused the Parmenidean view that all meaningful discourse (*logós*) must be *about a being* of some kind. Since winged horses and other nonexistent things can obviously be talked of meaningfully,[2] a rigid adherence to this doctrine would suggest for them a mode of being that is intermediate between the actually existent and the utterly nonexistent which could not even be talked about or thought of. Plato did not hesitate to draw this consequence, and his view of these matters is the precursor of all later treatments of the problem. We shall not, however, pursue these historical byways further on this occasion, referring the interested reader to other discussions.[3]

II

THE ONTOLOGICAL STATUS OF POSSIBILITIES

Putting aside historical observations, we turn now to the systematic issues. The central question of this paper can be posed in very old-fashioned terminology: What is the ontological status of nonexistent possibilities?

Possibilistic claims have their principal point where the contrast between the actually real and the hypothetically possible prevails, and where the domain of what is or what does happen is to be augmented by that of what can be or what might happen. Now the items of this second, hypothetical sphere clearly cannot just "objectively be" the case. It is my central thesis that by the very nature of hypothetical possibilities they cannot exist as such, but must be thought of: They must be hypothesized, or imagined, or assumed, or something of this sort. For unlike real acts, hypothetical ones, by their very nature, lack, *ex hypothesi*, that objective foundation in the existential order which alone could render them independent of conceiving minds.

---

[1] See especially **236 E** ff. "It is also plain, that in speaking of something (*ti*) we speak of being (*ontos*), for to speak of an abstract something naked and isolated from all being is impossible" (*ibid.*, 237 D, tr. Jowett). Cf. also the discussion in the *Theaetetus*, 189 A.

[2] However, positive statements about nonexistents will presumably be false according to the correspondence theory of truth of *Sophist*, 261 E-263 B, since reality cannot provide the corresponding circumstances. Cf. Francis Cornford, *Plato's Theory of Knowledge* (London: Routledge & Kegan Paul, 1936), p. 313. Compare however, J. Xenakis' article "Plato on Statement and Truth-Value," *Mind*, Vol. 66 (1957), pp. 165-172, where it is argued that for Plato, claims about nonexistents do not represent proper statements at all, and so do not have a truth value. However, see also the reply by J. M. E. Moravcsik, "Mr. Xenakis on Truth and Meaning," *ibid.*, Vol. 67 (1958), pp. 533-537.

[3] "The Concept of Nonexistent Possibles," *Essays in Philosophical Analysis* (Pittsburgh: University of Pittsburgh Press, 1969).

This critical point that the realm of the hypothetical is mind-dependent must be argued in detail. Just what can be said regarding the existential status of that which is possible but not actual? In considering this, let us begin by asking the question: What sorts of items are at issue with the locution "X is possible but not actual"? We can best answer this question by referring to the two traditional modes of modality, modality *de dicto* and modality *de re*. When we say that X is possible (but unactualized) then X is to be taken either (1) as a certain proposition (it is possible that-the-cat-is-on-the-mat) or (2) as a certain state of affairs (the cat's being on the mat is possible). But in dealing with the *ontology* of the possible, only this second category of possible states of affairs or things could conceivably concern us. For then we are certainly *not* concerned with the question of whether *propositions* exist as such: Our interest is in the existential status of *what is asserted by them*. Thus the *ontological* issues that concern us here are those posed by modality on the *de re* side; the question is not one of the existential status of the *proposition* "that the cat is on the mat" (*qua* proposition), but rather one of the existential status of the state of affairs that this proposition claims to obtain.

But just exactly what can the existential status of a possible-but-unrealized state of affairs be? Clearly—*ex hypothesi*—the state of affairs or things at issue does not exist as such: Only *actual* things or states of affairs can unqualifiedly be said to exist, not those that are possible but unrealized. By definition, only the *actual* will ever exist in the world, never the unactualized possible. For the world does not have two existential compartments, one including the actual and another that includes the unactual. Of course, unactualized possibilities can be conceived, entertained, hypothesized, assumed, and so on. That is to say, they can, in a way, exist—or "subsist" if one prefers— not, of course, unqualifiedly in themselves, but in a *relativized* manner, as the objects of certain intellectual processes. But it goes without saying that if their ontological footing is to rest on this basis, then they are clearly mind-dependent.

In the cases of actual existence we have a dualism. There is

(1)   The actually existing thing or state of affairs (for example, with "that dogs have tails" we have the tailed dogs)

and

(2)   The thought or entertainment of this thing or state of affairs.

But with nonexistent possibilities (such as, that dogs have horns) the ontological situation becomes monistic since item (1) is altogether lacking. And this difference is crucial. For, in the dualistic cases of actual existence, (1) would remain even if (2) were done away with. But with nonexistent possibles there is (*ex hypothesi*) no items of category (1) to remain, and so category (2) is determinative. Exactly this is the basis of the ontological mind-dependent of nonexistent possibles.

I insisted above that, in dealing with the *ontology* of the possible, our concern is not with modality *de dicto* (or rather *de cogitatione*) but with modality *de re;* not with the (very actual) *thought-of-the-possibility* but with *the possibility itself,* the (utterly nonexistent) state of affairs that is thought of. We must distinguish clearly between these two items:

> (i)   the thought of the (nonexistent) possibility (*der Gedanke des Nichtseiendes*)
> (ii) the (nonexistent) possibility thought of (*das nichtseiende Gedachte*)

When this distinction is duly observed, the "ontological" aspect of the matter becomes quite clear:

> (A)   The ontological status per se of item (ii), the possibility at issue, is simply zero: *ex hypothesi* the item in question does not exist at all.
> (B)   Clearly item (i), the thought of the possibility, exists unproblematically in the manner of thoughts in general. And while its object, item (ii), does not "exist" in reality, it does "exist" (or "subsist" or what have you) *as the object* of the thought.
> (C)   And then it is perfectly clear that *this* mode "being"—not as a reality but solely as an object of thought—is mind-dependent.

One point of caution is immediately necessary. We are not saying that to be a possible (but unactualized) state of affairs requires that this state must *actually* be conceived (or entertained, hypothesized, and so on)—so as in fact to stand in relation to some *specific* mind. Rather, what we are saying is that possible, albeit unrealized, states of affairs or things obtain an ontological footing, that is, they can be said to "exist" in some appropriately qualified way only insofar as it lies within the generic province of minds to conceive (or to entertain, hypothesize, and so on) them. Thus the ontological footing of unactualized possible states of affairs involves the mind in this generic sense that the very concept at issue is viable only with reference to concepts the analysis of which demands reference to the workings of minds.

The case for the mind-dependency of hypothetical possibilities is obviously not based on any sort of empirical considerations as to the workings of minds, but is purely a matter of a priori conceptual analysis. Possibilities are mind-dependent because the essential purport of the very conception of possibility is mind-involving. There simply can be no unrealized possibilities lying about in the real and "objective" world: unreal possibilities can only be imagined, supposed, and so on. They cannot be located but only *assumed* to be located; they cannot be handled, seen, heard, but only *supposed* to be handled, seen, heard. Of course, it is not a *property* of the imaginary dollar bill that it is not to be seen anywhere. Kant is quite right about this; the imaginary dollar bill is not to be imagined as an *invisible* dollar bill (then it would not be a dollar bill at all) but as one that is real—and so visible, and capable of being handled, among other things. But although invisibility is *ex hypothesi* not a descriptive *property* that characterizes an imaginary dollar, it is all the same a regulative *fact* about it. It is not by way of their internal and constitutive properties but by way of the external and regulative facts about them that hypothetical possibilities are mind-involving. (And these are not just contingent facts about them, but necessary ones that serve to make the items at issue what they are.)

The argument that hypothetical possibilities depend on the mind thus proceeds as follows:

(1) The natural world of mind-independent reality comprises only the actual. This world does not contain a region where nonexistent or unactualized possibilities somehow "exist." Unactualized hypothetical possibilities *ex hypothesi* do not exist in the world of objective reality at all.

(2) Nor do unactualized possibilities exist in some mind-accessible Platonic realm of mind-independent reality existing wholly outside the natural world order.

(3) The very foundation for the distinction between something actual and something merely hypothetically possible is thus lacking in a "mindless" world. Unactualized hypothetical possibilities lack an independent ontological footing in the

sphere of objective reality: They can be said to "exist" only insofar as they are *conceived*, or *thought of*, or *hypothesized*, and the like. For such a possibility to be (*esse*) is therefore to be conceived (*concipi*).[4] In consequence, possibility is mind-dependent.

The procedure described above outlines the general strategy for arguing in denial of the thesis that possibilities exist in some self-subsisting realm that is "independent of the mind." Inorganic nature—subrational nature generally—encompasses only the actual: The domain of the possible is the creation of intelligent organisms, and is a realm accessible to them alone. A "robust realism of physical objects" is all very well, but it just will not plausibly extend into the area of the hypothetical. We can plausibly argue that it would be foolish (or philosophically perverse) to deny the thesis: "This (real) stone I am looking at would exist even if nobody ever saw it." But we cannot reason by analogy to support the thesis: "This nonexistent but possible stone I am thinking of would be there even if nobody could imagine it." The existential objectivity and autonomy of the real world does not underwrite that of the sphere of hypothetical possibility. This sphere is mind-dependent, and so consequently are all those intellectual resources of whatever kind they be—that are hinged upon it.

I do not want to wander off into Bishop Berkeley's forest. For the present we are not concerned with the general idealist position that substance—real and unreal unlike—will in general require minds. We are prepared to recognize and admit the crucial distinction between the attribution of a property to an object by someone (which obviously requires a mind), and the *possession* of the property by the object (which is or may be presumed to be an "objective," mind-independent fact). But hypothetical possibilities are *inherently* mind-related: The hypothetical cannot just "objectively be" the case, but must be hypothesized, or imagined, or assumed, or whatever. Unlike real facts, merely hypothetical ones lack, *ex hypothesi*, that objective foundation in the existential order which alone could render them independent of minds.

The following line of objection is more or less inevitable: "To make possibility *in toto* mind-dependent is surely fallacious. Take physical possibility, for example. This acorn has the potentiality to

---

[4] To say this is not to drop the usual distinction between a thought and its object. If I imagine this orange to be an apple, I imagine it *as an apple* and not as an *imaginary* apple. But this does not gainsay the fact that the apple at issue *is* an imaginary apple that "exists only in my imagination."

develop into an oak. How can the possible development of a tree in such cases possibly be mind-dependent?" We reply: Regardless of the status of the acorn as being independent of the existence of the mind, and whatever the acorn *in fact* does, the strictly *modal* aspect of what it may or may not do is not and cannot be an aspect of objective reality. (The potentiality of function and teleology is invariably based upon *lawfulness* and this—as we shall argue below—represents an inherently mind-dependent conception.) The possibility of developmental processes involves the mind in just this respect that possibility (or indeed all modality outside the actual) requires the existence of minds.

On such a view, then, mere or strictly hypothetical possibilities are mind-made. Does it follow from this position that if there were no men—or rather no rational minds—that there would be no unreal possibilities? Are we driven to a possibility-idealism as the logical terminus of the line of thought we have been tracing out? These questions must, I believe, be answered affirmatively. If the conceptual resources that come into being with rational minds and their capabilities were abolished, the realm of supposition and counterfact would be abolished too, and with it the domain of unrealized, albeit possible, things would also have to vanish.

But to put the matter in this way is somewhat misleading. Our present preoccupation is not with a point of conjectural natural history, but is strictly *conceptual* in character. The conceptual unraveling of the idea of "hypothetical possibilities" demands deployment of mind-related conceptions. Thus the dependence at issue is conceptual and not causal. We are certainly not saying that the world (the extramental world) somehow becomes different with the introduction of minds.

The objection that "Surely it was possible before there were any minds in the universe that there should be minds; hence possibilities antedate minds and accordingly cannot be mind-dependent" thus misses its target if aimed at our position. The whole issue of historico-causal dependencies is quite beside the point, and even to talk of a mental *creation* of possibility is to set up something of a straw man. Doubtless there were colors (in the sense of phenomenal colors) in the universe before there were sight-endowed beings. But this in no way saves phenomenal color from being *conceptually* sight-referring. In fine, it is a *conceptual* dependency upon mind-referring notions rather than any *causal* dependency upon the functionings of minds that is at issue in our discussion.

It is crucial that our concern is not with assertions regarding or ideas about possibilities—which are obviously and trivially mind-involving—but the possibilities themselves. We recognize and admit—indeed regard as crucial—the distinction between the *attribution* of a property to an object by someone (which evidently requires a mind), and the *possession* of the property by the object (which is or may be supposed to be an "objective" fact that does not require any reference to mind). But unrealized possibilities are insuperably mind-related: The hypothetically possible cannot just "objectively be" the case; it must be hypothesized, or imagined, or assumed, and so on. Unlike real facts, hypothetical ones lack, *ex hypothesi*, that objective foundation in the existential order which alone could render them independent of minds.

Of course, in a trivial sense, everything that is discussed—real or unreal—bears *some* relationship to a mind. Unquestionably, no matter what truth *we* may think of, *somebody* thinks of; but what people think of is not the crux. Being thought of is not essential to the truthfulness of a truth. This whole way of approaching the matter—with reference to what "is thought" to be the case—loses sight of our specifically focal issue of unrealized possibilities. I have no desire to question the distinction between a fact, say that the cat is on the mat (which could continue unchanged in a world devoid of intelligence), and the thought or statement of a fact (which could not). My point is that the *condition* of possibility, unlike the *condition* of factuality, involves something (namely, a reference to the hypothetical) that would be infeasible in the face of a postulated absence of minds. Unrealized possibility is not something that we can meaningfully postulate objectively of a mindless world, that is, a world from which all mind-involving conceptions have been abstracted. For if the hypothetical element (which is clearly accessible only in a world endowed with minds) were *aufgehoben* (annihilated), possible things and states of affairs would be *aufgehoben* as well. Of course, *we* can think of an "alternative possible world" that is unpopulated, and so denuded of minds, but yet endowed with unrealized possibilities—so long as we do not postulate a genuinely mindless universe and abandon reference—however implicit—to the sphere of mind. But if we rigorously put aside minds and their capabilities, eliminating any and all reference to the mental, then the hypothetical element is lost, and unrealized possibility is lost with it.

We have no desire to be pushed to the extreme of saying that the "being" of nonexistent "possible beings" lies in their being actually *conceived;* rather, we take it to reside in their being *conceivable.* The "being" of an unactualized item does not inhere in its relation to this or that specific mind, but to its conceivability by mind-in-general, in terms of the linguistic resources that are a common capability of intelligence as we know it. This independence of any specific mind establishes the *objectivity* of nonexistent possibilities despite their mind-dependence. Just as an actual thing or state of affairs remains as such when not known, so an unactualized item is not affected if not conceived by any actual person. But this independence of specific minds does not render unactualized possibles independent of mind as such. Their mind-dependence is not *particularistic* (like that of a headache) but *generic:* a dependence on the capability of minds as such. (And, of course, generic mind-dependence is mind-dependence all the same.)

But are we not involved in a circle of some kind in saying that possibility resides in conceivability, something which in turn requires reference to the possible—to what *can be conceived?* Is not the qualification of possibility in terms of possibilities a nonproductive circumambulation? Not really. What we are saying is that the "reality" of certain possible states of affairs and things (that is, nonexistent possibilities) resides in the reality of possibility-involving *processes* [the *construction* of verbal descriptions, and the *hypothesizing* (assuming, postulating) of their existence]. We are saying that, when the-possibility-of-the-thing is its only "reality," this "reality" inheres in a possibilistic intellectual process. Here actuality is indeed prior to possibility—the actuality of one category of things, namely, minds with their characteristic modes of functioning, underwrites the *construction* of the totality of nonexistent possibles that can be contemplated.

Nonexistent possibilities thus have an amphibious ontological basis: They root in the capability of *minds* to perform certain operations—to describe and to hypothesize (assume, conjecture, suppose)— operations to which the use of *language* is essential, so that both thought processes and language enter the picture. The dependency of unrealized possibilities on language gives them the *objective* ontological foothold they undoubtedly possess. "The possibility existed alright only nobody thought of it at the time" is a perfectly viable locution, the import of which we might gloss as follows: "The means for its description exist and the possibility *could* therefore have been formulated, though in fact no one had then hypothesized it." And the statement, "There are possibilities no one will ever conceive of" is also perfectly viable and can be glossed along just the same lines. Actually is prior to possibility (as Aristotle was wont to insist), but we must amend this by the thesis that the possibility of a thing (that is, entity possibility) is posterior to the possibility of a process (that is, conceptual possibility). *It is the actuality of minds capable of deploying by way of hypotheses and assumptions the descriptive mechanisms of*

language that provides the ontological basis of nonexistent possibilities.
For such possibilities "exist" insofar as they can be stated or described
in the context of their being supposed, assumed, posited, or the like.

From this standpoint several conclusions emerge: (1) *Substantive*
possibility (the possibility of states of affairs and things) is conceptually consequent upon *functional* possibility (the possibility of process). (2) The processes at issue here are those intellectual processes
through which the descriptions of nonexistent things are constructed
and the existence of such things hypothesized. (3) Intellectual possibilities are fundamental; the basic category of possible things are
possible descriptions and thus are terms that are in large measure
linguistic in nature. Thus on our view the possibility-for-being is secondary to and consequent upon the possibility-for-description (construed rather broadly to include imaging and imagining. And finally
(4) whatever "being" or "quasireality" nonexistent possibilities have
is thus consequent upon the actuality of minds and their modes of
functioning.

The last point deserves special emphasis. It is important to distinguish between *existential* possibility, the possibility-of-item (that
is, the of states of affairs or things), which, at the "hard-core"
level underwrites the conception of such nonexistent possible items
as the Cheshire cat *functional* possibility, the possibility-of-process,
perhaps better designated as *contingent potentiality,* such as the possibility of an apple tree to bear certain fruit or of a speaker to utter
certain words. Our point is that even a "mere possibility" of the
existential type always can, and in the final analysis, *must* have a
grounding in the range of functional possibility—and indeed of functional possibility relating to mental functions. In affording the mechanisms of conceivability minds come to be functionally operative and
to render the whole range of possibility in general mind-involving.

What we are saying is the "mere" possibility of the existential
type is based upon and derivative from a real functional potentiality
of mental processes. It is in this sense that all possibility in general
involves some reference to the mental—namely because the *functional
possibility* of mental processes is basic to and fundamental for the
realm of possibility in general.

One very basic line of objection must be considered. Someone
might protest as follows:

"I grant," says the objector, "that it makes sense to speak of
possible nonexistent states of affairs, such as its being (merely)
possible that a cat be on the mat. But such a *propositional* possi-

bility posed by a that clause, surely does not give rise to possible *things*, and so does not justify us in speaking of *a* or *the* (non-existent) cat on the mat. To speak of possible things or entities is to reify, quite illegitimately, the strictly propositional possibility that a thing of that sort exists. But this substantizing move from a possible-that situation to the setting up of a *possible-thing* is wholly improper."

I wholly endorse this objection in all regards, except that it claims to being an objection. Nothing we have said gainsays its complaint as to the queerness and dispensability of a realm of possible *entities*. Throughout our discussion of ontology we have been careful to use such locutions as "possibilities," "possible state of affairs or things," or "possible item." The ontology of possibilities that has concerned us does not have a specifically thing-directed orientation in any sense that requires *entities*. The existence-claims with which we are concerned are posed by locutions of the propositional variety typified by:

that-there-be-a-cat-on-the-mat.

It does *not* require us to postulate some queer entity, a possibilistic cat, that is somehow present upon the mat. The mode of being or existence at issue in the thesis

It is (merely) possible that there be (exist) a cat on the mat

is the target of our discussion, and not the being or existence of that queer entity, the *ex hypothesi* nonexistent cat that is mysteriously placed upon the mat.[5]

III

The Linguistic Foundations of Possibility

Among contemporary logicians W. V. Quine especially has been concerned to attack the very idea of possible but nonexistent objects. Quine has assaulted this conception not only with weighty argument

---

[5] This section elaborates and develops some points made almost in passing in the section on "Lawfulness as Mind-Dependent" in my book on *Scientific Explanation* (New York: The Free Press, 1970), pp. 113–121.

but also with clever invective. In his influential paper "On What There Is," he has made great fun of possible nonexistent entities:

> Take for instance, the possible fat man in that doorway; and, again, the possible bald man in that doorway. Are they the same possible men, or two possible men? How do we decide? How many possible men are there in that doorway? Are there more possible thin ones than fat ones? How many of them are alike? Or would their being alike make them one? Are no *two* possible things alike? Is this the same as saying that it is impossible for two things to be alike? Or, finally, is the concept of identity simply inapplicable to unactualized possibles? But what sense can be found in talking of entities which cannot meaningfully be said to be identical with themselves and distinct from one another?[6]

Quine is seeking for a principle of individuation (*principium individuationis*) for nonexistent, yet possible, items. But—his inclination to the contrary notwithstanding—this problem does not in fact pose any insuperable obstacles. Presumably a nonexistent possible is to be identified by means of a *defining description*. And on this, the classical approach to the matter, the problems so amusingly posed by Quine encounters no decisive theoretical difficulties. How many possible objects are there? Clearly as many as can be described distinctly—presumably an *infinite* number. When are two possible objects identical? When their defining descriptions are "logically identical," that is, equivalent. The doctrine of possible objects entails no major logical anomalies. With nonexistents everything save existence alone (and its implications) remains precisely the same as it does with objects that "really" exist, subject to one exception only: Existents can be differentiated by purely ostensive processes—pointing or other means of placement within "this actual world"—whereas possibilities cannot be so indicated; they must be differentiated by purely descriptive means, that is, by indicating property differences.

The theory of nonexistent possibles in the sense of *merely possible things* is actually, as I see it, a somewhat misleading derivation from

---

[6] "On What There Is," *The Review of Metaphysics*, Vol. 2 (1948), pp. 21–38; reprinted in L. Linsky (ed.), *Semantics and the Philosophy of Language* (Urbana: University of Illinois Press, 1952), pp. 189–206. See pp. 23–24 (pp. 191–192 of the Linsky reprint). A cognate denial of nonexistent individuals and of the "reality" of unrealized possibilities is found in J. M. E. McTaggart, *The Nature of Existence*, vol. 1 (Cambridge: Cambridge University Press, 1921), Bk. I, Chap. 2.

the conception of *unactualized states of affairs,* which is itself super-venient upon certain actualities. Thus the actual state of affairs:

(1)   that there is no cat on the mat

automatically gives rise (under appropriate conditions) to the follow-ing unactualized states of affairs

(2)   that there should be a cat on the mat.

And it is because of the states of (2) as a "mere possibility" that we can appropriately speak of an unactualized possible entity such as

(3)   the possible cat on the mat

and in turn such more detailed (description-laden) variants as

(4)   the possible Siamese tomcat on the mat.

In the manner of this example, nonexistent particular things are in general parasitic upon unactualized states of affairs.

To say (as I have done) that the doctrine of nonexistent possibles poses no insuperable theoretical difficulties is not to deny that their introduction into our conceptual framework may complicate the logi-cal situation somewhat. Here one consideration comes to mind pri-marily—one connected with their mode of individuation—namely their *descriptive incompleteness.*

With respect to any existent (that is, any actual existent) x it will have to be the case that the principle

(P)   For any property ϕ: If "ϕx" is false, then "$[\sim\phi]x$" is true

obtains. This principle holds whenever x is an actually existent object. Moreover, it holds whenever x is a possible object described completely through its Leibnizian "*complete* individuation notion." Unlike the more realistic situation we envisage, *Leibnizian* possibilia are defined through their complete individual notions in such a way that for any such individual and any predicate ϕ, either "ϕx" is true or "$[\sim\phi]x$" is true. Now the thesis (P) will not hold for nonexistent

possibles that are individuated—on the approach adopted here—
through an identifying characterization that is descriptively incomplete. Thus to individuate a nonexistent particular is to provide a
description of it, but this description will, in general, have the feature
of logical incompleteness.[7] This inherent incompleteness of (non-
Leibnizian) possibilia serves to set them apart from paradigm (ex-
tant) things.

The essential role here of descriptive mechanisms indicates the
indispensable part played in this connection by language. However
closely the descriptive machinery of our language—its stock of adjectives, verbs, and adverbs—may be tied to reality, the link to reality
is broken when we move from universals to particulars and from
their features to the things themselves. Once we have enough descriptive machinery to describe real things (such as this pen, which is
pointed, blue, 6 inches long, and so on) we are *ipso facto* in a position
to describe nonexistents (a pen in other respects like this one but
10 inches long). It is in principle impossible to design a language
in which the descriptive mechanisms suffice for discourse about real
things alone, without affording the means for introducing nonexistents
into discussion. The mechanisms of reference to nonexistents are an
inherent linguistic feature. Any language adequate to a discussion
of the real cannot but burst the bounds of reality.

Our view of the "ontology" of the matter can now be put into
brief compass. Unrealized possibilities do not exist as such. What
exists are minds and their capabilities, and consequently languages
and their rules. Unrealized possibilities are *generated* by minds, and
so they can be said to "exist" only in a secondary and dependent
sense, as actual or potential objects of thought. Such possibilities
are the products of an *intellectual construction*. The ontological status

---

[7] Actually the description might be formulated more effectively on a three-valued
basis. From this standpoint, given an individual x and a predicate ϕ three
situations can obtain:

ϕx: ϕ holds of x ("4 is even")
$[\sim\phi]x$: non-ϕ (the primitive negation predicate of ϕ) holds of x ("4 is non-
     prime")
ϕ is inapplicable to x: the predicate ϕ is in principle inapplicable to x, that
     is, it fails to apply for categorial reasons because x is
     the kind of thing with respect to which the predicate
     ϕ as well as its negation predicate $[\sim\phi]$ are "just not
     in the running" (4 is neither green nor non-green)

If this trichotomy were adopted, then an ordinary (existing) thing—as well
as a Leibnizian possibility—would invariably determine the given predicate
within the framework of one of the three groups. But a nonexistent possible
can now fail to fit anywhere, exactly as with the initially simplified dichotomy
it could fail to fit either way.

of the possible is thus fundamentally mind-dependent, the domain of the possible being a mental construct.[8]

IV

HISTORICAL RETROSPECT

Basically four positions have been taken in the history of philosophy with respect to the ontology of hard-core possibilities.

Position	This Position Attributes the Reality of Non-Existent Individuals to	Exponent
Nominalism	language	Russell, Quine
Conceptualism	the mind	Stoics, Descartes, Kant, Brentano
Conceptualistic Realism	the mind of God	Some Scholastics, Leibniz
Realism	a realm of possibility existing independently of human language and thought	Some Arabic Mu'tazilites, MacColl, Meinong

Let us consider these positions with a contemporary perspective. Regarded from this point of view, realism is not an attractive position. Present-day philosophers have a (well-advised) aversion toward postulating a Platonic realm of being that is distinct from the worlds of nature and of thought. Nor would Conceptualistic Realism nowadays be viewed as a viable position, for contemporary philosophers are unwilling to follow in the path of their predecessors (both before and after Descartes, Leibniz, and Berkeley) and obtain by theft—that is, by falling back upon theological considerations—what they believe ought to be the fruits of honest philosophical toil. Moreover, a rigorous Conceptualism, with reference to nonexistent possibilities, would not, I think, be regarded as an appealing position. For such a view must hold, regarding nonexistent possibilities, that *To be is to be conceived*—their *esse* is *concipi*. But the notion of *unthought-of possibilities* is certainly too viable to be so easily dismissed. (Note that while "it is possible though not conceived," is a perfectly viable conclusion, "it is possible though not conceivable" is not viable, at any rate, not in the *quasilogical*, rather than *psychological*, sense of "conceiv-

---

[8] In this discussion we have taken a distinctly verbal (that is, description-centered) view of unrealized possibilities. I have neglected, for example, the prospect of unreal things or states of affairs as presented quasivisually (for example in hallucination). This is no serious deficiency because in such cases of *illusion* (rather than hypothesis) the mind-dependency aspect of the matter is all the more clear and noncontroversial.

ability" that is relevant in my present discussion.[9] For our concern here is not with what people will in fact conceive of but with what is conceivable in principle.) And nonexistent possibilities would seem to have a solidity and objectivity of status that we hesitate to subject to the vagaries of what is and is not in fact thought of. I have preferred to move in the direction of going from "to be *conceived*" to "to be *conceivable*"—construing this in a broad sense that includes imaging and imagining. And once this approach has been purged of its psychologistic connotations, we have moved near to the nominalistic realm of what can be described and discussed, assumed and stated. Just here, in the sphere of linguo-centric considerations, we reach the ground which is, in any rate, most congenial to contemporary philosophers. The fashionably "modern" view that the ultimate foundation for nonexistent individuals is linguistic comes close to returning in a full circle to the language-oriented conceptualism expounded in classical antiquity by the Stoics in the context of their theory of *lekta* ("meanings"). The problem of nonexistent possibles once more illustrates the fundamental continuities of *philosophia perennis*.[10]

POSTSCRIPT

Throughout, I have been dealing with *hard-core* possibilities that are altogether unreal. The paradigm of our "mere" possibilities relate to items that do not exist at all, with nonexistent possibilities rather than the merely unrealized possibilities that involve some assumed change in the actual (such as moving my birthday ahead by a day or two). We have taken this line because hypothetical changes in actual things do not pose ontological issues of equal seriousness. But the thrust of my present discussion, namely that the mind dependency of the merely possible, would be quite unaffected if I broadened my focus. My key point that "mere possibility" is dependent on the mind holds not just for the utterly unreal, but applies equally throughout the whole realm of supposition and counterfact—to "what would happen if." The "ontological" problems are less pressing here but the infusion of mind-dependency is just as pressing. Hypotheses regarding the unrealized circumstances regarding real things are just as hypothetical as those relating to altogether nonexistent states of affairs and things.

---

[9] On the issue of psychologism that arises here cf. Chapter VII of N. Rescher, *Essays in Philosophical Analysis* (Pittsburgh: University of Pittsburgh Press, 1969).

[10] Some of the materials of this paper—and particularly of this section—have been drawn from Chapter IV, "The Concept of Nonexistent Possibles," in my *Essays in Philosophical Analysis* (Pittsburgh: University of Pittsburgh Press, 1969), pp. 73–110.

Individuals in Possible Worlds

STEPHAN KÖRNER

Bristol University

The purpose of this paper is to explain the problem of the sense in which, and the conditions under which, individuals belonging to different possible worlds may be correctly identified with each other; to propose a solution of the problem; and to indicate some respects in which the suggested solution is relevant to wider epistemological questions. The problem of the transmundane identification of individuals is one of the few controversial issues between the proponents and the opponents of modal logics which has not been fully clarified by recent work on their appropriate semantic interpretation.[1] The paper is divided into three sections of which the first contains some preliminary and mainly taxonomical remarks on systems of possible worlds; the second analyzes various representability-relations which are applied when objects belonging to different worlds are identified with each other; the third briefly considers the role of these relations in scientific thinking and in the formation of concepts potentially.

I

Any classification of systems of possible worlds depends in the first place on the type of logic which underlies the statements describing the worlds. We may, in particular, distinguish between Augustinian or Leibnizian systems, in which the law of excluded middle is valid for all statements, including statements with a temporal refer-

[1] For an excellent concise survey see "Modal Logic" by R. Barcan Marcus in *Contemporary Philosophy*, edited by R. Klibansky (Vol. I, Firenze, La Nuova Italia Editrice, 1968).

ence; and Pelagian systems in which the law of excluded middle is not generally valid and which admit of open futures. To be more specific, we shall assume that the statements describing Leibnizian worlds are subject to the principles of classical propositional logic, quantification theory and theory of identity, briefly to the principles of L (so called after Leibniz and his logicist successors); and that the statements describing Pelagian possible worlds are subject to the principles of intuitionist propositional logic, quantification theory and theory of identity, briefly to the principles of I (so called after the intuitionist mathematicians and Iulianus of Eklanum, one of early protagonists of the Pelagian doctrine). It will be convenient to speak of L-systems and I-systems as well as of L-possible and I-possible worlds. Moreover, what will be said about the former applies with obvious modifications to the latter.

Another relevant classification of systems of possible worlds is based on the categorial structure of the worlds, that is, on the maximal kinds (*summa genera*) of objects they contain and the constitutive and individuating principles associated with these maximal kinds. A constitutive principle determines a simple or compound attribute the possession of which by an object is a logically necessary condition of the object's belonging to the maximal kind. An individuating principle determines a simple or compound attribute the possession of which by an object belonging to a certain maximal kind is a logically necessary and sufficient condition of the object's being a distinct individual object belonging to this kind. In a world of Kantian categorial structure the class of external material things is a maximal kind—its constitutive and individuating principles being exhibited in the transcendental logic and the transcendental aesthetics of the *Critique of Pure Reason*.

On the basis of their categorial structure we may distinguish between two L-possible worlds which are homogeneous, that is, have the same categorial structure and two L-possible worlds which are heterogeneous, that is, have different categorial structures. In a similar manner we might speak of homogeneous and heterogeneous L-systems. Principles which, like those of the transcendental philosophy of Kant, assert or require that every possible world "must," if it is to be "intelligible," "meaningful," "metaphysically sound," and so on, have a certain categorial structure are sometimes called "principles of coherence."[2]

Between homogeneous and completely heterogeneous systems of possible worlds there are, of course, a great many intermediate

---

[2] See S. Körner, *Categorial Frameworks*, (Oxford: Basil Blackwell, 1970).

varieties. For our purpose it will be convenient to have available an example of a homogeneous and an example of a strongly heterogenous system or, more precisely, of two suitable fragments of such systems. The example of a homogeneous system is taken from the end of Leibniz's *Theodicy*, where he describes fragments of three L-possible worlds of which one is the actual world. In the actual world Sextus Tarquinius, having left the temple of Jupiter in Dodona, goes to Rome where he is destined to a life of vice and misfortune. In the other two worlds he does not go to Rome. In one he goes to Corinth, in the other to Thrace—and in either to a life of honor and contentment. In each of the three worlds Sextus bears a number on his forehead which refers to the world to which he belongs. We may accordingly distinguish between $Sextus_0$, who belongs to the domain of individuals associated with the actual world, $Sextus_1$ who belongs to the individual domain of the first, and $Sextus_2$ who belongs to the individual domain of the second merely possible world. All three worlds contain a maximal kind of persons and are, we assume, homogeneous.

As our example of two strongly heterogenous worlds we consider, on the one hand, a commonsense world, say one of the three Leibnizian worlds; on the other, the world described by a scientific theory of a fairly sophisticated mathematical structure and of few maximal kinds, all of which differ considerably from the maximal kinds of the world or worlds of common sense. A typical world of this kind is described by classical dynamics and will be called a "Newtonian" world. The two examples illustrate familiar differences between possible worlds. In the second example, in which a commonsense and Newtonian world are contrasted, the question as to which of the two, if either, is the actual world, cannot be answered without bringing in some special metaphysical apparatus.

Having distinguished systems of possible worlds according to the logical and categorial structure of the statements describing them, we might feel tempted to classify them according to the extent to which the possible worlds contain the "same individuals." Examples would be a Carnapian L-system where every possible world contains the "same individuals" as every other, but where in every world at least one individual or n-tuple of individuals possesses some attribute which it possesses in no other world; systems of possible worlds where at least two possible worlds have no individuals in common; systems of possible worlds whose domains of individuals are partially ordered with respect to the relation of inclusion of one individual domain in the other; and so on. Yet, any such classification of systems of possible worlds already presupposes what we are looking for, namely a reasonably clear conception of the transmundane identity of individuals.

II

So far no criterion has been offered for deciding whether two individual objects belonging to two different possible worlds are, or are not, occurrences (appearances, aspects, embodiments, among others) of one and the same individual—whether, for example, they are manifestations of the same individual substance, which is uniquely characterized by certain essential attributes, or whether, in spite of some similarities, they are manifestations of different individual substances. We are in particular as yet unable to answer Chisholm's question whether, say, Sextus$_0$ and Sextus$_1$ are the same individual man, differing from each other like the young Adam and the old Adam of the biblical world or whether they are distinct individuals, differing from each other rather like the Adam and the Noah of the biblical world.[3]

The answer to these and similar questions, as well as an understanding of transmundane sameness and distinctness emerges from reflection on the general manner in which we actually, naturally, and habitually identify with each other objects belonging to different worlds such as the three Sextuses or a material object belonging to our commonsense world with a configuration of particles belonging to a Newtonian world. In order to draw attention to a crucial feature of transmundane identification, it will, moreover, be useful to contrast it with the intramundane identification of objects, a procedure which is hardly less natural and habitual to us. An example of such identification is the recognition of things and persons.

There are obvious similarities between intramundane and transmundane identification. Thus, whether we identify, say, the old and the young Noah, or the Sextus who goes to Rome with the Sextus who goes to Corinth, both identifications are made within some contexts rather than others and for some purposes rather than others. We might, for example, identify the young and the old Noah in the context of a folktale and for the purpose of explaining the uses of wine in an ancient culture. And we might identify Sextus$_0$ and Sextus$_1$ in the context of a child's moral education and for the purpose of explaining the nature of moral responsibility. There is, however, an important difference between identifying the old and the young Noah and identifying the first and the second Sextus. For, the two Noahs are, as I shall say, commensurable, whereas the two Sextuses are

[3] See R. M. Chisholm, "Identity through Possible Worlds: Some Questions," *Noûs*, Vol. 1, No. 1 (March 1967).

incommensurable individuals. These notions have to be made clear since intramundane identifications apply, or are intended to apply, to commensurable objects, whereas transmundane identifications are identifications of incommensurable objects.

We first define the incommensurability of propositions. Two propositions—such as 'Sextus leaves Dodona for Rome' and 'Sextus leaves Dodona for Corinth'—are incommensurable if, and only if, the assumption that they describe the same world is internally inconsistent, (according to L or some other accepted logic). The incommensurability of propositions is a generalization of their incompatibility. In other words, two incompatible propositions are *eo ipso* incommensurable, while two incommensurable propositions may or may not be incompatible. In terms of the incommensurability of propositions the incommensurability of objects is defined as follows. Two objects are incommensurable if, and only if, they are correctly described by two incommensurable propositions.

In accordance with this definition $Sextus_0$ and $Sextus_1$ are incommensurable objects since—unlike the old and the young Noah—they are correctly described by incommensurable propositions. More generally, let an object a_1 belong to a world W_1 but not to a world W_2, and let p_1 imply this fact; let an object a_2 belong to the world W_2 but not to the world W_1, and let p_2 imply this fact. Then p_1 and p_2 are incommensurable propositions (the assumption that they describe the same world is self-contradictory since it implies that a_1 and a_2 both belong and do not belong to $W_1 = W_2$); and a_1 and a_2 are, consequently, incommensurable objects.

We are now ready to consider the transmundane identification of incommensurable objects belonging to different possible worlds. It consists in purposefully ignoring their differences. More precisely, a person identifies an object a_1 with an incommensurable object a_2 for a certain purpose P if, and only if, he assumes that replacing a_1 by a_2 for the purpose P does, as a matter of fact, further this purpose and if he acts on this assumption. Let us call the relation which the person believes to hold between the represented object a_1, its representative a_2 and the purpose P "the representability of a_1 by a_2 for the purpose P," writing it schematically as "a_1 Rep $- P$ a_2." Returning to our previous examples, a moralist may believe in the representability of $Sextus_0$ by $Sextus_1$ for the purpose of understanding the chosen conduct of the former; and a scientist may believe in the representability of a cannon ball by a particle for the purpose of predicting the movement of the former.

The dependence of a_1 Rep $- P$ a_2 on a purpose P implies a distinction between attributes of a_1 and a_2 which are, and attributes of a_1 and a_2 which are not, essential to the purpose P. Such relative essentialism, which is characteristic of all practical and much factual thinking, is no more than a moderate version of pragmatism. It is quite different from the absolute essentialism of Aristotle which explains the nature of things by their dependence on eternal purposes. If an essentialism, which presupposes unchangeable, superhuman ends, is the pragmatism of God, then a pragmatism which presupposes changeable, human ends, is the essentialism of man.

The relation of representability x Rep $- P_y$ is not an equivalence relation. It is not transitive: We may, for example, agree with Leibniz that for the purpose of judging the chosen conduct of Sextus$_0$ he is representable by Sextus$_1$, that Sextus$_1$ is representable by Sextus$_2$, and that Sextus$_0$ is also representable by Sextus$_2$. Yet it is not difficult to imagine a Sextus$_3$ such that for our purpose Sextus$_0$ is representable by Sextus$_1$, Sextus$_1$ by Sextus$_3$, but not also Sextus$_0$ by Sextus$_3$. It may be that Sextus$_3$ is for our purpose not sufficiently similar to Sextus$_0$. Essential similarity for the purpose is like similarity in general not a transitive relation.

The relation x Rep $- Py$ is not symmetric: For the purpose of exploiting their slaves some nations believed certain human beings to be representable by subhuman animals, without at the same time believing these subhuman animals to be in turn representable by human beings. Finally, x Rep $- Py$ is not even reflexive: For certain religious purposes a living spirit may be representable by a statue without the statue being representable by itself. The illustrations of the nonsymmetric and nonreflexive character of the representability relation are unfamiliar and therefore seem artificial.

In terms of the representability of incommensurable objects we can define their mutual representability or interrepresentability in an obvious manner. Two incommensurable objects a_1 and a_2 are interrepresentable for a purpose P or, briefly, a_1 Inter rep $- Pa_2$ if, and only if, a_1 Rep $- Pa_2$ and a_2 Rep $- Pa_1$. Interrepresentability is symmetric and reflexive. That it is not transitive follows from the example by which the nontransitive character of representability was illustrated. It can, however, be turned into a transitive relation when its domain and counterdomain are suitably restricted. We simply define a class of incommensurable objects $\{a_0 \ldots a_n\}$ as an interrepresentability class with respect to the relation x Inter rep $- Py$ and the relation as restricted to the class if, and only if, any two members of the class are interrepresentable for the purpose P (that is, a_r Inter-rep Pa_s for $0 \leq r \leq n$ and $0 \leq s \leq n$). The restricted relation is symmetric, transitive, and reflexive, that is, an equivalence relation and the class $\{a_0, \ldots, a_n\}$ an equivalence class with respect to it.

Leibniz's three Sextuses were conceived by him to be interperresentable for a variety of purposes, such as the purpose of judging their conduct. Their interrepresentability class is clearly extendable in an infinite number of ways—for example by small variations of the route taken by them to Rome or their other destinations. Yet not every such extension will yield an interrepresentability class. The unions of some interrepresentability classes, for example, that consisting of $Sextus_0$ and $Sextus_1$ and that consisting of $Sextus_0$ and $Sextus_2$, are themselves such classes. But it would require a very wide purpose if we wished to combine the class of our Sextuses with a similar class of Napoleons into one interrepresentability class. All this is too obvious to deserve further elaboration.

Since an interrepresentability class is an equivalence class, we can form a new object by abstraction from its members. Thus if $\{a_0, \ldots, a_n\}$ is a class of $n + 1$ incommensurable and interrepresentable objects, say $n + 1$ Sextuses, we can form from it a new abstract object a, say Sextus, which is not a member of the class. This new object is commensurable with $a_0, \ldots, a_n$, does not belong to the separate worlds to which they belong, but is represented by these objects in these worlds. The incommensurable Sextuses, as it were, each represent one and the same supramundane Sextus in their world. The relation between the abstract object a and the $n + 1$ members of the interrepresentability class is analogous to the relation between a direction of a class of parallel lines and the lines themselves; or between the cardinal number of a class of equinumerous sets and the sets themselves.

In defining an interrepresentability class of objects belonging to different possible worlds, no distinction has been made between the object, if any, which belongs to the actual world and the objects which belong to merely possible worlds. Nor has any other privileged status been accorded to some other object or possible world. The Sextus who goes to Rome and the other Sextuses, as well as their worlds, are treated on a par. In order to make adequate allowance for the privileged status of some object or possible world—in particular an actual object and the actual world—we define what might be called a correpresentability class. The key notion of this definition is again the relation $x \text{ Rep} - Py$, that is, that representability of one of two incommensurable objects by the other for a certain purpose

Let us say that an object a_0 is for a certain purpose P correpresentable by two incommensurable objects a_1 and a_2 if, and only if, for this purpose a_0 is representable by a_1 and by a_2, and if a_1 and a_2 are not representable by each other. Schematically, a_0 Correp $- Pa_1, a_2$ if, and only if $a_0 \text{ Rep} - Pa_1$, $a_0 \text{ Rep} - Pa_2$, not $(a_1$

Rep $- Pa_2$) and *not* (a_2 Rep $- Pa_1$). We can then define a class
of n incommensurable objects $\{a_1, \ldots, a_n\}$ as a correpresentability
class with respect to a certain object a_0 and a certain purpose P
if, and only if, with respect to this purpose a_0 is correpresentable
by any two members of the class. Correpresentability classes are
hardly less frequently employed in factual and practical thinking
than are interrepresentability classes. If the class of possible Sextuses,
including the actual Sextus, is an interrepresentability class employed
for the purpose of, for example, explaining moral responsibility, then
the class of possible Sextuses excluding the actual Sextus, is, with
respect to the actual Sextus, a correpresentability class employed,
say, for the purpose of understanding the relation between actual
and potential conduct. If the task of this paper were exegetic, it
would be worth showing that in the *Theodicy* and elsewhere in discussing individual substances Leibniz employs and distinguishes the
two kinds of class.

The transmundane interrepresentability of objects must not be
confused with the identity of objects. While the former relation depends on a purpose in the furtherance of which the objects are identified with each other, identity is not so dependent. Again, while the
interrepresentability of two objects implies their incommensurability,
that is, that each of them possesses at least one attribute which is
incompatible with at least one attribute possessed by the other, "two"
objects are identical if, and only if, they possess the same attributes.
Lastly, the so-called "principle of identity," namely that every object
is identical with itself, is as a principle of logic true *in* every possible
worlds and irrelevant to nonlogical relations between incommensurable
individuals belonging to distinct possible worlds. Neglect of this point
has given rise to an alleged paradox concerning the "substitutivity
of identity in modal contexts." A few words about it are thus not
out of place here.

Using '$\Box$' to stand for 'it is true in every possible world W that'
we may express the principle of identity by means of a free variable as
(ia) $\Box x = x$, that is, 'it is true in every possible world W that $x = x$,
where x ranges over all the individuals of (the individual domain
associated with) W'. Alternatively we may express the principle by
means of a bound variable as (ib) $\Box \forall x(x = x)$, that is, 'it is true in
every possible world W that for all $x - x = x$, where the bound variable x ranges over all individuals of W. Now if e is a constant, say
"the evening star" of our world, we *seem* to arrive by substituting e
for x in (ia) or by applying (ib) to e at (ii) $\Box e = e$, that is, 'It is true
in every possible world W that $e = e$ where e is an individual belonging
to the individual domain of W'. Yet (ii) is clearly false since it asserts

that *e*, which belongs to the individual domain of the actual world, belongs to the individual domain of every possible world. (More generally, since the place of *e* can presumably be taken by any individual belonging to any world, (ii) implies that if an individual belongs to one world it belongs to all of them; hence it implies that all possible worlds have the same domain of individuals and thus that there are no incommensurable objects.)

The proposition (ii) may appear to be true only if we forget that (ia) and (ib), from which it seems to be derived, are incomplete without an indication of the individual domain over which their (free or bound) variable ranges. Once the falsehood of (ii) is clear, the following argument, in which '$e = m$' stands for the contingent proposition 'the evening star = the morning star' is seen to be not a subtle paradox, but a fallacy: "From the true premises $\Box e = e$ and $m = e$ there follows by the substitutivity of identity the paradoxical conclusion $\Box m = e$." The paradox is supposed to consist in the circumstance that from a logically necessary and a true contingent proposition (expressing respectively a necessary and a contingent identity) as premises, a logically necessary proposition (expressing a necessary identity) follows as a conclusion. However, since the allegedly necessary premises $\Box e = e$ is false, the conclusion is a *non-sequitur*.

III

The relations of representability, interrepresentability, and correpresentability have been distilled from reflection on familiar modes of identifying distinct objects with each other. In its turn the result of the analysis enables us to achieve a clearer understanding of the way in which these relations are employed in our thinking. They are, for example, constantly employed in scientific thinking, which creates and overcomes at least two kinds of incommensurability. One, which plays an important role in the application of scientific theories to experience, is the incommensurability of commonsense and theoretical propositions and, hence, of the objects described by them. The other is the incommensurability of propositions belonging to different theories.

Having investigated these matters in detail elsewhere[4] I shall content myself with some very general, impressionist remarks. The incommensurability of commonsense and theoretical propositions, and of the objects described by them, results from modifications imposed by the logical and conceptual structure of a theory on the different logical and conceptual structure of commonsense. In this way there

---

[4] See esp. S. Körner, *Experience and Theory* (2nd edition, London: Routledge and Kegan Paul, 1969).

arises, for example, the incommensurability between our commonsense, actual Sextus, Sextus Physicus (the commonsense Sextus, as modified on his incorporation into Newtonian dynamics), Sextus Economicus (the commonsense Sextus, as modified on his incorporation into, say, classical economics), Sextus Physiologicus, Sextus Psychologicus, and so on. To "apply" Newtonian physics to the commonsense Sextus for the purpose of predicting, say, his free fall from a tower is to assume the representability for this predictive purpose of the commonsense Sextus by Sextus Physicus. It is to apply the relation x Rep $- Py$ to the commonsense Sextus and Sextus Physicus. In the application of economics and other theories for predictive purposes, the relation x Rep $- Py$ is similarly applied.

For some purposes, such as for the purpose of a simple census, the commonsense Sextus and the various theoretical Sextuses might be regarded as forming an interrepresentability class and as defining a supramundane Sextus different from, and commensurable with, all of them. More frequently, however, the commonsense Sextus is accorded privileged status—the theoretical Sextuses being regarded as members of a correpresentability class with respect to him.

Representability and its cognates do not only relate incommensurable objects which are synchronic, but also incommensurable objects separated in time. When applied diachronically they play an important part in the formation of attributes which characterize objects as changeable in more ways than one. Such an attribute might be a constant disposition which characterizes the changeable object as a member of a certain kind, for example, the power of human beings to learn mathematics, or it might be a passing potentiality which characterizes a particular object strictly as a particular and at a certain time, for example, a person's option to do or not to do a certain deed. There is again no room for more than some very sketchy remarks. (This time, however, the sketchiness is not redeemed by a footnote referring to a detailed publication.)

The general structure of a person's options has been considered in the case of Leibniz's example. It involves an interrepresentability class and a correpresentability class. The interrepresentability class consists of the actual choosing Sextus and the potential, choosable Sextuses. Among the purposes furthered by the assumed interrepresentability is the unification of the Sextuses into one person. The correpresentability class consists of the potential, choosable Sextuses which are correpresentable with respect to the actual, choosing Sextus. Among the purposes furthered by the assumed correpresentability is the unification of the choosable Sextuses into the options of one person—the choosing Sextus.

The general structure of the passing potentiality of a material thing may be analyzed on similar lines. It involves an interpresentability class consisting of the actual object and various potential, expectable successors; and a correpresentability class consisting of the potential, expectable successors which are correpresentable with respect to the actual object Among the purposes furthered by the assumed interrepresentability is the unification of the actual object and its successors into one material thing. Among the purposes furthered by the assumed correpresentability is the unification of the object's expectable successors into what is expectable of one material thing. In examining the relevance of interrepresentability and correpresentability to the formation of the concept of a constant disposition or power, we would have to remember that the occurrence of the objects related, as well as the order of their occurrence, are repeatable.

So far, we have been concerned with the application of representability and its cognate relations in science and other modes of thinking, which are familiar in, and characteristic of, our culture. It may be fitting to conclude with the conjecture that these relations are no less habitually employed in magical thinking—although for purposes which are different from our own. This conjecture is strongly suggested by anthropological descriptions of prescientific thinking, for example by Evans-Pritchard's description of the way in which the Sudanese tribe of Nuer in certain sacrificial situations identify a cucumber with an ox, but not an ox with a cucumber.[5]

[5] See his *Nuer Religion* (Oxford, 1956), esp. Ch. V.

On Dispensing with Things and Worlds

HUGUES LEBLANC

Temple University

Some like their logic mixed with a lot of ontology. To them first-order logic, for example, adjudicates on basic matters of existence, and any semantic account of it should come with things, sets of things, and relations between things. They likewise think of modal logic as adjudicating on basic questions of possibility, and to them any semantic account of it should be complete with possible worlds, possible individuals, and so on.

Others prefer their logic straight: They view it as a handbook (of a highly sophisticated kind, to be sure) for drawing inferences. Of course, there are things, and if one is to discourse about them, he must—sooner or later—think of them as belonging to sets, bearing relations to one another, and so on. But first-order logic *can be, and hence is perhaps best*, explicated without recourse to "models": *What is dispensable simply is not of the essence*. And those who so wish may of course ponder over possible worlds, possible individuals, ways in which the latter preserve their identity from one possible world to another, and so on. But modal logic *can be, and hence is perhaps best*, explicated without recourse to (Leibniz' and) Kripke's musings.[1]

The present paper is a report on recent successes at ridding logic of much expendable ontology, and in particular at making of modal logic a sheer manual of inference.

[1] In some passages Kripke describes the K in his triple $\langle G,K,R \rangle$ as an arbitrary (nonempty) set, G as an arbitrary member of K, and R as an arbitrary reflexive relation on K [see, for example, Kripke [11], p. 84, lines 7 and 8]. In other passages, though, he talks of K as the set of all "possible worlds," of G as the "real world," and of R as a relation of "possible relativity between worlds"; and deleting the latter passages robs Kripke's account of its intuitive appeal (see page 256).

From a model-theoretic viewpoint, the formula

(1) $(\exists x)(f(x) \lor \sim f(x))$

demands that "bound" variables have values (or, as the matter has been put, that there exist things); and the formula

(2) $(\exists x)(f(x) \lor \sim f(x)) \supset (g(y) \supset (\exists x)g(x))$

demands that "free" variables have values (hence, that free variables stand for designating terms) when bound variables have values. Borrowing in part from Lambert, I shall study in Section I a variant of QC (the first-order quantificational calculus) which bars proof of formulas (1) and (2).[2]

The returns, however, are still modest ones. So, moving on, I shall present in Section II a new semantics for QC which does without models at all. Quantifications will be understood *substitutionally*, and validity explicated by means of truth-value assignments to the atomic well-formed formulas of QC. The semantics in question, known as *truth-value semantics*,[3] makes for innocuous readings of formulas (1) and (2). To meet all preferences, though, I shall include a variant of it suiting Lambert's QC.

Lastly, I shall treat in Section III of eight modal logics with quantifiers, and supply a truth-value interpretation of each. (In the first four of these logics *both* the "Barcan formula"

$$(\forall x)\Box f(x) \supset \Box(\forall x)f(x)$$

and its converse will be provable, whereas in the last four neither one will be.) Besides truth-value assignments I shall employ there sets of truth-value assignments and a relation R (like that of Kripke) on these sets. A recent paper by Dunn would suggest that R is dispensable.[4] But possible worlds and possible individuals will be gone, at any rate, and with them a good deal of needless ontology.

---

[2] See Lambert [12], Leblanc [15], and Leblanc and Meyer [19]. In previous writings I have understood the formula '$f(y) \supset (\exists x)f(x)$' as requiring that free variables have values (or stand for designating terms). However, '$(\exists x)(f(x) \lor \sim f(x)) \supset (g(y) \supset (\exists x)g(x))$', which under the account of pages 246–247 always evaluates to T when the domain is empty, but sometimes evaluates to F when it is not, suits my purpose better. (Whether any formula of QC requires that free variables have values when bound ones do not is a moot question which I would rather avoid here.)

[3] The appellation was suggested to me by Quine. For a short history of truth-value semantics, see Leblanc [17].

[4] See Dunn [3].

I

Most presentations of QC use just one run of individual variables, to wit: '*x*', '*y*', '*z*', and so on,[5] and then declare some of their occurrences—in well-formed formulas of QC—bound, the rest free. The first two occurrences of '*x*' in

$$(\forall x)f(x) \supset f(x)$$

for example, would be declared bound, the third one free; both occurrences of '*x*' in

$$(\forall x)f(x) \supset f(y)$$

would similarly be declared bound, the one occurrence of '*y*' free; and so on.

I implicitly adhered to that practice on page 242, but henceforth I shall use two runs of individual symbols: (1) '*x*', '*y*', '*z*', and so on, for which I save the appellation 'individual variables', and (2) '*a*', '*b*','*c*', and so on, to be known as *individual parameters*. In well-formed formulas of QC, '*x*', '*y*', '*z*', and so on will always "occur bound," whereas '*a*', '*b*', '*c*', and so on will always "occur free." So I shall write, say,

$$(\forall x)f(x) \supset f(a)$$

where others would '$(\forall x)f(x) \supset f(x)$', or '$(\forall x)f(x) \supset f(y)$', or '$(\forall x)f(x) \supset f(z)$'. However, in this part of the paper, formulas like '$(\forall x)f(x) \supset f(x)$', '$(\forall x)f(x) \supset f(y)$', and so on, though not acknowledged as well-formed, will nonetheless play some role, and I shall refer to them as *quasi*-well-formed formulas. So, '*x*', '*y*', '*z*', and so on, though never occurring free in well-formed formulas, will occasionally do so in quasi-well-formed ones.

For uniformity's sake I shall likewise call the letters '*p*', '*q*', '*r*', and so on *sentence parameters*, and the letters '*f*', '*g*', '*h*', and so on *predicate parameters*. These, of course, are not quantified in QC.

The primitive symbols of QC will thus be the two connectives '$\sim$' and '$\supset$', the one quantifier symbol '$\forall$',[6] the two parentheses '(' and ')', the comma ',', $\aleph_0$ individual variables (referred to by means of '*X*' and '*Y*'), $\aleph_0$ individual parameters (referred to by means of '*P*'),

[5] That is, '*x*', '*y*', '*z*', and their $\aleph_0$ accented variants '*x*″', '*y*″', '*z*″', '*x*‴', '*y*‴', '*z*‴', and so on.

[6] I presume the extra operators '&', '$\vee$', '$\equiv$', and '$\exists$' to be defined in the usual manner. So '$(\exists x)(f(x) \vee \sim f(x))$', for example, is short for '$\sim(\forall x)\sim(\{f(x) \supset \sim f(x))$'.

aleph$_0$ sentence parameters, and—for each k from 1 on—aleph$_0$ k-adic predicate parameters (referred to by means of 'F^k').[7] The formulas of QC will be, as usual, all finite (but nonempty) sequences of primitive symbols of QC. And, where A is a formula of QC, and I and I' are two individual symbols of QC, $(A)(I'/I)$ should be understood as the result of putting I' everywhere in A for I.

The well-formed formulas (wffs, for short) of QC will be all sentence parameters of QC, plus all formulas of QC of any of the following four kinds: (1) $F^k(P_1, P_2, \ldots , P_k)$, where F^k is a k-adic predicate parameter, and P_1, P_2, $\ldots$, and P_k are (not necessarily distinct) individual parameters, (2) $\sim A$, where A is a wff, (3) $(A \supset B)$, where A and B are (not necessarily distinct) wffs, and (4) $(\forall X)A$, where—for any individual parameter P—$(A)(P/X)$ is a wff. The quasi-well-formed formulas (qwffs, for short) of QC will be all formulas of QC of the kind $(\forall X)(X/P)$, where A is a wff or qwff, X is an individual variable that does not occur in A, and P is an individual parameter that does. Finally, the atomic wffs of QC will be all wffs—and the atomic qwffs of QC will be all qwffs—of QC that contain no connective or quantifier symbol.

Clause (4) in my account of a wff insures that, where $(\forall X)A$ is well-formed, any result of putting an individual parameter of QC for X in A is likewise well-formed. So parameters can be substituted for variables without any ado.[8]

The interpretation normally placed upon QC runs as follows. First, you acknowledge as *a domain* (alternatively, as a range of values for the individual symbols of QC) *any non-empty set*.[9] Second, D being a domain, you acknowledge as a D-*valuation* any result of assigning a truth-value to each sentence parameter of QC, a member of D *to each individual symbol of* QC, and a subset of the Cartesian product

$$\underbrace{D \times D \times \cdots \times D}_{k \text{ times}} (= D^k)$$

to each k-adic predicate parameter of QC, this for each k from 1 on.[10] Third, D being a domain, V_D and $V_D{}'$ being D-valuations, and X being

---

[7] Throughout 'f' and 'g' will serve as monadic predicate parameters.

[8] Because of clause (4) formulas like '$(\forall x)(f(x) \supset (\forall x)g(x))$' in which identical quantifiers overlap do not count as well-formed. But all of '$(\forall x)(f(x) \supset (\forall y)g(y))$', '$(\forall x)(f(x) \supset (\forall z)g(z))$', and so on do; these well make up for the missing '$(\forall x)(f(x) \supset (\forall x)g(x))$'.

[9] Note the italicized "*any*." It is a common misapprehension that only an "individual" should serve as a value of, say, 'x'. *Any*thing can.

[10] Each monadic predicate parameter of QC is thereby assigned a set of members of D, each dyadic one a set of pairs of members of D (that is, a dyadic relation), each triadic one a set of triples of members of D (that is, a triadic relation), and so on.

an individual variable of QC, you count $V_D{}'$ an X-*variant of* V_D if $V_D{}'$ agrees with V_D on all the parameters of QC and on all the individual variables of QC other than X.[11] Fourth, A being a wff or qwff of QC, D being a domain, and V_D being a D-valuation, you take A *to be true on* V_D if:

(1) in case A is a sentence parameter, $V_D(A) = $ T,

(2) in case A is of the kind $F^k(I_1, I_2, \ldots, I_k)$, $\langle V_D(I_1), V_D(I_2), \ldots, V_D(I_k)\rangle$—the k-tuple consisting of the members of D respectively assigned in V_D to the individual symbols $I_1, I_2, \ldots,$ and I_k—belongs to $V_D(F^k)$,

(3) in case A is a negation $\sim B$, B is not true on V_D,

(4) in case A is a conditional $(B \supset C)$, B is not true on V_D or C is, and

(5) in case A is a quantification $(\forall X)B$, B is true on every X-variant of V_D.

And, fifth, you declare a wff A of QC *valid*, (that is, *valid in the standard or model-theoretic sense*) if, no matter the domain D nor the D-valuation V_D, A is true on V_D.

(More model-theoretic sounding definitions can be had by taking A *to be true in a model* $\langle D, V_D \rangle$—D a domain and V_D a D-valuation—when A is true on V_D, and to be *valid* when A is true in every model. A wff of QC valid on either account will of course be valid on the other.)

Now count as your axioms all wffs of QC of the following kinds:[12]

(A1) $A \supset (B \supset A)$

(A2) $(A \supset (B \supset C)) \supset ((A \supset B) \supset (A \supset C))$

(A3) $(\sim A \supset \sim B) \supset (B \supset A)$

(A4) $(\forall X)(A \supset B) \supset ((\forall X)A \supset (\forall X)B)$

(A5) $A \supset (\forall X)A$[13]

(A6) $(\forall X)A \supset A(P/X)$, this for any individual parameter P of QC

and

(A7) $(\forall X)A$, where—for any individual parameter P of QC foreign to $(\forall X)A$—$A(P/X)$ is an axiom

and let *Modus Ponens* be your (sole) rule of inference.[14]

---

[11] And possibly X as well. Any D-valuation thus counts as one of its X-variants.

[12] To abridge matters I drop from now on a number of easily restored parentheses.

[13] With $A \supset (\forall X)A$ presumed here to be well-formed, $(\forall X)A$ is sure to be a "vacuous quantification."

[14] Because of (A7) no rule of generalization is needed here.

It can be shown, as in Gödel [5] or Henkin [6] (see the bibliography, page 258), that all and only those wffs of QC valid in the foregoing sense are provable. But, as was stressed on pages 244–245, domains must be nonempty, and—in D-valuations—members of these domains must be assigned to all of 'x', 'y', 'z', and so on, and all of 'a', 'b', 'c', and so on. So, *from a model-theoretic standpoint*, the axioms above do demand that the individual symbols of QC have values.

Lifting the requirement that 'x', 'y', 'z', and so on have values is easy. First, weaken (A6) to read:

$$(A6') \quad (\exists x)(f(x) \lor \sim f(x)) \supset ((\forall X)A \supset A(P/X))$$

Then, acknowledge $\varnothing$ as a domain; understand by a $\varnothing$-valuation any result of assigning a truth-value to each atomic wff or qwff of QC; take an atomic wff or qwff A of QC to be true on a $\varnothing$-valuation $V_\varnothing$ if $V_\varnothing(A) = T$; take a negation $\sim A$ of QC to be true on $V_\varnothing$ if A is not; take a conditional $A \supset B$ to be true on $V_\varnothing$ if A is not true on $V_\varnothing$ or B is; mindful that $(\forall X)A$ is equivalent to $\sim(\exists X)\sim A$, take a quantification $(\forall X)A$ of QC to be automatically true on $V_\varnothing$; and declare a wff A of QC *valid'* if—for any domain D, empty or not, and any D-valuation V_D—A is true on V_D. As simple additions to Gödel's argument or Henkin's will show, all and only those wffs of QC that are *valid'* are provable by means of (A1) through (A5), (A6'), (A7), and *Modus Ponens*,[15] and hence '$(\exists x)(f(x) \lor \sim f(x))$'—a wff false on any $\varnothing$ valuation—is no longer forthcoming as a theorem.

Note, however, that for any non-empty domain D each individual parameter of QC is still assigned, in any D-valuation V_D, a member of D. So our revised axioms still demand that 'a', 'b', 'c', and so on have values when 'x', 'y', 'z', and so on do.[16]

Lifting that requirement too calls for more drastic measures. (A6)—again the culprit—is readily weakened to suit the occasion. Run it as Lambert did in [12]:

$$(A6'') \quad (\forall Y)((\forall X)A \supset A(Y/X))^{17}$$

But the notion of a D-valuation for non-empty D, and that of an X-variant of a D-valuation, must be thoroughly revamped.

---

[15] For proof of the result, see Leblanc and Meyer [18], where (A6') made its first appearance.

[16] Note indeed that formula (2) on page 242 is still forthcoming as a theorem.

[17] Whether wffs of the kind $(\forall X)(\forall Y)A \supset (\forall Y)(\forall X)A$ remain provable when (A6'') substitutes for (A6) is still an open question. Should the answer turn out to be No, draft $(\forall X)(\forall Y)A \supset (\forall Y)(\forall X)A$ as an extra axiom schema for Lambert's version of QC and the four modal calculi QC$_M''$, QC$_B''$, QC$_5''$, and QC$_5''$ on pp. 252–253.

Talking now of a D-valuation *relative to a set Σ of individual parameters of* QC (said set Σ possibly empty), one allocates members of D *only to those individual parameters of* QC *that belong to* Σ, and then assigns a truth-value to each atomic wff or qwff of QC that contains an individual parameter of QC not in Σ. However, to preserve the equivalence of wffs like '$(\forall x)f(x, a)$' and '$(\forall y)f(y, a)$', we must require that —for any two individual symbols I and I' of QC—A and $A(I'/I)$ be assigned the same truth-value when I and I' are assigned the same member of D.

Turning to the other task, let D be a non-empty domain, Σ be a set of individual parameters of QC, $V_{D,\Sigma}$ and $V_{D,\Sigma}'$ be D-valuations relative to Σ, and X be an individual variable of QC. If $V_{D,\Sigma}'$ is to count as an X-variant of $V_{D,\Sigma}$, $V_{D,\Sigma}'$ must of course agree with $V_{D,\Sigma}$ on all the parameters of QC, all the individual variables of QC other than X, and all the atomic wffs or qwffs of QC that are assigned a truth-value in $V_{D,\Sigma}$ and do not contain X. Furthermore, when $V_{D,\Sigma}'(X)$ is not assigned in $V_{D,\Sigma}$ to any individual symbol of QC, $V_{D,\Sigma}'$ should also agree with $V_{D,\Sigma}$ on any atomic qwff A of QC that is assigned a truth-value in $V_{D,\Sigma}$ and contains X. Suppose, however, that $V_{D,\Sigma}'(X)$ is already assigned in $V_{D,\Sigma}$ to one or more individual symbols of QC. To preserve again the equivalence of wffs like '$(\forall x)f(x, a)$' and '$(\forall y)f(y, a)$', we must require that, for any individual symbol I of QC such that $V_{D,\Sigma}'(X) = V_{D,\Sigma}(I)$, A be assigned in $V_{D,\Sigma}'$ the truth-value assigned in $V_{D,\Sigma}$ to $A(I/X)$ (rather than the one assigned to A).[18]

This done, take a wff A of QC to be *valid"* if (1) for every $\emptyset$-valuation $V_\emptyset$, A is true on $V_\emptyset$ and (2) for every non-empty domain D, every set Σ of individual parameters of QC, and every D-valuation $V_{D,\Sigma}$ relative to Σ, A is true on $V_{D,\Sigma}$.

As a long (and somewhat complicated) argument will show, all and only those wffs of QC that are *valid"* are provable in QC,[19] and hence '$(\exists x)(f(x) \lor \sim f(x)) \supset (g(a) \supset (\exists x)g(x))$'—a wff false for non-empty D on any D-valuation relative to $\emptyset$ that assigns T to '$g(a)$' and $\emptyset$ to 'g'—is no longer forthcoming as a theorem.

So, touched up as in [12], QC no longer requires (model-theoretically speaking) that 'x', 'y', 'z', and so on have values, nor—when they do—that 'a', 'b', 'c', and so on also have values. But, as promised earlier, more substantial savings are in store.

---

[18] For fuller details on this matter, see Leblanc and Meyer [19].
[19] For proof of the result, see Leblanc and Meyer [19]. (The paper assumes that in Lambert's version of QC wffs of the kind $(\forall X)(\forall Y)A \supset (\forall Y)(\forall X)A$ are provable without further ado. The question, however, is still an open one, as pointed out in footnote 17.) A different, but equivalent, account of things will be found in van Fraassen [25].

II

When axiomatized as on pages 245–246,[20] QC can be shown to be complete by extending $\{\sim A\}$, A here any wff of QC not provable in QC, into a set S of wffs of QC which is maximally consistent and omega-complete.[21] A model $\langle D, V_D \rangle$ is then constructed in which every member of S—hence, in particular, $\sim A$—is sure to be true. So, if as presumed A is not provable in QC, then there is a model in which $\sim A$ is true and, by rebound, A is not. So, if a wff of QC is true in every model (that is, valid), then the wff is provable in QC.

The model $\langle D, V_D \rangle$ used in the foregoing proof has an important feature: each member of D is assigned in V_D to an individual symbol of QC. This peculiarity, when fully exploited, yields a whole new semantics for QC: It bridges the gap between models and (what I call) truth-value assignments, and thereby permits proof that all and only the wffs of QC true on all true-value assignments are theorems of QC.

To go more fully into the matter, understand by *a truth-value assignment (for* QC) any result of assigning one of the two truth-values T and F to each atomic wff of QC. Where A is a wff of QC and α a truth-value assignment, take A *to be true on* α if:

(1) in case A is atomic, $\alpha(A) = \text{T}$,
(2) in case A is a negation $\sim B$, B is not true on α,
(3) in case A is a conditional $B \supset C$, B is not true on α or C is,

and

(4) in case A is a quantification $(\forall X)B$, every result of putting an individual parameter for X in B (that is, every substitution instance of $(\forall X)B$) is true on α.

Call a model $\langle D, V_D \rangle$ a *Henkin model* if for every member d of D there is an individual parameter P of QC such that $V_D(P) = d$. And by *the truth-value counterpart of a Henkin model* $\langle D, V_D \rangle$ understand the result of assigning T to all atomic wffs of QC true on V_D, and F to the rest.

It is readily shown that a wff A of QC is true in a Henkin model $\langle D, V_D \rangle$ if and only if A is true on the truth-value counterpart α of

---

[20] That is, with (A6) [rather than (A6′) or (A6″)] serving as the *Specification Axiom*.
[21] This way of showing QC complete goes back to Henkin [6]. A set S of wffs of QC is said to be maximally consistent if S is *syntactically* consistent (that is, no contradiction is derivable from S) and would become syntactically inconsistent upon addition to S of any other wff of QC; and S is said to be omega-complete if a quantification $(\forall X)A$ is not derivable from S unless all the substitution instances of $(\forall X)A$ are also derivable from S.

$\langle D, V_D \rangle$. The proof is by mathematical induction on the number k of occurrences of '$\sim$', '$\supset$', and '$\forall$' in A. Suppose first that $k = 0$. Then A is atomic, and by the very construction of α is true on V_D if and only if true on α. Suppose next that the result to be proved holds true for any wff of QC with fewer than k occurrences of '$\sim$', '$\supset$', and '$\forall$'. When A is a negation $\sim B$ or a conditional $B \supset C$, the inductive. hypothesis immediately yields that A is true on V_D if and only if true on α. So only one case remains to be covered: that where A is a quantification $(\forall X)B$.

By definition $(\forall X)B$ is true on V_D if and only if B is true on every X-variant of V_D, whereas $(\forall X)B$ is true on α if and only if $B(P/X)$ is true on α for every individual parameter P of QC. However, it can be shown that—with $\langle D, V_D \rangle$ presumed to be a Henkin model—B is true on every X-variant of V_D if and only if $B(P/X)$ is true on V_D for every individual parameter P of QC. (For example, let V_D' be the X-variant of V_D such that $V_D'(X)$ is, say, $V_D(a)$. Then B will be true on V_D' if and only if $B(a/X)$ is true on V_D.) So the inductive hypothesis will again yield that A is true on V_D if and only if true on α.

The induction can thus be completed, and the members of the set S on page 248 are now sure to be true on the truth-value counterpart of $\langle D, V_D \rangle$ as well as on V_D. Hence any wff of QC true on all truth-value assignments is provable in QC. But, as the reader may wish to verify, any wff of QC provable in QC is true on all truth-value assignments. So, take a wff of QC to be *valid in the truth-value sense* if it is true on all truth-value assignments, and exactly the same wffs of QC as were valid in the standard sense will be valid in the truth-value sense.[22]

Discarded here is the whole paraphernalia of models in favor of just these:

(1) the two truth-values T and F

and

(2) assignments of the truth-values in (1) to the atomic wffs of QC [more formally, functions from the atomic wffs of QC to the truth-values in (1)].

So first-order validity *can* be explicated without recourse to things, sets of things, and relations between things, indeed without appeal to any but the twin notions of truth and falsehood. The result should be welcome news to anyone with a stake in "pure" logic.

Under the present account of things, an existential quantification $(\exists X)A$ of QC is certified true on any truth-value assignment on which

[22] For a detailed proof of the result, see Leblanc [17]; see also Leblanc [14].

one of $A(a/X)$, $A(b/X)$, $A(c/X)$, and so on is true. So wffs which from a model-theoretic viewpoint demanded that variables have values, or that parameters have values when variables do, are now innocuously valid. For example,

$$(\exists x)(f(x) \vee \sim f(x))$$

turns out to be valid because, say, '$f(a) \vee \sim f(a)$' is true on any truth-value assignment; and

$$(\exists x)(f(x) \vee \sim f(x)) \supset (g(a) \supset (\exists x)g(x))$$

turns out to be valid because '$(\exists x)g(x)$' is true on any truth-value assignment that assigns T to '$g(a)$'.

However, theorems like these might still jolt some who—however first-order validity be explicated—would count a sentence

$$(\exists x)(x \text{ is thus and so})$$

true only if putting a *designating* term for 'x' in

$$x \text{ is thus and so}$$

gave a truth. Readers of this persuasion could, of course, think of 'a', 'b', 'c', and so on as standing for designating terms only.[23] Or they could adjust the foregoing semantics to suit their understanding of '$\exists$' and their choice of theorems for QC.

Indeed, A being a wff of QC, α a truth-value assignment, and Σ a (possibly empty) set of individual parameters of QC, take A to be *true on* α_Σ, that is, take A to be *true on α as relativized to Σ*—if:

  (1′) in case A is atomic, $\alpha(A) = \text{T}$,
  (2′) in case A is a negation $\sim B$, B is not true on α_Σ,
  (3′) in case A is a conditional $B \supset C$, B is not true on α_Σ or C is,

and

  (4′) in case A is a quantification $(\forall X)B$, $B(P/X)$ is true on α_Σ for every member P of Σ:[24]

and take A to be *valid″ in the truth-value sense* if, no matter the truth-value assignment α nor the set Σ of individual parameters of QC, A is

---

[23] Readers of Leblanc and Wisdom [21] are asked to do just that. The text uses truth-value semantics as its official semantics.
[24] In case A is an existential quantification $(\exists X)B$, A proves to be true on α_Σ if only if $B(P/X)$ is true on α_Σ for at least one member P of Σ: the parameters in Σ can thus be thought of as standing for designating terms only. Note that when Σ is $\varnothing$, $(\forall X)B$ is automatically true, and $(\exists X)B$ automatically false, on α_Σ.

true on α_Σ. The argument in [14] is easily adapted to show that all and only the wffs of QC valid" in the truth-value sense are provable by means of (1) through (5), (A6''), (A7), and *Modus Ponens*. So '$(\exists x)(f(x) \vee \sim f(x))$' (which is false on any truth-value assignment relativized to $\varnothing$) and '$(\exists x)(f(x) \vee \sim f(x)) \supset (g(a) \supset (\exists x)g(x))$' [which is false on any truth-value assignment relativized to $\{b\}$ that assigns T to '$g(a)$' and F to '$g(b)$'] are no longer forthcoming as theorems; and 'a', 'b', 'c', and so on can now stand for *all* terms, that is, for *all* expressions which function as subjects or objects in sentences.

So far, I have exclusively talked of validity. Other semantic concepts can be explicated in terms of truth-value assignments. A key one is, of course, that of *simultaneous satisfiability* or—as some would rather say—*semantic consistency*. In standard semantics you take a set S of wffs of QC to be semantically consistent if there is a model in which every member of S is true; you readily have the proof that the set is semantically consistent if and only if no contradiction is derivable from it. In truth-value semantics you may likewise take S, *when S is finite*, to be semantically consistent if there is a truth-value assignment on which all the members of S are true [or, should (A6'') substitute for (A6), if there is a truth-value assignment α and a set Σ of individual parameters of QC such that all the members of S are true on α_Σ]. However, a problem arises in connection with some infinite sets of wffs.

Consider the set

$$\{f(a), f(b), f(c), \ldots , \sim(\forall x)f(x)\}$$

It is semantically consistent in the standard sense. Indeed, let D consist of, say, the two integers 1 and 2, and let V_D be any D-valuation that assigns 1 to all the individual symbols of QC and the subset $\{1\}$ of D to 'f'. The members of the set will all be true on V_D, and hence be true in the model $\langle D, V_D \rangle$. Yet there is no truth-value assignment on which all of '$f(a)$', '$f(b)$', '$f(c)$', \ldots , and '$\sim(\forall x)f(x)$' are true: one of '$f(a)$', '$f(b)$', '$f(c)$', and so on must be false on any truth-value assignment on which '$\sim(\forall x)f(x)$' is true, and '$\sim(\forall x)f(x)$' must be false on any truth-value assignment on which all of '$f(a)$', '$f(b)$', '$f(c)$', and so on are true. [Nor—in case (A6'') substitutes for (A6)—is there, for any truth-value assignment α, a set Σ of individual parameters of QC such that all of '$f(a)$', '$f(b)$', '$f(c)$', \ldots , and '$\sim(\forall x)f(x)$' are true on α_Σ.]

The difficulty can be met in a number of ways. The simplest is to certify S, *when S is infinite*, semantically consistent in the truth-value sense if at least one finite subset of S is semantically consistent in that sense. Since '$f(a)$' and '$\sim(\forall x)f(x)$' are true on any truth-value assignment (on any truth-value assignment relativized to $\{b\}$) that assigns

T to '$f(a)$' and F to '$f(b)$', set $\{f(a), \sim(\forall x)f(x)\}$ is semantically consistent in the truth-value sense, and hence so will be $\{f(a), f(b), f(c),$ $\ldots, \sim(\forall x)f(x)\}$. More sophisticated handlings of the matter will be found in [13] and [14].

Higher-order quantificational calculi (both ramified and unramified) admit, as does QC, of a truth-value interpretation, and hence can be semantically explicated at bargain rates. The subject is covered in Leblanc [16].

III

Modal logics with quantifiers have multiplied almost beyond reckoning since the publication of Barcan [1] and Carnap [2]. I shall study eight of them here, respectively labelled QC_M, QC_B ('B' for 'Brouwersche'), QC_4 ('4' for 'S4'), QC_5 ('5' for 'S5'), QC_M'', QC_B'', QC_4'', and QC_5''.[25] In all eight cases add '$\Box$' to the list of primitive symbols on pages 243–244, count $\Box A$ well-formed when A is, and use '$\Diamond A$' as short for '$\sim\Box\sim A$'. The axiom schemata of my eight calculi are to be as in the following table, with (A8) through (A14) respectively reading:

(A8) $\Box(A \supset B) \supset (\Box A \supset \Box B)$
(A9) $\Box A \supset A$
(A10) $\Box A$, where A is an axiom
(A11) $A \supset \Box\Diamond A$
(A12) $\Box A \supset \Box\Box A$
(A13) $\Diamond A \supset \Box\Diamond A$

and
(A14) $(\forall X)\Box A \supset \Box(\forall X)A$

And *Modus Ponens* is again to be the sole rule of inference.

TABLE OF AXIOM SCHEMATA

(A1)–(A5)	All eight calculi
(A6)	QC_M, QC_B, QC_4, and QC_5
(A6'')	QC_M'', QC_B'', QC_4'', and QC_5''
(A7)	All eight calculi
(A8)–(A10)	All eight calculi
(A11)	QC_B and QC_B''
(A12)	QC_4 and QC_4''
(A13)	QC_5 and QC_5''
(A14)	QC_M and QC_4

[25] I save the customary appellations 'M', 'B', 'S4', and 'S5' for modal logics without quantifiers [that is, for modal logics with just sentence parameters, '$\sim$', '$\supset$', '$\Box$', '(', and ')' as their primitive symbols].

As the reader doubtless knows, wffs of the sort $(\forall X)\Box A \supset$ $\Box(\forall X)A$ are provable by means of (A1) through(A10) *plus* either one of (A11) and (A13). And wffs of the sort $\Box(\forall X)A \supset (\forall X)\Box A$ are provable by means of (A1) through (A10) alone. So both the Barcan formula and its converse turn up as theorems in the first four of my calculi.[26] Neither formula, though, is provable in the last four.

Kripke's semantics is best studied in separate installments.[27] So limit yourself initially to S5; K being a non-empty set (to Kripke a non-empty set of "possible worlds") and G being a member of K (to Kripke a "world" in K), understand by *a valuation function for* K any function that pairs with each member G of K a truth-value assignment (to the sentence parameters of S5); K being as before, Φ being a valuation for K, and G being a member of K, take a wff A of S5 to be *true on the triple* $\langle K,\Phi,G\rangle$ if:

(1) in case A is a sentence parameter, A is assigned T in $\Phi(G)$,
(2) in case A is of the sort $\sim B$, B is not true on $\langle K,\Phi,G\rangle$,
(3) in case A is of the sort $B \supset C$, B is not true on $\langle K,\Phi,G\rangle$ or C is,

and

(4) in case A is of the sort $\Box B$, B is true on $\langle K,\Phi,H\rangle$ for every member H of K;

and take a wff A of S5 to be *valid* if A is true on every triple $\langle K,\Phi,G\rangle$ of the kind just described (that is, A is true on $\langle K,\Phi,G\rangle$ no matter the non-empty set K, given any K no matter the valuation function Φ for K, and given any K and any Φ no matter the member G of K).

Proof can be retrieved from Kripke [9] that all and only those wffs of S5 valid in the foregoing sense are provable in S5 [that is, are provable by means of (A1) through (A3), (A8) through (A10), (A13), and *Modus Ponens*].

When turning in [10] to M, B, and S4, Kripke intercalates a relation R on K. To use M as a sample, he takes a wff A to M to be *true on a quadruple* $\langle K,\Phi,R,G\rangle$, where R is an arbitrary *reflexive* relation on K, if:

(1) in case A is a sentence parameter, A is assigned T in $\Phi(G)$,
(2) in case A is of the sort $\sim B$, B is not true on $\langle K,\Phi,R,G\rangle$,
(3) in case A is of the sort $B \supset C$, B is not true on $\langle K,\Phi,R,G\rangle$ or C is,

---

[26] On this matter see Hughes and Cresswell [8], pp. 181–182.
[27] Kripke [9] deals exclusively with QC_5 (and hence S5); Kripke [10] extends the semantics of Kripke [9] to M, B, and S4; and Kripke [11]. Throughout I adapt Kripke's terminology and symbolism.

and

(4)   in case A is of the sort $\Box B$, B is true on $\langle K,\Phi,R,H \rangle$ for every
      member H of K *such that* $R(G,H)$.

(It follows from these clauses that if $R(G, H)$ and A are true on
$\langle K,\Phi,R,H \rangle$, then $\Diamond A$ is true on $\langle K,\Phi,R,G \rangle$, hence—informally—that
any wff "true in a world H" is "possible in any world" that bears R
to H.)

This done, Kripke takes a wff A of M to be *valid* if A is true on
every quadruple of the sort $\langle K,\Phi,R,G \rangle$, and goes on to show that all
and only those wffs of M valid in this sense are probable in M.

Like results hold for B when R is required to be reflexive *and*
symmetrical, for S4 when R is required to be reflexive *and* transitive,
and—expectedly enough—for S5 when R is required to be reflexive,
symmetrical, and transitive.

Now for Kripke's handling of quantifications. I limit myself initially to QC₅″, where R is dispensable.

(1) K being a non-empty set (of "possible worlds"), understand
      by *a domain function for* K any function that pairs with each
      ("world") G in K a non-empty set (said by Kripke to consist
      of "the individuals existing in world G");[28]

(2) K being a non-empty set, Ψ being a domain function for K,
      D being $\bigcup_{G \epsilon K} \Psi(G)$, and G being a member of K, understand
      by *a $\Psi(G)$-valuation* any result of assigning:

   (i)   a truth-value to each sentence parameter of QC₅″,
   (ii) a member of D to each individual parameter of QC₅″,
   (iii) a member of $\Psi(G)$ to each individual variable of QC₅″,[29] and
   (iv) a subset of D^k to each k-adic predicate parameter of QC₅″;

---

[28] Those individuals would of course be "real" ones when G is the "real" world,
"merely possible" ones when G is not, and deals with the last four of our modal
logics. How to determine whether individual d_G in world G and individual d_H
in world H are the same has been widely discussed.

[29] Note that in view of clauses (ii) and (iii) the entire set D serves as the range of
values of 'a', 'b', 'c', etc., whereas just its subset $\Psi(G)$ serves as the range of
values of 'x', 'y', 'z', etc. In effect, what Kripke has here are two domains: an
inner one ($\Psi(G)$) and an *outer* one (D *minus* $\Psi(G)$). See Leblanc and Thomason
[20], where versions of QC = with $(\exists X)(X = P) \supset ((\forall X)A \supset A(P/X))$ as
their *Specification Axiom* are accounted for in terms of inner and outer domains.

(3) K being a non-empty set and Ψ a domain function for K, understand by *a valuation function for* K *and* Ψ any function that pairs with each member G of K a $\Psi(G)$-valuation;[30]

(4) K being a nonempty set, Ψ being a domain function for K, D being $\bigcup_{G \in K} \Psi(G)$, Φ being a valuation function for K and Ψ, and G being a member of K, take a wff A of $\mathrm{QC_5}''$, to be *true on the quadruple* $\langle K, \Psi, \Phi, G \rangle$ if:

(i)   in case A is a sentence parameter, A is assigned T in $\Phi(G)$,

(ii) in case A is of the sort $F^k(I_1, I_2, \ldots, I_k), \langle d_1, d_2, \ldots, d_k \rangle$ —the k-tuple consisting of the members of D respectively assigned in $\Phi(G)$ to I_1, I_2, $\ldots$, and I_k—belongs to the subset of D^k assigned in $\Phi(G)$ to F^k,

(iii) in case A is of the sort $\sim B$, B is not true on $\langle K, \Psi, \Phi, G \rangle$,

(iv) in case A is of the sort $B \supset C$, B is not true on $\langle K, \Psi, \Phi, G \rangle$ or C is,

(v)   in case A is of the sort $\square B$, B is true on $\langle K, \Psi, \Phi, H \rangle$ for every member H of K, and

(vi) in case A is of the sort $(\forall X)B$, B is true on $\langle K, \Psi, \Phi, G \rangle$ no matter which member of $\Psi(G)$ is assigned in $\Phi(G)$ to X;[31]

(5) K, Ψ, Φ, and G being as in (4), take a wff A of $\mathrm{QC_5}''$ to be automatically *true$_\varnothing$ on* $\langle K, \Psi, \Phi, G \rangle$ if A is of the sort $(\forall X)B$; otherwise, take A to be true$_\varnothing$ on $\langle K, \Psi, \Phi, G \rangle$ if conditions (i) through (v) in (4) (with 'true' read 'true$_\varnothing$') are met.

This done, certify a wff A of $\mathrm{QC_5}''$ *valid* if A is both true and true$_\varnothing$ on every quadruple of the sort $\langle K, \Psi, \Phi, G \rangle$. A routine adaptation of Kripke's argument in [9] will show that all and only those wffs of $\mathrm{QC_5}''$ valid in this sense are provable in $\mathrm{QC_5}''$ [that is, provable by means of (A1) through (A5), (A6''), (A7) through (A10), (A13), and *Modus Ponens*].

Treatment in [11] of $\mathrm{QC_M}''$, $\mathrm{QC_B}''$, and $\mathrm{QC_4}''$ calls again for a (binary) relation R on K, which in the case of $\mathrm{QC_M}''$ you require to be reflexive, in that of $\mathrm{QC_B}''$ to be reflexive and symmetrical, and in that of $\mathrm{QC_4}''$ to be reflexive and transitive. Quintuples of the sort $\langle K, \Psi, \Phi, R, G \rangle$ will then do duty for the quadruples $\langle K, \Psi, \Phi, G \rangle$ above, and $\mathrm{QC_5}''$ can again be accommodated within this broader framework by requiring R to an equivalence relation.

[30] Note that one and the same $\Psi(G)$-valuation may be paired with two different worlds, so long as the same individuals exist in both worlds. The like holds true on page 253 of a G-valuation. Some like this feature of Kripke's semantics; others do not.

[31] A more formal account would talk here of X-variants of $\Phi(G)$, but the intent of clause (v) is clear enough.

As Kripke notes, wffs of the sort $(\forall X)\Box A \supset \Box(\forall X)A$ will turn out to be valid if, for any two members G and G' of K such that $R(G, G')$, $\Psi(G')$ is required to be a subset of $\Psi(G)$, and wffs of the sort $\Box(\forall X)A \supset (\forall X)\Box A$ will if, for any two such members of K, $\Psi(G)$ is required to be a subset of $\Psi(G')$.

Kripke does not attend to calculi like QC_M, QC_B, QC_4, and QC_5. To provide for these within his own semantics, drop the domain function Ψ in favor of an arbitrary domain D common to *all* the worlds in the set K (thus talking of a quintuple $\langle K,D,\Phi,R,G \rangle$ where I just talked of $\langle K,\Psi,\Phi,R,G \rangle$), disregard (5) on page 255, and take a wff A of, say, QC_M to be valid if A is true on every quintuple of the sort $\langle K,D,\Phi,R,G \rangle$ for reflexive R. A will then be valid if and only if provable in QC_M [that is, provable by means of (A1) through (A10), (A14), and *Modus Ponens*].[32]

Kripke's 1959 and 1963 papers were major breakthroughs, ranking with Gödel [5] and Henkin [6]. They teem, though, with references to "possible worlds," "possible individuals," and the like, and you cannot delete these without robbing the account of its intuitive appeal. So to readers with more frugal tastes an alternative treatment of things may be welcome.

Using QC_M'' as a sample, understand by *a truth-value assignment (for QC_M'')* any result of assigning a truth value to every atomic wff of QC_M''; K being a nonempty set of truth-value assignments, each relativized to a set of individual parameters of QC_M'', R being a reflexive relation on K, and α_Σ being a member of K, take a wff A of QC_M'' to be *true on the triple $\langle K,R,\alpha_\Sigma \rangle$* if:

(1) in case A is atomic, $\alpha(A) = \mathrm{T}$

(2) in case A is of the sort $\sim B$, B is not true on $\langle K,R,\alpha_\Sigma \rangle$,

(3) in case A is of the sort $B \supset C$, B is not true on $\langle K,R,\alpha_\Sigma \rangle$ or C is,

(4) in case A is of the sort $\Box B$, B is true on $\langle K,R,\alpha_{\Sigma'} \rangle$ for every member $\alpha_{\Sigma'}$ of K such that $R(\alpha_\Sigma, \alpha_{\Sigma'})$,

and

(5) in case A is of the sort $(\forall X)B$, $B(P/X)$ is true on $\langle K,R,\alpha_\Sigma \rangle$ for every individual parameter P of QC_M'' in Σ;

and take a wff A of QC_M'' to be *valid in the truth-value sense* if A is true on every triple of the sort $\langle K,R,\alpha_\Sigma \rangle$.

Note, by the way, that the individual parameters 'a', 'b', 'c', and so on may be treated here as they were on page 250. Kripke must think of them as drawing their values from possibly different worlds; we

---

[32] Kripke acknowledges only closed wffs as theorems of QC_M'', QC_B'', QC_4'', and QC_5''; but the restriction is inessential and—in my opinion—best lifted.

may think of them as simply standing for non-designating as well as designating terms. The savings are considerable.

The wanted definitions for QC_B'', QC_4'', and QC_5'' can be had the usual way: Require in the case of QC_B'' that R be reflexive and symmetrical, in that of QC_4'' that R be reflexive and transitive, and in that of QC_5'' that R be reflexive, symmetrical, and transitive (or, in this last case, dispense with R altogether, use pairs of the sort $\langle K,\alpha_\Sigma \rangle$ instead of triples, and take $\Box B$ to be true on $\langle K,\alpha_\Sigma \rangle$ if B is true on $\langle K,\alpha_{\Sigma'} \rangle$ for every member $\alpha_{\Sigma'}$ of K).

Finally, when it comes to QC_M, QC_B, QC_4, and QC_5, just think of K as a set of *unrelativized* truth-value assignments, use triples of the sort $\langle K,R,\alpha \rangle$ rather than the sort $\langle K,R,\alpha_\Sigma \rangle$, and certify $(\forall X)B$ true on $\langle K,R,\alpha \rangle$ if $B(P/X)$ is true on $\langle K,R,\alpha \rangle$ for every individual parameter P of your calculus.

Proof that any wff of, say, QC_M which is valid in my sense is provable in QC_M can be retrieved from Makinson [22] and Thomason [24]. So can proof that any wff of, say, QC_M'' which is valid in that sense is provable in QC_M''. In this case, though, some delicate maneuvers are needed to make up for the missing axiom schema (A14).[33] The two proofs are then easily adjusted to cover the remaining six of my calculi. Details, which are too lengthy for inclusion here, will be supplied in Leblanc [17].[34]

Another account of QC_M'', QC_B'', QC_4'', and QC_5'' which does without "possible worlds" and "possible individuals" can of course be found in Hintikka. It uses model sets in lieu of truth-value assignments, and sets of model sets (called *model systems*) in lieu of sets of truth-value assignments.[35]

So, the reader for whom the "real world" is already enough of a concern need not despair. The behavior of '$\Box$', like that of '$\forall$', can be explicated with a minimum of ontology, and inferences that employ '$\Box$' can be performed by all: those who deal in "other worlds" and the heathens who do not.[36]

---

[33] For hints on this matter, see Thomason [24], Hughes and Cresswell [8], pp. 174–176, and Leblanc and Meyer [19].

[34] The above completeness results for QC_M, QC_B, QC_4, and QC_5 were first announced at the Temple University Conference on Alternative Semantics, December 29, 1970. They were already known to Dunn, whose proof that R can be dispensed with in truth-value accounts of M, B, S4, and S5 was also presented at that conference.

[35] See in particular Hintikka [7]. For an extended variant of Hintikka's semantics, see Snyder [23].

[36] I wish to thank John Robert Cassidy (Ramapo College of New Jersey), Robert P. McArthur (Temple University), and George Weaver (Bryn Mawr College) for their helpful advice and suggestions. (The brash tone of the paper is my sole responsibility, though.) Excerpts from the paper were read at SUNY at Buffalo in October of 1971.

Bibliography

[1] Barcan, Ruth, "A Functional Calculus of First Order Based on Strict Implication," *The Journal of Symbolic Logic* (hereafter *JSL*), Vol. 11 (1946), pp. 1–16.

[2] Carnap, Rudolph, "Modalities and Quantification," *JSL*, Vol. 11 (1946), pp. 33–64.

[3] Dunn, J. Michael, "A Truth Value Semantics for Modal Logic," *Truth, Syntax and Modality, Proceedings of the Temple University Conference on Alternative Semantics*, Amsterdam, 1973.

[4] Dunn, J. M., and N. D. Belnap, Jr., "The Substitution Interpretation of the Quantifiers," *Noûs*, Vol. 2 (1968), pp. 177–185.

[5] Gödel, Kurt, "Die Vollständigkeit der Axiome des logischen Funktionenkalküls," *Monatshefte für Mathematik und Physik*, Vol. 37 (1930), pp. 349–360.

[6] Henkin, Leon, "The Completeness of the First-Order Functional Calculus," *JSL*, Vol. 14 (1949), pp. 159–166.

[7] Hintikka, Jaakko, *Models for Modalities*, Dordrecht-Holland, 1969.

[8] Hughes, G. E., and M. J. Cresswell, *An Introduction to Modal Logic*, London, 1968.

[9] Kripke, Saul A., "A Completeness Theorem in Modal Logic," *JSL*, Vol. 24 (1959), pp. 1–15.

[10] Kripke, S. A., "Semantical Analysis of Modal Logic I," *Zeitschrift für mathematische Logik und Grundlagen der Mathematik*, Vol. 9 (1963), pp. 67–96.

[11] Kripke, S. A., "Semantical Considerations on Modal Logic," *Modal and Many-Valued Logics, Acta Philosophica Fennica*, Fasc. XVI, Helsinki, 1963.

[12] Lambert, Karel, "Existential Import Revisited," *Notre Dame Journal of Formal Logic*, Vol. 4 (1963), pp. 288–292.

[13] Leblanc, H., "A Simplified Account of Validity and Implication for Quantificational Logic," *JSL*, Vol. 33 (1968), pp. 231–235.

[14] Leblanc, H., "A Simplified Strong Completeness Proof for QC =," *Akten des XIV. Internationalen Kongresses für Philosophie*, Vol. III (1969), pp. 83–96.

[15] Leblanc, H., "Truth-Value Semantics for a Logic of Existence," *Notre Dame Journal of Formal Logic*, Vol. 12 (1971), pp. 153–168.

[16] Leblanc, H., "Semantic Deviations," *Truth, Syntax, and Modality: Proceedings of the Temple University Conference on Alternative Semantics*, Amsterdam, 1973.

[17] Leblanc, H., *Truth-Value Semantics*, forthcoming.

[18] Leblanc, H., and R. K. Meyer, "Open Formulas and the Empty

Domain," *Archiv für Mathematische Logik und Grundlagenforshung*, Vol. 12 (1969), pp. 78–84.

[19] Leblanc, H., and R. K. Meyer, "On Prefacing $(\forall X)A \supset A(Y/X)$ with $(\forall Y)$: A Free Quantification Theory without Identity," *Zeitschrift für mathematische Logik und Grundlagen der Mathematik*, Vol. 16 (1970), pp. 447–462.

[20] Leblanc, H., and R. H. Thomason, "Completeness Theorems for Some Presupposition-Free Logics," *Fundamenta Mathematicae*, Vol. 62 (1968), pp. 125–164.

[21] Leblanc, H., and W. A. Wisdom, *Deductive Logic*, Boston, 1972.

[22] Makinson, David C., "On some Completeness Theorems in Modal Logic," *Zeitschrift für mathematische Logik und Grundlagen der Mathematik*, Vol. 12 (1966), pp. 379–384.

[23] Snyder, D. Paul, *Modal Logic and its Applications*, New York, 1971.

[24] Thomason, Richmond H., "Some Completeness Results for Modal Predicate Calculi," *Philosophical Problems in Logic: Some Recent Developments*, Dordrecht-Holland, 1970.

[25] van Fraassen, Bas C., "The Completeness of Free Logic," *Zeitschrift für mathematische Logik und Grundlagen der Mathematik*, Vol. 12 (1966), pp. 219–234.

Perception and Individuation[1]

RICHMOND H. THOMASON

University of Pittsburgh

I

INTRODUCTION: PERCEPTION AS A MODALITY

The themes I will take up in this paper were originated by Jaakko Hintikka in an article called "On the Logic of Perception."[2] I want to modify and generalize Hintikka's ideas, and to discuss various ways in which they can be applied to problems of philosophical interest. Since Hintikka's paper is not at present well known, I will begin by duplicating material already discussed in that paper. I will presuppose general familiarity with modal logic but will try to be as nontechnical as possible.

Throughout this paper I will follow tradition and concentrate on visual perception, on *seeing*. In their accounts of seeing, most epistemologists have taken the transitive use of the verb 'sees' to be basic; to put it crudely, they have taken sentences such as

(1.1)   Schwartz sees the footstool

[1] This research was supported by National Science Foundation Grants GS-1567 and GS-2517. The present paper was first written in May, 1970 and has since undergone many revisions, having been presented at Yale University, Indiana University, and New York University. I am indebted to all those who commented on the paper on these occasions. But Paul Benacerraf, Donald Davidson, David Kaplan, Geoffrey Sampson, Dana Scott, and Bas van Fraassen deserve special mention.
[2] Spirit duplicated and privately distributed, 1967. Published as Hintikka [12]. Hintikka has further developed his ideas and applied them philosophically in papers such as [16], [17], and [18].

to express some sort of relation between a percipient, Schwartz, and an object, the footstool. This relation may or may not be mediated by various "secondary" perceptual entities. In any case, the truth of

(1.2)   Schwartz sees that the footstool is broken

would then depend in some way on this relation.

Our use of the techniques of modal logic, however, suggests the strategy of taking *perceptual knowledge* to be basic and the relation to an object to be secondary—or at least, not more fundamental. This suggestion will bear fruit later, when we will find that expressions such as 1.1 can be defined using logical operators and expressions such as 1.2.

II

COMMITMENTS OF THE MODAL APPROACH

In general, the problem of providing a semantic interpretation of a formal language divides into two parts. First you have to figure out what structural information is needed in order to assign appropriate meanings to expressions of the language and, on the basis of these meanings, to give truth-values to atomic formulas. Second you have to devise semantic rules showing how the truth-values of complex formulas depend on the truth-values of simpler ones.[3]

According to the standard method of interpreting modal operators,[4] the structural information consists of a set $\mathcal{K}$ called the set of "possible worlds" or situations or points of reference, and a relation $\mathcal{R}$ on $\mathcal{K}$, called the relation of relative possibility. The ordered pair $\langle \mathcal{K}, \mathcal{R} \rangle$ is called a *model structure*. In the logic of 'seeing that' the relation $\mathcal{R}$ is construed so that a situation α bears the relation $\mathcal{R}$ to a situation β (that is, $\alpha \mathcal{R} \beta$) in case β is compatible with what a certain fixed percipient, say p, sees in situation α. If in a situation, α, I can't see exactly how many people are in the room with me but can see that there are more than four and fewer than seven, there is a situation "perceptually possible" with respect to α in which five other persons are there, and another in which six are there.

Let's suppose that a connective S in our formal language stands for 'sees that'. According to the semantic rule for S, a formula SA will be true in a situation α of a model structure $\langle \mathcal{K}, \mathcal{R} \rangle$ if for all β in $\mathcal{K}$ such that $\alpha \mathcal{R} \beta$, A is true in β.

This isn't a very complicated theory yet, but it has some conse-

---

[3] See Thomason [27].
[4] See Hintikka [14], Scott [23], or Thomason [26].

quences that are worth mentioning. It renders any formula of the sort

(2.1) $S(A \supset B) \supset (SA \supset SB)$

valid, as well as making SA valid whenever A is valid. Together, these commit us to the principle that if $SA_1, \ldots , SA_n$ are all true and B is a logical consequence of $\{A_1, \ldots , A_n\}$, then SB is true.

Commitments of this kind can be questioned on the ground that they assume a "logically omniscient" percipient. This objection may then be countered by adjusting the interpretation of logical consequence, as Hintikka does in [10], so that it represents what a percipient would conclude were he logically omniscient. Or, in a similar vein, one can adapt a ploy of Aristotle's and say that there is an active and a potential kind of seeing, the second being the sort described by the logical theory. Recently Hintikka has been exploring still another response to this problem, one involving a formal distinction between "surface" and "depth" notions of consequence.[5] But rather than delaying over this point, I feel that it is more useful to go forward and see what the theory has to offer.

If we assume that the relation $\mathfrak{R}$ is transitive, any formula of the sort

(2.2) $SA \supset SSA$

becomes valid. As usual, there are few intuitive resources to mobilize in resolving the question of whether this is desirable or not. Provisionally, however, I will make the assumption that $\mathfrak{R}$ is transitive.

Another important question is whether $\mathfrak{R}$ should be reflexive. To require that it be reflexive will make all formulas of the sort

(2.3) $SA \supset A$

valid. On the other hand, if we allow $\mathfrak{R}$ to be nonreflexive, then many such formulas, such as

(2.4) $SP \supset P$

are rendered invalid. (In 2.4, P is a sentence parameter, an atomic formula.) In other words, we're asking whether seeings-that are always successful, so that if SA is true then A is true.

[5] See Hintikka [13] and the references given therein.

As long as we don't confuse 'seeing that' with 'seeing', English usage strongly supports a positive answer to this question; one can't see that a thing is so without it actually being so. If someone claims that he sees that there are pumpkins in the field, he will be forced to withdraw this claim once he is shown that there aren't pumpkins in the field. In this respect 'sees that' resembles 'knows that', 'realizes that', 'is surprised that', and 'forgets that'.[6] (Its resemblance to the first two locutions is even stronger, since in many contexts it is interchangeable with them. I will return to this point below, in Section 6.) There is no need to collect further evidence on this point, since it is so plentiful and unequivocal; there is really no choice but to make ℛ reflexive.

To forestall misunderstanding, however, I should emphasize that our commitment to the validity of scheme 2.3 by no means implies that statements such as

(2.5) If Arnold sees a pink elephant in the bathtub, then there is a pink elephant in the bathtub

are valid. This is because 2.5 can't be formalized by means of a formula of the sort 2.3. In particular, the sentence

(2.6) Arnold sees a snake crawling up his leg

can't be represented by the formula SP because P can stand only for declarative sentences, and 'snakes crawling up his leg' is not a sentence but a noun phrase.

Of course, things might have been arranged differently. Many current transformational grammars treat sentences as noun phrases, and under the influence of these we might have disregarded the difference between 2.6 and

(2.7) Arnold sees that snakes are crawling up his leg

and so sanctioned a formalization such as SP. But this, I think, would be a mistake. Not only logical, but syntactic evidence indicates that

---

[6] There is a question as to whether the relation between 'Greg sees that his watch has stopped' and 'His watch has stopped' is really one of presupposition rather than implication. My present feeling is that, despite the fact that 'Greg does not see that his watch has stopped' seems also to imply 'His watch has stopped', this is not a true implication but a phenomenon to be explained by Grice's notion of conversational implicature. (See Grice [8], which also contains numerous points about perception relevant to our subject.) This applies also to 'knows that' and perhaps to 'realizes that,' 'is surprised that,' and 'forgets that'. In this case the source of the presupposition would be pragmatic rather than semantic, and so can be ignored in the present paper.

'see' has two very different uses when it takes sentential and nominal complements. An example of such evidence is the fact that the expression

(2.8)   Tom sees a seagull and that the tide is rising

is ungrammatical because of zeugma.

These considerations show how narrow the scope of our present theory is: we are dealing only with uses of 'see' taking sentential complements, with 'sees that' where this is taken to be a special and restricted use of 'sees'. Later in this paper we will be concerned with ways in which this initial theory can be extended to include other cases.

III

PERCEPTUAL AND PHYSICAL INDIVIDUATION[7]

According to Hintikka, the distinctive and novel features of perceptual modalities emerge only when quantifiers are taken into consideration. These arise, he feels, from the fact that there are two ways of individuating at work in the interpretation of these modalities.

What does this suggestion mean and what reasons are there for it? Let's consider an example. Suppose that John has lost a letter in a dimly lit room. He searches for it, looking through piles of papers and under furniture. Finally, he sees something white behind a wastebasket; it's the right shape, it could be the letter, but he isn't sure. Suppose that in this case what he is looking at is indeed the letter; even so, John doesn't see that it is the letter he is looking at.

Here, let Qu stand for '. . . is behind the wastebasket'. Is it correct to say

(3.1)   John sees something behind the wastebasket

here? This would be formalized as

(3.2) $(\exists x)SQx$.

[7] The argument of this section presupposes what can now be called the standard theory of modality and quantifiers. This theory is by now well enough established, it seems to me, to deserve a methodological status analogous to that of the calculus of probability. Certainly this calculus does not constitute a solution to philosophical problems concerning the interpretation of probability. Nevertheless, any philosopher interested in these problems must respect and be thoroughly familiar with the calculus. For one thing, any such interpretation that conflicts with the calculus is automatically invalidated. For accounts of the theory itself see the references given in Note 4, above.

Strangely enough, 3.2 is false when the quantifier is taken to range over physically individuated objects. The reason for this is that John hasn't recognized the letter. There is a situation compatible with what he sees in which it's the letter that is behind the wastebasket, but also there is a situation compatible with what he sees in which it's just, say, an empty envelope there.

Now, in each situation compatible with what John sees, something or other is there behind the wastebasket, so that

(3.3) $S(\exists x)Qx$

is true, though 3.2 is false. My own first reaction to Hintikka's examples of this sort was that this was the right way to formalize 3.1. But on further reflection this solution isn't acceptable. For one thing, you can see that there is something or other behind the wastebasket on indirect evidence: for instance, by seeing shadows or by seeing and hearing thrown objects bounce off of it. Such evidence suffices to support 3.3, but not 3.1.[8]

Also, familiarity with the standard theory of quantification and modality suggests that 3.3 is not the correct formalization of 3.1. According to this theory the difference between

(3.4)   Someone or other will always be on call

and

(3.5)   A specific person will always be on call,

or between

(3.6)   Two is necessarily greater than some number or other

and

(3.7)   Two is necessarily greater than some specific number,

is treated as a difference in the scope of a quantifier. Examples 3.4 and 3.6 have the form

(3.8) $M(\exists x)Qx$

[8] This is a little tricky, since one might say 'I see something behind the wastebasket' on such indirect evidence. But though this complicates matters it does not constitute an objection; our point only requires that there be a sense of 3.1 in which this sentence is false unless there is something behind the wastebasket such that John sees it.

and 3.5 and 3.7 the form

(3.9) $(\exists x)MQx$

where M is an appropriate modal operator. But we have a similar distinction between

(3.10)   John sees something or other behind the wastebasket

and

(3.11)   John sees a specific thing behind the wastebasket.

It's natural, then, for a modal logician to use 3.2 to formalize 3.11, and yet we find that this formalization is inadequate when the quantifiers range over physically individuated objects. To resolve this impasse, let's consider the matter from the standpoint of the semantic theory.

To interpret 3.11 correctly we must make it mean that in each situation compatible with what John sees there is an object behind the wastebasket which in some sense is the same: a single thing to which, in each situation, his attention is directed. This, of course, presupposes some way of individuating objects, of identifying them across situations.

Since physical individuation is inadequate in explaining 3.11, we must allow two sorts of individuation. Corresponding to these, we'll need two sorts of variables in our formal language, one for physically individuated objects and the other for perceptually individuated objects. Using Roman letters for physical variables and Greek letters for perceptual variables, we can then formalize the two senses of 3.1 as follows.

(3.12) $(\exists\varphi)Q\varphi$
(3.13) $(\exists x)Qx$

The first of these says that there is an object, identified perceptually, which in each visually possible situation is behind the wastebasket. The second says that there is an object, identified physically, which in each visually possible situation is behind the wastebasket.

Another example may help to clarify the difference between the two kinds of quantifiers and to reinforce the arguments that led us to introduce them. Suppose we're at a cocktail party and there is someone across the room you're trying to point out to me. I look, attending to your description, and successfully determine who you mean. I then can say truthfully that I see who you mean. This use of

(3.14)   I see who you mean

can be represented by

(3.15) $(\exists\varphi)\mathrm{S}a = \varphi,$

where a stands for 'the person you mean'. This formula is true if and only if there is an object in my vision, perceptually the same in all situations, and which in all situations compatible with what I see is identical to the person you mean.

It's easy to arrange the example so that $(\exists x)\mathrm{S}x = a$ is false; let the person you indicate have his back to us, so that I don't see who he is. In that case, there is no physically individuated object identical to the man you mean in all situations, and so

(3.16)   I don't see who the person you mean is,

which would be formalized as $\sim(\exists x)\mathrm{S}a = x$, is true. Our two kinds of variables are designed to permit a means of formalizing perceptual locutions so that 'I see who you mean, but I don't see who he is' can be represented as consistent.

This example can be inverted to make 3.14 and 3.16 both false. Here we want a case in which I don't see who you mean, but I do see who he is. Suppose that from your description I realize who he must be; he's a person well known to me whom I know to be at the party. But the light is bad, people are milling around, and I haven't been able to pick him out from the crowd. The natural thing to say in these circumstances is

(3.17)   I see who you mean, but I don't see him.

To someone attentive to logical form this is perilously close to paradox; if you replace the pronoun 'him' by the phrase to which it refers, 'who you mean', you get an outright contradiction:

(3.18)   I see who you mean, but I don't see who you mean.

Again the use of two styles of variables enables us to solve the problem. The formalization of 3.17 is

$$(3.19) \quad (\exists x)Sa = x \wedge \sim(\exists \varphi)Sa = \varphi.\,[9]$$

IV

EXISTENCE IN PERCEPTUAL LOGIC[10]

To represent this idea in our semantic theory we'll have to build modes of individuation into the notion of a perceptual model structure. But before turning to this task we should look more closely at the meaning of *existence* in 3.12 and 3.13. In particular, is there any semantic difference between

$$(4.1) \quad (\exists \varphi)\varphi = a$$

and

$$(4.2) \quad (\exists x)x = a$$

4.1 will be true in those situations in which a denotes an object which exists physically. For example, if a stands for 'Buckingham Fountain', 4.2 will be true; if a stands for 'The Fountain of Youth', 4.2 will be false. If this is so, it is reasonable to regard 4.1 as true in those situations in which a denotes an object which *exists visually* for the

---

[9] There is a difficulty with the arguments I have given here to support the resort to many-individuated logic, one that eventually must be cleared up if the theory is to be well founded on linguistic evidence. This is the fact that there are other kinds of locutions that give rise to phenomena similar to those cited in this section. And yet no one, least of all me, would wish to infer that specific modes of individuation need to be posited for these. To expand an example from Partee [22], we have sentences such as 'My home was once in Maryland, but now it's in Los Angeles', 'John thinks my home is in Maryland but Bill thinks it's in Los Angeles', and 'One of the places I always like best is my home'. If the interaction of 'my home' here with pronouns were explained as we accounted for the interaction of 'the man you mean' with pronouns in contexts such as 3.16 and 3.17, we would soon find ourselves having to introduce so many modes of individuation that the device would lose all plausibility. So I would like to account for these cases differently. Many of them, for example, can be explained as instances of what Geach calls "pronouns of laziness" in [7]. The remainder, I think, can be explained by generalizing this idea; they can be regarded as cases of substitutional quantification (see, for example, Dunn and Belnap [5]). But treating these phenomena differently from perceptual examples must be justified by differences in the evidence they present. As far as I know, the linguistic data has not been sufficiently cataloged to show whether the perceptual cases are more complex and essentially different from "pronouns of laziness" and related phenomena. My expectation is that the evidence will support this conclusion; but at present this is only an expectation.

[10] It is at this point that my treatment begins to differ significantly from Hintikka's.

percipient p, something which is a visual object _for_ p. Provisionally, then, we can say that 4.1 is true in situation α if and only if p sees the thing denoted in α by a; this is only a rough formulation, however, and we will have more to say about it later.

This interpretation of 4.1 means that its truth-values, unlike the truth-values of 4.2, will depend for a large extent on acts of p: motor acts involving the visual apparatus as well as "acts of consciousness" having to do with attention. Our theory, however, is very schematic. It only commits us to there being a set of objects that are seen, not to any particular account of the structure of these objects. No notion of visual space and no "visual field" are presupposed, and no psychological claims (such as the principle that if a thing is seen, and seen as a complex of parts, then the parts are seen) are made by the theory. I myself would prefer to apply the theory so that only a few individuals—four or five at the most—are seen at a given time. But I will not argue for this preference here.

It is no surprise that the formula

$$(4.3) \quad (x)(\exists \varphi) x = \varphi$$

is invalid; there is nothing wrong about a situation in which some physically existing things are unseen, and in fact such situations are the norm. The converse principle,

$$(4.4) \quad (\varphi)(\exists x) x = \varphi,$$

is more interesting. According to 4.4, everything which is seen exists physically. The question whether 4.4 is valid is very like the problem we discussed above, of whether 'seeing-that' should always be successful, since 4.4 expresses another way in which seeing can be veridical.

The counterexamples to 4.4, if any, are cases of hallucination or illusion. But we must be careful here in picking an example; we don't want illusions in which a physical object is seen as something else. For instance, if I'm hunting deer, the pattern of light and shadow on a cluster of leaves may organize itself into the figure of a buck. This isn't a counterexample to 4.4, since here what I see is in fact a cluster of leaves. There physically exists an object (the cluster of leaves) which is identical with what I see, so that if a stands for 'what I see' then $(\exists x) x = a$ is true.

What we want is an example like Macbeth and the dagger. In a way, Macbeth sees something—he has an impression of a dagger—and yet there is no physical object with which the dagger can be identified. Here, it's plausible to say that Macbeth sees the dagger, so that

(4.5) $(\exists\varphi)\varphi = b$

will be true, where b stands for 'this dagger', but to deny that the dagger is to be identified with any physical object, so that

(4.6) $(\exists x)x = b$

will be false. Since 4.5 and the negation of 4.6 together imply $(\exists\varphi)(x)\!\sim\!x = \varphi$, this provides a counterexample to 4.4.

Although I want to say that 4.4 is invalid, I believe that it is *prima facie* true, or true as a rule. But this is not reflected by the semantic theory developed in this paper, which has no mechanism for dealing with *prima facie* truth. Indeed, it's doubtful whether this notion falls within the scope of semantics at all.

V

MODEL STRUCTURES, MODES OF INDIVIDUATION, SATISFACTION

Our intuitions should now be sufficiently mobilized to make possible a rigorous semantics for perceptual logic. We have already discussed the elements $\mathcal{K}$ and $\mathcal{R}$ of a perceptual model structure and how they are used to interpret the connective S. Our problem here is how to interpret the perceptual and physical quantifiers. We will deal with this problem by introducing new elements into perceptual model structures and explaining how these determine the truth-values of quantified formulas.

First, our structures must tell us what things exist perceptually and physically in each situation. We therefore stipulate that a model structure $\mathfrak{M}$ having a set $\mathcal{K}$ of situations must possess functions $\mathfrak{D}^{\mu}$ and $\mathfrak{D}^{\nu}$ which take $\mathcal{K}$ into sets of objects. Where α is any situation in $\mathcal{K}$, $\mathfrak{D}_{\alpha}{}^{\mu}$ is the *domain of perceptual objects in α*, and $\mathfrak{D}_{\alpha}{}^{\nu}$ the domain of *physical objects in α*.

The domains $\mathfrak{D}_{\alpha}{}^{\mu}$ and $\mathfrak{D}_{\alpha}{}^{\nu}$ give us enough information to determine the truth-values of formulas such as $(\exists\varphi)\varphi = a$ and $(\exists x)x = a$. The former is true in a situation α if and only if in that situation a denotes a member of $\mathfrak{D}_{\alpha}{}^{\mu}$; the latter is true in α if and only if in that situation a denotes a member of $\mathfrak{D}_{\alpha}{}^{\nu}$.

But this is inadequate when we come to formulas such as $(\exists x)Sx = a$. This formula will be true in α in case there is a physical object which in all β such that $\alpha\mathcal{R}\beta$ is the denotation of a. To determine whether this is the case, we need to know what the physical objects of the model structure are, in a sense of "object" which is invariant under change of situation. In other words, we need a way of physically individuating objects across situations. We will now generalize this and make it more precise.

If we collect together all the domains $\mathfrak{D}_\alpha{}^\mu$ and $\mathfrak{D}_\alpha{}^\nu$, we obtain a set D,

$$D = \bigcup_{\alpha \in \mathfrak{K}} (\mathfrak{D}_\alpha{}^\mu \cup \mathfrak{D}_\alpha{}^\nu),$$

called the *domain* of the model structure. (There may also be a domain $\mathfrak{D}'$, disjoint from all the $\mathfrak{D}_\alpha{}^\mu$ and $\mathfrak{D}_\alpha{}^\nu$, associated with the model structure, in case it is desirable to have individuals which do not exist in any situation. If so, the members of this domain $\mathfrak{D}'$ are also included in D.) A mode of individuation is supposed to provide a complete list of objects for the domain D and set $\mathfrak{K}$ of situations of a model structure. We can identify such an object[11] with a *rule* which from the standpoint of each α in $\mathfrak{K}$ gives a member d of D; this individual d is understood as the perspective presented by the object, viewed from the situation α.[12] In other words, every object will be what I have elsewhere called a *world-line* on D and $\mathfrak{K}$: a function from $\mathfrak{K}$ into D.

But not every world-line on D and $\mathfrak{K}$ will be an object, relative to a given mode of individuation. Indeed, the job a mode of individuation is supposed to do is to pick from the class of all world-lines just those which are objects. Furthermore, these objects must be chosen systematically, so that they do not intersect: two different objects of the same mode of individuation cannot present the same perspective in the same situation. And to be complete, a mode of individuation on D and $\mathfrak{K}$ must associate an object with each perspective: that is, if d is a member of D and α a member of $\mathfrak{K}$, then there must be an object presenting the perspective d in the situation α.

Let's make this material explicit in the form of definitions.

(5.1) A *world-line* on D and $\mathfrak{K}$ is a function d from $\mathfrak{K}$ into D.

(5.2) A *mode of individuation* on D and $\mathfrak{K}$ is a set μ of world-lines on D and $\mathfrak{K}$, such that (*i*) for all d, $d' \in \mu$, if $d_\alpha = d_\alpha'$ for any $d \in \mu$ and $\alpha \in \mathfrak{K}$ then $d = d'$ and (*ii*) for all d $\in$ D and $\alpha \in \mathfrak{K}$, there is a $d \in \mu$ such that $d_\alpha = $ d.

Clauses *i* and *ii* both express things that in recent years have been puzzlesome for, if not controversial among, modal logicians.[13] Never-

---

[11] In Thomason [26] I used the term 'substance' where I here use 'object'. I've adopted the latter word because it is less heavily freighted with connotations from ordinary and philosophical usage. Although many of these connotations are illuminating, others are unfortunate.

[12] There is considerable philosophical interest nowadays in the topic of individuation or cross-worlds identification, and to avoid misunderstanding I want to emphasize that what I am doing here is primarily technical, not philosophical. My present view on the interpretation of these notions is that objects, not world-lines, are to be found in experience. I agree with Kripke that the viability of semantic theories of individuation does not require that criteria be found for cross-world identification.

[13] See, for instance, Føllesdal [6], Hintikka [11], and Scott [23].

theless, though I won't attempt to justify the claim here, I feel that these commitments can be defended as consequences of the concept of objectivity and, in particular (to put the matter less metaphysically), as giving a proper account of validity for languages with quantifiers, modal operators, and identity.[14]

I would not wish to commit myself to *ii*, however, in an unqualified way, since I am prepared to admit that there are situations in which objects of other situations will not have "counterparts." If Leibniz was right, for instance, in his dispute with Clarke, then the times of our world cannot be identified with the times of radically different possible worlds. It makes no sense, for example, to speak of God creating the universe earlier than he did.[15] So I am willing to generalize this definition by allowing the elements d of a mode of individuation to be *partial* functions on $\mathcal{K}$. But I would then want to use van Fraassen's method of "supervaluations" to define satisfaction.[16] This method gives rise to truth-value gaps, but does not affect the valid formulas. The nice thing about it, as applied to this problem, is that it enables us to relax the very strong requirement *ii*, while leaving the logical theory essentially unchanged. Hintikka's solution to the same problem, in [15], affects drastically the formulas sanctioned as valid.

With it understood that clause *ii* of 5.2, in its present form, is an idealization that may need to be modified, we can proceed to other matters and characterize perceptual model structures. Such a structure $\mathfrak{M}$ must include, besides a set $\mathcal{K}$ of situations, a relation $\mathfrak{R}$, and domain-functions $\mathfrak{D}^{\mu}$ and $\mathfrak{D}^{\nu}$, two modes μ and ν of individuation on D and $\mathcal{K}$. These components of $\mathfrak{M}$ can then be used to formulate a semantic rule for the truth-values of formulas $(\varphi)A^{\varphi}/w$ and $(x)A^{x}/u$.[17]

By a *valuation* V of a formal language on $\mathfrak{M}$, we mean an assignment of appropriate values to variables and constants of the language. In particular, individual parameters w are assigned members of μ, and individual parameters u members of ν. Where $d \in \nu$, V^{d}/u is the valuation like V except in giving u the value d. The truth-values $\mathrm{V}_{\alpha}((\varphi)A^{\varphi}/w)$ and $\mathrm{V}_{\alpha}((x)A^{x}/u)$ of $(\varphi)A^{\varphi}/w$ and $(x)A^{x}/u$ in situation α are then determined as follows.

$\mathrm{V}_{\alpha}((\varphi)A^{\varphi}/w) = \mathrm{T}$ if and only if $\mathrm{V}^{d}/w_{\alpha}(A) = \mathrm{T}$ for all $d \in \mu$ such that $d_{\alpha} \in \mathfrak{D}_{\alpha}^{\mu}$.

$\mathrm{V}_{\alpha}((x)A^{x}/u) = \mathrm{T}$ if and only if $\mathrm{V}^{d}/u_{\alpha}(A) = \mathrm{T}$ for all $d \in \nu$ such that $d_{\alpha} \in \mathfrak{D}_{\alpha}^{\nu}$.

---

[14] There are arguments in Kripke [20] tending to support this position.
[15] See Alexander [1], pp. 75–77.
[16] See van Fraassen [29], pp. 94–96, 154–172.
[17] See Thomason [25], pp. 176–178, for an explanation of this notation. The other syntactic notations and terms used in this paper are also explained there; see the index on p. 326.

All of this raises a number of routine technical questions, such
as how the notion of validity arising from these definitions can be
axiomatized. None of these problems presents any special difficulty
and we can well afford to turn to a more interesting topic: what
is the relationship of this theory to natural language?

VI

NATURAL LANGUAGE AND THE LOGIC OF PERCEPTION

In this section we will discuss the relationships of the following
eight formulas to English locutions.

(6.1) $(\exists\varphi)\varphi = a$

(6.2) $(\exists x)x = a$

(6.3) $(\exists\varphi)S\varphi = a$

(6.4) $(\exists x)Sx = a$

(6.5) $(\exists\varphi)(\exists x)(\varphi = x \wedge x = a)$

(6.6) $(\exists\varphi)(\exists x)(\varphi = x \wedge Sx = a)$

(6.7) $(\exists\varphi)(\exists x)(\varphi = x \wedge S\varphi = a)$

(6.8) $(\exists\varphi)(\exists x)S(\varphi = x \wedge x = a)$

When we discussed 6.1 in Section 4, we interpreted this formula
as saying that the object named by a is seen by the percipient p.
But if we attend to the difference between 6.1 and 6.3, we can sharpen
this interpretation. Consider once again the example of the man who
looks at a cluster of leaves and has an impression of a deer, and
let a name the cluster of leaves. Then 6.1 will be true: the cluster
of leaves is in fact identical with a perceptual object for the man.
But 6.3 is false, since there is a situation compatible with what the
man sees, in which what he sees is not a cluster of leaves, but a
deer.

The fact that in this case 6.1 is true of a indicates that $(\exists\varphi)\varphi = a$
expresses a *weak* sense of 'sees', in which it is possible to have no idea
of what one is actually seeing: the man sees the cluster of leaves, but
doesn't see it as a cluster of leaves. The locution 'looks at' suggests itself
in cases of this kind. Here, for instance, it is suitable to say that the
hunter is looking at the cluster of leaves but doesn't really see it. The
sense of 'sees' which is contrasted here with merely looking at a thing
is the sense caught by 6.3. If 6.3 is true, what is named by a is not only
visually present, but in all situations compatible with what is seen, a
names the same visual object; that is, a names something which the
percipient has visually identified.

Formula 6.2 expresses physical existence; 6.2 is true in case a
names a physically existing individual. Again, 6.4 is stronger than

6.2; in order for 6.4 to be true, not only must the individual denoted by *a* exist, but in all situations compatible with what is seen, *a* must name the same physical object. For example, suppose that *a* stands for 'that man'; for 6.4 to be true, the percipient p must realize who the man is. In terms of our theory there must be a person who in all situations compatible with what p sees is that man. (For this, it will certainly suffice if p *knows* who that man is, but since in interpreting S we are considering situations compatible with what is *seen*, not just with what is known, perhaps this is not a necessary condition.)

It's useful to contrast 6.4 with 6.3 in this situation. For 6.3 to be true, p must visually identify that man, or "see who is indicated." If you say to me, "that man is a newcomer," it isn't necessary for me to realize who the man is in order for me to see who is indicated.

Notice that 6.4 can be true when p is not looking at the object referred to by *a*: that is, 6.4 does not imply 6.1. All that is needed for 6.4 to be true is that the object should exist and be physically the same in all situations compatible with what p sees. Since in English we commonly use locutions such as 'seeing what' or 'seeing who' to express 6.4,[18] this fact helps to explain how 'seeing' can take on nonvisual overtones akin to 'knowing'. For me to see who that man is, it is not necessary for me to be looking at him; the realization may strike me while my back is turned to him. Thus, 6.4 does not imply 6.1.[19]

6.5 is a mixed formula, involving both sorts of quantifiers. For it to be true, the individual named by *a* must exist physically and perceptually; that is, it must be a physically existing object of vision. There seems to be no locution in English corresponding to 6.5, but we can explain why this is so. There is no special need for a way of saying this because a direct object of 'looks at' is understood as a matter of course to be the name of a physical existent. The sense of 6.5 is thus conveyed implicitly by sentences using 'looks at' (for

---

[18] If in English 'seeing what' does not carry a commitment to existence, there is a discrepancy here with the logical theory, since 6.4 implies 6.2. But I am not persuaded that this discrepancy is terribly important.

[19] For some reason, many philosophers with whom I have discussed this claim have found it peculiar and somehow objectionable. Nevertheless, it's the way we all use the language: 'seeing that' and 'seeing who' are conditioned by knowledge, without regard to how this knowledge was obtained. Someone who is blind can "see that" and "see who" as well as anyone else, and no metaphors are involved here—any more than metaphor is involved when we say we see that burglars have robbed our house without seeing the burglars. "Seeing a thing," however, is another matter. I regard the fact that the present theory explains these data about 'sees' as an advantage. A theory of perception, logical or otherwise, that is not able to account for these phenomena is worse off than one that can.

example, 'John is looking at the house on the corner' conveys the impression that the house on the corner exists), and cases where this presupposition fails are usually treated by using special locutions which cancel presuppositions ('Macbeth was looking at an unreal dagger').

6.6, on the other hand, will be true if the individual named by a exists physically and perceptually, and in all visually possible situations a names a physically unique object. Again, there is no special English locution which expresses 6.6, and for similar reasons. Generally, an English noun or noun phrase is understood to refer to a single physical object in all possible situations. The indications that this presupposition has failed are usually contextual, and this feature of English gives rise to a deep-seated ambiguity which seems to affect all modalities.[20]

6.7 is true in case the individual named by a exists physically and perceptually, and in all visually possible situations a names the same perceptual object. We can express this in English: these are cases of "seeing an X which in fact is a Y." The sophistical puzzle of the masked man is a good example of this.[21] Let's make Socrates the butt of the joke; suppose that the sophist puts a masked man, who in fact is Socrates' father, in front of Socrates. Here, if a stands for 'that man', 6.3 will be true and 6.4 false; Socrates will see the man but will not see who he is. Since, however, Socrates' father exists physically and in fact is identical with that man, 6.7 will be true: Socrates will see a man who in fact is his father.

Our theory suggests an explanation of the source of the puzzle itself. When Socrates denies that he sees his father there is a sense in which what he says is true. Namely,

$$(6.9) \quad \sim(\exists\varphi)S\varphi = b$$

is true, where b stands for 'Socrates' father'. This is 'seeing' in the sense represented by 6.3. On the other hand there is also a sense in which what the sophist says is true when he claims that Socrates does see his father:

$$(6.10) \quad (\exists\varphi)\varphi = b$$

[20] For an extended examination of this ambiguity, see Thomason and Stalnaker [28].
[21] See Aristotle's *De Sophistics Elenchus*, 179[a] 25 ff. The puzzle reappears in Buridan's *Sophismata;* see [3], pp. 124–128. It is attributed to the Megarian logician Eubulides, who is also credited with the Liar Paradox. See Kneale and Kneale [19], p. 114, and the references therein.

is true. This is the 'seeing' represented by 6.1. If our account is correct it should be natural to say in such a situation that Socrates is looking at his father but doesn't see him, or is looking at his father but doesn't really see him. But this is just another way of saying that Socrates is looking at but doesn't recognize someone who in fact is his father. Here again, the evidence tends to support the formal theory.

6.8 is semantically equivalent to the conjunction of 6.3 and 6.4, and so is true in a situation α if and only if there is a world-line which is both a perceptual and physical object, which exists physically and perceptually in α, and which is named by a in each visually possible situation. Suppose again, for example, that a stands for 'that man'; then 6.8 says that p not only sees that man, but sees who he is. He has been wholly successful in identifying that man, or has *recognized* him. Locutions using 'recognizes' correspond to 6.8.

I was greatly encouraged and a little surprised at the above results; it's seldom that a new formal language purporting to relate to a kind of discourse will turn out to correlate so nicely to its intended subject matter. The results show that certain expressions generated by the formal syntax resemble and illuminate a variety of English locutions used in perceptual discourse. In cases where there is no correspondence, we can point to circumstances which explain this lack. Further, the enterprise of relating the formalism to natural language yields insights of the sort that bolster confidence in the theory. The explanation of why 'seeing who' takes on nonvisual connotations and the solution to the paradox of the masked man are examples of this.

Reassured by these developments, we can hope to use the theory in sorting out the logical relationships of locutions such as 'looks at . . .', '. . . exists', 'sees . . .', 'sees what . . . is', 'sees a thing which in fact is . . .', and 'recognizes . . .'. That is, we can proceed to reap the usual benefits accruing from formalization. But to me, the philosophical implications of the theory and the prospects it offers for further development are more exciting, and in the remainder of this paper I want to discuss these matters.

VII

KINDS OF INDIVIDUATION AND KINDS OF INDIVIDUALS

To its very toes, our formal system suggests dualism. If, with Quine, we regard the ontological commitments of a theory as indicated by the values of its bound variables, then the presence of two sorts of bound variables immediately suggests a commitment to dualism. Once this appellation is stripped of misleading overtones, however, I believe there is little fault with it. There is a grain of truth in epistemological dualism, though it is easily misconstrued and distorted, even by its advocates. The rigor of our logical model provides a great advantage here, permitting us to preserve this grain of truth while avoiding the pitfalls that lead to unwelcome consequences.

Above all, we must distinguish *many-individuated* from *many-sorted* logic. Consider, for instance, a two-sorted logic having the following two sorts of quantifications.

(7.1) $(x)A^x/u$

(7.2) $(y)A^y/u$

As is well known, these two quantifications can be replaced by one sort of quantification and two properties. Thus,

(7.3) $(z)(Pz \supset A^z/u)$

and

(7.4) $(z)(Qz \supset A^z/u)$

can be exchanged for 7.1 and 7.2 without affecting logical characteristics. It therefore is appropriate to say that a two-sorted logic divides the universe of discourse up into classes of things.

But in two-individuated logic the situation is very different. In particular, the "sorts" of the logic of perception are *referentially opaque*. In two-sorted logic,

(7.5) $s=t \supset (Ps \equiv Pt)$

will be valid, where P is one of the sorts, that is, where Pu is equivalent to $(\exists x)x=u$ or to $(\exists y)y=u$. But in the logic of perception,

(7.6) $s=t \supset ((\exists x)Sx=s \equiv (\exists x)Sx=t)$

and

(7.7) $s=t \supset ((\exists\varphi)S\varphi=s \equiv (\exists\varphi)S\varphi=t)$

are *invalid*. Since, for instance, $(y)A^y/u$ is equivalent to $(y)((\exists x)Sx=y \supset A^y/u)$,[22] the "sort" corresponding to $(y)A^y/u$ cannot be represented by an atomic formula such as Pu, because such formulas are *referentially*

---

[22] Here x and y are being used, as in previous sections, as quantifiers ranging over physically individuated objects.

transparent: that is, they satisfy 7.5. But it can be shown that no formula free of ν-quantifiers will serve to represent ν-quantification: it is not possible to eliminate the quantifications of a many-individuated logic in favor of predicates and a single quantifier. This suggests that something deeper and more subtle is involved in passing from one to many modes of individuation than from one to many sorts of individuals.

In describing the difference between sorts of individuals and modes of individuation, we may contrast *intramural* with *intermural* characteristics. If we deal only with differences among individuals which arise just from the point of view of one situation α, we can distinguish two sorts of existence using the domains $\mathfrak{D}_\alpha{}^\mu$ and $\mathfrak{D}_\alpha{}^\nu$. This is an intramural and purely two-sorted affair. But although this distinction is built into the μ- and ν-quantifiers of perceptual logic, this isn't what is most characteristic of them.

To emphasize this we may suppose for the moment that for all situations α the domains $\mathfrak{D}_\alpha{}^\mu$ and $\mathfrak{D}_\alpha{}^\nu$ are identical. This means that any formula having the form

$$(7.8) \quad (x)A^x/u \equiv (\varphi)A^\varphi/u$$

will be valid, as long as u has no occurrences in A within the scope of a modal operator, and x and φ are free for u in A. The μ- and ν-quantifiers will thus behave identically as far as quantifications into transparent contexts are concerned. (This is because the semantic behavior of such quantifications depends only on "intramural" considerations.)

But formulas involving quantifications into opaque contexts depend, in general, on "intermural" factors, and especially on modes of individuation, or identification across situations. The semantic effect which these factors have on formulas is what makes a multiplicity of modes of individuation much more than a set of pigeonholes. And the lesson to be learned from our discussion in Section 6 of natural language is that many important visual locutions should be regarded as involving quantifications into opaque contexts. These locutions are thus profoundly dependent on "intermural" factors such as individuation. It is therefore more appropriate to say of the logic of perception that it involves two *modes of being* rather than two kinds of things.

VIII

THE ARGUMENT FROM ILLUSION

This well-known philosophical "argument" is actually a cluster of arguments which have been formulated in many different ways, and to support many various lines of thought. We are interested here in those versions of the argument used to support the *existence* of sense-data. We need not bother with versions that are used, for example, to support the claim that there can be no certainty concerning the existence of physical properties of material objects. We are thus concerned only with those arguments which proceed from the existence of illusions, hallucinations, and other perceptual mishaps to the existence of sense-data. Notice that we ourselves have used a form of the argument from illusion to suggest that $(\varphi)(\exists x)x = \varphi$ is invalid. We also used a version of what Hintikka calls the "argument from incomplete identification," to establish the existence of a distinct mode of perceptual individuation.[23]

But traditional forms of the argument from illusion don't stop here. Their thrust is that since in some cases there are no physical objects corresponding to perceptual objects, this is so in *all* cases. I think it's fair to say that a sense-datum theorist who accepted our logical theory would go on to espouse the validity of

$$(8.1) \quad (x)(\varphi) \sim x = \varphi$$

which asserts that no visually present object is also a physical object. Semantically, this amounts to saying that $\mathfrak{D}_\alpha{}^\mu \cap \mathfrak{D}_\alpha{}^\nu$ is empty for all situations α.

Our formalism presents no reason for adopting a sense-datum theory in the strong sense captured by 8.1. Not only does the semantic theory render 8.1 invalid, but the intuitive interpretation we presented of the formal language suggests that it *ought* to be invalid. In case one is looking at an object which exists physically,

$$(8.2) \quad (\exists x)(\exists \varphi)x = \varphi$$

is true, so that 8.1 will be false. The logic of perception allows perceptual objects to be the same as physical objects. If, because it does distinguish between perceptually and physically individuated objects, this is a sense-datum theory, then it follows that not all sense-datum theories are incompatible with a realistic epistemology. It also differs from many sense-datum theories in a way which we stressed in Section 7: it is not a naïve dualism. Rather than distinguishing two kinds of objects, it delineates two modes of individuation.

Actually, our account of perception does more than just invalidating 8.1. It suggests that in ordinary cases, those in which perception

[23] Hintikka's argument is much closer to Eubulides' puzzle of the masked man than to the traditional argument from illusion.

is functioning successfully, not only will 8.1 be false, but

(8.3) $(\varphi)(\exists x)Sx = \varphi$

will hold true. 8.3 says that every perceptually individuated object is recognized as a physical object. Although cases of hallucination and "incomplete perceptual identification" force us to admit the two modes of individuation and allow the invalidity of 8.3, we can expect this formula to be true in normal, everyday situations.

Our logical theory, far from creating an impassable gulf between perceptual and physical objects, regards the identification of such objects as a goal of perception, a goal that as a rule is reached. (Recognition is certainly one of the goals of perception.) This point may be helpful to those who have had difficulty in seeing what we have meant by "perceptually identified objects." In ordinary cases, these will coincide with physical objects; there will be no difference between the two. The necessity for the distinction is to be found only in unusual cases; a lack of coincidence between perceptual and physical objects indicates a perceptually incomplete state, which ordinarily is to be remedied by further information limiting the supply of visually possible situations. (For example, Socrates comes to recognize his father by eliminating the situation in which the man is Crito, the situation in which the man is Callicles, and so on.) In very extraordinary cases (those sometimes called "conceptual revolutions") this coincidence may be brought about by readjusting the mode of physical individuation itself.

IX

OTHER PHILOSOPHICAL APPLICATIONS

I have spoken of our logical theory as "the logic of perception," but its philosophical uses extend well beyond the theory of perception. In order to convey an idea of these applications, I will briefly discuss three examples.

First, the theory provides a way of distinguishing "double-aspect" theories from other sorts of dualisms. It provides a good means of differentiating, for instance, between theories of mind and body such as Descartes' and Spinoza's. As we pointed out above, we can use the logical distinction between kinds of individuals and kinds of individuation to model the difference between two sorts of substances and two *attributes*, or ways in which substances appear.

Second, the theory applies to examples of "conceptual revolution" from the history of science. To take a simple case, consider the many astronomers who had Uranus in their telescopes prior to Herschel's observation of this planet. These men saw something which in fact was Uranus, but saw it as a star; in the situation α they took to be actual, what they saw was a star. They didn't recognize what they were looking at (that is, Uranus, a physical object), since in situation α the object they were looking at, being a star, could not be identified with the planet Uranus. Since these men didn't recognize what they saw, they were not credited with the discovery. Herschel himself at first took what he saw to be a comet, but this characterization led to closer scrutiny which eventually led Lexell to suggest that the thing was a planet. Thus, though Herschel is officially credited with the discovery, I would think it more appropriate to give Herschel and Lexell joint honors: Herschel being credited for the "seeing" and Lexell for the "seeing what" of the recognition.

This example shows why, when we award honors of discovery, a man whose picture of the universe differs greatly from ours isn't likely to come off well. Since his preconceptions will color his perceptually individuated objects in a way which makes it impossible to identify them with our physical objects, we will not credit him with recognition of these objects. This is why Priestley, for instance, is disputed in his claim to the discovery of oxygen. Though he successfully isolated it, there is nothing among the objects which he took to exist physically with which we can comfortably identify the substance oxygen. For many reasons, it is unsuitable to identify our oxygen with Priestley's dephlogisticated air.

Third, we want to say that a "conceptual revolution" is a change of *conceptual frameworks*. The recent philosophical literature contains much discussion of change of conceptual frameworks, but almost none of conceptual frameworks themselves. It is bad methodology to thus expect a serious, fruitful discussion of the dynamics of a phenomenon to precede an account of the statics. Perhaps modes of individuation can help here; I believe they should be viewed as components of conceptual frameworks. The above examples had to be restricted in scope because modes of individuation are only one of many components. But in spite of their simplicity, I believe they show we are on the right track. This is what is urgently needed in philosophy of science: a way of taking conceptual revolutions seriously without talking nonsense. A good logical model should afford us such an opportunity, in philosophy of science as well as other areas of philosophy.

X

FURTHUR DEVELOPMENTS OF THE THEORY

Perceptual discourse is very rich, and gives rise to many locutions beyond the scope of the present theory: 'seeing as', for instance, and 'seeing an event'. In particular, an adequate logic of perception should be able to distinguish between the following two sentences.[24]

(10.1)   I saw a man shaved in Oxford.

and

(10.2)   I saw a man born in Jerusalem.

In other words, the task is to distinguish 10.1 from

(10.3)   I saw a man who was shaved in Oxford.

The formal language developed above can handle 10.2 and 10.3; the latter, for instance, can be formalized by

(10.4) $(\exists x)(Qx \wedge (\exists \varphi)S\varphi = x)$

where Qu stands for ' . . . is a man who was born in Jerusalem'. (For the sake of simplicity, all considerations having to do with tense have been ignored here.)

But 10.2, on the other hand, seems to resist formalization, at least if we regard it as expressing a way of seeing a man. The most promising approach, I believe, is to treat it as expressing the seeing of an event, namely, of a shaving of a man in Oxford. Then the seeing of events can be formalized along the lines developed in preceding sections, provided that variables ranging over events are introduced into the formal language.

If this is done, I think it will be found that our previous arguments can be generalized to include events; it will be necessary to distinguish between the perceptual and physical individuation of events, and the perceptual and physical existence of events. Seeing an event, for instance, does not logically imply that the event happens: Macbeth saw a dagger marshalling him onwards to Duncan's murder, or in the optometrist's chair we may see a red circle moving on the wall across a green circle. If this generalization holds up, the formalization of 10.1 will simply be

(10.5) $(\exists \varphi)Q\varphi$

where Qw stands for '. . . is a shaving of a man in Oxford'.

---

[24] See Anscombe [2], p. 176, where this example is credited to J. L. Austin. Anscombe's article, by the way, contains a rewarding and insightful discussion of the data which we have been considering.

This formalization needs to be made adequate by founding it on a logical theory of events, whose task will be to display the formal relationships between predicates like '. . . is a shaving of a man in Oxford' and '. . . shaves a man in Oxford'. Two such theories are now available, Davidson's and Montague's,[25] and their relative merits in the present context must be compared.

This account of 10.1 is sketchy and tentative, and I offer it only as a suggestion for further consideration. Even more uncertain is the question of 'seeing as' as discussed, for example, by Hanson in [9], Chapter 1. I suspect that this phenomenon may raise entirely new problems calling for semantic devices not discussed in the present paper. In particular, Dana Scott's theory of approximate individuals might be useful in this connection.[26]

However this turns out, I find the prospects for applications of the logical techniques to epistemology very exciting. I will be pleased if the present paper stimulates other philosophers to criticize or apply and extend Hintikka's ideas on the subject.

Bibliography

[1] Alexander, H. (ed.), *The Leibniz-Clarke Correspondence*. Manchester, 1956.

[2] Anscombe, G., "The Intentionality of Sensation: A Grammatical Feature," *Analytical Philosophy*, Second Series, R. Butler (ed.). Oxford, 1965, pp. 158–180.

[3] Buridan, J., *Sophisms on Meaning and Truth*, K. Scott (tr.). New York, 1966.

[4] Davidson, D., "The Logical Form of Action Sentences," *The Logic of Decision and Action*, N. Rescher (ed.). Pittsburgh, 1966, pp. 81–95.

[5] Dunn, J., and N. Belnap, Jr., "The substitution interpretation of the quantifiers," *Nous*, Vol. 2 (1968), pp. 177–185.

[6] Føllesdal, D., "Knowledge, Identity, and Existence," *Theoria*, Vol. 33 (1967), pp. 1–27.

[7] Geach, P., *Reference and Generality*. Ithaca, 1962.

[8] Grice, H., "The Causal Theory of Perception," *Proceedings of the Aristotelian Society*, Suppl. Vol. 35 (1961), pp. 121–152.

[9] Hanson, N., *Patterns of Discovery*. Cambridge, 1958.

[10] Hintikka, J., *Knowledge and Belief*. Ithaca, 1962.

[11] Hintikka, J., "Existence and Identity in Epistemic Contexts," *Theoria*, Vol. 33 (1967), pp. 138–147.

[12] Hintikka, J., "On the Logic of Perception," *Perception and Per-*

---

[25] See Davidson [4] and Montague [21].
[26] Scott [24].

sonal Identity, N. Care and R. Grimm (eds.). Cleveland, 1969, pp. 140–173. Reprinted in J. Hintikka, *Models for Modalities*, Dordrecht, 1969, pp. 151–183.

[13] Hintikka, J., "Surface Information and Depth Information," *Information and Inference*, J. Hintikka and P. Suppes (eds.). Dordrecht, 1969, pp. 263–297.

[14] Hintikka, J., "Semantics for Propositional Atttiudes," *Models for Modalities*. Dordrecht, 1969, pp. 87–111.

[15] Hintikka, J., "Existential Presuppositions and Uniqueness Presuppositions," *Models for Modalities*. Dordrecht, 1969, pp. 112–147.

[16] Hintikka, J., "Objects of Knowledge and Belief: Acquaintances and Public Figures I," *Journal of Philosophy*, Vol. 67 (1970), pp. 869–884.

[17] Hintikka, J., "On the Different Constructions in Terms of the Basic Epistemological Concepts," *Contemporary Philosophy in Scandanavia*, R. Olsen and A. Paul (eds.). Baltimore, 1971.

[18] Hintikka, J., "Knowledge by Acquaintance—Individuation by Acquaintance." Mimeographed.

[19] Kneale, W., and M. Kneale, *The Development of Logic*. Oxford, 1962.

[20] Kripke, S., "Naming and Necessity," *Semantics of Natural Languages*, D. Davidson and G. Harman (eds.). Dordrecht, 1971.

[21] Montague, R., "On the Nature of Certain Philosophical Entities," *The Monist*, Vol. 53 (1969), pp. 159–194.

[22] Partee, B., "Opacity, Coreference, and Pronouns," *Synthese*, Vol. 21 (1970), pp. 359–385.

[23] Scott, D., "Advice on Modal Logic." *Philosophical Problems in Logic*, K. Lambert (ed.). Dordrecht, 1970, pp. 143–173.

[24] Scott, D., "Can We Have a Theory of Approximate Individuals?" Paper delivered at N.Y.U. Ontology Seminar, 1971, unpublished.

[25] Thomason, R., *Symbolic Logic: An Introduction*. New York, 1970.

[26] Thomason, R., "Modal Logic and Metaphysics," *The Logical Way of Doing Things*, K. Lambert (ed.). New Haven, 1969, pp. 119–146.

[27] Thomason, R., "Philosophy and Formal Semantics," *Truth, Syntax and Modality*, H. Leblanc (ed.). Amsterdam, 1972.

[28] Thomason, R., and R. Stalnaker, "Modality and Reference," *Nous*, Vol. 2 (1968), pp. 359–372.

[29] van Fraassen, B., *Formal Semantics and Logic*. New York, 1971.

Ontological Relativity and Relative Identity

P. T. GEACH

University of Leeds

In this paper I return to a topic I have discussed several times before and try to make connections with recent work of Quine's. I also shall make some comments on recent criticisms of my thesis that identity is relative.

I begin by saying what sort of term I take "identity" to be. This term, or rather the corresponding concrete term "identical" or "the same," belongs to the family of terms that medievals called transcendental: it belongs with "exists" and "something" and "one" and "true" and "good." "Transcendental" referred to the way these terms jump across any conceptual barriers between different kinds of discourse; they are, in Ryle's word, topic-neutral. (The term "good," traditionally one of this company, might appear an odd man out; for one thing, it might appear to be of less concern to logic than the others. But after all "good" cannot be kept out of logic; some inferences are good and others are not, and it is for logic to sort them out.) Of any pair of transcendentals the medievals say they convert, *convertuntur*. I have not actually found this said of "exists" and "same," "*ens*" *et* "*idem*"; but it is said of "one" and "exists," "*unum*" and "*ens*"; and as the phrase "one and the same" suggests, "one" and "the same" are very near akin. Of course we get nowhere if we try to construe the converting of transcendentals as logical convertibility, coextensiveness, or again as interchangeabil-

287

ity *salva veritate;* but if we look at the Latin etymology of "convert," we get an apt and helpful metaphor. The transcendentals turn together, like a train of gear wheels. Given these relations between transcendentals, I need not apologize for a paper on identity in a series devoted to ontology. For, as Quine has said, no entity without identity; he and I agree in regarding as *entia non grata* those philosophically postulated entities for which there is simply no telling whether men are talking about the same thing or not. And again Quine and I would both say: No identity without entity. Nonentities are not there to be the same or different; if the obligation to recognize this is what 'free logic' promises to free us from, then 'free logic' is thus far sophistry and delusion. In the first edition of my *Reference and Generality* insufficient emphasis on these points led to the idea that I countenanced 'intentional objects' which lacked a criterion of identity; I do not and never did, and I added a sentence in the emended edition to say so. More lately I have written about intentional identity. All I need say here on that perplexing topic is that intentional identity, like alleged identity, is not a variety of identity; if a lot of people *mean* to refer to the same thing, they may not manage to do so.

The term "criterion of identity," which I have just used, is closely tied up with the way I take identity to be relative; but this is a nasty ambiguity about the term, which I must now try to clear up. It may on the one hand be a matter of what standard we judge by when we judge that identity obtains—or equally, what standard we hypothesize by when we merely suppose, without judging, that identity obtains. (For here, as in other regions of philosophy, we must remember Frege's all too easily forgotten point about assertion, we must not construct a theory that only fits judgments or assertions of identity, forgetting mere suppositions that identity holds.) This is how I shall be using "criterion of identity." Or, on the other hand, it may be a matter of how we recognize identity. I recognize a man by his face and voice, not by his brain; but the criterion of identity, in my sense, answering to the phrase "the same man" is one to which the brain is far more relevant than the face or voice. Switching brains might raise some difficulties as to which man was which after the operation; but if a man suffers facial damage but no brain damage, and plastic surgery gives him a different face and voice, then he is nevertheless plainly the same man as before—the case is not marginal and doubtful—even though his friends may find the change uncanny. This distinction between two senses of "criterion" may not always be easy to draw; it is not therefore illusory.

With "criterion of identity" thus explained, I have to say yet once more that the thesis that identity is always relative to such a criterion seems to me a truism, like Frege's connected thesis that a number is always relative to a *Begriff*. It is as nonsensical to speak of identification apart from identifying some *kind* of thing, as to speak of counting apart from counting some kind of thing. A numerical word demands completion with a count noun; similarly for "the same" and "another." ("The same" also goes with mass terms, as when we say that the same gold was a crown and then a shapeless lump and then a crown again. Little has been published on the complex logical likenesses and differences between mass terms and count nouns; most logicians have followed the precedent of Aristotle's *Prior Analytics*, where snow and swans figure alike as examples of what is white, and pitch and crows, as examples of what is black. An unpublished doctoral dissertation by Helen Cartwright contains valuable work on this problem. It would take me too far to discuss mass terms further in this paper.)

But *is* counting a nonsensical procedure if it is not applied to objects brought under the same *Begriff?* Some philosophers have thought otherwise: all those, in fact, who have denied the Identity of Indiscernibles (to give the doctrine its slightly misleading traditional name). "Objects *x, y,* and *z*" they would say "may be merely numerically distinct; and even if they are also different in characteristics, they will have self-identity and numerical distinction logically prior to such dissimilarities."

Even apart from my thesis about relative identity, I should dismiss this view as incoherent. Here as elsewhere, the notion of logical priority that is introduced is far from being clear and distinct. In modern logic texts we find very little mention of logical priority. I suspect that appeals to logical priority are a hangover from the era when Euclid's geometry was to all intents the only deductive system that had been worked out. It was thus natural to think that in a system some terms are indefinable, others inherently definable; some propositions are axiomatic or self-evident, others essentially derivative. We now know that one and the same deductive system may be formulated with different choices of primitive terms and axioms; what is primitive in one formulation may be a defined term, or, as the case may be, a proved theorem, in the other formulation. Knowing this much, we should take a hard look at any appeal to considerations of logical priority; such considerations are not necessarily worthless, but should not move us too readily.

The doctrine of an individual's having self-identity, and distinctiveness from others, logically prior to having any characteristics is anyhow absurd; apart from its characteristics an individual is nothing, and the talk of bare particulars, which still oddly survives, is manifest nonsense. Adroit shifts of wording or of stresses may enable a philosopher to persuade himself and others that he is not contradicting himself when he says that an individual, or some ontic core of an individual, is a qualityless particular, qualityless precisely *because* IT is what HAS the qualities; somehow the emphasis, instead of making the self-contradiction manifest, serves to conceal it.

It does not follow that otherwise an individual is a bundle of qualities. I suppose people are driven to the bare-particular theory by finding the bundle theory incredible; however bedizened the lady may be, she cannot be clothes all the way through—we must come to bare skin at last. And some of course are driven the opposite way—Brand Blanshard for one. But we are not tied down to these alternatives. Think of a triangular area and its sides. We need neither identify the triangle with its sides, nor hypostatize a sideless triangle that owns or wears the sides and is sideless precisely on that account. It was my great good fortune that I read McTaggart's *Nature of Existence* at a formative age and was thus made immune for life to these opposing errors. In this vein of thought, again like McTaggart, I find the idea of distinctness without distinguishing characteristics an absurd one; you might as well try to think of two distinct plane triangles bounded by the same three sides. And, yet once more like McTaggart, I am not saying distinctness requires qualitative difference; difference in relations is enough.

I have gone into these murky regions only because I am sure some of the resistance to the relative identity thesis has its source here; this is clear as regards some published criticism. Even when people do not explicitly accept, or would explicitly reject, the idea of bare 'numerical' difference, I think the idea sometimes works in them subterraneously; if so, it is well to bring it into the open.

I return, then, to the Fregean idea: the idea of counting, not 'numerically different' things, but things brought under a *Begriff*. Counting, or rather numerical quantification, is explained in logic books by way of identity: "there are three . . . " let us say by "for some x, y, and z, $x \neq y$ and $y \neq z$ and $z \neq x$ and . . . ," where of course "$\neq$" is read "is not identical with." I have to maintain that the identity is relative. I shall first show that we can and do use relative identities to count by and that this procedure need raise no theoretical difficulties.

But first I need to specify which predicables can express relative identity. It would be useless to say: those predicables which are formed by substituting a count noun for "A" in "the same A as." For such an answer would just raise further problems: What is a count noun? What is the syntactical liaison between such a noun and the prefix "the same"? Why can some nouns enter into the liaison and not others?

We escape these difficulties by saying that predications of a count noun "*A*" does not serve to form the predicable "is the same *A* as," but the other way around: as I said in *Reference and Generality* (§ 109) the one-place predicable "is an *A*" is definable as meaning "is the same *A* as something or other." This explanation may seem to go the wrong way round. But it is formally just like defining "is a brother" (say) is "is brother of somebody." Here also we could not proceed the other way around; we could not supply a logic and semantics for the phrase "of Jane" so as to explain how this fuses with "is a brother" to form "is (a) brother of Jane." (In this case then we *can* say that logical priority obtains: "brother of" is logically prior to "brother").

We shall treat "the same" in "is the same *A* as" not as a syntactically separable part, but as an index showing we have here a word for a certain sort of relation: just as "of" in "is brother of" does not signify a relation by itself (as if the phrase were "is a brother, who belongs to") but serves to show that the whole, "is brother of," stands for a relation. For logical purposes, a *count noun* is a word related to this sort of relational term in just the way that "brother" is to "is brother of." And here we have no need to bring in any syntax more complicated than can be expressed in standard first-order quantification theory.

What sort of relation, then, do these phrases "is the same *A* as" express? Plainly it must always be an equivalence relation—one that is symmetrical and transitive, and consequently reflexive in its field. Thus the definition of "is an *A*" by "is the same *A* as something or other" could be replaced by a neater definition: "is the same *A* as itself." I had already seen this possibility when I wrote *Reference and Generality;* but some odd psychological quirk makes the use of this *definiens* appear a piece of trickery, so for expository purposes I used the more complicated form.

Could any expression for an equivalence relation serve to define a count noun? When I read this paper in New York, Donald Davidson suggested a reason to the contrary: Areas and time stretches can be identified but not counted. This connects with a difficulty, already raised by Frege (*Gundlagen der Arithmetik* page 66), as to which *Begriffe* determine a cardinal number. It has to do with the divisibility of what is *A* into parts that are also *A*, or again with the combinability of parts that are *A* into a whole that is again *A*. (And here we might have to return to the topic of mass terms.) I shall not try to resolve this problem here, for we need not doubt that predication of a count noun is always explicable, in the way I have stated, in terms of *some* equivalence relation; it is only that *not all* equivalence relations will serve this purpose, and the exact restriction required is not yet clear.

The equivalence-relation expression "is the same *A* as" is of course not paraphrasable by "is an *A* and is (absolutely) the same as"; this equivalence will not hold definitionally, nor will it be provable. Some thinkers (such as David Wiggins) have put forward theories of 'relative' identity from which it would follow as a logical consequence that 'relative' identity is simply absolute identity restricted to a certain field. Obviously any such theory differs only in a trivial way from a theory of absolute identity—that is, so far as the *logic* of identity goes: I cannot here discuss the philosophy in which this logic gets imbedded. My theory does not admit of such a trivialising twist.

Let me now show how we can use the relative identity of "is the same *A* as" to fix an answer to the question "How many *As*?" and thus justify me in saying that "*A*," defined in my style, is a count noun in the logical sense. I shall specify a way of assigning numbers to such objects in a domain as are *As*—each of them the same *A* as something or other. We assign 1 to an object *x*, and to whatever is the same *A* as *x*, and to nothing else; we assign 2 to an object *y*, and to whatever is the same *A* as *y*, and to nothing else; and so on. We must not assign two numbers to any object in the domain; this condition can be fulfilled because the things that are the same *A* as *x* cannot overlap the things that are the same *A* as *y*; equivalence classes must either coincide or be disjoint. The number *n* eventually reached will be the count of *As* in the domain under consideration. It is easy to see that if "*A*" and "*B*" represent different count nouns, the count of *As* in a domain may be different from the count of *Bs* even if everything in the domain both is an *A* and is a *B*—that is to say, both is the same *A* as something and is the same *B* as something. This may seem to introduce nonextensional contexts, "is the same . . . as" and "the count of . . . S," for count nouns. But a moment's thought should dispel this appearance. Quite similarly, in a domain in which whoever is a father is an uncle and conversely, "is father of" and "is uncle of" need by no means coincide; but this does not mean that in the construction "is . . . of" there is a nonextensional argument place for nouns like "father" and "uncle."

In the light of this theory of count nouns, we see once more how very wrong is the two-name theory of predication—the theory that the fundamental sort of predication is the joining of two names with a copula, names that may be empty or nonempty, shared or unshared, and that the predication is true iff we thus join two names of one and the same thing. Leśniewski's 'ontology' was a revival of this medieval view (The epsilon generally used as a copula in 'ontology' is nonsymmetrical, and has a more complicated semantics than that I have just given; but 'ontology' *could* be formulated with a symmetrical copula, as Lejewski has shown; and then we could say, as I did, that this copula *truly* joins two names iff they name the same object.) But it is hopeless to try and explain "is the same A as" in terms of the shared name "A"; we might as well try to explain "is uncle of" in terms of the shared name "uncle." In both cases, the true explanation goes the other way. In the last paragraph of *Reference and Generality,* emended edition, I expressed a hope of some day investigating a program, inspired by Leśniewski's work, wherein shared and unshared names could alike be inserted in the blank of "is the same . . . as." I have now carried out this investigation; my verdict is that the program is theoretically unsound because this class of predicables are not derived from names by any logical procedure.

Speaking of names' designating the same thing, we may here remark how futile is a certain controversial move of semantic ascent (to use Quine's handy term). People have challenged me to say whether two designations designate the same thing, or again, whether a list is nonrepetitive: yes or no! But of course a relativizer of identity, if he has his wits about him, will refuse the challenge; if the question "Are x and y the same?" needs relativizing, if the plain "the same" must be replaced by a specific identity predicable, there also we must complete the question "Do these designations designate the same?" by adding a count noun at the end; and likewise the question "Is this a nonrepetitive list?" must be changed—we must say "list of As," where "A" is a count noun. (For the record, *I did* have my wits about me on this matter when I wrote *Reference and Generality:* see page 82 and page 177, footnote.)

The objection may be raised (it has been) that I have no right to talk as I have done about a domain of quantification, a universe of discourse; a domain must be given by an absolutely nonrepetitive bit or not at all. The objectors seem to misunderstand the business of assigning interpretations in predicate logic. In the first place, we may need to consider indenumerable domains. Such domains just cannot be listed, be the list finite or infinite. Second, interpretation by means of a finite and listed domain in no way requires that the list be nonrepetitive. Universal quantification will then answer to a finite conjunction and existential quantification to a finite disjunction, and neither conjunction nor disjunction gets different truth-conditions from repetition of a conjunct or disjunct. (This feature, idempotency, distinguishes conjunction and the ordinary disjunction from exclusive disjunction; exclusive disjunction is commutative and associative like the other two connectives, so that we may write (say) "*p* aut *q* aut *r*" without bracketing and in any order, but "*p* aut *p* aut *q*" reduces to "*q*," not to "*p* aut *q*.")

Let me now bring these abstract considerations down to earth by going over some examples I have previously used in this controversy. The word "word," I pointed out, is ambiguous. It may mean "token word" or "type word," or "dictionary-entry word," or various other things. Despite this, I may specify as the universe of discourse the words in a given volume in my room at Leeds; for I could give each word in the volume a proper name and get a finite list of them. The ambiguity I have just mentioned is an ambiguity over what shall count as *the same* word; but since a list specifying a domain anyhow need not be nonrepetitive, this need not worry us. The count of token words, of type words (identified by sheer sameness of spelling), and of dictionary-entry words, may be different in each case; all the same, each thing in the universe is the same token word as itself *and* the same type word as itself *and* the same dictionary-entry word as itself, and thus *both* is a token word *and* is a type word *and* is a dictionary-entry word. I dismiss the protest that this result is incoherent because the entity in question must be of only one of these three kinds; there is no "must" about it. We have in view an entity that belongs to the field of those different equivalence relations, and therefore comes under three different counts using different count nouns; *each* of the count nouns applies—that is how count nouns are used. It is on the contrary the question "But which is it *really?*" that is incoherent and unintelligible.

Similarly for the matter of men and surmen. I defined "——— is the same surman as———" to mean "——— and ——— are both men and have the same single surname." Accordingly, if every inhabitant of Leeds has just one surname, then every inhabitant of Leeds both is a man and is a surman; he (or she) is the same man as somebody and also the same surman as somebody. And further, just as I said, if *x* is a surman in Leeds, then *x* has a heart in his breast, guts in his belly, and so on, just as I said. These predicables will be true of *x* in their ordinary everyday sense; to make these predications true, we need not use words in some artificial sense that I have negligently failed to specify. All the same, if we count the men in Leeds and the surmen in Leeds, we shall get different counts; the count of surmen will be smaller. But this does not mean that the surmen in Leeds are only a subclass of the men, or perhaps are a class of nonhuman androids. I cannot have intended the definition of "is the same surman as" that I actually gave; whatever I *said*, I must have *meant* that a surman is a class of men, or perhaps a whole with men as parts! And then how could a surman have a heart in his breast and guts in his belly, except in some quite unnatural sense of the words? How indeed? But after all the term was mine, defined by me; and nobody has shown such incoherence in the definition as calls for conjectural emendation of my text to restore sense. If a definition that was not mine is wished upon me, then things get into a mess; but that is hardly my fault.

I claim, then, to have explained relative-identity predicables, their connection with count nouns (in the predicative use), and the procedures of counting, without internal incoherence and without any departure from standard predicate logic; moreover, I have avoided making "is the same A as" equivalent to "is an A and is *absolutely* the same as." At this point someone may say: "Why, Geach has simply trivialized his relative-identity thesis!" But this claim may reveal a state of the discussion that I should be glad to have brought about. For a logical thesis of this kind ought to look trivial when it is once properly understood. What is not always trivial is the work of removing obstacles to understanding. What could be more banal than what I have elsewhere styled *the* Frege point, namely that a proposition's sense and truth-value do not depend on whether it is actually asserted or merely considered? And yet, as I have argued elsewhere, failure to grasp this point has led to the writing of confused and misguided philosophy by the ream. So here: If at the end of the day my account appears trivially true, all the same the confusions that made it seem unacceptable were indeed great, and their removal was a worthy task. Moreover, we have gained a positive insight into the logic of count nouns.

What I have so far said relates to certain one-place and two-place predicables; I now have to make some remarks about proper names. Quine has often insisted that proper names need not come into predicate logic; so agreement on what I have thus far said need not be prejudiced if what I say about proper names should prove less acceptable. I have long maintained that any given successful use of a proper name is tied to identification by some definite criterion of identity. I see no reason to change my mind or to repeat my old arguments; I shall simply attack two particular errors. First, it is certainly not enough to regard a proper name as clinging to something spatiotemporally continuous with what was originally christened or labelled with the name. Starting with the region occupied by a certain newly baptized baby, one could trace a continuously varying series of regions ending up with the region occupied by any arbitrarily chosen man a year later (a strip cartoon would serve to bring out my meaning); it does not follow that every man has an equal right to count as the bearer of the name thus conferred on the baby. Again, if we could believe in Epicurean sempiternal atoms, the very collection of atoms that was the baby's body at the moment of baptism would still be there forty years on though afar and asunder; and this scattered collection would not be lawful heir to the name either. Of course there is in this case only one continuously varying series of regions that is occupied throughout by the same *human being;* and of course the intention of the name-conferring ceremony is just that the name shall stick to one and the same human being.

Secondly, from time to time people doubt whether it need be an equivalence relation that is expressed by (say) "is the same person as" and by the continual use of a proper name. Might not the relation fail to be, for example, unrestrictedly transitive? Those who suggest this do not know what they would be at. If we think in terms of proper names, then personal identity is *shown* (to use the language of Wittgenstein's *Tractatus*) by repetition of a proper name; so lack of transitiveness would mean that we might have "*Fa* and *Ga*" and "*Ga* and *Ka*" both true but "*Fa* and *Ka*" false. Or perhaps it would be fairer to think of a temporal "and" meaning "and then" or "and later on." Perhaps it is being suggested that "*Fa* and later on *Ga* and later on *Ka*" could be true but "*Fa* and later on *Ka*" false. These are not minor revisions in the logic of proper names; those who propose nontransitive personal 'identity' have assuredly not seen the need for such revisions, let alone, thought them through.

What is supposed to have shown that we ought to regard nontransitive identity as possible is scientific information about the fission and fusion of unicellular organisms, together with science fiction about the way memory might survive the changes if they happened to a higher species like ours. But of course the biological facts about fusion and fission in no way call for a revised logic of identity. A *Punch* cartoonist once supplied a series of pictures of an amoeba in fission with the captions: "I'm all alone in the world—so I've got to be—father and mother—to you two kids"; he clearly grasped the logic of identity in its application far better than some philosophers. (I suppose they would wish to replace "to you two kids" by "to myselves"!)

As for science fiction, we must notice that fiction in general, science fiction in particular, even when 'convincingly' written, often contains inconsistencies; *The Time Machine* is quite grossly incon-sistent, which does not stop it from being a good and 'convincing' story. Indeed, when the inconsistencies are spelled out we may admire Wells all the more for having got away with them by his narrative skill. If one person remembers himself doing the deeds of each of two different coexisting people, or if two different coexisting people each remember doing the deeds of one and the same person, then at least one set of memories is deceptive and both may be; and there's an end of it. (There is, by the way, no objection to saying that some memory is deceptive or wrong or muddled or positively inventive; we can and do say such things, whatever ordinary-language philosophers may con-tend, and whether or not the dictionary backs them up.) The argu-ments against memory as a criterion of personal identity are old, well known, and to my mind conclusive; I need not repeat them. And memory eked out with the imperfect bodily continuity that would survive fusion or fission is no better as a criterion than memory by itself. Even in face of actual strange cases, the logic of identity and of proper names is too central to our conceptual scheme to be lightly revised; we are not likely to revise it merely in order to concede a piece of science fiction describes a possible state of affairs.

I now turn to the final topic of my paper. Someone may object that even if I have made good sense of relative identity, I have not shown that a theory is incapable of expressing absolute identity. In-deed, if any theory is to be interpreted, must there not be an absolute identity and nonidentity for the objects that are being quantified over? (I use Quine's term "quantify over," as he does, quite differently from "quantify"; what we *quantify* are the expressions we prefix quantifiers to—as in "Hamilton quantified the predicate"—but what we *quantify over* are the things we are talking about.) Can we have an ontology at all without absolute identity? And if identity can only be relative, how much ontological relativity does this let in?

In the first place, our theory need not be capable of expressing absolute identity conceived as the contradictory of 'purely numerical' difference, for there is no such relation. It is a particularly futile semantic ascent to stipulate that a predicable of a language shall express this sort of identity, and then call this "a complete semantical characterization in the metatheory."

Next, we can of course define for a given language what it is for a predicable to be an identity predicable (I-predicable) of that language. For our present purposes, the definition may be given in words as follows: A predicable is an I-predicable in L iff, whenever this predicable is true in L of x and y, any predicable of L whatsoever is true of x iff it is true of y. Quine has shown how to construct an

I-predicable for a first-order extensional language L, even if no undefined predicable of L is an I-predicable. But if x and y satisfy an I-predicable of L, that guarantees only that they are indiscernible so far as the predicables of L can show—not that they are absolutely indiscernible.

For absolute indiscernibility we should need to have: Whatever is true of x is true of y, and conversely. Here, the domain of "true of" would not be restricted to the predicables of some specified language. Now the types of paradox that Grelling and Richard constructed certainly seem to show that an unrestricted "true of" is inadmissible; unless the domain of "true of" is restricted to predicables of some specified language L, "true of" just cannot figure safely in our semantic vocabulary. So if we say "Whatever is true of x is true of y, and conversely" without restricting "true of" to the predicables of some language L, it is not clear that we have managed to say anything. The absolute identity that was opposed to merely numerical difference is a chimera; absolute indiscernibility is a will-o'-the-wisp that we pursue in vain.

Is there any other way of salvaging absolute identity? In an earlier paper I suggested one. I got the idea for this by reading Quine's works, but textual discussion of them to decide whether I understood them aright would be a tedious irrelevance. Let us just consider the suggestion on its own merits. Could we perhaps systematically construe the quantifications in each language L so that entities x and y which we are quantifying over are *absolutely* identical where the I-predicable of L is true of them; that is to say, when x and y are indiscernible in L?

I tried to show that this suggestion leads to a baroque Meinongian ontology. It is largely my own fault that my argument was misunderstood, for I failed to bring out the important differences between a language and a theory. A language normally contains the negations of all its sentences; a theory, one hopes, will not contain the negations of all its theses. A language, or its speaker, need not be ontologically committed to whatever a sentence of the language affirms to exist; but a theory, or its holder, is ontologically committed to whatever a thesis in the theory affirms to exist. (Some people have certainly at least slurred over this distinction in discussing Quine's view of ontological commitment.)

A language may contain sublanguages, and a theory, subtheories; in each case the relation is the *timeless* set-theoretical relation of a class to a proper subclass. It is quite normal set-theoretic jargon to speak of obtaining one class from another by adding or omitting members; of course, this jargon does not refer, as some critics seem to suppose, to acts of adding and omitting members, or even to events of members' coming to be added or removed. (I am reminded of an Italian critique of Bertrand Russell that I once read; after putting the *Principia* definition of the successor function reasonably well into the vernacular, the author protested that we men were in no position to obtain a thirteen-membered class by adding a new apostle of Christ, marshal of Napoleon, or sign of the Zodiac to the twelve original ones!) When I spoke of adding predicables to a language, my critics took me to be speaking of a development of knowledge; when I spoke of omitting predicables, was this taken to mean something like the 1984 situation, in which the vocabulary of Newspeak is being progressively impoverished by order of the Ministry of Truth? Since one critic spoke of "loss of knowledge" in this connection I fear even this degree of misunderstanding may have occurred.

A subtheory may be stated in the same language, and have the same vocabulary, as the main theory. But if a sublanguage omits part of the vocabulary of a language, then those sentences of the main theory that contain the omitted predicables may themselves be omitted from the theory so as to get a subtheory. (The word "omitted" must be taken in the way just explained.)

The relation between a language and a sublanguage, or a theory and a subtheory, requires not only equiformity but also correspondence of truth conditions between any sentence in the smaller class and some sentence in the larger class. This is most important, for it is because of this that any ontological commitment of a subtheory carries over to the main theory. Of course this would not hold if a sentence of the subtheory, though spelled the same way, were reinterpreted in the main theory so as to get different truth conditions; but that is not how I conceived the relation between a subtheory and the main theory. It is, of course, flatly inconsistent to say that as a member of a larger theory a sentence retains its truth conditions but not its ontological commitment.

Given this relation between a theory and its subtheories, we can see what unacceptable results follow from the attempt to construe the quantifiers in a given language as ranging over entities for which the I-predicable of the language expresses *absolute* identity. Suppose, for example, that we have in a sublanguage no predicables to distinguish two men with the same surname. Then if a theory T in the main language is ontologically committed to the existence of men, the fragment of T in the sublanguage will be ontologically committed, *if construed this way*, to the existence, not just of surmen, but of creatures for whom the predicable "is the same surman as," as I defined it, supplies a criterion of absolute identity. Let us say, for short, on the suggestion we are discussing, this fragment of T is committed to the existence of *absolute surmen*. If so, then T itself is likewise committed, since a theory picks up the ontological commitments of each subtheory it contains. But the existence of absolute surmen, I shall argue, is an absurd supposition. This and an infinity of like absurdities follow from the construal of quantifiers in each language as ranging over entities for which the I-predicable of the language gives a criterion of absolute identity; therefore we cannot construe quantifiers according to this principle.

I am not arguing that there is any absurdity in the assertion "There are surmen." It is easy to check that by my definition there are surmen iff there are men each of whom has just one surname. So there is no absurdity about a subtheory ontologically committed to the existence of surmen; the main theory can pick up this commitment without coming to shipwreck. A subtheory that lacked the resources of vocabulary to distinguish x and y when x and y were the same surman might nevertheless have quite a rich vocabulary; it could contain any predicable that holds good in common for two men, regardless of any differences that do not come out when we only know the surnames of x and y: predicables like "has a heart," "has a liver," and "has the surname *Jones.*" If, however, we read this theory as committed to the existence of absolute surmen—or creatures for whom "is the same surman as" expressed absolute identity—then what sort of creatures would these be? Would they be androids—creatures resembling men in many ways, for example, in having hearts and livers, but differing from men in their criterion of identity? We can in fact rule this out in short order; whatever is a surman is by definition a man. Then suppose, to the contrary, that absolute surmen are in fact men. Then, since, as we saw, the count of surmen comes out smaller than the count of men, absolute surmen will be just some among men. There will, for example, be just one surman with the surname "Jones"; but if this is an absolute surman, and he *is* a certain man, then *which* of the Jones boys is he? Surely we have here run into absurdity, just as we did when we tried out the suggestion that absolute surmen are nonhuman androids.

Let me re-emphasize that here I am not throwing any doubt on my previous claim that the equivalence relation *is the same surman as* had been properly and coherently explained. What I have just reduced to absurdity is the notion of absolute surmen, that is, beings for whom the holding of this relation constitutes absolute identity. Therewith, I claim, I have also reduced to absurdity the proposal for construing the quantifiers of any given language L so that the I-predicable of L gives a criterion for the *absolute* identity of the

objects quantified over L. Let us thus contentedly revert to the view
that what the holding true of the I-predicable in a language L guarantees is always and only: indiscernibility relative to the predicables
of L. If L has a sub-language L', the I-predicable for L' may not
be an I-predicable for L, because L may have predicables to discriminate things that are indiscernible in L'. Plainly there is no difficulty
about this.

This view chimes in very well with the way Quine treats identity
in his *Philosophy of Logic*. Quine proposes that the sign of identity
in first-order logic be treated not as a logical constant but as merely
schematic like the schematic letters *F*, *G*, and so on. In any concrete
interpretation, "=" will be read as the I-predicable of the language
in question; and given an extensional language, with a finite vocabulary of undefined predicables, we can actually define "=" for this
language by constructing an I-predicable in this vocabulary. This
dodge of Quine's painlessly dominates the boundary between first-
order logic and identity theory. Further, we eliminate the anomalous
feature of "=" as compared with other logical constants: namely,
that it looks as though "=" enabled us to write down, not just valid
schemata, but actual true sentences containing only logical vocabulary
like "For all *x*, *x* = *x*" and "For all *x* and *y*, if *x* = *y* then *y* = *x*."
With Quine's proposal, such formulas would become more schemata
like "For all *x*, *Fx* or not *Fx*."

Finally, then, to how much ontological relativity does this relativized identity theory commit us? We can never so specify what
we are quantifying over that we are secure against an expansion
of our vocabulary enabling us to discriminate what formerly we could
not. (In saying this I am in no way revoking my previous insistence
that the relation between a language and a sublanguage be treated
as timeless. I *am* here considering linguistic developments from an
increase of knowledge; this is not a change of mind, but a change
of subject.) And if we list the things we are quantifying over by
their names, one of these names may turn out to be not a proper
name but a shared name, of objects that we now can discriminate
by previously could not. This suggests, after all, some justification
for Leśniewski's idea that proper names and shared names be assigned
to the same syntactical category, for we may wish to guarantee that
the syntax, as opposed to the semantics, of words in our language
need *not* be revised in view of new discriminatory powers. (Readers
of *Reference and Generality* may remember that I favored this aspect
of Leśniewski's views, while I opposed the two-name theory of
predication.)

It was therefore not quite right on my part to say that with relativized identity theory our ontology is firmly under control; but it is as well under control as we could possibly hope. So long as we merely fail to discriminate things that are in truth indiscernible in our language, we are not condemned by this defect in our language and information to say the thing that is not. Thus I do not think there is much of a threat here: only a fangless worm, a paper tiger.